APR -- 2017

THE BRITISH TABLE

THE
BRITISH
TABLE

A New Look at the Traditional Cooking of ENGLAND, SCOTLAND, AND WALES

COLMAN ANDREWS

photography by
HIRSHEIMER & HAMILTON

Abrams, New York

For Terence, who changed the game

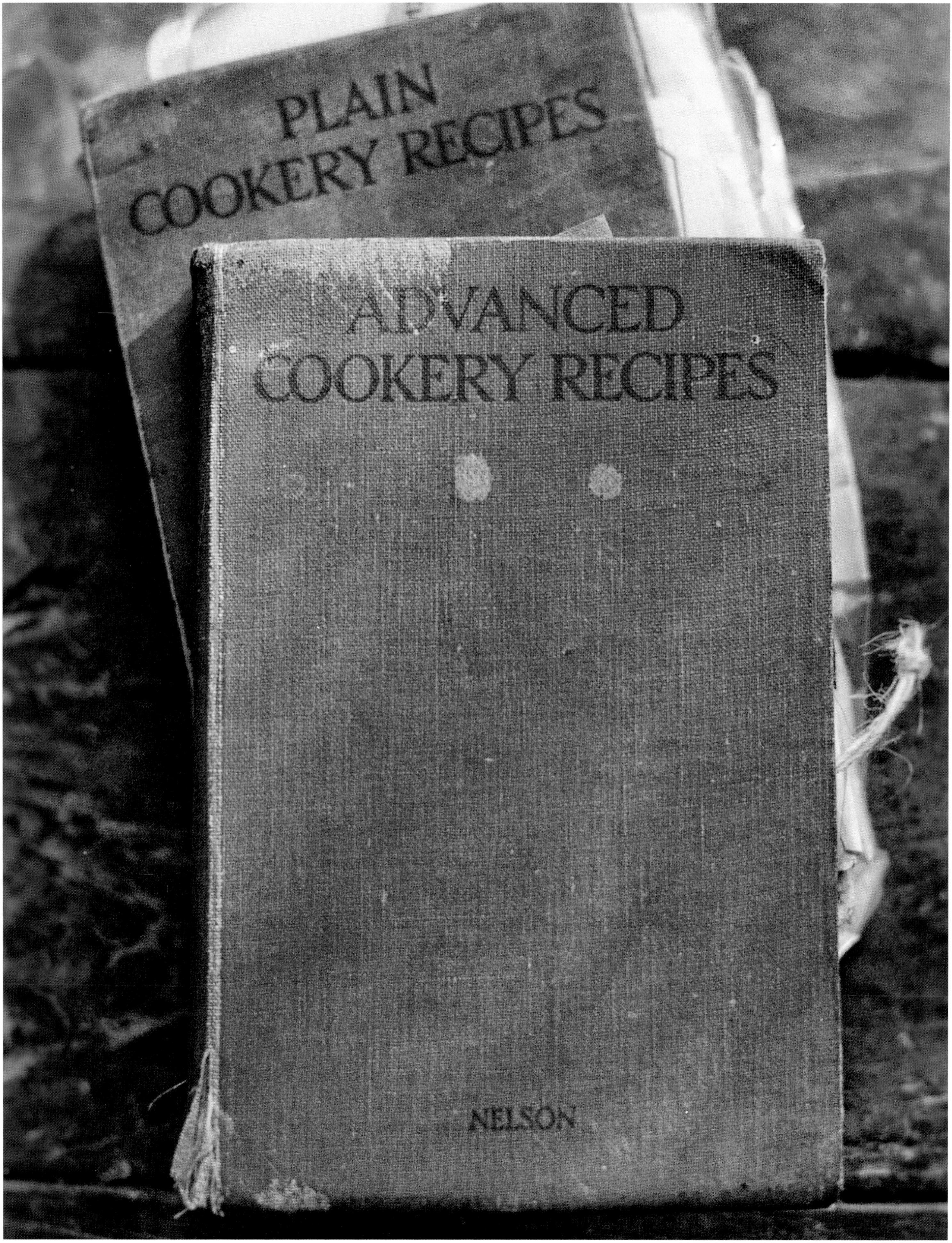
PLAIN
COOKERY RECIPES
ADVANCED
COOKERY RECIPES
NELSON

CONTENTS

"TO TASTEFUL PALATES, KEEN APPETITES, AND HEALTHFUL AND CAPACIOUS STOMACHS."

—WILLIAM KITCHINER, *Apicius Redivivus: Or, The Cook's Oracle* (1817)

INTRODUCTION

"... ENGLISH FARE I WOULD DEFINE AS BEING THE VERY BEST NATIVE MATERIAL, COOKED IN THE PLAINEST POSSIBLE MANNER."

—LIEUT. COL. NEWNHAM-DAVIS, *The Gourmet's Guide to London* (1914)

"TRADITION IS ONE OF THE MAINSPRINGS OF INNOVATION; WE USE THE PAST AS A SPRINGBOARD TOWARDS THE NEW."

—HESTON BLUMENTHAL, *Historic Heston* (2013)

In 1965, living in my native Los Angeles, I became an Anglophile. This had nothing to do with my partially English and Scots-Irish genealogy, but rather was inspired by my love for the music of the so-called British Invasion (led by those four mop-topped lads from Liverpool) and, probably more so, by my attraction to one of my coworkers in the bookshop of the newly opened Los Angeles County Museum of Art, an English girl named Ann.

Ann seemed to me the very embodiment of Swinging London (as *Time* was soon to dub the British capital). She introduced me to Mary Quant (she had the miniskirts), the art of Allen Jones and Bridget Riley, the films of Richard Lester and John Schlesinger. We listened to LPs of *The Goon Show* and got the tissue-paper airmail edition of the *Observer* every week. She taught me how to make a proper pot of tea (she'd get *so* cross if I forgot to warm the pot first).

And when we went off to Europe for a month that summer, my first trip across the Atlantic, she took me straight to Manchester, where her parents lived. It was perhaps an unconventional introduction to England—I'd heard the commonplace by then that Manchester was famous most of all for "sausages and rain"—but I was enchanted: by the bold red telephone boxes and double-decker buses, by the little stone cottages trellised with climbing rose canes in the villages we visited, by the dank gothic churches where plaques named every pastor in succession for the past five hundred years, by the sugary petits fours and crumbly scones we ate with our inevitable afternoon cuppa.

Unfortunately, I don't remember anything else about the food I encountered on that trip (I don't think I ever got the sausages), but I do have memories of things I consumed in London on my next few visits to the U.K. They are not fond memories. I ate glutinous spaghetti with ketchupy tomato sauce in hotel dining rooms around Victoria Station; meat pies with dense, lard-soaked crusts bought cheap from street vendors in Soho; scrawny gray Wimpy burgers on damp buns. Occasionally, when I could afford it, I did what everybody said, in those days, was the only sensible thing to do in London if you had a discerning appetite: ate Indian food—usually in brightly lit restaurants with flocked wallpaper and piped-in Ravi Shankar (I still recall a meat *phall* I ate at one of these places as being quite possibly the spiciest food I've ever tasted).

That was the secret of dining well in England in those days: Eat foreign. I did admittedly have some delicious meals in London in the 1970s, sometimes at Indian restaurants, but more especially when I was taken out to dinner by my parents' friend Tony, the Viscount Furness. That's because we always went to places serving some non-British cuisine or other—Le Coq d'Or for tournedos Masséna, the White Tower for taramosalata and moussaka, the Gay Hussar for cold pike with beetroot sauce and *gulyás*. I don't think we ever had anything "British" at all, other than an occasional pint of Bass Ale or tumbler of Glenfiddich.

Today, of course, it's a very different story. London is widely acknowledged as one of the world's great food cities—as the prolific London chef-restaurateur Mark Hix puts it, "France has gone backward, we've gone forward"—and chefs in nearly every corner of the country are winning acclaim (the *Guide Michelin* awarded 181 stars around England, Scotland, and Wales in 2015), often for food strongly based in local traditions and almost always employing the rich bounty of their regions. And *rich* is the right word. With almost twenty thousand miles of coastline, counting the larger offshore islands, the country boasts a great wealth of seafood, some of which (Colchester oysters, Scottish Salmon, Dover sole; cured fish like

An Indian restaurant and Union Jack in London's Soho

kippers and finnan haddie) is famous worldwide. Its land is blessed with many kinds of soil and numerous micro-climates, variously well suited to the raising of livestock (including many so-called heritage breeds), the ranging of hooved and feathered game, and the cultivation of everything from wheat and rye and oats to ancient varieties of tree fruit, from onions and asparagus and carrots to savory herbs and even wine grapes, supplying a British wine industry that is beginning to be taken seriously even in France. The country's cheeses are renowned and widely copied around the world. Its beer is legendary. Its pickles and chutneys and sauces are sold in shops across the globe.

The mystery isn't so much why British food is so good today, but why it ever *wasn't*, why a once diverse and abundant cuisine degenerated for more than a century to the point of becoming an international punch line. As recently as 2005, French president Jacques Chirac, following a visit to Scotland for a summit meeting, cracked that, "after Finland, [the U.K.] is the country with the worst food." He was perhaps channeling his countryman Jean Anthelme Brillat-Savarin who, in the early 1800s, when British food was probably not bad at all, dismissed Britain as "a nation of beef-eaters and beer-swillers."

And yet . . . ancient cooking in the British Isles was probably as sophisticated as it was anywhere else in northern Europe, and the Romans, who arrived in 43 CE, improved it further, bringing at least the spirit of Mediterranean fare to Britain, along with a host of new ingredients, including walnuts, cherries, pears, onions, leeks, cucumbers, radishes, turnips, fennel, peas, mint, thyme, rabbits, pheasants, and partridges, as well as the arts of making sausage, rennet-based cheese, and possibly wine, and the technique of baking bread in ovens rather than cooking it on griddles. They even imported olive oil.

A serious food culture developed here in the ensuing centuries—though the Romans took the olive oil with them when they decamped after almost four hundred years ("boil in butter" became a common recipe instruction in medieval Britain). In his definitive history *British Food*, the English author and artist Colin Spencer writes that when he first read some of the earliest known Anglo-Norman recipes, he realized how "extraordinarily stylish, tasteful and contemporary the dishes were." This was food, he notes, "designed to please and satisfy very sophisticated palates. . . . It was food full of exotic ingredients and Mediterranean influences, with spices and flavourings from all over the then civilised world."

The English have long been enthusiastic carnivores, and that enthusiasm extended far beyond their now emblematic roast beef. Gervase Markham, whose best-known book was *The English Hus-wife, Containing the Inward and Outward Virtues Which Ought to Be in a Compleat Woman* (1615), offered an account of a "Little Dinner" he hosted for friends, where the menu included "shield of brawn [wild boar meat cooked in a cylinder of boar skin]; boiled capon; boiled beef; roast beef; neat's [cow's] tongue; roast pig; baked chewets [a kind of hash, probably in a pastry shell]; roast goose; roast swan; roast turkey; roast venison; pasty [pie] of venison; [and] roast kid, stuffed with dumplings. . . ." Such protein-rich feasts were commonplace.

In eighteenth-century London, according to the prolific English author and poet Thomas Burke in his 1937 book *Dinner Is Served! Or, Eating Round the World in London*, "sweetbreads, cocks'-combs, salamis [presumably salmis, rich game stews, as opposed to dried Italian sausages] and ragoûts were regularly served at taverns; also truffles, goose-liver, and a larger assortment of salads, made from many more herbs, than we get to-day. Every kind of game-bird and river-fish was served; of pies you had eel-pie, squab-pie, umble-pie [made with offal], partridge-pie, pheasant-pie; and as removes, jugged hare, pettitoes [pig's feet], lambs' tails, and varieties of local sausage." And such bounty was hardly confined to London. The splendor and variety of Scottish banquets in the eighteenth century, for instance, was legendary. An Englishman named John Chamberlayne, who visited Scotland in 1708, reported of the Scots that, at least among the upper social classes, "No people eat better, or have greater varieties of flesh, fish, wild and tame fowl."

What happened? Why did this variety and profusion and apparent quality diminish? Why had the popular idea of British food, by the mid-twentieth century, come to include overcooked meats, bland boiled vegetables, greasy fish and chips, and a handful of specialties with quaint, silly names like bubble and squeak, bangers and mash, and spotted dick? (In his recent book *The Road to Little Dribbling*, the American author Bill Bryson posits that such "strange and unseductive names" are a problem in themselves and that "if the British had given their foods pretentious names like 'galantine of pork saucisson en croûte' or 'julienne of vegetables Wellington,' people would gobble them up and there would be no jokes about British cooking.")

An Early Locavore

In Scottish author and poet Tobias Smollett's pica-resque satire *The Expedition of Humphry Clinker* (1771), the Welsh squire Matthew Bramble describes, in a letter to his physician, Dr. Lewis, the way he eats and drinks at his country house, Brambleton-hall:

I drink the virgin lymph, pure and chrystalline as it gushes from the rock, or the sparkling beveridge, home-brewed from malt of my own making; or I indulge with cyder, which my own orchard affords; or with claret of the best growth, imported for my own use, by a correspondent on whose integrity I can depend; my bread is sweet and nourishing, made from my own wheat, ground in my own mill, and baked in my own oven; my table is, in a great measure, furnished from my own ground; my five-year old mutton, fed on the fragrant herbage of the mountains, that might vie with venison in juice and flavour; my delicious veal, fattened with nothing but the mother's milk, that fills the dish with gravy; my poultry from the barn-door, that never knew confinement, but when they were at roost; my rabbits panting from the warren; my game fresh from the moors; my trout and salmon struggling from the stream; oysters from their native banks; and herrings, with other sea fish, I can eat in four hours after they are taken—My sallads, roots, and pot-herbs, my own garden yields in plenty and perfection; the produce of the natural soil, prepared by moderate cultivation. The same soil affords all the different fruits which England may call her own, so that my dessert is every day fresh-gathered from the tree; my dairy flows with nectarious tides of milk and cream, from whence we derive abundance of excellent butter, curds, and cheese; and the refuse fattens my pigs, that are destined for hams and bacon. . . .

What Is an Epicure?

William Kitchiner (1775–1827) was the son of a successful London coal merchant who inherited a small fortune upon his father's death. He became a professional optician (his specialty was tele-scopes) and was elected to the Royal Academy on the basis of his scientific skills, but he was also an amateur musician, a prolific author, and a serious cook, who was said to travel with a "cabinet of taste," in which he kept an array of sauces and condiments. His most famous book, published in 1817, was *Apicius Redivivus: or, The Cook's Oracle* (Apicius is the name given to several famous gourmets in ancient Rome, and perhaps used as a synonym for epicure; *redivivus* means "brought back to life"). The book was a great success, going into numerous editions—and more than thirty years after Kitchiner's death, the far more celebrated Mrs. Beeton lifted a number of his recipes for her own books. In his introduction to *Apicius Redivivus*, Kitchiner ruminates on the nature of the epicure:

The term gourmand, or epicure, has been strangely perverted; it has been conceived synonimous with a gluttony like that of the great eater of Kent [see page 150]; or a fastidious appetite only to be excited by fantastic dainties, as the brains of peacocks or parrots, the tongues of thrushes and nightingales; or the teats of a lactiferous sow. In the liberal acceptation of the term epicure, and as I use it, it means only the person who relishes his food cooked according to scientific principles, so prepared that the palate is delighted, rendered of easy solution in the stomach, and ultimately contributing to health. . . . The pleasures of the table have always been highly appreciated and carefully cultivated in all countries and in all ages; and, in spite of the Stoics, every one will allow they are the first we enjoy, the last we leave, and those we taste the oftenest.

Heston Blumenthal believes that the Georgian era (1714–1837) was the last great period of English cuisine, and it is likely that the Georgians' immediate successor, Queen Victoria, with her abstemious moral code, bears some of the responsibility for its decline. The Victorian middle class, as Colin Spencer puts it, "was nervous of pleasure." The notion of finding sensual enjoyment in what you ate seemed untoward, even vulgar. The idea, he says, was that "food should be tamed to make it powerless, and the only effective way of doing that was to make it uninteresting and unattractive." Around the same time, the factories of the Industrial Revolution were luring agricultural workers away from the land, a task made easier by a series of Inclosure Acts in the mid-1800s that gave landowners permission to increase rents for tenant farmers. This attenuated what Spencer calls "the constant stimulus that peasant cooking gives to any nation's cuisine."

Eliza Acton, the early nineteenth-century poet who wrote one of the first English cookbooks meant for ordinary households (as opposed to professional kitchens), decried the sorry state of British cooking as early as 1845, noting that while "England is, beyond most other countries, rich in the varied and abundant produce of its soil, or *of its commerce*, which in turn supply to it all that the necessities or the luxury of its people can demand; yet, until within very recent years, its cookery has remained far inferior to that of nations much less advanced in civilization; and foreigners have been called in to furnish to the tables of our aristocracy, and of the wealthier orders of the community, those refinements of the art which were not to be obtained from native talent."

Other factors that contributed to the downhill slide of British cooking were a fashion for French cuisine, seen to be far superior to the homegrown stuff, especially among the upper classes—Thomas Burke noted that by the 1930s, the restaurants of London were overwhelmingly French, with Simpson's-in-the-Strand being "indeed the only large purely *English* restaurant we have"—and the advent of labor-saving technologies like canning and freezing. Around the same time, the British medical establishment declared war on undercooked food—it could harbor germs—and prescribed long cooking times for meat, fish, and vegetables.

George Orwell, best known as the author of *1984* and *Animal Farm*, was a food lover who proposed, in the *Evening Standard* in 1937, that "it is not a law of nature that every restaurant in England should be either foreign or bad, and the first step towards an improvement will be a less long-suffering attitude in the British public itself." The same year, in a book called *Cheddar Gorge: A Book of English Cheeses*, the English poet, historian, and editor Sir John Squire wrote that while "the causes of our present lack of pride in home produce and interest in the subtleties of the palate may be left for others to trace," it was likely that puritanism and utilitarianism were in part responsible, as "each despises art and taste."

Then there were the two World Wars. The first of them further decimated the rural population, taking able-bodied men from farms in every corner of Great Britain, and not sending many of them back. During World War II, rationing—of meat, cheese, butter, sugar, cooking fat, and tea, among other things—hobbled home cooks and professional chefs alike (it continued long after the war's end; meat was still rationed in Great Britain until 1954), and the war itself broke up, temporarily if not permanently, the households in which home cooking had once thrived. "It is hard to overstate the damage the war did to Britain's food culture," says the London-based journalist and restaurant critic Jay Rayner. "A whole generation forgot how to cook." Rationing, postwar economic hardship, even the country's ingrained puritanism "made completely redundant," as Rayner puts it, "any sort of interest in food beyond its importance for basic survival."

The occasional culinary bright spots of the late 1950s and the '60s weren't British, for the most part: The influx of immigrants from all over Great Britain's dissolving or recently dissolved colonial empire meant the arrival of new "ethnic" restaurants and foodstuffs that would hitherto have been considered exotic if they were obtainable at all (soy sauce, fish sauce, Indian spices, pita bread). Around the same time, the books of Elizabeth David introduced—or reintroduced—the Mediterranean palate (and palette) to the British, rescuing olive oil (among other ingredients) from obscurity. Idiosyncratic restaurateurs like George Perry-Smith at the Hole in the Wall in Bath, Brian Sack and Francis Coulson at Sharrow Bay in the Lake District, and Franco Taruschio at the Walnut Tree in the Welsh town of Abergavenny, among others, did turn things inward at least a little, using good British raw materials and taking at least tentative steps towards developing a local (even if internationally accented) cuisine. It wasn't really until the 1970s and '80s, though, that things began to change dramatically.

The motivating forces behind the transformation included an upbeat economy (at least some of the time), a spike in world travel by the British after the austerity of the '60s (when British tourists were banned from taking any more than £50 per person out of the country), and even the transatlantic example set by the first generation of "New American" chefs. But the backbone of the revived British food scene was quite possibly the way in which young British chefs began to look back, and look around.

Mark Hix credits Swiss-born chef Anton Mosimann with having pioneered the renaissance of British cooking when he took over the kitchen at London's Dorchester Hotel Grill Room in 1975. "It was really very English," Hix says. Mosimann's menu promised "a selection of traditional British National and Regional dishes." That translated to things like potted shrimp ("a Lancashire delicacy"), the Scottish lamb and lentil soup called hairst bree, poached turbot with egg sauce, calves' liver and bacon, sherry trifle, and lemon syllabub. This was highly unusual for an upscale restaurant at a time when France was still looked upon as the center of the culinary universe.

French influence endured (as it does to this day), but something else started happening in the late 1980s and into the '90s. Chefs like Simon Hopkinson, Alistair Little, Brian Turner, Sally Clarke, and, later, Fergus Henderson, Jeremy Lee, Mark Hix, Rowley Leigh, Gary Rhodes, and Nigel Haworth began incorporating traditional British foodstuffs and dishes into their repertoires. The many restaurants opened by the legendary designer/restaurateur Terence Conran were massively influential in this regard, even when their accent was French. So were the old-guard London classics—The Caprice, The Ivy, J. Sheekey—revivified by Jeremy King and Chris Corbin. Traditional English fare like kipper pâté, steak and kidney pie, and jugged hare began appearing on trendy menus alongside cassoulet and steak frites—not as nostalgia, but as pleasingly edible reminders of the depth and breadth of Britain's culinary heritage.

The so-called gastropub movement (the term was coined by *Evening Standard* restaurant critic Charles Campion) energized the London, and then the national, restaurant scene in a different way. It started in 1991, when a couple of young restaurant veterans named David Eyre and Mike Belben refurbished and reopened a derelict pub called The Eagle in London's Clerkenwell district. Many British pubs were closing for economic reasons in that period (they still are), and the real estate was cheap, so such premises offered novice restaurateurs a way to set up

Scottish-born chef Jeremy Lee of Quo Vadis in London

shop with minimal investment. The idea of the gastropub, as it has developed, is to serve good, simple food at reasonable prices in an informal, unpretentious setting. That food isn't necessarily British—there might be fish and chips or a Sunday roast on the menu, but there is also likely to be bruschetta, moussaka, or curry—but the sensibility is, and gastropubs have given many young British chefs and restaurateurs their start.

This isn't a book about British restaurants per se. It's a book about the traditional and modernized-traditional cooking of Great Britain (which is to say, of England, Scotland, and Wales) as I've discovered and experienced it over the years—in restaurants, yes, but also in private homes and through books and other published sources, historical and modern. (Northern Ireland is part of the United Kingdom, but not of Great Britain; I'm omitting it here not because there isn't plenty of good food there, both classic and contemporary, but because I covered that food extensively in an earlier book, *The Country Cooking of Ireland*.) In putting together this compendium

Clouds at dusk over Lancashire

of recipes, stories, excerpts, and more, I've drawn on fully a half century's worth of trips I've made to Great Britain—probably an average of one per year at the least—since that visit so long ago to Manchester, trips that have taken me from Land's End at the tip of Cornwall to Unst at the very top of the Shetland Islands, from Holyhead in Wales to Whitstable in eastern Kent, and of course all around London (most of all), Glasgow, Cardiff, and other major cities. Along the way, I've benefited greatly from the kind cooperation of dozens of British chefs, restaurateurs, food and drink producers, and food writers.

I call this book, in its subtitle, a "new look" for two reasons: First, because many British chefs today are considering the cooking of the past in a fresh light and finding ways to reproduce or reinterpret it, and second, because I have been looking at British cuisine myself, with an American's eye (and with whatever advantages or disadvantages of distance that may imply), in an effort to come up with a kind of definition of good British cooking as I've found it in the second decade of the twenty-first century.

Jay Rayner warned me one day not to "mistake what people are doing now for food our grandparents would have eaten." They would not, for instance, have recognized what Fergus Henderson is serving at the estimable St. John in London, he said. "Fergus will tell you," added Rayner, "that Marcella Hazan, not Mrs. Beeton, was his inspiration." (Henderson confirmed this.)

Fair enough. But I'd suggest that whatever its origins or inspirations, what's now going on in the country's best kitchens is often uniquely and genuinely British, grown out of fertile tradition, shaped by an astounding natural bounty, and refined through the efforts of many centuries of men and women who have understood food well and pursued its creation passionately. The British table today, at its best, is as good as any in the world.

A Note on Ingredients and Metric Conversions

Butter means unsalted butter, preferably European or European-style. My preferred butter is Kerrygold from Ireland (now widely available in American supermarkets), which has a richness and elastic texture particularly suited to these recipes.

Eggs are large (about 2 ounces / 60 g each) and should be as fresh as possible. Use organic eggs if available.

Fruit and vegetables are medium- or standard-size and are always washed and trimmed, unless otherwise specified.

Oats are Scottish oats, which are stone-ground and have a finer texture than steel-cut Irish oats.

Pepper should be good quality coarse-ground black pepper, preferably freshly ground, unless otherwise specified.

Salt should be fine sea salt or kosher salt, or else Maldon crystals, crushed between your fingers.

Sugar is standard granulated sugar unless confectioner's (powdered) or superfine (caster) is specified.

Unless otherwise specified, all ingredients should be brought to room temperature before using.

For the convenience of readers who use metric measurements, quantity and temperature equivalents have been given in the recipes that follow. Please note that the conversions are approximate, and have been rounded off for reasons of practicality (1 pound of weight, for instance, has been translated as 450 g, not 454 g, which is more accurate; an oven temperature of 400°F becomes 200°C, not the more precise 204°C). British and American teaspoons, tablespoons, and cups hold slightly different quantities, but they are close enough for most dishes, so I have used those measurements wherever practical. Diameter and volume measurements for pots and baking dishes correspond to sizes that are actually available (e.g., Americans would use a 2-quart vessel, while the British would employ a 2-L one).

CHAPTER 1

—

BREAKFAST

"BREAKFAST IS EVERYTHING. THE BEGINNING, THE FIRST THING. IT IS THE MOUTHFUL THAT IS THE COMMITMENT TO THE NEW DAY."

—A. A. GILL, *Breakfast at the Wolseley: Recipes from London's Favorite Restaurant* (2014)

"POT OF HARE; DITTO OF TROUT; POT OF PREPARED SHRIMPS; DISH OF PLAIN SHRIMPS; TIN OF SARDINES; BEAUTIFUL BEEF-STEAK; EGGS, MUFFIN; LARGE LOAF, AND BUTTER, NOT FORGETTING CAPITAL TEA. THERE'S A BREAKFAST FOR YOU!"

—GEORGE BORROW, *Wild Wales* (1862)

Sir Winston Churchill—or was it Somerset Maugham?—is said to have remarked that the only way to have a decent meal in England was to eat breakfast three times a day. Dr. Johnson, on the other hand, was particularly taken with the morning meal in Scotland. "If an epicure could remove by a wish, in quest of sensual gratifications," he wrote, "wherever he had supped, he would breakfast in Scotland."

English literature is full of descriptions of breakfasts in various parts of Great Britain so grand that they might almost be called heroic. Tobias Smollett, in his novel *The Expedition of Humphry Clinker* (1771), describes a hunt breakfast encompassing "one kit [a small barrel] of boiled eggs; a second, full of butter; a third full of cream; an entire cheese, made of goat's milk; a large earthen pot full of honey; the best part of a ham; a cold venison pasty; a bushel of oat meal, made in thin cakes and bannocks, with a small wheaten loaf in the middle for the strangers; a large stone bottle full of whisky, another of brandy, and a kilderkin [a cask containing about 22 gallons / 83 L] of ale." Charles Lamb mentions in *The Essays of Elia* (1823), as part of a wedding celebration, "a protracted *breakfast* of three hours—if stores of cold fowls, tongues, hams, botargoes [i.e., bottarga, dried tuna or mullet roe], dried fruits, wines, cordials, &c., can deserve so meagre an appellation. . . ." Closer to our own time, George Orwell, in his unpublished 1946 essay "British Cookery," proposed that "breakfast . . . for nearly all British people . . . is not a snack but a serious meal," and suggested that a proper breakfast should begin with "sodden" porridge or breakfast cereal; continue on with fish ("usually salt fish"), meat ("fried bacon . . . grilled kidneys, fried pork sausages, or cold ham"), or eggs; and conclude with bread or toast with butter and orange marmalade or honey.

Of course, the British didn't always eat large breakfasts, and certainly don't indulge in them as a matter of course today. In medieval times, the typical morning meal—called the *morgenmete* (literally "morning food") in Old English; the word *breakfast* wasn't used until the mid-fifteenth century—would have been bread (or oatcakes or porridge in Scotland and northern England), cold meat of some kind, and ale.

The extravagant English breakfast started taking shape in the latter part of the seventeenth century, in the houses of the gentry, where an abundant morning groaning board became a sign of social status and a way of showing off the produce of the property—cured meats from the squire's pigs, cured fish from his river, fresh fruit from his orchards. In the Victorian era, an emergent middle class took up the traditions of country hospitality, including the ample breakfast. During the Industrial Revolution, even the working class began to eat large meals before leaving home in the morning, needing fuel to get through their arduous day. Serious breakfasts were pretty much ubiquitous in Great Britain by the end of the nineteenth century—and by the early 1950s, according to the website of an organization called the English Breakfast Society, about half the British population began their day with what is commonly known as "the full English" or "the fry-up" (see page 36)—a hearty combination-plate repast heavy on the pork.

That's no longer the case. Britons are breakfasting, just like their American cousins, on bagels, croissants, Krispy Kreme doughnuts, Bacon & Egg McMuffins. . . . Porridge is still popular, especially in the north, but so is granola, so is Greek yogurt, so is the full Kellogg's catalog. Hotel dining rooms, unreconstructed urban cafés, and certain modern restaurants do keep old traditions alive, however, serving things like grilled kippers, deviled lambs' kidneys, maybe the Indian-inspired smoked-fish-and-rice dish called kedgeree (page 39)—and many places do still offer "the full English" or some regional variation thereof.

"Any type of breakfast can be had in England," wrote Florence White in her invaluable *Good Things in England: A Practical Cookery Book for Everyday Use*. "All one has to do is to know what one wants, order it in good time, and have the money to pay for it." That was in 1932, but the same is true today.

BACON ROLL

MAKES 2

I love having breakfast at The Wolseley, across Arlington Street from The Ritz in Piccadilly, with its light and airy high-ceilinged dining room always full of handsome people, and I never have breakfast there without ordering the crispy bacon roll. This is simply a soft, floury roll enclosing crisp-cooked American-style bacon, the kind made from pork belly, known as "streaky bacon" in the U.K. It's delicious, but it's not what you'll get in most places if you order a bacon roll—also known variously as a bacon sandwich, a bacon sarnie, or a bacon butty (though a butty, properly speaking, is just a slice of buttered bread, or, at the most, a half sandwich made by folding over a piece of buttered bread around a filling). The typical bacon roll will be filled instead with leaner English bacon, or back bacon, cut from the loin of the pig, with just an edge of the pork belly attached. This is not to be confused with Canadian bacon, which is simply cured pork loin; what makes English bacon (and its counterparts elsewhere in the U.K. and in Ireland) so good is the ratio of lean meat to sweet fat, with the former in preponderance.

5 tablespoons (75 g) butter, softened
2 soft, crusty rolls, halved, or 4 thick slices multi-
    grain bread
4 slices English or Irish back bacon (see Sources,
    page 316)
HP Sauce or some other English or Irish brown
    sauce (see opposite)

Generously butter both halves of the rolls or all 4 slices of bread (on one side only).

Heat a large skillet over medium heat. Cook the bacon, in batches if necessary, until it begins to brown and grow crisp around the edges, turning the slices once.

Make sandwiches with the rolls or bread, dividing the bacon slices evenly between them, folding the bacon over if necessary to fit. Serve with HP Sauce on the side.

TATTIE SCONES

MAKES 16 TO 20 SCONES

These are griddlecakes, fried rather than baked. Related to potato pancakes and to the fadge or parleys of Northern Ireland, they have little to do with the leavened quick bread, often studded with currants, also known as scones. Both types of scones, however, may be made as rounds or triangles. I've been told that the triangles are more traditional—but on the other hand, F. Marian McNeill gives a recipe for round potato scones in *The Scots Kitchen*, published back in 1929. Tattie scones of whatever shape are frequently included in a "full Scottish" (as opposed to English) breakfast.

½ recipe Mashed Potatoes (page 211)
¾ cup (95 g) all-purpose flour, sifted, plus more
    for dusting
6 tablespoons (¾ stick / 85 g) butter, softened,
    plus more for serving
Salt

In a medium bowl, mix the mashed potatoes and flour together well, then stir in half the butter and salt to taste.

Turn the dough out onto a floured work surface and divide it into four or five pieces of equal size. Roll each one out into a disk about ¼ inch (6 mm) thick, then cut each disk into four triangular pieces.

Melt the remaining butter on a griddle or in a large skillet over medium-high heat. Fry the scones, working in batches if necessary, for about 2 minutes on each side, turning them once.

The scones may be eaten as is, as a side dish with eggs, or by themselves, slathered with butter. If you're having tattie scones as part of a full breakfast, fry them again quickly in bacon fat in the same pan you used to fry the bacon just before serving.

Brown Sauce

Tomato ketchup is certainly popular enough in Great Britain (the modifier *tomato* is useful to append here, as there is also mushroom ketchup, a much older condiment that survives today), but it wouldn't seem wholly inaccurate to describe the tart, fruity, mahogany-hued condiment called brown sauce as "British ketchup." It is on hundreds of thousands—probably millions—of tables around the country, both at home and in restaurants and fast food emporiums, and is widely considered an essential complement to steaks and chops, chips (french fries), bacon and sausage sandwiches, and the full English breakfast, among other things.

What's in it? The brown sauce sold under the Wilkin & Sons Ltd. Tiptree label contains tomatoes, sugar, barley malt vinegar, wine vinegar, apples, sultanas, oranges, citrus fiber, salt, tamarind, lemon juice, and a bouquet of unnamed spices. The constituents of the best-known brand, HP Sauce, are slightly different: tomatoes, barley malt vinegar, molasses, glucose-fructose syrup, spirit vinegar, sugar, dates, modified corn flour, rye flour, salt, spices, "flavourings," and tamarind.

HP Sauce was invented by a Nottingham grocer named Frederick Gibson Garton in the 1890s; he called it "HP" because somebody told him that it was being used in a dining room in the Houses of Parliament (a partial image of that famous building appears on the label). Garton sold the formula and the name to one Edwin Moore, a vinegar maker, and Moore launched the sauce on a commercial basis.

Today, the HP Sauce brand is owned by the H. J. Heinz Company (speaking of ketchup) and is produced in the Netherlands. Heinz introduced a reduced-salt and -sugar version of the sauce in 2007, which Britons were free to take or leave. But the company caused a stir in 2011 when it surreptitiously altered the then 116-year-old original recipe as well, apparently at the request of British government health authorities. Newspaper stories at the time quoted scores of unhappy Britons who claimed that the new sauce was too sour or somehow "off" and that it was ruining their breakfasts. Health experts predicted that the sodium reduction would prevent four thousand premature deaths a year, but didn't mention that the changes in the recipe also added calories and carbohydrates.

For whatever reasons, sales of brown sauce of all kinds—popular brands besides Wilkin & Sons and HP include Branston and O.K.—were down almost 20 percent in 2015 from the previous year.

Oatcakes

OATCAKES

MAKES 12

Wheat grows well in eastern Scotland, but historically, especially in the northern reaches of the country, in the Highlands and Islands, oats and barley were the most important cereal crops. Oats thrive in the Scottish north, with its long summer days, cool evening temperatures, and ample rainfall, but they have become a kind of emblematic foodstuff for the entire country. Among other things, they're essential to haggis (see page 142), various soups, desserts, and beverages, and, of course, baked goods, including breads and oatcakes.

Oatcakes were first described in the fourteenth century in *Chronicles*, an account of the Hundred Years' War by Jean Froissart, a French court historian, who wrote of seeing Scottish soldiers eating an oatmeal gruel cooked over a fire on a metal plate. There are countless variations on the oatcake today, including versions flavored with honey, enriched with egg, and made with the addition of rye or barley flour. In western Scotland, oatcakes are commonly called bannocks (in the rest of the country, bannocks are generally sweeter and include wheat flour). To obtain the proper texture, it is important to use stone-ground Scottish oats, not the steel-cut Irish variety. Oatcakes sometimes take the place of toast for an English—and, above all, Scottish—breakfast; even Queen Elizabeth is said to favor them for her morning meal. They are also a natural accompaniment to good cheese at any time of day.

10 ounces (280 g) stone-ground Scottish oats,
   plus more for dusting
5 tablespoons (75 g) butter, plus more for greasing
1 teaspoon salt

Preheat the oven to 350°F (175°C). Lightly grease a large baking sheet with butter.

Spread the oats out in a thin layer on a baking sheet and toast it in the oven for about 10 minutes, shaking the sheet occasionally. Keep the oven on.

Meanwhile, melt the butter with ¾ cup (180 ml) water in a small saucepan over low heat.

Transfer the toasted oats to the jar of a blender, add the salt, and pulse until the oats resemble fine bread crumbs mixed with flour.

Bring the water and butter just to a boil over high heat, then drizzle it into the oats, stirring continuously to form a dough that resembles dry cookie dough. Add a bit more water if necessary so that the mixture holds together.

Dust a work surface with oats, then transfer the dough to it. Divide the dough into two equal pieces, then roll or use your hand to flatten each piece into a round about ¼ inch (6 mm) thick. With a damp knife, score each cake into sixths without cutting all the way through the dough.

Carefully transfer the dough to the baking sheet and bake for 30 to 35 minutes, or until the oatcakes are firm and brown.

Carefully transfer the oatcakes to a wire rack to cool. When just cool, gently cut down into the lines scored in the oatcakes, turning each round into six triangular pieces. Return the pieces to the wire rack and leave them to harden overnight, uncovered, before serving.

BEREMEAL BANNOCKS

MAKES 2

Bere (pronounced "bear") is an ancient variety of barley, said to be the oldest cultivated grain in Great Britain (it was probably introduced by the Vikings), and is grown mostly on the archipelago of Orkney, off the far northern tip of Scotland. Baked goods made from it are dark and slightly smoky (the barley husks are smoked over peat fires) and have a unique flavor, earthy and a little bit acidic. Bannocks are unleavened bread cooked on a griddle. They're made around Scotland and the north of England of conventional barley or wheat flour or a

recipe continues

combination of the two; some are sweet. (In western Scotland, the term is sometimes applied to oatcakes.) The beremeal bannock, though, is found only on Orkney, where it is typically eaten with butter and/or cheese, often for breakfast.

1½ cups (225 g) beremeal (see Sources, page 316), plus more for dusting
¾ cup (65 g) all-purpose flour, plus more for dusting
Pinch of salt
1 teaspoon baking soda
1 teaspoon cream of tartar
1¼ cups (300 ml) buttermilk, plus more if needed
Good butter or cheese, for serving

Mix the beremeal, flour, salt, baking soda, and cream of tartar together thoroughly in a medium bowl. Make a well in the middle of the mixture and pour in the buttermilk. With a wooden spoon or plastic spatula, mix the ingredients together until they form a damp, soft dough. (Add a little more buttermilk if necessary.) Cover the bowl and set the dough aside for 30 minutes.

Dust a work surface lightly with flour and flour your hands, then divide the dough into two pieces of equal size and roll each one out into a round about 7 inches (18 cm) in diameter.

Heat a griddle or cast-iron skillet over medium heat until a drop of water sizzles on it. Reduce heat to medium-low, dust the griddle lightly with beremeal, then cook the bannocks, one at a time if necessary, for about 3 minutes on each side, or until they're golden brown.

Cool the bannocks to room temperature, then serve with good butter or cheese.

OATMEAL PORRIDGE

SERVES 4

"The healsome Parritch, chief o' Scotia's food." Thus Robert Burns hailed oatmeal porridge in his poem "The Cotter's Saturday Night." Dr. Johnson once defined oats as "a grain which in England is generally give to horses, but in Scotland supports the people"—to which his contemporary, the Scottish author and economist Patrick Murray, is said to have replied, "Yes, and where else will you see such horses and such men?" Oats have for centuries been a staple of Scottish life. They fattened the country's famous black cattle, were used as currency to pay rent and wages, and formed part of many a Scots lass's dowry. Oats even had medicinal value, as poultices for insect bites and skin infections.

Most of all, though, oats in Scotland were and are eaten in the form of porridge. There are various methods of making porridge, but traditionally, it was cooked up in the evening—always stirred clockwise, for good luck—to be reheated for consumption at breakfast time. Scots often take their oatmeal salted, possibly with some cream. If they sweeten it, they're more likely to use treacle or honey than sugar, and a splash of ale or porter is not unheard of.

2 teaspoons salt, plus more if needed
1 cup stone-ground Scottish oats (see Sources, page 316)

Bring 3½ cups (840 ml) water to a boil in a medium pot over high heat. Add the salt, then remove the pan from the heat, add the oatmeal, and stir well. Cover the pot and set it aside for at least 6 hours, or overnight.

Reheat the oatmeal over medium heat, stirring frequently and adding a bit more water if necessary to prevent sticking. Adjust the salt if necessary.

Dangerous Porridge

In Thomas Hardy's novel *The Mayor of Casterbridge*, a hay-trusser named Michael Henchard visits a fair outside Casterbridge (Hardy's fictional stand-in for Dorchester) with his wife, Susan, and daughter, Elizabeth-Jane. There are two refreshment tents on the fairgrounds, one offering "Good Home-brewed Beer, Ale, and Cyder," the other "Good Furmity Sold Hear." Henchard wants to head for the beer tent, but Susan says no, she always likes furmity. Furmity—better known as frumenty (page 30), and also called frumentee or fermenty—takes its name(s) from the Latin *frumentum*, wheat, and is a kind of wheat porridge, either savory or sweet. That sounds harmless enough, but the "hag" who tends the furmity tent at Hardy's fair spikes hers with rum. Henchard has so much of the porridge, and thus of the rum, that he ends up selling his wife and daughter to a sailor for five guineas, thus launching Hardy's complicated plot.

A Novel Omelet

The English novelist and journalist Arnold Bennett (1867–1931) is largely forgotten today, or remembered only for a single novel, *The Old Wives' Tale* (named by Modern Library as one of the twentieth century's hundred best works of fiction). He was, however, a prolific, best-selling author in his time, with about forty novels and short-story collections and half as many works of nonfiction to his credit. Bennett was a man-about-town in his heyday, and one of his regular haunts was London's celebrated Savoy Hotel, opened in 1889 by Gilbert and Sullivan producer Richard D'Oyly Carte and once run by César Ritz, with no less than Auguste Escoffier overseeing the kitchen.

Bennett set two of his novels in a hotel very much like The Savoy: *The Grand Bablyon Hotel* and *Imperial Palace*, the latter both a rather mannered love story and an almost journalistic portrait of the inner workings of a great institution like the Savoy, kitchen included. (In an essay in *Those United States*, Bennett claimed that his "secret ambition had always been to be the manager of a grand hotel.")

In The Savoy dining room, at some point in his career, Bennett apparently asked for an omelet that would involve smoked haddock, and the kitchen—almost certainly after Escoffier's time—created one for him and named it in his honor (page 33). While not as well known around the world as Escoffier's signature creations for The Savoy—Melba toast and pêche Melba (both named for the Australian soprano Nellie Melba)—it has endured into our era, even as Bennett's renown has faded, and may still be found at The Savoy and at a handful of other London restaurants, including The Wolseley and The Delaunay.

FRUMENTY

SERVES 4

Frumenty dates from medieval times—Florence White, in *Good Things in England: A Practical Cookery Book for Everyday Use*, calls it England's "oldest national dish"— and the savory version, cooked with meat broth, was considered a suitable accompaniment to venison as early as the fourteenth century. (A meatless version made with almond milk and flavored with saffron would have been eaten during Lent and on days of religious abstinence.) Plain though it may seem, frumenty was traditionally a festive dish, served at village fairs and festivals (see page 29) and on such occasions as Christmas Day and Easter Monday. This is a sweetened version, complete with rum, which makes an unusual offering for brunch or a weekend breakfast.

1 cup golden raisins
½ cup (120 ml) dark rum
1 cup cracked wheat
1 cup (240 ml) whole milk
2 tablespoons brown sugar
Pinch of salt

Put the raisins in a small bowl and pour the rum over them. Stir the raisins, then cover the bowl and let the raisins sit for 4 to 6 hours or overnight, stirring them occasionally.

Bring 4 cups (960 ml) water to a boil over high heat. Stir in the cracked wheat, reduce the heat to low, cover the pot, and cook until the wheat has softened, 20 to 30 minutes.

Transfer the wheat to a medium bowl (if the wheat is cooked but hasn't absorbed all the water, drain it in a fine-mesh sieve). Stir in the milk, sugar, and salt. Stir in the raisins and rum, then divide the frumenty evenly between four bowls.

EGGS AND SOLDIERS

SERVES 2 TO 4

This is a "nursery food" classic, but a dish still enjoyed for breakfast by many for whom the nursery is a distant memory. Thin strips of toast are called soldiers because they are thought to resemble military men on parade, trim and upright. (They are also sometimes called dippies—for obvious reasons.) It is possible to find, in Great Britain, an implement that cuts toast into forms resembling actual human soldiers.

4 large eggs
4 slices good-quality white bread
2 tablespoons (30 g) butter
Salt and finely ground black pepper

Bring a medium pot of water to a boil over high heat, then reduce the heat to medium to keep the water at a slow rolling boil. Carefully put the eggs into the pot and cook them for 3 minutes.

Meanwhile, toast the bread lightly, then trim the crusts, butter it, and cut each slice into four "soldiers."

To serve, put the eggs into eggcups and tap the top of each shell gently with a dinner knife to crack them. Remove the tops, season the eggs with salt and pepper, and eat by dipping the soldiers into the egg.

OMELETTE ARNOLD BENNETT

SERVES 2

The omelette Arnold Bennett has been on the menu at London's Savoy Hotel ever since the author asked the kitchen to serve him smoked haddock in omelet form sometime around the turn of the twentieth century (see page 29). Today, The Savoy's version has strayed from the original recipe (among other things, it includes garlic and thyme, and uses a mix of cheddar and Gruyère), and other variations on the formula abound. Some call for the omelet to be folded over like a classic French omelet, though the original was served open-faced. This is a reasonably simple interpretation, worked out by trial and error, which nonetheless captures what I believe to be the spirit of the original.

1¼ cups (300 ml) whole milk
8 ounces (225 g) smoked haddock, skin and bones
   removed
4 tablespoons (½ stick / 55 g) unsalted butter, plus
   more for greasing
2 rounded tablespoons all-purpose flour
Salt and freshly ground white pepper
½ cup (50 g) grated Parmigiano-Reggiano cheese
6 large eggs, lightly beaten

Heat the milk over medium-high heat (do not let it boil) in a saucepan large enough to hold the haddock. Add the haddock, reduce the heat to medium, and cover the saucepan. Cook the haddock, for about 4 minutes, turning it once.

Remove the haddock from the milk and set it aside. Reserve the milk.

Preheat the broiler. Grease a small baking sheet or dish lightly with butter.

In a separate saucepan, melt 2 tablespoons (30 g) of the butter over low heat, then stir in the flour to make a roux. Stir in the reserved milk to make a thick sauce. When the haddock is cool enough to handle, flake it into the sauce and stir well. Remove the pan from the heat. Season the

The Savoy hotel kitchen, London, 1928

haddock mixture with a little salt (the haddock will be salty) and white pepper, and stir in about 1 tablespoon of the cheese.

Melt 1 tablespoon (15 g) of the butter in a nonstick omelet pan or skillet over medium heat and pour in half the beaten eggs. Stir the eggs with a wooden spoon, then cook for about a minute, or until the bottom is set but the top is still runny. Spoon half the haddock mixture onto the omelet, spreading it out gently with the back of a wooden spoon to cover the omelet's surface.

Carefully transfer the omelet to the prepared baking sheet or dish, then repeat the process with the remaining ingredients to make a second omelet.

Scatter the remaining cheese evenly over the omelets, then broil for 1 to 2 minutes, or until the cheese is golden brown and bubbling.

Mrs. Beeton Starts the Day

What was served for breakfast in an affluent, well-run home in the Victorian era? We can get a good idea from the sections on the morning meal in *Mrs. Beeton's Book of Household Management*, the most famous Victorian cookbook and domestic instruction manual, written by the celebrated Mrs. Beeton (née Isabella Mary Mayson), and first published in book form in 1861.

It will not be necessary to give here a long bill of fare of cold joints, &c., which may be placed on the side-board, and do duty at the breakfast-table. Suffice it to say, that any cold meat the larder may furnish, should be nicely garnished, and be placed on the buffet. Collared and potted meats or fish, cold game or poultry, veal-and-ham pies, game-and-Rump-steak pies, are all suitable dishes for the breakfast-table; as also cold ham, tongue, &c. &c. . . . The following list of hot dishes may perhaps assist our readers in knowing what to provide for the comfortable meal called breakfast. Broiled fish, such as mackerel, whiting, herrings, dried haddocks, &c.; mutton chops and rump-steaks, broiled sheep's kidneys, kidneys à la maître d'hôtel, sausages, plain rashers of bacon, bacon and poached eggs, ham and poached eggs, omelets, plain boiled eggs, oeufs-au-plat, poached eggs on toast, muffins, toast, marmalade, butter, &c. &c. . . . In the summer, and when they are obtainable, always have a vase of freshly-gathered flowers on the breakfast-table, and, when convenient, a nicely-arranged dish of fruit: When strawberries are in season, these are particularly refreshing; as also grapes, or even currants.

Opposite: A Victorian advertising poster, 1899

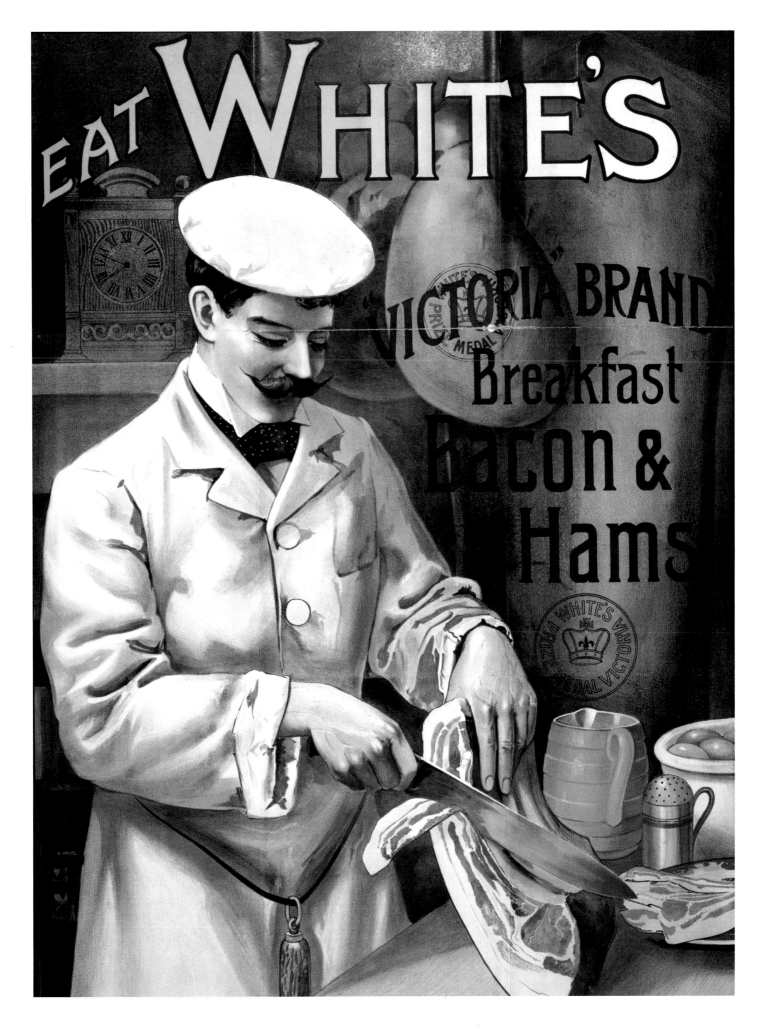

The Full English

The modern-day emblematic British breakfast—known as "the full English" (or "Scottish" or "Welsh"), or simply "the fry-up"—is a plate crowded with pork products, vegetables, and eggs. (Its calorie and cholesterol counts lend it another sobriquet: "the cardiac special.") The exact constituents of the meal vary according to region and individual preference, but basically it includes fried back bacon, sausages, black pudding (i.e., blood sausage), fried button mushrooms, fried or broiled tomato halves, baked beans, and fried or poached (sometimes scrambled) eggs, with toast—white or brown—on the side and coffee or tea to drink. There may be bread fried in bacon fat or butter instead of toast, and potatoes may be included in the form of chips or hash browns (purists frown on the latter).

In Scotland, additions to or substitutions for the standard fare might include haggis, lorne sausage (a square patty of ground pork and beef and rusk crumbs), the mild pork sausage called white pudding, oatcakes, or the potato griddle cakes called tattie scones (page 24), and sometimes finnan haddie is served in place of bacon. In some parts of the country, fruit pudding is also served; this is a sausage-shaped boiled pudding made with flour, suet, sugar, and currants or sultanas, then cut into slices and fried.

In earlier times, the Welsh used to add laverbread (see page 204), a gelatinous seaweed puree that can be coated in oatmeal and fried, to the breakfast plate, but this is uncommon today. Steamed cockles, the favorite shellfish of Wales, were sometimes added to the morning menu, too, but this also is rare today. Thick-cut bacon remains a standard, though.

Whatever the particulars, it is an impressive repast; when you get up from a full English, you know you've eaten. The Hawaiian-born, Oxford-educated social anthropologist Kaori O'Connor, who wrote a whole book on the subject (*The English Breakfast: The Biography of a National Meal with Recipes*), calls the full English "the best-known national meal in the world," and it's hard to argue with that assessment.

No Mushrooms, Please, We're British

How did fried mushrooms end up being part of "the full English"? They're a curious addition. The English traditionally have never been particularly fond of these fungi. The sixteenth-century botanist John Gerard, in his popular *Herball, or Generall Historie of Plantes*, wrote of mushrooms that "some are very venomous and full of poison," and that even among those that weren't, "few of them are good to be eaten, and most of them do suffocate and strangle the eater." In 1811, tavern-keeper John Farley, in his *London Art of Cookery*, warned that "the common esculent [i.e., edible] kinds, if eaten too freely, frequently bring on heart-burns, sicknesses, vomitings, diarrhoeas, dysenteries, and other dangerous symptoms. It is therefore to be wished, that they were banished from the table. . . ."

Mrs. Beeton, in 1861, lists more than twenty hot dishes (in addition to cold and potted meats) as possible constituents of "the comfortable meal called breakfast" but mushrooms are not mentioned. The full English (see opposite), in more or less its modern form, dates only from around the time of World War I, and it is reasonable to assume that mushrooms, along with two other perhaps curious additions, fried or broiled tomatoes and baked beans (preferably from a can), were added only then. Or perhaps they came later, when rationing during and after World War II took bacon and eggs off many tables. In any case, they are today considered pretty much essential to the meal.

Breakfast Mushrooms

BREAKFAST MUSHROOMS

SERVES 4

In making this essential part of the full English breakfast, some recipes call for cooking the mushrooms in vegetable oil in the same pan as the sausages; some suggest frying them in the leftover fat after you've fried the bacon; one fancy recipe I found involves browning them in butter, then braising them in chicken stock with garlic and thyme—a process that would appall purists, I'm sure. I like the idea of cooking them in the bacon fat, but butter works, too.

2 to 3 tablespoons (30 to 45 g) bacon fat or butter
16 white button mushrooms, cleaned, trimmed, and quartered
Salt

Melt the bacon fat or butter in a medium saucepan over medium heat. Add the mushrooms and cook, stirring frequently, until they release some of their liquid and begin to brown, about 10 minutes.

Season with salt.

KEDGEREE

SERVES 4

The *Oxford English Dictionary* offers a dozen different spellings for this Anglo-Indian dish, including *kitsery*, *ketchery*, *quichery* (which sounds like a good name for a brunch place), *cutcherry*, and *khichri*. The last of these is the Hindi word, meaning a dish of rice and sesame, from which these various forms derive. English travelers were aware of the Indian version of the dish as early as the 1660s, and by the mid-1800s a British interpretation had

become a popular breakfast dish back home. There are many variations on the recipe, some involving sultanas or currants, some made with fresh or smoked salmon or other fish.

2 cups (480 ml) whole milk
1 pound smoked haddock or finnan haddie (see Sources, page 316), rinsed, any skin and bones removed
3 cups cooked long-grain rice
1 teaspoon curry powder
1 teaspoon cayenne
Salt and freshly ground black pepper
3 tablespoons (45 g) butter
1 onion, finely chopped
2 hard-boiled eggs, chopped
2 tablespoons chopped fresh parsley

Heat the milk in a small saucepan over medium heat (do not boil). Add the fish, breaking it up with a fork into large pieces. Reduce the heat to low and poach the fish for about 10 minutes. Remove the fish from the pot, discarding the milk, and set aside to cool slightly. When the fish is cool enough to handle, remove and discard any skin and bones and break the flesh into small pieces with your hands.

Put the rice in a large bowl, breaking it up with your hands if it has clumped together, and stir in the curry powder, cayenne, and salt and black pepper to taste.

Melt 1 tablespoon (15 g) of the butter in a large skillet over medium heat. Add the onion and cook, stirring frequently, until it has softened but not browned, 5 to 6 minutes.

Melt the remaining 2 tablespoons (30 g) butter in a small pan, then drizzle it over the rice. Add the onion and the butter it was cooked in, then stir in the fish. Add the eggs and parsley and mix everything together well. Adjust the seasoning, if necessary.

Scotch Broth (see page 58)

CHAPTER 2

SOUPS

"BEAUTIFUL SOUP, SO RICH AND GREEN /
WAITING IN A HOT TUREEN!"

—LEWIS CARROLL, *Alice's Adventures in Wonderland* (1865)

"THERE IS A CATEGORY OF SOUP THAT ATTAINS
A ROBUSTNESS ONE DOESN'T EXPECT, A DENSITY
OF FLAVOR AND OFTEN OF TEXTURE. . . .
THESE SOUPS ARE LIKE THOSE WORKS OF ART . . .
IN WHICH A FILIGREED DELICACY OF LOCAL
DETAIL ADDS UP TO AN AGGLOMERATED SOLIDITY
OF EFFECT."

—JOHN LANCHESTER, *The Debt to Pleasure* (1996)

Soup is the most protean of foods. It can be a simple broth, flavored only with a few plebian vegetables (onions and carrots, say) and possibly the bones of a spent chicken, or it can be a virtual stew, meaty with lamb or opulent with lobster. It is the most personal of foods, as its main ingredients or at least its seasonings are determined by each cook's preferences and each kitchen's larder; it is also the most forgiving, allowing for endless last-minute additions or adjustments in the quest for perfection. It is also, not incidentally, the most economical of foods: Whatever lamb or lobster or other rich foodstuffs it may contain, its main ingredient is free, or nearly so: water.

The British attitude toward soup seems, to the outside observer at least, to be somewhat schizophrenic. As in most (if not all) cultures, it has been part of the daily diet for as long as people have known how to cook. The ancient Celts and later the Saxons in Britain ate a gruel or pottage of barley or oats flavored with vegetables and herbs, often with scraps of pork added—a kind of soup-stew combination—as well as thinner broths. The fourteenth-century *Forme of Cury* gives recipes for soups of white beans with almond milk and honey, and of leeks "seethed" in wine, among others. Soup was common on British tables in the eighteenth and nineteenth centuries (Jane Austen mentions it repeatedly in her novels, from the creamy chicken-based white soup at the ball supper in *Pride and Prejudice* to the "basin" of unspecified soup Mrs. Norris offers Sir Thomas in *Mansfield Park*), and such defining regional dishes as Scotland's cock-a-leekie and Scotch broth, though they are often dinner, are also in effect soups (and as such are included in this chapter).

On the other hand, the influential cookery writer Eliza Acton was able to say unequivocally that "the art of preparing good, wholesome, palatable soups, without great expense, which is so well understood in France, and in other countries where they form part of the daily food of all classes of the people, has hitherto been very much neglected in England. . . ." The great English gourmand and man-about-town Lieutenant Colonel Newnham-Davis agreed, writing in 1899 that "I mistrust the Brittanic soup, for we are not a nation of soupmakers. . . ." And a quarter-century later, Hilda Leyel, founder of the Society of Herbalists, had no qualms about recommending tomato, oxtail, green pea, asparagus, and celery soups as produced and canned by the Campbell Soup Company of Camden, New Jersey. ("There is no soup at the price to

An ad for soups that could be sent to the front for British soldiers during World War I, 1916

compare with Campbell's," according to *The Gentle Art of Cookery* by Leyel and Olga Hartley.)

And yet . . . historical cookbooks are full of recipes for savory soups in great variety (Elizabeth Raffald's mid-eighteenth-century Green Peas Soup [page 49], though probably needlessly complicated, caught my eye, for instance), and distinctly non-Campbell's versions are omnipresent on modern British menus, from a bright green Forager's Soup with Goat Cheese Gnocchi (page 51) at Northcote in Lancashire to a refinement of the smoky Scottish specialty Cullen Skink (page 54) at The Ubiquitous Chip in Glasgow. I doubt that the art of good soup-making was ever really neglected in Britain, *pace* Mrs. Acton, but if it was, it certainly seems to be thriving today.

Cold Pea and Lovage Soup

COLD PEA AND LOVAGE SOUP

SERVES 6

Restaurateurs Chris Corbin and Jeremy King animated the London restaurant scene in the 1980s and '90s by intelligently reviving three classic properties from earlier eras: Le Caprice, The Ivy, and J. Sheekey. In 1998, they sold the restaurants and, five years later, began again by opening The Wolseley, in what was once the Wolseley automobile showroom, across the street from The Ritz.

Other restaurants followed (The Delaunay, Brasserie Zédel, Colbert, and more), and in 2014 they became hoteliers as well, with The Beaumont in Mayfair. The Beaumont has a restaurant, of course: The Colony Grill Room, a comfortable, clubby, handsomely appointed dining room with a menu that is mostly mid-Atlantic traditional (oysters, chicken liver parfait, fish stew, several steaks and chops), with some American accents ("New York shrimp cocktail," mac and cheese, lobster roll, bananas Foster). One unusual offering, though, is this cold soup, created by head chef Christian Turner, made—conveniently—with frozen peas and given an English twist through the inclusion of lovage. Available at some farmers' markets and specialty stores, lovage gives a pronounced celery-like flavor to the soup. Celery leaves could be substituted if necessary, though they won't have as much effect.

Extra-virgin olive oil
2 medium Spanish onions, sliced
1¾ ounces (50 g) fresh lovage leaves
2 bay leaves
6¼ cups (1.5 L) vegetable stock, store-bought or
    homemade (page 315)
2 pounds (900 g) frozen green peas
Salt and freshly ground white pepper
6 to 8 leaves fresh mint, finely chopped
1 cup crème fraîche

Heat about 3 tablespoons olive oil in a large pot over medium-low heat. Add the onions and cook, stirring frequently, for about 5 minutes. Add the lovage and bay leaves and cook for 5 minutes more.

Add the vegetable stock, raise the heat to high, and bring to a boil. Immediately remove the pot from the heat and stir in the peas. Season with salt and white pepper. Carefully transfer the soup to a food processor and puree it, with the peas still frozen. (If you're not going to serve the soup immediately, transfer it to a bowl, cover with plastic wrap, and refrigerate until ready to serve.)

Stir the mint leaves into the crème fraîche.

Divide the soup evenly between six chilled serving bowls, then, with a soupspoon, scoop out quenelles of crème fraîche and put one in the middle of each serving. Drizzle a bit of olive oil over the top before serving.

JOAN STIRLING'S COLD CURRIED APPLE SOUP

SERVES 4

The original Hat and Feather in Knutsford, just southwest of Manchester in Cheshire, was a seedy pub, torn down in the early 1900s by a well-traveled glove merchant named Richard Harding Watt to make way for his gifts to the city, the landmark Gaskell Memorial Tower and King's Coffee House. The name was revived in the mid-1960s by Joan and Arthur Stirling, who were influenced by Elizabeth David and later Robert Carrier, and served serious French- and British-inspired food for several decades. (The Stirlings' son, Andrew, now runs the Wolfscastle Country Hotel in Haverfordwest, Wales.) For some months in the early 1970s, one of the young cooks at the Hat and Feather was Simon Hopkinson, later to become one of the best-known and most influential chefs in London. This is one of the dishes he learned to cook there—and one he served at a memorable lunch I enjoyed at his flat all too many years ago. Hopkinson maintains that this soup must be made with bouillon cubes or canned chicken broth, not homemade stock—which, he

recipe continues

points out, will likely contain enough gelatin to cause the soup to set.

2 tablespoons (30 g) butter
1 medium yellow onion, chopped
1 tablespoon hot curry powder
2 chicken bouillon cubes, dissolved in 4 cups (960 ml) hot water, or 4 cups (960 ml) store-bought chicken stock
3 medium Gala apples or other sweet eating apples, peeled, cored, and chopped
2 medium Granny Smith apples, peeled, cored, and chopped
¼ teaspoon sea salt, plus more if needed
Juice of 1 large lemon
2 cups (480 ml) heavy cream
Leaves from 4 sprigs mint, chopped
Cayenne

Melt the butter in a large saucepan over medium heat. Add the onion and cook, stirring occasionally, until it's translucent but hasn't begun to brown, about 5 minutes. Add the curry powder and cook, stirring, for 2 minutes. Add the chicken stock, apples, and salt. Bring the mixture to a boil, then reduce the heat to medium-low and simmer, stirring frequently, until the apples are very soft, 30 to 45 minutes. Set the soup aside to cool.

Working in batches, puree the soup in a blender or food processor until very smooth, then pour it through a fine-mesh sieve (it should be the consistency of heavy cream). Whisk in the lemon juice and cream. Adjust the seasoning, if necessary.

Refrigerate the soup, covered, until it is very cold. Divide the soup between four chilled bowls and garnish each serving with some mint and a little cayenne.

SUMMER LOBSTER SOUP

SERVES 6

For a summer lunch early in the twenty-first century at Barton Court, his country house in Berkshire, Sir Terence Conran and his wife, Vicki, with the help of chef Jeremy Lee (who was then cooking at Conran's Blueprint Café in London), prepared us this extraordinary soup—a kind of warm-weather version of lobster bisque, but brightened by fresh summer vegetables.

Salt
1 tablespoon sugar
3 (1-pound / 450-g) lobsters
3 tablespoons vegetable oil
1 medium yellow onion, chopped
1 large leek, washed well and chopped
1 large carrot, chopped
3 stalks celery, chopped
2 ripe tomatoes, cored and chopped
2 sprigs fresh thyme
1 bay leaf
4 whole white peppercorns
1½ cups (360 ml) dry white wine
1 cup (240 ml) brandy
1 cup (240 ml) heavy cream
Freshly ground white pepper
1 cup shelled fresh peas, blanched
1 cup shelled young fava beans, blanched and peeled
12 to 18 baby carrots, blanched

Put 4 quarts (3.8 L) water, 3 tablespoons of salt, and the sugar into a pot large enough to hold the lobsters. Bring the water to a boil over high heat.

Add the lobsters and return the water to a boil. As soon as it boils, turn off the heat, cover the pot, and allow the lobsters to cool in the water.

Meanwhile, heat the oil in a separate large pot over medium heat. Add the onion, leek, chopped carrot, and

recipe continues

Summer Lobster Soup

celery and cook until they soften, 6 to 8 minutes. Add the tomatoes, thyme, bay leaf, white peppercorns, and wine. Reduce the heat to medium-low and simmer gently for 30 minutes.

Preheat the oven to 400°F (200°C).

Remove the lobsters from the pot, reserving the poaching water. Remove the lobster meat and the roe from the shells. Set the roe aside; coarsely chop the meat and set it aside separately. Put the shells in a roasting pan and roast for 10 minutes. Transfer the pan to the stovetop over medium heat, then add the brandy and carefully ignite it with a kitchen match. When the flames die out, add the shells and any pan juices to the pot of vegetables.

Add 6 cups (1.4 L) of the reserved poaching water to the pot and bring it to a boil over high heat. Reduce the heat to low and simmer for 30 minutes. Strain the soup through a sieve into another large pot, pressing on the shells to extract any juices. Add the cream to the strained soup. Bring the soup to a boil over medium-high heat, then reduce the heat to low and simmer for 5 minutes. Season with salt and white pepper.

Add the lobster meat, lobster roe, peas, favas, and baby carrots to the soup. Turn off the heat and allow the soup to cool to room temperature in the pot. When it has cooled, transfer it to a large bowl or soup tureen, cover, and refrigerate until slightly chilled but not cold, 20 to 30 minutes. Divide the soup evenly between six chilled bowls or soup plates, or serve in a tureen with a ladle at the table and let diners serve themselves.

PALESTINE SOUP

SERVES 4 TO 6

This soup has nothing to do with the Middle East; it takes its name from its principal ingredient, the Jerusalem artichoke—which has nothing to do with the Middle East, either. The vegetable, native to North America, is the tuberous root of a variety of sunflower (*Helianthus tuberosus*). The prevailing theory is that "Jerusalem" is

a corruption of the Italian word for sunflower, *girasole*. An alternative etymology, that the Puritans gave the root its name in reference to the "New Jerusalem" of the New World, is surely false: The Puritans set sail for Massachusetts in 1630, and the *Oxford English Dictionary* cites a reference by the Somerset physician Tobias Venner in his *Via Recta Ad Vitam Longam* (1620) to "artichocks of Ierusalem."

An early recipe for Palestine soup appears in *Mrs. Beeton's Book of Household Management* (1861), and there's also a version in Escoffier's *Le guide culinaire* (1903), which calls for hazelnuts in addition to Jerusalem artichokes. This recipe is based on ones appearing in *Recipes of the Highlands and Islands of Scotland* (originally *The Feill Cookery Book*, 1907) and *The Gentle Art of Cookery* (1929).

½ cup (1 stick / 115 g) butter
1 onion, coarsely chopped
2 pounds (900 g) Jerusalem artichokes, peeled and halved
1 teaspoon ground mace
2 cups (480 ml) vegetable stock, store-bought or homemade (page 315), plus more if needed
2 cups (480 ml) whole milk, plus more if needed
Salt and freshly ground white pepper
2 slices country-style white bread, crusts removed, cut into ½-inch (1.25-cm) cubes

Melt half the butter in a large saucepan with a lid over low heat. Add the onion and Jerusalem artichokes, cover the pan, and cook for about 5 minutes, stirring two or three times. Stir in the mace, then add the stock and milk. Bring the mixture to a boil over high heat, then reduce the heat to low and cook, covered, for 30 minutes, or until the Jerusalem artichokes are very tender.

Meanwhile, melt the remaining butter in a small saucepan over low heat. Stir in the bread cubes and cook, stirring frequently, until golden brown. Drain them on paper towels.

Season the soup with salt and white pepper, then carefully transfer it to a blender or food processor and puree, adding a bit more milk or stock if it's too thick. Serve in warmed soup bowls, with croutons scattered on top of each serving.

MRS. RAFFALD'S GREEN PEAS SOUP

SERVES 6

I went back and forth about whether to include this recipe from the eighteenth-century housewife-turned-entrepreneur Elizabeth Raffald's book *The Experienced English Housekeeper*. It's needlessly complicated and calls for one ingredient (veal shank) that has become pricey—and is used only to flavor the broth. Raffald's style of recipe writing, too, approaches stream of consciousness ("put in a lump of sugar the size of a walnut, take a slice of bread and cut it in little square pieces, cut a little bacon the same way, fry them a light brown in fresh butter . . ."), and is challenging to tame to modern-day recipe standards. The result of the bother and expense required, however, is impressive; this tastes very different, in a good way, from any other fresh pea soup I've ever tasted, and I highly recommend it.

Salt
6 cups shelled fresh peas (about 5 pounds / 2.25 kg unshelled)
1 pound (450 g) veal shank (osso buco)
3½ ounces (100 g) cooked ham, in 1 or 2 pieces
2 carrots, coarsely chopped
1 turnip, coarsely chopped
4 leaves (not stems) green Swiss chard, julienned
1 cup spinach leaves
White heart of 1 bunch celery, finely chopped
1 tablespoon sugar
2 tablespoons (30 g) butter
3½ ounces (100 g) thick-cut bacon, cut into small cubes
1 thick slice country-style bread, cut into small cubes
1 small head butter lettuce, coarsely chopped
6 to 8 leaves fresh mint, julienned

Bring a large pot of salted water to a boil over high heat, then add 5 cups of the peas. Reduce the heat to medium and cook until the peas are very soft, about 20 minutes.

Drain the peas, reserving the cooking water, then transfer the peas to a blender or food processor and liquefy. Set aside.

Return 6 cups of the cooking water to the pot and add the veal shank, ham, carrots, turnip, chard, and spinach. Bring the water to a boil over high heat, then reduce the heat to medium and cook, uncovered, for 1½ hours.

Meanwhile, bring a small pot of salted water to a boil over high heat. Add the remaining 1 cup peas and cook until just done, 6 to 8 minutes. Drain the peas, refresh them with cold water, and set them aside.

Strain the broth into a large bowl, discarding the solids, then stir in the pureed peas and return the soup to the pot. Bring to a boil over high heat, then reduce the heat to low, add the celery and sugar, and simmer for about 20 minutes, or until the celery is very soft.

Meanwhile, melt the butter in a medium skillet over medium heat. Fry the bacon, stirring frequently, until it begins to brown. Add the bread cubes to the pan and cook until the bread cubes are golden brown and the bacon is well browned, 6 to 8 minutes.

Put the fried bacon and bread and any pan juices into a large soup tureen. Stir the lettuce and mint into the soup, then pour it into the tureen and serve.

FORAGER'S SOUP *with* GOAT CHEESE GNOCCHI

SERVES 4

Probably every society that has foragers has some version of forager's soup—a (usually) green potage based on assorted wild herbs and grasses. At the luxurious North-cote, a country house hotel in Langho, near Blackburn in Lancashire, Lancashire-born, Swiss-trained "chef-patron" Nigel Haworth and executive head chef Lisa Allen create elegant interpretations of traditional local fare. This is a slight adaptation of Northcote's forager's soup, which is fancied up by the use of butter and cream, the substitution of chicken stock for the water that would likely be the base of such a soup in a forager's kitchen, and an unusual form of gnocchi as garnish.

FOR THE SOUP:
6 tablespoons (¾ stick / 85 g) butter
1 small onion, sliced
1 medium russet potato, peeled and thinly sliced
1 small clove garlic, finely chopped
½ cup (120 ml) heavy cream
4¼ cups (1 L) chicken stock, store-bought or homemade (page 314)
8 ounces (225 g) assorted greens, preferably wild, such as watercress, dandelion greens, nettles, chervil, green garlic leaves, etc.
Salt and freshly ground white pepper

FOR THE GNOCCHI:
¼ recipe Mashed Potatoes (page 211)
1 large egg, lightly beaten
1 cup (125 g) pasta flour, plus more for dusting
1 cup grated firm or semifirm goat cheese, such as Ticklemore (Devon), White Lake Rachel (Somerset), Arina (Holland), Montchevré Cheddar (Wisconsin), Haystack Mountain Sunlight (Colorado)
Salt
3 tablespoons extra-virgin olive oil

MAKE THE SOUP:
Melt the butter over low heat in a Dutch oven or large skillet. Add the onion and cook, stirring frequently, for 4 to 5 minutes, until the slices begin to soften. Add the potato and garlic and cook for a minute more. Add the cream and chicken stock, cover, and cook for about 10 minutes, or until the potatoes are very soft.

Add the greens and bring the soup to a boil. Remove the soup from the heat, carefully transfer it to a blender or food processor, and liquefy it. Season with salt and white pepper.

Fill a large bowl with crushed ice and set a slightly smaller bowl in it. Strain the soup through a fine-mesh sieve into the bowl and set aside.

MAKE THE GNOCCHI:
Put the mashed potatoes in a medium bowl. Add the egg, pasta flour, goat cheese, and salt to taste and stir until well combined.

Turn the dough out onto a lightly floured work surface, roll it into a long cylinder about 1 inch (2½ cm) in diameter, then cut the cylinder into 1¼-inch (3-cm) lengths. You should have 8 to 12 gnocchi.

Flatten each gnoccho slightly with the back of a dinner fork, leaving shallow grooves in the top, and gently shape it into a square or rectangle.

Bring a medium pot of salted water to a boil over high heat. Add the gnocchi and cook until just done, 3 to 4 minutes. Drain them, then set them aside on paper towels to dry, blotting the tops lightly with another paper towel.

Heat the olive oil in a large skillet over medium-high heat. Fry the gnocchi for about 2 minutes on each side until they are golden brown, turning them once. Drain them on paper towels.

To serve, bring the soup to a boil over high heat, then reduce the heat to low and simmer for about 2 minutes. Divide it evenly between four warm soup bowls, then divide the gnocchi into equal portions and serve them on the side.

A Man and His Smoke

It isn't hard to find Iain Spink at the Dundee Flower & Food Festival, a sprawling outdoor fair full of food stalls, cooking contests, exhibition gardens, product displays, and more held every September at Dundee's Camperdown Country Park. A plume of woodsmoke rises from his corner of the fairgrounds, and its aroma winds through the air seductively, leading me to his stand.

He's there, doing what he does: smoking pairs of haddock, strung together by their tails and hung from racks, over smoldering oak and beech logs in shallow wooden tubs that look like truncated wine casks. Damp burlap bags thrown over the racks hold in some of the smoke. When the fish are done—the process takes roughly forty minutes—they're lightly bronzed, with flaky flesh and a surprisingly mild flavor, unmistakably smoky but sweet and clean.

These are Scotland's famous Arbroath Smokies, a product more uniquely Scottish and arguably more interesting to the gastronome than even the country's famous smoked salmon. The official definition of the Arbroath Smokie for its European Union PGI (Protected Geographical Indication) certification states that it must be "a hot-smoked, headless and gutted whole haddock processed in Arbroath. . . . In size, [Smokies] weigh between 350–550g [about ¾ to 1¼ pounds] and are sold in pairs as processed tied with jute string. In colour they are deep golden to mid brown externally, creamy white internally. In texture they are dry on the outside, moist and juicy on the inside with flesh which flakes and removes easily from the bone. They have a very pleasant, mild, fishy flavour with a light smoky taste and slight salt enhancement. . . . The Arbroath Smokie has been described as being to the humble haddock what prosciutto crudo is to the hind leg of a pig."

The process, said to be of Scandinavian origin (though some say the Picts developed it), involves gutting the haddock at sea—"The Vikings would have smoked any kind of fish they could find," Spink told me when I visited him at the Dundee fair, "but eventually the Scots settled on haddock because it was available year-round"—and then dry-salting them before tying them together for smoking. In the old days, they were smoked over tubs, the way Spink does them; today, according to Spink, the big commercial smokers "do basically the same thing, but in six-foot brick pits."

Strangely enough, the Smokie didn't originate in Arbroath, which is about fifteen miles northeast of Dundee, but in a smaller fishing town three miles farther along called Auchmithie. Locals there refined the process in the nineteenth century—but in the early 1900s, they began migrating to Arbroath, drawn by better housing, a bigger harbor, and various enticements offered by the Arbroath Town Council. Production virtually stopped in Auchmithie, and the Arbroath name got appended to the fish.

Though there are several smokehouses in Arbroath bearing the Spink name (which *is* of Scandinavian origin), Iain Spink no longer produces his fish on a commercial scale. Instead, he demonstrates the traditional process at fairs, food shows, and other public events, selling copies of his little book *The Arbroath Smokie Bible* as well as the Smokies he prepares then and there. They're delicious—full of flavor but not overpowering like so much smoked fish. "I offer these as an alternative to hamburgers and hot dogs," Spink told me.

ARBROATH SMOKIE ⦿ PARSNIP SOUP

SERVES 6

The sweet, earthy flavor of parsnips and the mild smokiness of Arbroath Smokies go very well together, and there are several modern recipes for soups or salads combining these ingredients. This is a very slight adaptation of a recipe from Edinburgh-based food writer and television personality Sue Lawrence's book *A Cook's Tour of Scotland*, which I first found on the website of Abroath Smokie craftsman Iain Spink (see opposite). It is used with Lawrence's kind permission.

2 tablespoons extra-virgin olive oil, plus more
    for drizzling
1 onion, chopped
2 cloves garlic, chopped
2 stalks celery, chopped
2 teaspoons ground cumin
2 pounds (900 g) parsnips, chopped
5 cups (1.2 L) chicken stock, store-bought or
    homemade (page 314)
¼ cup (60 ml) dry white wine or dry white
    vermouth
Salt and freshly ground black pepper
1 pair Arbroath Smokies (see Sources, page 316),
    boned and skinned

Heat the oil in a large pot over medium-low heat. Add the onion, garlic, and celery and cook, stirring occasionally, for 10 minutes, or until the vegetables begin to soften.

Preheat the oven to 250°F (120°C).

Add the cumin and the parsnips and stir them in well, then cook for about 5 minutes. Add the stock and wine, bring the liquid to a boil, then reduce the heat to low, cover the pot, and cook for about 30 minutes, or until the parsnips are very soft. Season with salt and pepper, remembering that the Smokies are salty already.

While the soup cooks, wrap the Smokies in foil and bake them for 10 to 15 minutes, or until completely warmed through.

Carefully transfer the soup in a blender or food processor and puree. Divide it evenly between six warmed bowls. Flake the Smokies and scatter the meat evenly over the soup. Drizzle a little olive oil over the Smokies before serving.

MULLIGATAWNY SOUP

SERVES 4

The name of this Anglo-Indian specialty—first recorded in English in 1784 as Mullaghee-tanny—is a corruption of the Tamil compound *miḷaku-taṇṇi*, meaning black-pepper water. However it was spelled, the basic preparation was originally a sauce, apparently thinned into a soup to satisfy British dining habits in the nineteenth century. There are many recipes for mulligatawny, involving such ingredients as garlic, cumin, turmeric, cinnamon, coconut, tomatoes, lentils, and rice. I've seen recipes from Northern Ireland in which rabbit or fish are substituted for lamb or chicken. This is a very basic recipe, producing the kind of soup I used to be served in the homes of English friends before they all converted to *pappa al pomodoro* or *tom kha gai*.

2 tablespoons (30 g) butter
1 tablespoon vegetable oil
1 pound (450 g) lamb necks or lamb stew meat
    (with bones) or chicken thighs (with bones
    and skin)
1 onion, finely chopped
1 apple, unpeeled, cored and finely chopped
1 small carrot, finely chopped
1 tablespoon all-purpose flour
1 tablespoon curry powder
4 cups (960 ml) chicken stock, store bought or
    homemade (page 314)
Juice of ½ lemon
Salt and freshly ground white pepper

recipe continues

Melt the butter with the oil in a large pot over medium heat. Add the lamb and cook, stirring frequently, until nicely browned, 10 to 12 minutes. Remove the lamb from the pot and set aside. Add the onion, apple, and carrot and cook, stirring frequently, until they soften but don't brown, 4 to 5 minutes. Add the flour and curry powder and stir well, then cook for about 1 minute more.

Reduce the heat to low. Add the chicken stock and return the lamb to the pot. Stir well, cover the pot, and simmer for about 2 hours.

Remove the lamb from the pot and set it aside to cool. Strain the soup, discarding the solids. Rinse out the pot and return the soup to it. When the lamb is cool enough to handle, shred it with your fingers, discarding the bones and skin (if any), then add the meat to the soup.

Add the lemon juice and season with salt and white pepper.

CULLEN SKINK

SERVES 4

The name of this classic Scottish soup involves a joke along the lines of "Welsh rabbit" or "Scotch woodcock." A skink is a soup flavored with beef shin or some other portion of meaty leg bone (the word shares common origins with our *shank* and the German word for ham, *Schinken*). In the village of Cullen on Scotland's Moray Firth, though, fish was more common than meat, so finnan haddie, or smoked haddock, supplanted the shin. This recipe was given to me in 2005 by the late Ronnie Clydesdale, proprietor of the estimable Ubiquitous Chip in Glasgow.

1 pound (450 g) smoked haddock or finnan haddie
    (see Sources, page 316)
2 cups (480 ml) whole milk
2 cups (480 ml) plus 1 tablespoon clotted cream
    (see Sources, page 316)
1 small russet potato, peeled

2 teaspoons butter, softened, plus more for
    greasing
2 tablespoons vegetable oil
1 large yellow onion, finely chopped
Freshly ground black pepper
Leaves from ½ bunch parsley, finely chopped

With your hands, remove any skin and bones from the haddock and set them aside. Trim the edges of the fish off and add those to the skin and bones. Cut enough of the remaining fish into ¼-inch (6-mm) cubes to fill 2½ cups and add the rest to the skin and bones.

Combine the milk and 2 cups (480 ml) of the clotted cream in a medium saucepan and bring the mixture to just under a boil over medium-high heat, then lower the temperature slightly to keep it at that point for 2 to 3 minutes. Remove the pan from the heat and add the fish trimmings, skin, and bones. Let them soak until the mixture cools, about 30 minutes.

Meanwhile, put the potato into a small pot, cover it with cold water, and bring the water to a boil over medium-high heat. Cook until soft, about 15 minutes, then drain the potato, put it in a medium bowl, and mash until smooth. Mix in the butter and the remaining 1 tablespoon clotted cream, then cover the potatoes and set them aside.

Preheat the broiler. Lightly grease a baking sheet.

Heat the oil in a medium pot over medium-low heat. Add the onion and reserved 2½ cups fish and cook, stirring occasionally, until the onion is soft and translucent, about 10 minutes. Strain the cooled cream mixture into the pot, discarding the solids, and simmer the soup over medium heat for about 10 minutes. Season with pepper.

Spoon the mashed potato into four equal mounds on the prepared baking sheet, gently flattening each mound slightly. Broil the potatoes until their tops are golden, 3 to 5 minutes.

Divide the soup evenly between four warmed wide soup bowls. Put a potato mound in the center of each bowl and sprinkle the soup with the parsley.

Cullen Skink

A Philosopher in the Kitchen

The influential Scottish philosopher David Hume (1711–1776) was an empiricist, arguing that human knowledge is based solely on our sense perception, and that we derive moral distinctions not from reason but from our basic instincts or feelings. He also loved food, though he reportedly once said, "Ye ken I'm no epicure, only a glutton." Hume sometimes used references to food or drink to make points in his essays, perhaps most famously in his retelling of a story from *Don Quixote*, in discussing the notion of taste, in which two of Sancho Panza's kinsmen detect the flavor of metal and of leather in a hogshead of wine (it is eventually revealed that a key on a leather thong had been dropped into the barrel). And in a letter from Edinburgh, dated October 16, 1769, to his friend the poet and philosopher Sir Gilbert Elliot, Hume wrote in part:

I live still, and must for a twelvemonth, in my old house in James's Court, which is very cheerful, and even elegant, but too small to display my great talent for cookery, the science to which I intend to addict the remaining years of my life! I have just now lying on the table before me, a receipt for making soupe à la reine [see opposite], *copied with my own hand: for beef and cabbage, (a charming dish), and old mutton and claret, nobody excels me. I make also sheep-head broth, in a manner that Mr. Keith speaks of it for eight days after; and the Duc de Nivernois would bind himself apprentice to my lass to learn it. I have already sent a challenge to David Moncrief: you will see that in a twelvemonth he will take to the writing of history, the field I have deserted; for as to the giving of dinners, he can now have no further pretensions. I should have made a very bad use of my abode in Paris, if I could not get the better of a mere provincial like him. All my friends encourage me in this ambition; as thinking it will redound very much to my honour.*

COCK-A-LEEKIE

SERVES 4

"And my lords and lieges, let us all to dinner," wrote Sir Walter Scott in 1822 in *The Fortunes of Nigel*, "for the cockie-leekie is a cooling." Scott's protégée, Christian Isobel Johnstone, in her guise as Meg Dods, noted a few years later that "the leek is one of the most honourable and ancient of pot-herbs. In the old poetry of the northern nations, where a young man would now be styled the *flower*, he was called 'the *leek* of his family, or tribe.'" Though the fowl and the leek are saluted in the name of this dish, it is the combination of chicken and prunes (which recalls the prune-stuffed chicken called hindle wakes; page 95) that seem to most saliently define it. This marriage of ingredients is an old one; F. Marian McNeill quotes the English travel writer Fynes Moryson (1566–1630) as noting that in Scotland in 1589, he was given "a Pullet with some prunes in the broth." Cock-a-leekie was traditionally served in Scotland on November 30, St. Andrew's Day—Andrew being Scotland's patron saint.

1 (2½- to 3½-pound / 1.15- to 1.35-kg) chicken,
    quartered
4 leeks, white and pale green parts only, washed
    well and coarsely chopped
1 bunch parsley
2 bay leaves
4 ounces (115 g) pitted prunes
Salt and freshly ground black pepper

Put the chicken, about three-quarters of the leeks, the parsley, and the bay leaves into a large pot and add enough water to just cover them. Bring the water to a boil over high heat, then reduce the heat to low, cover the pot, and simmer for 2 hours.

Remove the chicken pieces from the pot with a slotted spoon and set them aside to cool. Strain the stock through a cheesecloth-lined colander into a large bowl. Rinse out the pot, then return the stock to it.

When the chicken is cool enough to handle, pull off and discard the skin, then pull the meat from the bones and coarsely chop it; discard the bones. Return the chicken to the pot with the stock, then add the prunes and the remaining leeks and season the stock with salt and pepper. Bring to a boil over high heat, then reduce the heat to low, cover the pot, and simmer for 15 minutes. Serve in warmed bowls.

SOUPE À LA REINE

SERVES 4 TO 6

The original French recipe for this soup, which dates from 1651, calls for stock made from mushrooms and capons or partridges mixed with almond milk, with the addition of finely chopped meat from the birds and a garnish of cockscombs, pistachios, and pomegranate seeds. Some version of the soup was apparently known in Scotland by the latter eighteenth century, when no less than the philosopher David Hume (see opposite) mentioned having a recipe for it.

An interpretation published in 1826 by Christian Isobel Johnstone (writing as Meg Dods), under the name "The Old Scots White Soup or Soup à La Reine" involved a strong broth made with chicken, veal, bacon, and assorted vegetables, flavored with lemon thyme, and served with "perfectly soft" macaroni or small French rolls. Eliza Acton, in 1845, offers a potage à la reine made with strong veal broth, and appends a recipe for oyster soup à la reine. More recent recipes simplify the soup greatly. This one—the following of which would doubtless have been far below David Hume—is based on one ascribed to a family called Champneys, collected by the late Michael Barry, a prolific English cookbook writer and the longtime host of BBC Two's popular *Food and Drink* show.

recipe continues

5 cups (1.2 L) chicken stock, store-bought or
    homemade (page 314)
½ cup white rice
1 chicken breast, coarsely chopped
Salt and freshly ground white pepper
1 cup (240 ml) heavy cream
½ cup small celery leaves

Put the stock into a large pot, then add the rice and chicken breast. Bring the liquid to a boil over high heat, then reduce the heat to low, cover, and cook for 35 minutes.

Remove from the heat and allow the soup to cool slightly, then carefully transfer it to a food processor or blender and puree until very smooth. Return it to the pot and season it generously with salt and white pepper. Stir in the cream, then cook over medium heat for about 5 minutes (do not allow the soup to boil).

Divide the soup evenly between four warmed soup bowls and garnish each serving with celery leaves.

SCOTCH BROTH

SERVES 4

This hearty soup (see photo, pages 40–41), so much more than a mere "broth," is the Lancashire hotpot, the cawl, the Irish stew of Scotland; one Scot once called it "our goulash." It is so popular that it has become a canned-food standard; there are dozens of brands of Scotch broth in tins—even a version produced as a Campbell's soup. (And speaking of Irish stew, a website called FoodIreland.com, which sells Irish foods and gifts, publishes a recipe for Scotch broth labeled "traditional Irish soup"—arguably an indication of just how universal the dish has become.) Boswell notes that Dr. Johnson consumed several servings of Scotch broth "with barley and peas in it" en route to the Hebrides in 1773. "I said, 'You never ate it before,'" writes Boswell. "JOHNSON, 'No, sir; but I don't care how soon I eat it again.'" It is, Johnson's dig notwithstanding, a delicious dish. Most recipes today don't include peas, but since Dr. Johnson had them, I'm adding them here.

1 pound (450 g) lamb neck or lamb shank, cut into
    pieces by the butcher
¼ cup pearl barley
1 onion, finely chopped
1 small rutabaga, peeled and finely chopped
2 carrots, finely chopped
2 leeks, white and pale green parts only, washed
    well and coarsely chopped
4 ounces (115 g) white cabbage, shredded
¾ cup shelled fresh peas (about 12 ounces / 340 g
    in the pod) or frozen peas
Leaves from 3 or 4 sprigs parsley, coarsely chopped
Salt and freshly ground white pepper

Put the lamb and barley into a large pot and add enough water to cover by about 1 inch (2.5 cm). Bring the water to a boil over high heat, then reduce the heat to low, cover, and simmer for 30 minutes.

Add the onion, rutabaga, carrots, leeks, and cabbage, cover, and simmer for 1¼ hours. Remove the lamb from the pot with a slotted spoon and set aside to cool.

When the lamb is cool enough to handle, pull the meat off the bones and return it to the pot (discard the bones). Add the peas and parsley. Return the broth to a simmer and cook, covered, for 15 minutes more. Season generously with salt and white pepper. Serve in four warmed bowls.

France in the Scottish Kitchen

"A man who visits [Scotland], after having been in France," wrote the English journalist and playwright Edward Topham (1751–1820), "will find, in a thousand instances, the resemblance which there is betwixt those two nations. That air of mirth and vivacity, that quick and penetrating look, that spirit of gaity which distinguishes the French, is equally visible in the Scotch."

There was more to it than mirth and gaiety. France and Scotland were political and economic partners for centuries. The so-called Auld Alliance between the two (the common enemy they were allied against was England) dates from 1295, though tradition dates the first military collaboration between these kingdoms to the time of Charlemagne, more than five hundred years earlier. Over the centuries, the link between the two countries was broken and repaired on several occasions, but for many years Scottish soldiers served in the French army and the country's scholars studied at French universities. (A University of Manchester historian proposed in 2011 that the alliance may never have been officially ended, making it the oldest in the world.) For hundreds of years, the French exported salt and wine, along with other less comestible items, to Scotland, and Scottish merchants bringing cloth and animal hides to France paid no customs fees at certain ports.

Wine was a particularly important commodity. In the late Middle Ages, it was said that no country drank more claret than Scotland, and that wine was "the bloodstream of the Auld Alliance." Alexander III, the thirteenth-century King of Scots, famously died with an outstanding wine bill (the Bordeaux merchant to whom it was owed took him to court, but died himself before he could collect). According to a law passed in 1431, half the Scottish salmon exported to France had to be paid for in wine from Gascony.

French was once widely spoken in Scotland, too, not least in the kitchen, where certain French dishes became popular (see Soupe à la Reine, page 57), and terms of French origin were adopted into everyday discourse. F. Marian McNeill lists some 139 examples of French loan words for food and cooking terminology and miscellaneous household items in *The Scots Kitchen*. Among those still occasionally heard, or at least recognizable, today are *jiggot* or *gigot* for a leg of lamb or mutton (*gigot* in French); *ashet*, a platter on which meat is served (*assiette*, plate); *grosset*, gooseberry (*groseille*); *cannel*, cinnamon (*cannelle*); *syboes*, green onions (*ciboules*); *howtowdie*, pullet (from the Old French word for the same thing, *hétoudeau*); *purry*, from *purée*; *tassie*, cup (*tasse*); *pecher*, pitcher (*pichet*); *collop*, (meat) scallop (*escalope*); and maybe *petticoat tails*, shortbread cakes (possibly from the Middle French *petit gastel*, or little cake—though the *Oxford English Dictionary* thinks this "very unlikely").

CHAPTER 3

FISH & SHELLFISH

"THE FISHMONGER IS A KIND OF BENEVOLENT TRITON; A CREATURE BRINGING THE TREASURES OF THE DEEP TO EARTH . . ."

—DOUGLAS WILLIAM JERROLD ET AL., *Heads of the People: or, Portraits of the English* (1841)

"SEAFOOD IS EXCITING BECAUSE IT'S HEALTHY, TASTES FANTASTIC AND IS SIMPLE TO COOK— IT IS TODAY'S STAR INGREDIENT, AND THERE'S NOTHING NICER THAN SITTING DOWN TO A FRESHLY COOKED PIECE OF LOCAL FISH."

—MITCH TONKS, *Fish: The Complete Fish & Seafood Companion* (2009)

The best-known and most popular British dish internationally is almost certainly fish and chips—battered and deep-fried cod, haddock, or some other white-fleshed variety accompanied by thickish lengths of fried potato and typically garnished with tartar sauce and mushy marrowfat peas. Perhaps equally famous, if not exactly a "dish," per se, is the exquisite smoked salmon of Scotland. Add in grilled or sautéed Dover sole and some kind of fishcakes, and you've got pretty much the entire British seafood repertoire as far as much of the planet is concerned.

Of course, there's a lot more to it than that. From the Shetland Islands in the far northeast to the evocatively named Land's End at the southernmost tip of the nation and the nearby Isles of Scilly, Great Britain boasts more than nineteen thousand miles of coastline, and its waters—even today, as fish stocks plummet everywhere—are abundantly stocked with seafood.

A volume called *The Angler's Book of British Sea Fish*, published in 2013 by the English fisherman and nature writer Paul Duffield, lists almost 150 kinds of fish, from almaco jack to wreckfish, found off the coasts of England, Scotland, and Wales—and that's leaving shellfish out of it.

Such piscatorial bounty is nothing new. While archeological evidence of fish-eating in prehistoric Britain is scanty, it is certain that by the time the Romans arrived in the early years of the Christian era, seafood had become an important part of the local diet. The Romans were particularly fond of shellfish, including the cockles for which Wales later became famous, and they established oyster beds in a number of places, some of which are still in use today.

By the fourteenth century, according to food historian Colin Spencer, the range of fish eaten in England was "so large it has the power to amaze us now." He mentions, among other varieties, bass, cod, conger, cuttlefish, coalfish, dogfish, flounder, garfish, gunard and red gurnard, haddock, hake, halibut, lamprey (back in 1135, King Henry I is said to have died after eating a surfeit of lampreys, despite his doctor's orders), mackerel, grey mullet, plaice, rayfish, salmon, salmon trout, sea shad, skate, sole, smelt, sturgeon, turbot, and whiting—and from freshwater, barbel, crayfish, chub, eel, dace, perch, pike, and tench. The royal household, in medieval times, added porpoise (roasted whole) and whale to the menu. (Trout wasn't much prized until the early twentieth century, and salmon was mostly the concern of Scotland.)

Religious laws promulgated by the Roman Catholic Church and then the Church of England—and bolstered by acts of Parliament—forbade the consumption of meat not just on Fridays but on Wednesdays and Saturdays, too, and also for the forty days of Lent and during the vigils of various holy days. (The motives for these strictures weren't entirely religious, at least on the part of the government: The increased demand for fish that these rules implied benefited the ship-building and fishing industries).

An unsigned article in the August 1891 issue of *Blackwood's Edinburgh Magazine* notes that while meat was proscribed three days a week and on a number of other occasions, "there does not appear to have been much penance involved in this, for the *menus* of fast-days, although they consist wholly of fish, are in every respect as abundant as those on festivals . . ." The author describes as one of the best meals he has ever eaten an Ash Wednesday dinner at a Catholic club in Savile Row, of which he had "a pleasant remembrance of the *bisque*, the *filets de sole aux truffes*, the omelette, the *beignets d'abricot*, the *tomates au gratin*, and the 'Roederer '68', which formed part of this penitential feast."

Things weren't as pleasant for the poor, who, especially in the medieval era, had no access to fresh fish and who were thus limited, when they could not eat meat, to a diet of vegetables or of preserved cod, herring, and the like, either imported in bulk from Norway or Iceland or brought down from the Scottish islands. In the Shetlands, cod and ling, fished from small boats, was cleaned, split, salted, and dried right on the stony beaches before being sent south.

By the Victorian era, with the network of railways that crisscrossed Great Britain and the faster boats plying its waters, fresh fish became easier to obtain around the country. In *Enquire Within Upon Everything* (1856), Robert Kemp Philp is quite specific on the matter: Mackerel "must be perfectly fresh, or it is a very indifferent fish," he notes. (Writing from Tunbridge Wells in 1724, Daniel Defoe noted that he ate mackerel landed at nearby Hastings "within three hours of their being taken out of the sea, and the difference which that makes in their goodness, I need not mention.") Salmon, too, must be extremely fresh, as "no method can completely preserve the delicate flavour that salmon has when just taken out of the water." His catalog goes on.

Bluefin tuna is not a fish typically associated with Great Britain, but from the 1930s through the 1950s, big-game

English oystermen carry their catch ashore, 1903

fishermen off Scarborough, on the coast of North Yorkshire, landed many examples of this leviathan—the largest of them weighing in at 851 pounds (386 kg). The most famous participant in the competition to land ever larger tunny (as the fish was then called in Britain) was an aristocratic big-game hunter named Lorenzo Mitchell-Henry, but a host of political figures, members of the nobility, and even celebrities like the actor Charles Laughton were avid participants. François Latry, the head chef at The Savoy, apparently offered a tuna recipe to readers of *The Observer* in 1933, but this was considered quite a novelty, as the point of the Scarborough fishery was sport, and most of the fish itself was sold to dog-food producers.

Today, in England, Scotland, and Wales, as in America, fish and shellfish, both fresh and smoked or cured by "artisans," is highly regarded and widely available. Chefs like Mark Hix in London and Lyme Regis (and his chef in the latter place, Charlie Soole); James Cornwall at J. Sheekey and Jordan Sclare at Bouillabaisse, both in London; Roy Brett at Ondine in Edinburgh; and Mitch Tonks, Nathan Outlaw, Rick Stein, and Ben Tunnicliffe at their various establishments around Cornwall are treating seafood right and ever broadening the repertoire (Hix's British translation of risotto, which he calls Fisherman's Spelt, page 79, is one example). And while purists may bemoan the demise of the old-style chipper—fish-and-chips shop—the fact is that in both new-style shops and the more serious restaurants that are now venturing to put this plebian pleasure on their menus, the fish itself is probably better than it ever was, and the science behind frying the chips has been refined.

When the Potato Met the Plaice

Fish and chips (page 67) is considered a quintessential English—and Scottish—dish, and it remains one of the most popular forms of fast food in Great Britain. This emblematic combination of deep-fried battered fish—today commonly cod, haddock, plaice, or pollock (but sometimes also salmon, skate, or other fish)—and fried potatoes, however, probably didn't exist until the latter 1800s. It is a melding of two culinary traditions.

Fish battered and fried—without its now inevitable accompaniment—is old news in England. The idea seems to have been introduced to London by Marranos, Sephardic Jews, who migrated to the city from Spain and Portugal in the sixteenth and seventeenth centuries. By the nineteenth century, the preparation had become commonplace. Charles Dickens mentions a "fried fish warehouse" in *Oliver Twist* (1837), and the celebrated London-based French chef Alexis Soyer gives a recipe in his *Soyer's Shilling Cookery for the People* (1859) for "Fried Fish, Jewish Fashion." The recipe, "constantly in use by the children of Israel," involves a simple flour and water batter and frying in "fat, lard, or dripping (the Jews use oil)." According to a "memoir" compiled by his former secretaries, Soyer used to duck out from the opera and "quietly and slyly often dive into some obscure place and purchase two-pennyworth of fried fish! eating it with the greatest relish as he walked along . . ."

The term *chip*, meaning slice, in the culinary sense, dates from the mid-eighteenth century, but was apparently first applied to potatoes by the aforementioned Mr. Dickens, who refers, in *A Tale of Two Cities* (1859) to "every farthing porringer [a shallow bowl] of husky chips of potato, fried with some reluctant drops of oil" as a symbol of hunger in Revolutionary Paris. Indeed, fried potatoes in this style probably came to England from Belgium by way of France.

The question, then, is who thought to unite Jewish fried fish with fried potatoes of Gallic origin? One Mr. Chatchip, in a book called *The Fish Frier and His Trade*, published in 1902, believed that while the fried fish business began in London, the fried potato business took root in Lancashire. (Mr. Chatchip was in fact William Loftus, a onetime fish-and-chip shop owner and president and general secretary of the Federation of Fish Caterers.)

The earliest citation linking fish and chips in the *Oxford English Dictionary* dates only from 1923, but the combination was common long before that. Numerous attempts have been made over the years to discover who opened the first fish-and-chips shop—and where it was located. Most authorities give the honor to one Joseph Malin, who may have started serving the two fried foods together at his shop in Bow, in East London (or perhaps from a handcart in the same area), as early as 1860. Alternative claims, though, are made for Lees's of Mossley on the edge of Lancashire, and for a woman in Bradford, in West Yorkshire, named "Granny" Duce, who apparently owned several greengrocer shops selling fish and chips on the side in the later 1860s.

By 1910, it is said that there were more than twenty-five thousand fish-and-chips establishments around England, Scotland, and Wales, and as faster ships and extended railway lines made transportation of fish easier, the number grew to something closer to thirty-five thousand. In 1926, according to one government source, more than half the annual catch of fish in British waters ended up in the fryer. While the number of fish-and-chip shops around the country has fallen to fewer than ten thousand today, there are still close to 300 million servings of the specialty consumed every year in Great Britain—about four and a half portions for every man, woman, and child.

FISH <small>AND</small> CHIPS

SERVES 4 TO 6

If you ask most people from outside the United Kingdom to name a typical British dish, I'll bet fish and chips comes up first in most cases. It's a cliché, a commonplace, almost a cartoon of a dish—but it is genuinely loved and frequently eaten all over Great Britain. A poll conducted by Discover Cornwall, the Cornish tourism initiative, found that a majority of Britons named fish and chips—preferably eaten out of a newspaper, the traditional way, and at the seaside—as their favorite British dish, edging out the Sunday roast dinner with Yorkshire pudding and the full English breakfast. Fish and chips isn't hard to make, but its success depends on the use of fresh, high-quality fish.

1 to 1½ recipes Mushy Peas (page 201)
1 recipe Tartar Sauce (page 276)
2 cups (250 g) all-purpose flour
2 cups (480 ml) good-quality English ale
6 to 8 cups (1.4 to 1.9 L) vegetable oil, for frying
2 pounds (900 g) cod, haddock, pollock, plaice, whiting, hake, or some other firm-fleshed white ocean fish, cut into 8 to 12 pieces of approximately equal size
Salt and freshly ground black pepper
1 to 1½ recipes Chips (page 206)
Malt vinegar, for serving

Prepare the mushy peas and tartar sauce according to the directions. Cover the peas in their pan with aluminum foil or a lid to keep them warm.

Put the flour in a large bowl, then slowly whisk in the ale until well combined. Set the batter aside to rest for 15 minutes.

Eating fish and chips on the street in Manchester, 1930s

Pour the oil into a deep-fryer or large, deep, heavy-bottomed saucepan to a depth of 4 to 5 inches (10 to 13 cm) and heat it over high heat until it registers 375°F (190°C) on a deep-fry thermometer.

Season the fish generously on all sides with salt and pepper, then dip the pieces in the batter, letting the excess drip off, and fry them in batches for 5 to 6 minutes, or until the batter is crisp and golden-brown. Turn the pieces a few times with tongs if necessary to ensure even cooking.

At the same time, prepare the chips according to the directions.

As they're done, drain the fish pieces and the chips on paper towels. Adjust the seasoning on the fish if necessary.

Serve hot, with the peas, tartar sauce, and malt vinegar on the side.

POACHED WHOLE SALMON

SERVES 6 TO 8

Salmon is Scotland's most famous fish, in both smoked and fresh form, and this is one of the best ways to prepare it, simple though the recipe may be. No less an authority on things Scottish (food most definitely included) than Sir Walter Scott describes, in *Saint Ronan's Well* (1823), a traditional local dish called "kettle of fish"—which was simply just-caught salmon boiled in water salted to the level of brine. "This is accounted the best way of eating salmon," he writes, "by those who desire to taste the fish in a state of extreme freshness . . ." This recipe includes another ingredient, but accomplishes the same effect. To cook this dish correctly, it is essential to use a fish poacher or deep elongated baking dish (with a cover) large enough to hold the salmon with a little room around the sides—typically at least 20 inches (50 cm) long and 5 inches (12.5 cm) deep.

2½ to 3 quarts (2.4 to 2.8 L) fish stock or court bouillon, store-bought or homemade (page 315)
2 cups dry white wine
Salt
1 (5- to 6-pound / 2.25- to 2.75-kg) whole salmon, preferably head-on, cleaned and scaled
Slices from 1 lemon (optional)

Put 2 quarts (1.9 L) of the court bouillon and the wine into a large fish poacher and generously salt the liquid. Cover the fish poacher, then put it over two burners on the stovetop. Bring the liquid just to a boil over high heat. Bring the remaining court bouillon to a boil in a small pot over high heat.

Meanwhile, wrap the salmon in several thicknesses of cheesecloth, then tie the ends with kitchen twine. Carefully lower the salmon into the poacher. Add more hot court bouillon, if needed, to cover the salmon entirely, then reduce the heat to medium-low and simmer until the salmon is just cooked through, about 30 minutes. Remove the poacher from the heat and set aside until the salmon and poaching liquid have cooled to room temperature.

Carefully remove the salmon from the poacher, holding the cheesecloth by the ends, and transfer it to a cutting board. Gently cut off and discard the cheesecloth.

Serve the salmon with its skin on, or carefully peel the skin from one side of the fish, leaving it intact on the head and tail. Garnish the salmon with lemon slices, if you like. Serve at room temperature or chilled.

A Salmon in Welsh

George Borrow was a nineteenth-century English author and translator who traveled widely around Europe, chronicling one of his trips in a book called *Wild Wales: Its People, Language and Scenery* (1862). Borrow was an accomplished linguist, who studied Greek and Latin and subsequently became fluent in a number of disparate languages, including Irish, Manchu, Romany, and—as this passage reveals—obviously Welsh as well. Borrow and his traveling companion have stopped at an inn for breakfast, and he is frustrated in his attempts to communicate in Welsh with the elderly woman who is in charge.

"Are you sure that you understand Welsh?" said I.

"I should think so," said the woman, "for I come from the Vale of Clwyd, where they speak the best Welsh in the world, the Welsh of the Bible."

"What do they call a salmon in the Vale of Clwyd?" said I.

"What do they call a salmon?" said the woman.

"Yes," said I, "when they speak Welsh."

"They call it—they call it—why a salmon."

"Pretty Welsh!" said I. "I thought you did not understand Welsh."

"Well, what do you call it?" said the woman.

"Eawg," said I, "that is the word for a salmon in general—but there are words also to show the sex—when you speak of a male salmon you should say cemyw, when of a female hwyfell."

"I never heard the words before," said the woman, "nor do I believe them to be Welsh."

"You say so," said I, "because you do not understand Welsh."

"I not understand Welsh!" said she. "I'll soon show you that I do. Come, you have asked me the word for salmon in Welsh, I will now ask you the word for salmon-trout. Now tell me that, and I will say you know something of the matter."

"A tinker of my country can tell you that," said I. "The word for salmon-trout is gleisiad."

The London Cure

Smoking is an ancient means of preserving food, and oily fish—like herring, mackerel, and, of course, salmon—take particularly well to the treatment, as they are less likely to dry out. The Romans smoked salmon (the fish was once common in Italian rivers) and so, with different techniques, did the Native Americans of the Pacific Northwest. Curiously, though they smoked other kinds of fish, the Scots don't seem to have taken their own famous salmon to the smokehouse very often until the twentieth century.

Brined, cold-smoked salmon, or lox, was a traditional food in the Jewish communities of Eastern Europe, and it was immigrants from Russia and Poland to London's East End who, in the late 1800s, introduced the idea to Britain. At first, they brought their own fish from the Baltic, but once they discovered wild Scottish salmon, that became the standard.

H. Forman & Son, by the River Lea near London's Olympic Stadium, is the lone survivor of the first London Jewish smokehouses; established in 1905, it calls itself the world's oldest salmon smoker. Unlike many producers, it uses wild Scottish salmon exclusively—it is said that more than 90 percent of the salmon sold today at the city's Billingsgate wholesale fish market comes from Norway—and fillets the fish by hand. Forman is also a leading exponent of the so-called London Cure. Brined with rock salt (no sugar) and smoked over oak, London Cure salmon uses smoke almost as a seasoning, subtle and mild.

There is certainly high-quality smoked salmon made in Scotland, from wild Scottish fish, but there isn't a lot of it. Ambiguous labeling laws permit fish from Norway and elsewhere that is processed in Scotland to be labeled as "Scottish smoked salmon," and the vast majority of what comes out of Scotland, whatever the provenance of the fish, is farmed. I've had excellent smoked salmon in the past from Uig Lodge on Lewis and Harris, Ardtaraig Fine Foods in Ayrshire, and Dundonnell in Dingwall, in the Highlands, among other places, but supplies of wild fish even to right-thinking firms are often irregular, and the Scots generally prefer a heavier smoke flavor. Some smokers even use peat fires.

BAKED WHOLE SALMON

SERVES 6 TO 8

Like poaching (see right), this is an extremely simple way to cook salmon. The quality of the fish is paramount, and wild-caught salmon is infinitely preferable to even the best of the farmed variety. This recipe will produce salmon cooked through and flaky, in the traditional manner, not rare or rosy in the contemporary style.

3 tablespoons (45 g) butter
1 (5- to 6-pound / 2.25- to 2.75-kg) whole salmon, preferably head-on, cleaned and scaled
½ bunch parsley
Juice of 1 lemon
Salt and freshly ground black pepper

Preheat the oven to 375°F (190°C).

Lightly grease a fish roaster or roasting pan large enough to hold the whole fish with some of the butter.

Stuff the parsley into the cavity of the fish, then lay the fish in the roasting pan. Drizzle lemon juice over the whole fish, then dot it with pieces of the remaining butter. Season the top of the fish generously with salt and pepper.

Bake the fish for 8 to 10 minutes per pound, basting occasionally with the pan juices. Serve warm, at room temperature, or chilled.

POACHED SALMON STEAKS WITH WHISKY SAUCE

SERVES 4

With boiled salmon, "the more judicious gastronomes eat no other sauce than a spoonful of the water in which the salmon is boiled, together with a little pepper and vinegar," at least according to Sir Walter Scott in *Saint Ronan's Well*. That said, the addition of a little cream and whisky to the recipe, injudicious or not, indisputably enhances the salmon.

1 cup (240 ml) fish stock or court bouillon, store-bought or homemade (page 315)
¼ cup (60 ml) heavy cream
¼ cup (60 ml) good-quality blended Scotch whisky
Sea salt and finely ground white pepper
2 tablespoons (30 g) butter
1 medium onion, sliced into thin rings
2 teaspoons white wine vinegar
4 (6- to 8-ounce / 170- to 225-g) salmon steaks

Bring the fish stock to a boil in a small saucepan over medium-high heat. Add the cream and whisky and stir them into the stock. Reduce the heat to medium and cook, stirring frequently, until the liquid has reduced by about half. Season with salt and white pepper.

Meanwhile, melt the butter over medium heat in a pan big enough to hold the salmon steaks without them touching. Add the onion and cook, stirring occasionally, until it softens but doesn't brown, 7 to 8 minutes. Add 3 cups (720 ml) water, the vinegar, and ¼ cup of sea salt. Bring the mixture to a boil over high heat and boil for about 3 minutes. Reduce the heat to maintain a simmer, distribute the onion slices evenly around the bottom of the pan, and put the salmon steaks on top of the onion. Cook for about 5 minutes, uncovered, then remove the salmon from the pan, pat it dry, and put 1 steak on each of four heated plates. Spoon the sauce and onions over the salmon.

DAVID NIVEN'S SALMON FISH CAKES

SERVES 6

In a letter to Julia Child in 1953, her friend the cookbook editor Avis DeVoto promised to send Child "positively the worst cookbook I have ever seen"—a collection of recipes from celebrities, called *Stars in Your Kitchen*. "I particularly recommend," wrote DeVoto sarcastically, "Mr. David Niven who discusses fish cakes in a very sophisticated (sic) manner."

The suave London-born Niven's recipe reads as follows: "Take any old piece of left over fish (the better the fish the better the cake). Mix it up with boiled potatoes. Pop in a raw egg to bind it and a little anchovy paste because I say so. Add a chopped onion just for the hell of it, then make little cakes of this shambles. Sprinkle some flour around the general area of the cakes and park some bread crumbs atop them. FRY IN DEEP FAT."

Some twenty years after the publication of Niven's "very sophisticated" recipe, Maxime de la Falaise, the fashion designer and onetime food editor of *Vogue*, offered a recipe in her book *Seven Centuries of English Cooking* under the title "Salmon Fish Cakes (from David Niven)." It's very different from the one in *Stars in Your Kitchen* (no potato, onions, or anchovy paste, to begin with), so presumably Niven refined his recipe over the years. This is my version, closely following de la Falaise's (and Niven's?). It calls for leftover simple poached or baked salmon, though good-quality canned salmon may be substituted.

½ cup (1 stick / 115 g) butter, softened
1 pound white mushrooms, cleaned, trimmed, and finely chopped
Juice of 1 lemon
1 cup White Sauce (page 277)
2 egg yolks
Salt and finely ground white pepper
¼ teaspoon mild paprika
Pinch of freshly grated nutmeg

1½ pounds (700 g) leftover cooked salmon (see page 71), bones and skin removed, flesh coarsely flaked
2 large eggs, beaten
2 cups fine bread crumbs
¼ cup (60 ml) vegetable oil
Boiled or mashed potatoes, for serving

Melt half the butter in a medium skillet over low heat. Add the mushrooms and lemon juice and cook, stirring frequently, until the mushrooms have given up their liquid and the liquid has almost evaporated.

Meanwhile, heat the white sauce in a large pot over low heat, then stir in the egg yolks and cook, stirring frequently, for 2 to 3 minutes, until the sauce has thickened (do not allow it to boil). Season the sauce generously with salt and white pepper, then stir in the paprika and nutmeg. Add the mushrooms, then gently fold in the salmon, breaking up the flakes as little as possible.

Using about 1 tablespoon (15 g) of the butter, lightly butter two sheets of aluminum foil, each about 16 inches (40 cm) long, on one side. Set one sheet, butter side up, on a baking sheet. Allow the salmon mixture to cool slightly, then transfer it to the sheet of foil on the baking sheet, spreading it out gently with the back of a wooden spoon. Put the other sheet of foil on top of the salmon mixture, butter side down, then carefully transfer the baking sheet to the refrigerator. Refrigerate for 2 to 3 hours.

Put the beaten eggs in one shallow bowl and the bread crumbs in another. Form the salmon mixture into patties about ¾ inch (2 cm) thick and 4 inches (10 cm) wide. Dip each fish cake in the beaten egg, then dredge it well in the bread crumbs, returning each to the foil after it has been coated.

Heat the remaining 3 tablespoons (45 g) butter and the vegetable oil in a large skillet over medium-high heat. Working in batches, fry the fish cakes until they are golden brown and heated through, turning them once. Serve with boiled or mashed potatoes.

Grilled Dover Sole

GRILLED DOVER SOLE

SERVES 4

Dover sole (*Solea solea*)—the fish found in the eastern Atlantic and the Mediterranean, not the unrelated Pacific species that sometimes borrows Dover sole's name—is one of the great food fishes. Its meat is firm and mild but flavorful, with a hint of sweetness, and it's easy to cook and to fillet. Though it may be prepared in a number of ways (it is sometimes rolled and stuffed with a shellfish forcemeat, for instance), it is best when treated simply.

The two most common methods of cooking sole are grilled and à la meunière. The latter involves dredging the fish in flour (a *meunière* is a miller's wife), panfrying it in butter, and garnishing it with brown butter, parsley, and lemon. The idea of the former method, especially popular in the U.K., used to vex me a little. For years, when I'd order grilled sole in London, it never betrayed grill marks. It eventually dawned on me that this was because grilled sole in Britain was usually what Americans would call *broiled* sole; that is, the contrivance that applies high heat to food from above, which we call a broiler, is called a grill by the British. The grilled sole I would typically be served, then, wasn't cooked on a grill, in the sense of a brazier, at all.

More recently, I've seen actual grilled sole, in the American sense, on more and more menus. Both methods of cooking work fine, and both may fairly be called "grilled." I give both options below. (Dover sole has dark skin on one side and white on the other. It is traditionally cooked with the dark skin removed, a task your fishmonger can accomplish for you if you find it daunting.)

4 tablespoons (½ stick / 55 g) butter, melted, plus more if needed
4 (¾-pound / 340-g) whole Dover sole, cleaned, heads and dark skin removed
Salt and freshly ground white pepper

If using a grill, preheat a gas grill to 400°F (200°C) or light a charcoal grill and wait until all the coals are lit and any flame has died down.

Brush the butter over both sides of the fish, then season them generously with salt and white pepper.

Grill the fish for about 4 minutes on one side, then carefully turn them over and grill for 4 to 6 minutes more.

If using a broiler, preheat it with the rack about 4 inches (10 cm) from the heat.

Line a baking sheet or baking dish large enough to hold the fish with aluminum foil and lightly butter the foil. Put the sole skin side down on the foil.

Cook the fish for about 4 minutes, then carefully turn them over. Brush the butter over the skinned side of the sole, then season them with salt and white pepper. Cook for 4 to 6 minutes more, or until the fish is cooked through and lightly browned on top.

FILLET OF COD ꟿ PARSLEY SAUCE

SERVES 4

This is a simple recipe, based on one from London-based chef-restaurateur Mark Hix, that depends for its success on the freshness of the cod. Hix notes that it's best made with freshly picked parsley, if possible.

4 tablespoons (½ stick / 55 g) unsalted butter, softened
2 shallots, finely chopped
2 tablespoons dry white wine
½ cup (60 ml) fish stock or court boullion, store bought or homemade (page 315)
1½ cups (360 ml) heavy cream
¼ cup chopped fresh parsley
Salt and freshly ground white pepper
4 pieces cod loin, about 6 ounces (180 g) each

recipe continues

Preheat the oven to 400°F (200°C).

Melt half the butter in a heavy pan over low heat. Add the shallots and cook, stirring continuously, for about 1 minute. Stir in the wine and fish stock, raise the heat to medium, and cook, stirring frequently, until the sauce has reduced to about 1 tablespoon.

Add the cream and cook, stirring continuously, until the liquid has reduced by about half and thickened, then stir in the parsley. Reduce the heat to maintain a simmer and cook for about 1 minute. Season with salt and white pepper, and set aside, covered.

Rub the remaining butter over all surfaces of the cod, then put the cod into a baking dish and season it generously with salt and white pepper. Roast for about 15 minutes, or until cooked through but still moist.

Drain the cod on paper towels, then reheat the sauce over low heat if necessary. Divide the cod between four warmed plates and spoon the sauce over it.

GRILLED MACKEREL WITH CUCUMBER AND DILL

SERVES 4

Mackerel is a fish not much appreciated these days, but it is full of flavor and can be less oily and milder in flavor than diners sometimes expect it to be. When Jeremy Lee serves it at Quo Vadis, he sears it on a grill pan. "Let the fish cook undisturbed," he counsels. "Strengthen your resolve and do not be temped to lift the fish to peek. This will lessen the crust and, heaven forbid, encourage the fish to stick. Courage is necessary here. . . ." Don't overcook the fish, he warns, as "cooking less makes for much better eating." He adds that the dish is equally good with the fish hot from the pan, cooled to room temperature, or even cold.

1 small cucumber, peeled, sliced lengthwise, seeded, and cut on an angle into slices about ⅓ inch (8 mm) thick
Coarse sea salt
½ teaspoon sugar
½ teaspoon table salt
½ teaspoon finely ground black pepper
1 tablespoon apple cider vinegar
1 tablespoon Dijon mustard
½ cup (120 ml) extra-virgin olive oil
1 tablespoon chopped fresh dill
4 (1- to 2-pound / 450- to 900-g) whole Boston mackerel or some other smaller mackerel, cleaned, scaled, and patted dry
4 lemon halves, for garnish

Toss the cucumber slices in a bowl with 3 to 4 teaspoons of sea salt and set aside for 1 hour. Rinse the cucumber slices thoroughly under cold running water, then set them aside.

Whisk the sugar, table salt, and pepper into the vinegar in a medium bowl, then whisk in the mustard. Add the oil a little at a time, whisking continuously, then stir in the dill.

Drain the cucumber pieces and squeeze them dry in a clean kitchen towel. Add them to the dressing and mix.

Heat a grill pan over medium heat, then scatter sea salt over it generously. Cook the fish for 7 to 8 minutes without moving it, so that it develops a nice crust. Carefully turn it over and cook for 5 minutes more.

Put the cooked mackerel on a warmed plate and garnish with a lemon half. Serve the cucumber and dill dressing on the side.

FISHERMAN'S SPELT

SERVES 4

The newly trendy grain called spelt is an ancient form of wheat (*Triticum spelta*), first cultivated as early as the fifth millennium BC in the Caucasus. The Greeks disseminated it around the eastern Mediterranean and the Romans probably brought it to Britain, where there are records of it being grown by around 500 BC. It fell out of fashion as conventional wheat (*Triticum aestivum*), which offers higher yields, became increasingly popular. There was a brief vogue for it in the nineteenth century, and then it largely disappeared from the U.K. By the latter part of the twentieth century, commercial plantings of spelt in England had all but disappeared.

Since 2005, the grain has begun appearing on a small scale again, almost always grown organically. At his Hix Oyster and Fish House in Lyme Regis, Mark Hix cooks spelt risotto-style, with whatever seafood is best at the moment. He also adds locally foraged seasonal seashore vegetables (the green leaves in the photograph), unlikely to be available to most cooks, but these are not essential.

FOR THE STOCK:

1 tablespoon extra-virgin olive oil
1 medium onion, coarsely chopped
6 cloves garlic, halved
1 teaspoon fennel seeds
10 whole black peppercorns
Pinch of saffron threads
1 tablespoon (15 g) butter
4 or 5 parsley stems, leaves reserved for the spelt
½ (14½-ounce / 400-g) can chopped tomatoes
6 cups court bouillon or fish stock, store-bought or homemade (page 315)
Salt and freshly ground black pepper

FOR THE SPELT:

1 tablespoon extra-virgin olive oil
1 medium onion, finely chopped
1 cup spelt, soaked in cold water for 2 hours
8 medium shrimp
8 ounces (225 g) cleaned squid, cut into ¾-inch (2-cm) squares
8 medium scallops, shucked
½ pound (225 g) mussels or clams in their shells, or a mixture, cleaned and debearded
Reserved parsley leaves, chopped
Salt and freshly ground black pepper

MAKE THE STOCK:

Heat the oil in a Dutch oven or a large skillet with a cover over medium heat, then add the onion, garlic, fennel seeds, peppercorns, and saffron. Cook, stirring occasionally, for 3 to 4 minutes, then add the butter, parsley stems, tomatoes, and court bouillon. Bring the stock to a boil, then reduce the heat to low and simmer, covered, for 45 minutes. Strain the stock through a fine-mesh sieve and season it with salt and pepper. Set the stock aside.

MAKE THE SPELT:

Heat the oil in a Dutch oven or a large skillet with a cover over low heat, then add the onion and cook, stirring occasionally, for 3 to 4 minutes. Drain the spelt, add it to the pan, and stir continuously for about 30 seconds. Add about a quarter of the reserved stock, stirring the spelt occasionally, until the stock has been absorbed. Repeat the process three times, until you have used all the stock.

When the final portion of stock is about half absorbed, stir in the shrimp, squid, scallops, and mussels and/or clams. Add the parsley leaves and season with salt and pepper. Cover the pan and cook for 3 to 5 minutes, or just until the clams and/or mussels open (discard any that do not open). The spelt should still be slightly soupy. Serve in soup plates or shallow bowls.

MONKFISH CURRY

SERVES 4 TO 6

Curry has been known in Great Britain since the mid-eighteenth century (see page 105), not just through Indian restaurants opened by immigrants—the first of which appeared in 1759, in London—but as prepared by chefs at non-Indian establishments, and even by home cooks. Thackeray has one fed to an unsuspecting Becky Sharp by the Sedleys, for instance, in *Vanity Fair*, his 1847-vintage satire on British society (see page 103). Queen Victoria was introduced to curry by her Indian secretary, Abdul Karim, who also taught her Urdu; according to Heston Blumenthal, she ate curry every day for the last thirteen years of her life. Curries prepared in the U.K. by chefs who are not themselves South Asian tend to employ that ubiquitous seasoning known as curry powder. In his own curries, like this one from Hix Oyster and Fish House in Lyme Regis, chef Mark Hix prefers individual spices instead. "I like to use firm fish for this," he says, "like monkfish, huss [a kind of small shark or dogfish, sometimes called rock salmon, popularly used for fish and chips], or ling."

3½ pounds (1.5 kg) monkfish, cut into thick
　　cubes about 1¼ inches (3 cm) square
Salt and freshly ground black pepper
¼ cup (55 g) clarified butter (page 312) or
　　vegetable oil
3 medium onions, coarsely chopped
5 large cloves garlic, crushed
1 tablespoon grated fresh ginger
2 jalapeños, seeded and finely chopped
1 teaspoon cumin seeds
½ teaspoon fenugreek seeds
1 teaspoon ground cumin
1 teaspoon ground turmeric
Pinch of saffron threads
Pinch of ground curry leaf
½ teaspoon paprika
1 teaspoon fennel seeds
1 teaspoon mustard seeds
2 teaspoons tomato puree
Juice of ½ lemon

5 cups (1.2 L) court bouillon or fish stock,
　　store-bought or homemade (page 315)
Leaves from 4 or 5 sprigs cilantro, chopped
Cooked basmati rice, for serving

Season the fish generously with salt and pepper.

Heat half the clarified butter in a Dutch oven or a large skillet with a lid over high heat. Fry the fish cubes, working in batches if necessary, turning them frequently with tongs until they are lightly browned, 3 to 4 minutes.

Remove the fish from the Dutch oven with a slotted spoon and set it aside. Add the remaining clarified butter to the pan, reduce the heat to medium, and add the onions, garlic, ginger, and jalapeños. Cook, stirring frequently, for 4 to 5 minutes, or until they begin to soften. Add the cumin seeds, fenugreek seeds, ground cumin, turmeric, saffron, curry leaf, paprika, fennel seeds, and mustard seeds, cover, and cook for 2 to 3 minutes more.

Add the tomato puree, lemon juice, and court bouillon and bring to a boil over high heat. Season with salt and pepper, then reduce the heat to low, cover, and simmer for 45 minutes.

Carefully transfer 1 cup of the sauce to a blender or food processor, puree it, then stir it back into the rest of the sauce. Add the fish to the sauce and simmer for 15 minutes, then stir in the cilantro and simmer for 5 minutes more. Adjust the seasoning if necessary.

Serve with basmati rice.

Worth Its Salt

We look out over the vast marshes, split-pea green and yellow-brown in winter. "Every two weeks, the spring tides completely cover them," Clive Osborne tells me (spring tides are the flood tides that rise, in all seasons, around the time of the full and the new moon). "That's one of the reasons we're here."

"Here" is the banks of the River Blackwater estuary (for *black*, read *brack*, meaning salty), in the town of Maldon, near Chelmsford in Essex. Sea salt is an ancient product, still made today in pretty much the traditional manner, all over the world, from Maine to Alaska, Canada to Australia, Denmark to South Africa. For many years, the best sea salt, the one chefs called out on menus, was considered to be the fleur de sel, "flower of salt," made around Guérande in France's coastal Loire region. In the past fifteen or twenty years, though, its place has been taken increasingly by Maldon salt. Ferran Adrià was one chef who fell in love with the product. Maldon is whiter and lighter in texture than fleur de sel, and lacks the faint bitterness the latter sometimes has. Large flakes of it look dramatic scattered over salads, simply-cooked fish, and other foods (it's indispensible on ripe sliced summer tomatoes), and it grinds easily between the thumb and forefinger of the cook.

The Osborne family and their immediate antecedents have run the Maldon Salt Company since 1922. Salt production here goes back far longer, however. "This is the driest part of the U.K.," says Osborne, "so ideal for this purpose." There is a colorful if unlikely anecdote about a Roman legionnaire stationed here, named Cassius Petox, accidentally discovering salt crystals in a seawater bath that had been heated for too long. There is also the possibility that East Saxons, in the fifth and sixth centuries, made salt here, boiling brine in red earthenware pots, shards of which are still found buried in local earth.

What is indisputible is that the *Domesday Book*, completed in 1086, lists some forty-five salt pans in the Maldon area. Later records show that salt-making flourished here and elsewhere on the Essex coast during the Middle Ages and on into the nineteenth century, when first onerous salt taxes and then, after the taxes were abolished, cutthroat competition drove many producers out of business. One of the most prominent of Maldon families, the Coes, owned the Maldon saltworks for generations. A local wine and spirits merchant, Thomas Elsey Bland, took possession of the enterprise in 1882, establishing the Maldon Crystal Salt Company. James Rivers and his wife, Nellie Eliza, bought the firm in 1922, and their stepson, Cyril Osborne, began managing it ten years later. It was his son Clive who showed me around (Clive's son Steven is now managing director).

Inside the old processing room nearest the river, one of several Maldon uses, filtered seawater simmers in salt pans, large open brick tubs heated by gas furnaces. It has previously been brought to a full boil and skimmed, then it bubbles for fifteen hours or so and the salt crystals precipitate out and sink to the bottom. A worker with a broad wooden hoe rakes them to the sides of the pan as the water cools. Then they're shoveled into drainage bins for forty-eight hours before being sent to dry.

"All the salt we make is for human consumption," Osborne says—no road salt or bath salts here. Ferran Adrià, he adds, wanted particularly large crystals, "so of course we made them for him."

LANGOUSTINES _with_ GARLIC BUTTER

SERVES 2

Possibly the best langoustines I've ever had were fished from Orkney's Scapa Flow—the immense sheltered bay, said to be the world's second-largest natural harbor after Sydney's, better known as a major petroleum port and former naval base but also a source of first-rate shellfish. I enjoyed these at a place called Skerries Bistro, on South Ronaldsay, at Orkney's southernmost tip. Langoustines (_Nephrops norvegicus_), which look a bit like miniature lobsters, are what the Irish call Dublin Bay prawns and the Italians call scampi; they're found all over the northern Atlantic and in parts of the Mediterranean (there is a related species in Pacific waters off Australia and New Zealand), and I've had them many times in various places, but these were the sweetest I can remember, firm but tender, and just briny enough—perfect.

Of course, the experience of getting to Skerries might have increased my appreciation. One summer evening, I drove down to the place from Kirkwall, the Orcadian capital. It was an eerie journey. The sun sets late this far north in summertime, but the twilight is long and ghostly. There was mist in the air, alternately gauzy and dense. The road traverses four causeways, each signposted with large red placards warning DRIVERS CROSS AT OWN RISK (huge waves sweep over the road sometimes, and cars have been washed into the sea), and here and there, off to the sides, rusting hulks of shipwrecks poked above the waterline. On one hunk of land, called Lamb Holm, I stopped to see a small frescoed chapel built by Italian prisoners of war in 1943, open but forlorn and empty. By the time I got to the restaurant, I was more than ready for a glass of wine and some comforting fare. I had an assortment of cured and smoked seafood to start, and then a simple plate of whole langoustines bathed in garlic butter. I couldn't have asked for anything better. The restaurant declined to share their recipe with me, but this one isn't too far off.

Fresh langoustines are difficult to find in the United States, and are expensive. There are several mail-order sources for quick-frozen ones from Scotland or the Pacific (see Sources, page 316). These are expensive, too, but worth it for a rare treat. Be sure to save the shells and heads to make stock. If the langoustines are frozen, they are also excellent when thawed then simply boiled for 2 or 3 minutes and served cold with homemade mayonnaise (page 274).

1 clove garlic, very finely chopped
1 teaspoon fresh oregano or thyme leaves
2 tablespoons (30 g) butter, melted
2 to 2¼ pounds (900 g to 1 kg) fresh or frozen
    langoustines (see Sources, page 316), 8 to 12
    in all
Juice of 1 lemon
2 tablespoons extra-virgin olive oil
Salt

Preheat the broiler.

Stir the garlic and oregano into the butter and set it aside.

If using frozen langoustines, submerge them in a large bowl of room-temperature water for 10 minutes. If using fresh langoustines, rinse them well.

With a sharp knife or cleaver, split the langoustines in half lengthwise from head to tail. Place them cut side up on a baking sheet large enough to hold them all in a single layer.

Drizzle the lemon juice and then the olive oil lightly over the exposed meat, then sprinkle the meat with salt.

Broil for 2 minutes, then remove from the oven and spoon a bit of the garlic butter over each langoustine half. Return to the broiler for 1 minute. Serve immediately.

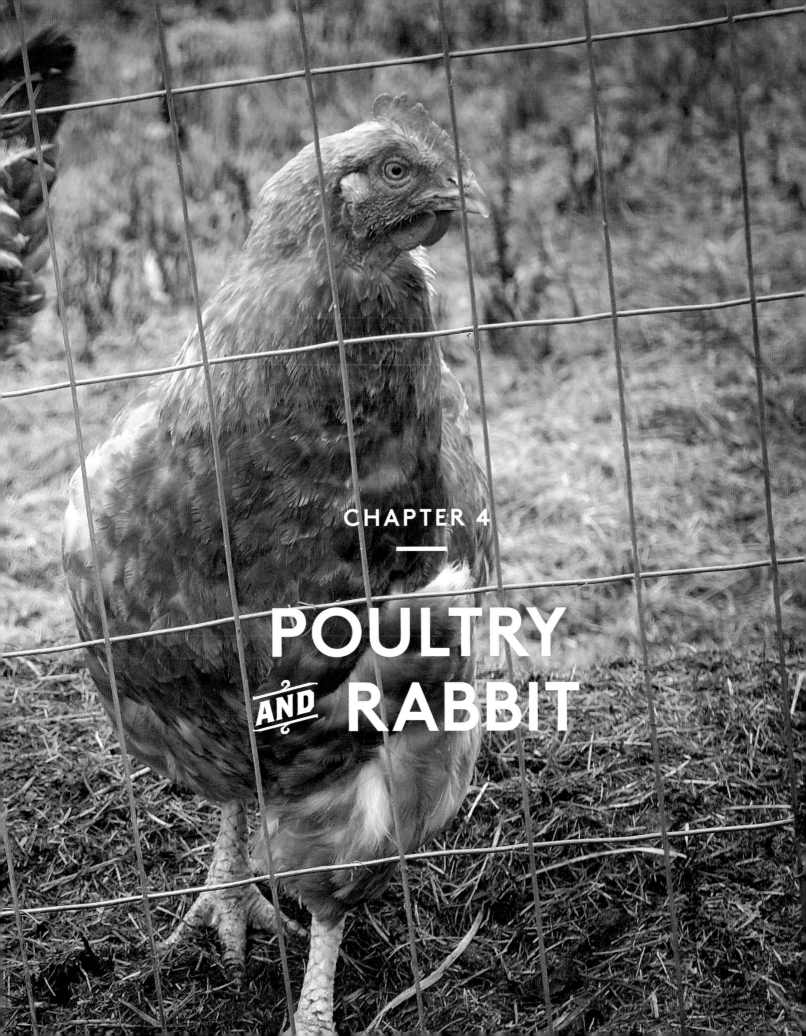

CHAPTER 4

POULTRY
AND RABBIT

"YOUNG, PLUMP, WELL-FED, BUT NOT
OVER-FATTED POULTRY IS THE BEST."

—ELIZA ACTON, *Modern Cookery, in All Its Branches* (1845)

"COUNTRY PEOPLE HAVE ALWAYS KNOWN
THE FOOD VALUE OF RABBIT, OFTEN PICKING
OFF A COUPLE FOR THE POT AT SUNSET."

—ROSEMARY SHRAGER, *Rosemary: Castle Cook* (2001)

Just how long the British have been eating chicken isn't certain. In the *Cambridge World History of Food*, Colin Spencer writes that the Celts raised hens, ducks, and geese in the eighth century BC, but other sources refer to hen bones found at Glastonbury dating from 250 BC as the earliest evidence of domesticated fowl in Britain. The Celts may have been interested in chickens more for religious sacrifice and for cockfighting than for food, in any case. It is certain that the Romans brought their own breeds of chicken from Italy in the first century AD. They also introduced ducks and geese of their own, as well as domesticated pigeons and doves—though these latter creatures never seem to have caught on with the populace.

For whatever reasons, chicken never became as popular in Great Britain as it did in the United States. The wine writer Jancis Robinson told me one day that, at least until the 1960s, "chicken was a luxury here, not something you ate too often, more or less equal to roast beef." Chef Jeremy Lee confirms this: "When I was growing up in Scotland,"

he says, "we only had chicken once every two or three months." Even today, the chicken dish most often found on restaurant tables around the country (leaving aside American-style fast-food fried chicken and the Sunday roasted variety) is probably the "fusion" concoction called chicken tikka masala (see pages 90 and 91). Regional specialties like Yorkshire's parmo (an over-the-top relation of the Italian American "chicken parm") and the mysterious hindle wakes of Lancashire (pages 92 and 95) have never caught on in other parts of Britain. (And sorry, but the curried salad called coronation chicken, invented at the London branch of the Cordon Bleu cooking school in honor of Queen Elizabeth II's coronation in 1953, is just not a chicken dish worth bothering with; it's basically deli chicken salad.)

It probably didn't increase chicken's popularity when a 2014 study revealed that some two-thirds of all fresh British chicken sold in the U.K. was contaminated with campylobacter bacteria, thought to sicken almost three hundred thousand people around the country each year and to kill about a hundred of them. (The National

An English farmer feeding his hens between two haystacks, early 1930s

A boy in Pencaenewydd, Wales, holds a duck spared from Christmas slaughter, 1959

Farmers Union of England and Wales's Red Tractor campaign seek to reassure consumers in the face of such revelations by identifying birds raised under high standards of animal welfare, food safety and hygiene, and traceability.)

The most famous domestic British bird for eating might well be—or at least have been—the Aylesbury duck, a white-feathered breed (the feathers were prized as fillers for pillows and quilts) descended from birds farmed around Aylesbury in Buckinghamshire, west of London, and known since at least the late seventeenth century. For much of the eighteenth and nineteenth centuries, the Aylesbury was considered the standard for tasty duck, in London itself and around Britain. The introduction of the Pekin breed to the country in 1873, however, was bad news for the Aylesbury. It was a hardier fowl and fattened more quickly, and soon Pekins or Pekin-Aylesbury crosses ruled the roost. Today, there is said to be only one remaining purebred Aylesbury flock in the U.K.

The duck names to look for today on menus are Gressingham and Goosnargh (pronounced approximately "goozenaw"). Both come originally from Lancashire, though

the Gressingham—a mallard-Pekin cross—is now raised exclusively in East Anglia. The Goosnargh label applies to both ducks and chickens, raised by the Johnson & Swarbrick company near Preston, on the Lancashire coast. Lancashire chefs Paul Heathcote and Nigel Haworth were early champions of the Goosnarghs, encouraging the late poultry farmer Reg Johnson to raise corn-fed birds in the French style, and they have become popular all over the country. Gordon Ramsay is a fan of the ducks, reportedly buying at least a hundred Goosnargh breasts a week for his London restaurants. Neither Gressingham nor Goosnargh fowl are sold in the United States, but they're names worth looking for on menus on their native turf.

The Romans farmed rabbits as early as 200 BC in Spain, where the animals originated, and first brought them to Britain. (The remains of a rabbit butchered for cooking, nearly two thousand years old, were found in Norfolk in 2005.) Medieval monks raised rabbits and bred increasingly healthy and meaty specimens, with new fur colors, and at least through the early Victorian era rabbits were raised for both their flesh and their pelts. Attitudes toward rabbits began to change in the mid-nineteenth century, as they became popular pets, especially in the cities; one theory holds that this was because they were a low-maintenance reminder of the country life so many people had left behind in the urban migrations that followed the Industrial Revolution. Beatrix Potter's Peter Rabbit books in the early twentieth century helped move the animals farther from the kitchen, as did the cartoon image of Thumper, the bunny in the 1942 Walt Disney film *Bambi* (the character did not appear in the original book). Though the British government encouraged the citizenry to raise rabbits during World War II, to help provide food and clothing for themselves and for soldiers, the use of rabbit as a foodstuff around the country declined steadily during the twentieth century.

Today, as more and more British chefs extol the virtues of rural cookery and seek to establish or intimate connections with their country's older culinary traditions, rabbit appears frequently on menus. The shabby-chic Pig-near Bath hotel and restaurant in Pensford, serving what it describes as "uncomplicated and simple British garden food," brings rabbit and chicken together in a sense: One of its standard offerings is "Kentucky-fried rabbit."

ROAST CHICKEN with SKIRLIE STUFFING

SERVES 6 TO 8

"Meg Dods" wrote that fowls (she was speaking specifically of boiled ones) "must be very neatly trussed . . . nothing can be more indecorous than to see unfortunates on the table 'whose dying limbs no decent hands composed.'" (I'm guessing that the last phrase is a citation, but I've been unable to track it down.) This reminds me of a remark Julia Child once made when a student asked what was wrong with leaving chickens untrussed and allowing their legs to splay: "It makes them look wanton." That said, I rarely bother to truss chickens myself; while many authorities maintain that trussing allows the birds to cook more evenly, in my experience binding the legs to the body of the bird is more likely to leave them slightly underdone when the breast is at the perfect point.

Skirlie is a old-fashioned Scottish dish of seasoned oats with onions, cooked in lard, suet, or drippings, served as a side dish or as the main course in a simple country dinner, usually accompanied by tatties and neeps (mashed potatoes and mashed rutabaga). The name is short for skirl-in-the-pan; *skirl* is a Scots and northern English dialect word meaning "to shriek or cry shrilly," and is perhaps used in this sense as an analogue to the English bubble and squeak—a reference to the noise the food makes cooking. Note that this recipe calls for a roasting chicken, or roaster—not a broiling chicken. The difference in flavor is noticeable.

⅓ cup lard or bacon fat
1 medium onion, finely chopped
2 cups stone-ground Scottish oats
2 cups chicken stock, store-bought or homemade
    (page 314)
Salt and freshly ground black pepper
1 (4- to 5-pound / 1.8- to 2.25-kg) roasting
    chicken, free-range, if possible
1 tablespoon all-purpose flour

Melt the lard in a medium skillet over medium heat. Add the onion and cook until it softens, 6 to 8 minutes. Stir in the oats and mix well. Cook for 6 to 8 minutes more, or until the oatmeal begins to turn brown. Add ½ cup of the stock and continue cooking, stirring continuously, until the oats have absorbed the stock. Season the oats generously with salt and pepper, then set aside.

Preheat the oven to 400°F (200°C).

Season the chicken generously, inside and out, with salt and pepper, then spoon the stuffing into the cavity, being careful not to pack it too tightly as the oats will expand as they cook. Secure the opening with a small skewer or damp toothpick, then roast the chicken on a rack in a heavy roasting pan for 20 minutes. (Put any extra stuffing into a baking dish and roast it along with the chicken, if you like.) Reduce the heat to 350°F (175°C) and continue roasting for about 20 minutes per pound (450 g) of the bird's weight (not counting the first 20 minutes).

When the chicken is cooked, remove the rack from the baking pan with the chicken on it and set it aside to cool. Put the baking pan on the stovetop over low heat, then sprinkle the flour into the chicken fat that remains, stirring until a roux forms. Add the remaining stock. Increase the heat to high and deglaze the pan, scraping up the brown bits from the bottom of the pan. Cook, stirring continuously, until the gravy is thick.

Transfer the chicken to a carving board and carve it, removing the skewer and spooning out the skirlie. Serve with the gravy and any additional skirlie on the side.

Indian Food, Glasgow Style

What is chicken tikka masala (opposite), and where did it come from? *Tikka* is a Punjabi preparation, generally consisting of poultry, meat, or vegetables marinated with spices and yogurt and cooked in a tandoor oven; it differs from other tandoori food in the composition of the spice mixture used and in that it is usually made with smaller, often boneless cuts of meat. *Masala* is a spice mixture—basically what much of the world calls "curry powder." Chicken tikka masala is chicken tikka (more or less), served in a rich tomato-cream sauce, and whether or not it is genuinely Indian in origin is a matter of some dispute.

According to some authorities, it is indeed Indian, dating from the mid-nineteenth century. The seminal Moti Mahal restaurant in New Delhi, on the other hand, claims to have created it in the midtwentieth. Then there's Ali Ahmed Aslam, who always maintained that he introduced CTM, as it is popularly known, in 1971 at his Shish Mahal restaurant in Glasgow—a city where Indian restaurants are so popular and so plentiful that it calls itself "Great Britain's Indian food capital." Aslam is said to have improvised the dish one evening when a customer complained that his chicken tikka was too dry. Aslam had an ulcer, it seems, and was warming himself some Campbell's tomato soup. He had the idea of mixing a little of it into the chicken. The customer loved it and came back to order it again, bringing his friends. The restaurant refined the recipe, and the next thing anyone knew it had become a nationwide obsession. In 2009, Aslam's grandson even petitioned the European Union (unsuccessfully) to grant CTM Protected Designation of Origin status.

CHICKEN TIKKA MASALA

SERVES 4 TO 6

Though it has since been dethroned by Chinese-style stir-fry and surpassed by several other dishes, there was a point, in the late twentieth and early twenty-first centuries, when chicken tikka masala was said to be the most popular dish in Great Britain. A study conducted in 1997 reported that some 11 million Britons, more than 20 percent of the population, ordered it regularly. The British foreign secretary Robin Cook made headlines in 2001 when he proposed, in a speech to the Social Market Foundation in London, that "chicken tikka masala is now a true British national dish" and "a perfect illustration of the way Britain absorbs and adapts external influences."

The dish is best made with real chicken tikka, from a tandoor, but there are scores, if not hundreds, of alternate recipes that variously call for broiling, baking, or frying the chicken. This is an easy way to cook the dish, an amalgam of half a dozen other recipes.

Juice of 1 lime
1 cup (240 ml) plain yogurt
½ teaspoon ground cumin
½ teaspoon ground ginger
½ teaspoon ground turmeric
½ teaspoon cayenne
Salt
3 tablespoons vegetable oil, plus more if needed
2 pounds (900 g) boneless, skinless chicken breasts
1 onion, finely chopped
2 cloves garlic, finely chopped
1 teaspoon chili powder
1 tablespoon curry powder
1 tablespoon tomato paste
1 cup (240 ml) Campbell's tomato soup
½ cup (120 ml) heavy cream
White rice, for serving (optional)
Major Grey's Chutney, for serving (optional)

In a large nonreactive bowl, combine the lime juice, half the yogurt, the cumin, ginger, turmeric, cayenne, 2 teaspoons of salt, and 1 tablespoon of the vegetable oil and stir well. Add the chicken breasts and turn several times to coat them thoroughly in the marinade. Cover the bowl with plastic wrap and refrigerate for 1 to 2 hours.

Heat the remaining 2 tablespoons vegetable oil in a large skillet over medium heat. Use tongs to transfer the chicken breasts from the marinade to the skillet, allowing the excess marinade to drip back into the bowl. Fry the chicken breasts for 6 to 8 minutes on each side, or until they begin to brown, turning once. Remove them from the pan and set them aside to cool.

Add about ½ cup (120 ml) water to the skillet, increase the heat to high, and deglaze the pan, scraping up any browned bits on the bottom. Pour any remaining marinade into the pan and cook, stirring continuously, for about 1 minute, then reduce the heat to low and add the onion and garlic. Cook, stirring occasionally, for 6 to 8 minutes, or until the onion begins to soften (add a little more oil if necessary).

Stir in the chili powder, curry powder, tomato paste, tomato soup, and cream, mixing them together well. Cover the skillet and cook for about 10 minutes.

Cut the chicken into bite-size pieces, then stir it into the sauce. Cook for about 5 minutes more, or until the chicken is warmed through. Serve with white rice and Major Grey's Chutney, if you wish.

PARMO

Parmo, the culinary pride of Middlesbrough—an industrial town in northeastern Yorkshire, south of Newcastle-upon-Tyne—is a kind of schnitzel (or chicken parm) gone wild. Said to have been invented by an American chef named Nicos Harris at a local restaurant called The American Grill in 1958, it is simply a thin chicken cutlet (Harris may have originally made it with veal) coated in bread crumbs and fried, then slathered with béchamel sauce—known locally as "besh"—and covered with cheddar cheese, then toasted in the oven.

A typical parmo is ten or twelve inches (20 to 25 cm) in diameter (when it's sold as takeout food, it comes in a pizza box), and is almost always accompanied by a healthy portion of chips (in the English sense) and a green salad. A study of local fast food dishes conducted by the North Yorkshire Trading Standards bureau computed that the average parmo, with sides, contains 2,600 calories and 150 grams of fat. Those statistics have hardly hurt its reputation. Local branches of the Asda supermarket chain claim to sell more than six thousand parmos a week, and a Parmo World Championship competition has been held annually since 2007 as a part of the Stockton Summer Show near Middlesbrough. Variations include the parmo hotshot, topped with pepperoni and jalapeños, and the parmo Kiev, involving garlic butter and mushrooms. This is the classic version.

4 boneless, skinless chicken breasts, about 1½
    pounds (700 g) in all
½ cup (60 ml) canola or vegetable oil
2 large eggs, lightly beaten
1 cup bread crumbs
3 tablespoons (45 g) unsalted butter
3 tablespoons all-purpose flour
2 cups (480 ml) whole milk
Pinch of freshly grated nutmeg
Salt and freshly ground white pepper
1 cup grated cheddar cheese

Cut each breast in half crosswise, leaving it attached on one side, so that it opens like a book. Working with one at a time, place each split breast, opened up, between two large sheets of waxed paper. With a meat mallet or rolling pin, pound or roll the chicken out to a diameter of 10 to 12 inches (25 to 30 cm) and a thickness of about ½ inch (1.25 cm), or a little less.

Heat the oil in a large skillet over medium-high heat.

Place the beaten egg in one shallow bowl and the bread crumbs in another. Dip 1 chicken breast at a time in the egg, then dredge it in the bread crumbs on both sides. When the oil is very hot but not smoking, fry one chicken breast at a time, turning it once with tongs. As each chicken breast is done, transfer it to a baking sheet large enough to hold all four breasts (use two baking sheets, if necessary).

Preheat the broiler.

Melt the butter over medium heat in a medium saucepan. Slowly add the flour and cook, stirring continuously, to form a roux, until the mixture turns light golden brown, about 6 minutes.

Meanwhile, heat the milk in another saucepan to just below boiling, then pour it slowly into the roux, stirring continuously until the mixture is very smooth. Bring the sauce to a boil over high heat, then reduce the heat to medium and continue cooking, stirring continuously, for 10 minutes. Remove the sauce from the heat, add the nutmeg, and season generously with salt and pepper.

Spoon the sauce over each chicken breast, covering it completely. Scatter the cheddar over the chicken breasts, dividing it evenly. Broil the chicken breasts until the cheese has melted but not yet begun to brown, 2 to 4 minutes depending on the broiler.

Serve with chips (page 206) and a small green salad.

Poached Chicken with Tarragon Gelée

POACHED CHICKEN ᴡɪᴛʜ TARRAGON GELÉE

SERVES 4 TO 6

Sir Terence and Vicki Conran served this dish to photographer Christopher Hirsheimer and me at their home in Berkshire on a summer day in 2000, when we had come to work on a story for *Saveur*. The dish remains memorable. The onion skins give the gelée its rich golden color.

2 large leeks, washed well and halved crosswise
4 stalks celery, halved crosswise
1 carrot, halved crosswise
2 medium yellow onions, unpeeled, halved
4 sprigs parsley
2 sprigs thyme
5 whole black peppercorns
1 bay leaf
1 calf's foot
1 (4-pound / 1.8-kg) chicken, trussed
1 (750-ml) bottle good dry white wine
Leaves from 3 branches tarragon
Salt and freshly ground white pepper

Put the leeks, celery, carrots, onions, parsley, thyme, peppercorns, and bay leaf in a large pot. Put the calf's foot and the chicken on top of the vegetables, then add the wine and enough water to just cover all the ingredients. Bring to a boil over medium-high heat, periodically skimming off any foam that rises to the surface. Reduce the heat to low and simmer for 1 hour, continuing to skim off any foam that appears.

Remove the pot from the heat and allow the chicken to cool in the broth for about 1 hour.

Transfer the chicken from the pot to a platter and cover it with a clean, damp kitchen towel. Refrigerate the chicken.

Strain the broth through a colander lined with a triple layer of cheesecloth into a medium pot, discarding the calf's foot and other solids. Simmer the broth over medium heat, periodically skimming off any foam that rises to the surface, for about 1½ hours, or until it has reduced to about 4 cups (960 ml). Pour the broth into a

ceramic dish, stir in the tarragon leaves, cover the dish, and refrigerate it until the gelée sets, about 2 hours.

To unmold the gelée, run a warm knife around the edges, center a large platter on top of the dish, and invert the dish. Carve the chicken, arrange it on the platter around the gelée, and season it with salt and pepper.

HINDLE WAKES (STEAMED CHICKEN ᴡɪᴛʜ PRUNES AND LEMON SAUCE)

SERVES 4 TO 6

In her 1932 recipe compendium *Good Things in England: A Practical Cookery Book for Everyday Use*, which seems to be the first cookbook in which a recipe for hindle wakes appears, Florence White recommends serving this curious dish (see page 97), from Lancashire, as part of an "English Dinner" for the month of November, along with Chesterfield soup (made with calf's tail), something called Scottish fish custard, Oxford sausages and mashed potatoes, pumpkin pie, port wine jelly, and a savoury of deviled sardines. Hindle wakes, she says, is "a good way of cooking an old hen." Other sources suggest that even an old rooster could be cooked this way with good results.

It may take a little looking around to find a stewing or boiling chicken—these large, older fowl, generally with at least a year of age on them, are little appreciated in this age of boneless, skinless chicken breasts from six- or eight-week-old birds—but small producers at farmers' markets and, conversely, large supermarkets catering to ethnic clienteles, are good bets. If you can't find one, a large roasting chicken may be substituted. The noted Lancashire chef Nigel Haworth spins an elaborate fantasy on this dish at the luxury country house hotel Northcote,

recipe continues

involving steamed chicken wings, chicken mousse, dried plums, and sticky rice. It's delicious, but not exactly the kind of thing most home cooks would want to try to reproduce. This recipe, much more traditional and less complicated, is based on the one Florence White published, which she credits to a Mrs. Kate A. Earp of Brighton, far from its putative Lancastrian home.

2 lemons
1 pound (450 g) dried prunes
1 cup coarse bread crumbs
Salt and freshly ground black pepper
1 (4- to 6-pound / 1.75- to 2.75-kg) boiling or
　　stewing chicken
1 to 1¼ cups (240 to 300 ml) Brown Gravy
　　(page 280)

Pare the rind thinly from one of the lemons and put it into a small saucepan with 2 cups (480 ml) water. Bring the water to a boil over high heat, then reduce the heat to low and simmer for 15 minutes.

Juice the lemons, then add the juice to the lemon-rind water. Transfer the lemon water to a large bowl, then add the prunes. Add a little more water if necessary to completely cover them. Cover the bowl and let the prunes soak in the refrigerator overnight.

Preheat the oven to 350°F (175°C).

Drain the prunes, reserving the lemon water. Pit the prunes, if necessary, and chop them coarsely. Mix them with the bread crumbs and season the mixture generously with salt and pepper.

Season the chicken generously on all surfaces with salt and pepper, then stuff the cavity with the prune mixture. Sew the cavity shut with kitchen twine.

Place a rack into a large, deep pot with a tight cover, large enough to hold the chicken. Add half the lemon water to the bottom of the pan (it should not touch the chicken), then cover the pan and steam the chicken in the oven until its internal temperature reaches 145°F (63°C), 2 to 2½ hours.

Remove the pot from the oven and carefully lift out the chicken. Pour off and reserve any pan juices. Raise the oven temperature to 425°F (215°C). Return the chicken to the pot and roast it, uncovered, until its internal temperature reaches 165°F (75°C), 20 to 30 minutes more.

Remove the roasting pan from the oven and carefully lift out the chicken and transfer it to a carving board to rest.

Place the pot over two burners on the stove, add the reserved lemon water, and return the pan juices to the pan. Cook over high heat, deglazing the pot and scraping up any browned bits. Cook, stirring continuously, until the liquid has reduced by half. Stir in the brown gravy, then adjust the seasoning if necessary. Strain the sauce into a bowl or sauceboat.

Cut open the cavity of the chicken and scoop out the stuffing. Put it in the middle of a heated serving platter. Carve the chicken into serving pieces, then add it to the platter. Drizzle some of the sauce over the chicken and stuffing, and serve the rest on the side.

The Curious Story of Hindle Wakes

Hindle wakes (page 95)—an old hen stuffed with prunes, steamed, then cloaked in lemon sauce—is a strange dish with a strange name and a strange story behind it. According to a number of cookbooks and countless magazine and newspaper articles, it is a traditional Lancashire specialty, supposedly imported to this part of England by Flemish weavers in the fourteenth century. A popular folk etymology for the unusual name of the dish—accepted even by the estimable Alan Davidson in his *Oxford Companion to Food*—holds that it is a concatenation of the bilingual phrase *hen de la wake*, meaning a fowl cooked on the occasion of the village fête. (A wake or "wakes day" in this sense is a country fair.)

Why Flemish-speaking weavers—or English-speaking Lancastrians—would throw French words into the name of the dish, or, if they did, why they wouldn't translate *hen* as well, is not clear. In any case, it turns out that "hindle" has nothing to do with hens, but was the name of a fictitious Lancashire town—perhaps inspired by that of a real town, Hindley, near Wigan—in Manchester playwright Stanley Houghton's 1912 romantic drama called . . . *Hindle Wakes*. Houghton's play concerned an independent-minded female textile worker who shares a sexy wakes weekend with a man of higher social station and then spurns his proposal of marriage (as one précis put it, "A mill girl leaves home rather than marry the owner's son, with whom she spent a holiday").

It's possible, of course, that in naming his play Houghton was punning on the name of a popular local specialty—but the earliest written reference to a dish called hindle wakes seems to be a recipe appearing in Florence White's *Good Things in England*, published twenty years after the play appeared. White got the recipe, she says, from a Mrs. Kate A. Earp of Brighton, who told her, "We as a family in Lancashire called these fowls 'Hindle Wakes'—why I do not know, unless it was because old hens were sold at the 'wakes' (fairs)."

In 1954, a social historian named Dorothy Hartley published her best-known book, the influential *Food in England*, which Alan Davidson hailed as "the greatest book on English food." In it, she offers a far more complicated version of hindle wakes than White's, a recipe she says was collected from a Lancashire family near, ahem, Wigan around 1900. She calls it "Hindle Wakes ('Hen de la Wake' or 'Hen of the Wake')" and says it is a "very old English recipe [that] has come down through many centuries unchanged." Chicken blood was once mixed with the stuffing, she says. Unfortunately, she cites no sources other than the anonymous family from whom her recipe supposedly came.

In considering whether it's likely that this unusual preparation did indeed have medieval origins, the skeptic might wonder why there is no mention of it or anything like it in the near-encyclopedic recipe compendiums of Hannah Glasse (1747), Elizabeth Raffald (1769), William Kitchiner (1817), Eliza Acton (1845), Robert Kemp Philp (1856), Mrs. Beeton (1861), Harriet Anne De Salis (1898), or anywhere else until Florence White in 1932. (The only other well-known combination of chicken with prunes in British cookery is in the Scots soup cock-a-leekie.)

That same skeptic might also point out something else: Houghton's play was a success, and its proto-feminist plot was apparently appealing enough that it was subsequently filmed six times, first as a silent movie in 1918 and most recently as a television play directed by Sir Laurence Olivier in 1976. One version came out in 1952, and thus would have been in the theaters just about the time that Dorothy Hartley was working on *Food in England*. Is it possible that the film inspired her to flights of culinary fancy in elaborating the dish?

Why a Goose?

Throughout Great Britain (and in Ireland, too), goose used to be indelibly associated with Michaelmas, September 29, a day observed in western Christianity as the feast of St. Michael the Archangel, archfoe of Satan. (It is also called the Feast of Michael and All Angels.) Michaelmas had—and in some quarters still has—considerable nonreligious significance, too: It is one of the so-called quarter days dividing the year (the others being Lady Day, March 25; Midsummer, June 24; and Christmas). In earlier times, these days marked the beginnings of new cycles in the British Isles—the occasions on which debts and rents were paid, servants were hired, land was sold, and judges were elected. To this day, the so-called Michaelmas Term, beginning in late September or early October, is the first academic term in many British schools and universities, and also the start of the legal year in British jurisprudence.

All very well and good. But why a goose? One reason is that Michaelmas was traditionally the day on which the annual harvest was completed, and goose is considered a festive food, one suitable for roasting on celebratory occasions. It happens that geese typically became fat enough to slaughter around this time, too. (They may have enjoyed one last meal before being dispatched: They were sometimes called "stubble geese," because they fed on the remains in the fields after the harvest.) Farmers were also known to offer geese to their landlords as partial payment of their quarterly rent, and by extension a folk belief grew that eating a goose on Michaelmas would ensure financial prosperity for the next twelve months. There is also an apocryphal story that the Michaelmas-goose association grew out of the fact that Queen Elizabeth heard news of the defeat of the Spanish Armada while eating a goose on Michaelmas Day in 1588—but since the Armada was destroyed in July of that year, this seems unlikely.

Since the latter twentieth century, goose in Great Britain has been relegated mostly to the Christmas banquet table, but in recent years, the British Goose Producers, an arm of the British Poultry Council, has campaigned to bring back the Michaelmas goose tradition, and some restaurants now serve the bird for the occasion. Eddie Hegarty, who runs Norfolk Geese in Diss, northeast of London, told the *Guardian* a few years back that Michaelmas geese were "a leaner bird, more like a wild goose." Geese grow fatter in cold weather, he added, and "the Michaelmas ones haven't gone through that process."

MICHAELMAS GOOSE

SERVES 8

The end of September generally signals the beginning of the apple harvest in Great Britain, and so the goose cooked for Michaelmas, on September 29 (see opposite), is often roasted with that fruit.

1 (9- to 11-pound / 4- to 5-kg) goose, with giblets,
    completely thawed if frozen
1 large carrot, chopped
1 large stalk celery, chopped
3 medium onions, chopped
Bouquet garni (2 sprigs parsley, 2 sprigs thyme,
    and 1 bay leaf, wrapped and tied in cheesecloth)
4 slices American (streaky) bacon, minced
2 tablespoons (30 g) butter
3 cooking apples, peeled, cored, and chopped
1 recipe freshly made Mashed Potatoes (page 211)
1 tablespoon chopped fresh sage
1 tablespoon chopped fresh thyme
1 tablespoon chopped fresh parsley
Salt and freshly ground black pepper

Separate the liver from the giblets and set it aside. Put the giblets, minus the liver, into a medium saucepan with a lid. Add the carrot, the celery, about a third of the onions, and the bouquet garni, then add enough water to cover all the ingredients. Bring the water to a boil over high heat, then reduce the heat, cover the pan, and simmer for 2 hours. When it's done, strain it into a medium bowl, discarding the solids. Set the stock aside.

Fry the bacon over medium heat in a large skillet with a lid until brown, then remove it with a slotted spoon and set it aside. Reduce the heat to medium-low, add the butter to the bacon fat in the pan, and, when it has melted, add remaining the onions and cook them, stirring frequently, until they grow soft and translucent but haven't begun to brown, about 5 minutes.

Finely chop the goose liver, then add it to the onions. Cook for 3 to 4 minutes, then add the apples to the skillet. Cover the skillet and cook, stirring occasionally, until the apples are very soft, 20 to 30 minutes. Stir in the mashed potatoes, sage, thyme, and parsley, and season with salt and pepper. Remove from the heat and set aside to cool.

Preheat the oven to 400°F (200° C).

Pat the goose dry thoroughly with paper towels. Pull out any fat inside the cavity and reserve it to render later for cooking fat. Prick the skin of the goose all over with a fork, then rub salt all over the skin. Season the cavity with salt and pepper, then fill with the stuffing. Truss the goose with kitchen twine, binding its legs and wings close to its body.

Put the goose into a heavy roasting pan large enough to hold it with a little room around the sides and roast it for 30 minutes. Remove the pan from the oven and, using a bulb baster or large spoon, draw off the rendered fat, reserving it for another use. Return the pan to the oven and reduce the oven temperature to 325°F (160°C). Roast the goose for about 2½ hours more, drawing off rendered fat at least once more as it cooks. Test for doneness by pricking the thigh at its thickest point with a skewer. If the juices run clear, the goose is done; if they're pink, roast the goose for another 15 minutes, then check again.

When the goose is done, transfer it to a large serving platter to rest. Draw off any remaining fat, reserving it for cooking, then set the roasting pan over two burners on the stovetop over medium-high heat and deglaze the pan with the stock, scraping up any browned bits on the bottom of the pan. Cook until the stock has reduced by about one-third, then strain it into a gravy boat or bowl.

Carve the goose at the table, and serve with the gravy on the side.

BRAISED DUCK WITH PEAS

SERVES 4

The idea of stewing or braising duck with garden peas as a summertime dish dates back at least to the eighteenth century. In 1769, Elizabeth Raffald gave a recipe for half-roasted duck stewed with "good gravy, a little mint, and three or four sage leaves"; boiled green peas are added as soon as the gravy has thickened. Eliza Acton, seventy-six years later, offers instructions for stewing ducks, then notes that "they may be served with a small portion only of their sauce, laid in a circle, with green peas à la Francaise, heaped high in the center . . ." In her 1879 volume *The Cookery Book* (later called *Margaret Sim's Cookery*), described by a contemporary magazine as being "no unworthy sequel to that of the classical Meg Dodds [*sic*]", the Scottish writer Margaret Sim calls for braising the bird "in the usual way" and separately cooking peas with shredded lettuce, green onions, and parsley as a garnish. According to the early twentieth-century restaurant chronicler Lieutenant Colonel Newnham-Davis, Lord Dudley (presumably the thirteenth Baron Dudley, Ferdinando Dudley Henry Lea Smith) considered the dish as one of the possible main courses for a typical British dinner "fit for an emperor," along with neck of venison and chicken with asparagus. The combination of duck and peas is hardly fashionable today, but the dish is delicious.

1 (5- to 6-pound / 2.25- to 2.75-kg) duck, cut into
    4 pieces
Salt and freshly ground black pepper
3 tablespoons (45 g) butter
4 shallots, quartered
1 (3-ounce / 85-g) piece thick-cut bacon, cut into
    ½-inch (1.25-cm) cubes
2 cups (480 ml) beef stock, store-bought or
    homemade (page 314)
6 to 8 large leaves romaine lettuce, julienned
4 scallions, chopped
Leaves from 3 or 4 sprigs parsley, chopped
2 cups shelled fresh peas (about 1½ pounds / 700 g
    in the pod)
Leaves from 6 to 8 sprigs mint, cut into chiffonade

Prick the duck skin all over with a fork, then season it generously on all sides with salt and pepper.

Melt the butter in a Dutch oven or large skillet with a cover over medium heat. Working in batches if necessary, add the duck, skin side down, and cook for 6 to 8 minutes, or until the skin is lightly browned and some of the fat has rendered. Pour off the fat and butter and reserve for another use.

Add the shallots and bacon to the Dutch oven, then add the stock. Bring the stock to a boil over high heat, then reduce the heat to low, return the duck to the pot, cover, and simmer for about 1 hour, or until the duck is cooked through.

Remove the duck pieces from the Dutch oven and set them aside on a platter, covered loosely with aluminum foil. Add the lettuce, scallions, and parsley to the broth, bring it to a boil over high heat, then add the peas. Cook, stirring occasionally, for about 3 minutes, or until the peas are just done.

Drain the peas, reserving the broth. Return the broth to the Dutch oven and cook over high heat, uncovered, for 3 to 4 minutes to reduce it slightly. Return the peas to the pot and stir in the mint.

Divide the peas with some broth evenly between four large warmed plates and arrange a piece of duck on top of each serving. Drizzle any remaining broth over the duck.

WELSH SALT DUCK *WITH* ONION SAUCE

SERVES 2 TO 4

Lady Llanover, born Augusta Waddington (1802–1896), was a wealthy Welsh arts patron, a dedicated anti-alcohol campaigner (she was notorious for turning all the pubs in her part of Wales into tearooms), and the author of a curiously charming book called *The First Principles of Good Cookery*. Though there are recipes in the book, it is mostly taken up by a series of conversations between a hermit she calls the Master of the Cell of Gover and a traveler who happens past his quarters. The hermit, "93 years old at least," feeds the man an admirable repast, and then makes him an offer: If he continues on his way for fourteen days, returning with "an exact report of [his] bad dinners, whether at inns or private houses," the hermit—who is not *that* much of a hermit, as he is attended to by four Welsh women of advanced age—will then cook exactly the same food for the traveler, correctly this time, thereby imbuing him with the titular principles of good cookery.

The traveler accepts the offer and returns with his notes, and the hermit guides him through the preparation of numerous dishes, along the way offering disquisitions on many topics, from hedgerows to bees. The recipes are presented as an appendix. They are said to be taken from a daybook kept by one of the hermit's attendants, and this in turn has been transcribed from the "original Welsh memoranda in white chalk, on the door of the Larder. . . ."

The most famous recipe in Lady Llanover's book is this one, for duck marinated in salt and then steamed or boiled in the oven (an almost identical method is used on the Isle of Man). She employs a kind of double boiler, a roasting pan filled with water set inside another roasting pan filled with water. It is a curious technique, but the duck emerges moist and flavorful. Some modern versions of the recipe finish the duck out of the water, roasting it for a short time to crisp the skin. I like this refinement of the original—and I think the duck cooks just as well in a single vessel as in a double one. (The onion sauce is mine, not Lady Llanover's; she talks about such a condiment but doesn't offer a recipe for it, other than to note that "Onion sauce is made of new milk and flour, flavoured with scalded onions".)

1 (5- to 6-pound / 2.25- to 2.75-kg) Pekin duck (see Sources, page 316)
1¼ cups (360 g) plus 1 tablespoon coarse kosher salt
2 small onions, chopped
1 recipe White Sauce (page 277)
½ cup (120 ml) whole milk

Rub the duck all over with 1¼ cups (360 g) of the salt, then put it breast side down in a nonreactive container, cover it with a lid or aluminum foil (not touching the duck), and refrigerate for 24 hours.

Turn the duck over, breast side up, and rub any salt that's loose in the container into the bird. Cover it again and refrigerate for 24 hours more.

Preheat the oven to 300°F (150°C).

Rinse the duck very thoroughly under cold running water, brushing off all the salt.

Put the duck into a deep baking dish or roasting pan large enough to hold it and pour in cold water to completely cover the bird.

Bake the duck, uncovered, for 2½ hours.

Remove the baking dish from the oven and increase the oven temperature to 450°F (230°C). Carefully transfer the duck from the cooking liquid onto a rack set inside a shallow roasting pan and roast for 30 minutes.

Meanwhile, add the remaining 1 tablespoon salt to a medium saucepan full of water. Bring the water to a boil over high heat. Add the onions and boil for 15 minutes, or until they're soft. Combine the white sauce and the milk in a small saucepan over low heat, stirring them together well. Drain the onions and stir them into the sauce.

Carve the duck into serving pieces and serve with the onion sauce on the side.

Becky Eats a Curry

That curry was commonplace in England, at least among the upper classes, by at least the early nineteenth century is suggested by a scene in William Makepeace Thackeray's satire on English society, *Vanity Fair*. Dining with the well-to-do Sedley family, into which she has insinuated herself, Thackeray's heroine (anti-heroine?) Rebecca (Becky) Sharp encounters the dish and finds it . . . surprising.

Now we have heard how Mrs. Sedley had prepared a fine curry for her son, just as he liked it, and in the course of dinner a portion of this dish was offered to Rebecca. "What is it?" said she, turning an appealing look to Mr. Joseph.

"Capital," said he. His mouth was full of it: his face quite red with the delightful exercise of gobbling. "Mother, it's as good as my own curries in India."

"Oh, I must try some, if it is an Indian dish," said Miss Rebecca. "I am sure everything must be good that comes from there."

"Give Miss Sharp some curry, my dear," said Mr. Sedley, laughing.

Rebecca had never tasted the dish before.

"Do you find it as good as everything else from India?" said Mr. Sedley.

"Oh, excellent!" said Rebecca, who was suffering tortures with the cayenne pepper.

"Try a chili with it, Miss Sharp," said Joseph, really interested.

"A chili," said Rebecca, gasping. "Oh yes!" She thought a chili was something cool, as its name imported, and was served with some. "How fresh and green they look," she said, and put one into her mouth. It was hotter than the curry; flesh and blood could bear it no longer. She laid down her fork. "Water, for Heaven's sake, water!" she cried. Mr. Sedley burst out laughing (he was a coarse man, from the Stock Exchange, where they love all sorts of practical jokes). "They are real Indian, I assure you," said he. . . .

SCOTS RABBIT CURRY

SERVES 4

The first recipe for curry (more or less) published in English was Hannah Glasse's "To Make a Currey the India Way," which appeared in 1747; it called for "fowls or rabbits" and was flavored only with black peppercorns and toasted coriander seeds. The Scots, who went to India in droves as soldiers, administrators, and entrepreneurs following the 1707 Acts of Union, which joined Scotland and England into a single kingdom, developed a taste for spiced Indian stews on their own; the earliest recipe for curry in Scotland was apparently one set down in 1791 by Stephana Malcolm in a handwritten recipe book from Burnfoot House, the Malcolm family's estate near Langholm in the Scottish border country. This one included many more spices, among them cardamom, ginger, cayenne, cloves, mace, mustard seed, and cinnamon. By the end of the eighteenth century, commercial curry powders began to be available, and the pseudonymous Meg Dods uses some in her recipe for this dish, published in 1826. This is my adaptation of it.

3 tablespoons (45 g) butter
1 tablespoon vegetable oil
1 (2- to 3-pound / 900 g- to 1.4-kg) rabbit, cut
    into 8 pieces
Salt and freshly ground black pepper
24 pearl onions, peeled
1 (6-ounce / 170-g) piece thick-cut bacon, cut into
    ½-inch (1.25-cm) cubes
2 tablespoons curry powder
1 tablespoon all-purpose flour
1 teaspoon mushroom powder (optional; see
    Sources, page 316)
1 teaspoon cayenne
½ teaspoon ground turmeric
1½ cups (360 ml) chicken stock, store-bought or
    homemade (page 314)
Juice of 1 large lemon
Boiled rice, for serving (optional)

Melt the butter with the oil in a Dutch oven or large skillet with a cover over medium heat. Season the rabbit generously with salt and pepper, then add the rabbit, onions, and bacon to the Dutch oven. Cook, turning the rabbit pieces frequently and stirring the onions and bacon occasionally, until the rabbit is golden brown on all sides and the onions are beginning to brown, 6 to 8 minutes.

Reduce the heat to low and stir in the curry powder, flour, mushroom powder (if using), cayenne, and turmeric, stirring to coat the rabbit, onions, and bacon well. Add the chicken stock. Bring the stock to a boil over high heat, then reduce the heat to low, cover, and simmer for 30 to 40 minutes, or until the rabbit is done.

Transfer the rabbit pieces to a warmed platter with a slotted spoon, then add the lemon juice to the sauce, raise the heat to high, and cook, stirring frequently, until it has reduced slightly and thickened. Pour the sauce over the rabbit pieces.

Meg Dods says, "Serve with plain boiled rice in a separate dish."

CHAPTER 5

BEEF, PORK, AND LAMB

"AFTER A SURFEIT OF MADE UP DISHES . . .
WHAT A JOY TO RETURN TO THE SIMPLE
JOINT, ROAST SIRLOIN OF BEEF OR LEG
OF MUTTON."

—"DINER-OUT," *London Restaurants* (1924)

"THINK ABOUT THE WAY YOU COOK MEAT.
DO YOU RESPECT IT? DO YOU DO IT JUSTICE?"

—HUGH FEARNLEY-WHITTINGSTALL, *The River Cottage Meat Book* (2004)

The British are famous meat-eaters. Roast beef is one of the country's emblematic foods, so much so that the French used to call their neighbors across the Channel *les rosbifs*, either because they ate so much "rosbif" or because, as Heston Blumenthal believes, British cooks taught the French how to roast the meat. The Sunday roast, in fact—typically beef, but also lamb or pork (or sometimes chicken)—is such an institution that it can be hard to find anything else to eat in restaurants on the Sabbath in Great Britain. Meat figures in many of the definitive regional dishes of British cuisine, too, from Lancashire hotpot to Welsh cawl to Scotch broth.

There were domesticated cattle in Britain at least six thousand years ago. The British Celts measured wealth by cattle owned, as did their Irish cousins, and battles were fought over them. Cows were kept for milk and cheese and various hybrids of the two, and aging bulls were periodically slaughtered for food. At least two-thirds of the meat eaten by Iron Age Britons, between about 1200 BC and the dawn of the Christian era, was beef.

The Celts domesticated pigs and sheep, as well; pork, both fresh and cured, was the next most popular meat after beef, with lamb almost a footnote. (The Celts also ate horsemeat, though consumption began dying out when early Christian missionaries discouraged it on the grounds that horses were sometimes used in pagan religious sacrifices.) The Romans brought new breeds of all the principal domesticated animals to Britain, along with improved methods of husbandry.

By the seventeenth century, cattle were being raised in the vast pasturelands of Scotland, Wales, and northern England, fattened in southeastern England on grass and turnips, then driven into London for slaughter and sale. Daniel Defoe, in 1724, describes "Scottish runts" from the Highlands who were pastured at St. Faiths near Norwich, where they "feed so eagerly on the rich pastures in these

A butcher's shop in London's East End

marshes that they thrive in an unusual manner, and grow monstrously fat. . . ." By the mid-1700s, the average Londoner was eating half a pound of meat per day—more than twice as much as the average Parisian. Visiting London, Count Cosimo, the grand duke of Tuscany, gave Britain's Yeomen of the Guard their nickname when he noted that they were "great eaters of beef, of which a very large ration is given them daily at the court, and they might be called 'Beef-eaters.'" The twentieth-century British attitude toward beef is neatly summarized in the 1945 edition of the *Encyclopaedia Britannica*, which states unequivocally that the meat "contains the highest form of protein for human consumption, in the most palatable, stimulating and digestible form."

While roasted suckling pig has long been much appreciated in Britain (see the non-eponymous Charles Lamb on the subject, page 132), and pork chops and roasted pork loin are popular, the meat of pigs has been eaten above all in Britain in the form of bacon, sausage, and ham, at least since the time of the Saxons. Regional pork sausage varieties—including black pudding, or blood sausage—abound around England, Scotland, and Wales. Since the first commercial bacon-curing plant was set up in Wiltshire in the 1770s, bacon in the British style has figured in morning meals all over the nation.

The most famous lamb in Britain is probably that of Wales—though it's not always lamb, per se: Technically, lamb is the meat of a sheep less than a year old; an animal between one and two is called a hogget, and that term sometimes appears on menus; the meat of sheep older than two years is mutton, much disparaged (and rarely available) in America, but still appreciated in some quarters in Britain for its forthright, slightly gamy flavor. George Borrow, a Victorian traveler in Wales, wrote that "the leg of mutton of Wales beats the leg of mutton of any other country . . . rich but delicate. . . ." However, he warned, "Welsh leg of mutton is superlative; but with the exception of the leg, the mutton of Wales is decidedly inferior to that of many other parts of Britain."

I've never managed to have Welsh mutton, but have had excellent Welsh lamb, fed in salt marshes. The late Gareth Jones, however, once warned me that "Welsh upland and salt marsh lamb are among the best in the world, but much of what's labeled 'Welsh' is lowland lamb brought into Wales for finishing and a better price ticket." (He added that during lambing season, Welsh farmers like to eat "lamb fries"—the testicles of castrated rams, fried

A policeman stops traffic for a herd of pigs crossing the road near London's Spitalfields Market, circa 1930

in bacon fat.) Two other places with famous lamb are Scotland's Orkney and Shetland Islands, where the lamb feeds partially on seaweed—but their meat is rarely found outside its home region and, even there, is sold mostly in butcher shops, not restaurants. Both places also produce first-rate grass-fed beef, however, and that is readily available to visitors. Beef still rules in Britain.

Meat Fruit and Sambocade

"I'm proud to be British," Heston Blumenthal, the London-born chef-restaurateur, author, food scholar, and television personality, told me not long ago—not that there was any doubt. Known as the most avant-garde of British chefs, Blumenthal—whose three-Michelin-star restaurant, The Fat Duck in Bray-on-Thames, pushes culinary boundaries with scientific techniques and multimedia presentations as surely as Ferran Adrià ever did at elBulli—has also embraced the past: He is a passionate student of British culinary history, and has long worked old culinary ideas into his menus at The Fat Duck and his two Bray pubs, The Hinds Head and The Crown.

Even more to the point, he dedicates his London restaurant, Dinner by Heston Blumenthal (at the Mandarin Oriental Hotel), to centuries of classic British recipes, rediscovered and redeveloped by him and his executive chef, Ashley Palmer-Watts, with the help of culinary historians and the collections of the British Library.

At Dinner, Blumenthal and Palmer-Watts serve food that is unique in today's world and is presented with a finesse that perhaps even its various originators, centuries ago, wouldn't recognize. Or perhaps they would. The dishes with the oldest provenance on the current menu date from around 1390: "rice & flesh" (rice with saffron, red wine, and calf's tail); a version of frumenty (page 30) made with spelt instead of cracked wheat and combined not with sugar and golden raisins but with grilled octopus, pickled dulse, and lovage in a "smoked sea broth"; and sambocade, a goat's milk cheesecake with elderflower, apple, perry-poached pear, and smoked candied walnuts.

The most famous dish at Dinner is "meat fruit" (circa 1500), a chicken liver parfait shaped to resemble a mandarin orange and coated with an orange frosting. (Such decoratively deceptive presentations were once common.) Among the other offerings are spiced pigeon with ale and artichokes (circa 1780); roast turbot with mussel and seaweed ketchup, salmon roe, and sea rosemary (circa 1830); and a dish of poached rhubarb with hibiscus, rosehip jam, yogurt cream, and olive oil (circa 1590). The most recent dish, so new that it almost seems out of place, is cod with cider, chard, onions, and smoked artichokes—a real youngster from only about 1940.

The interesting—and particularly appealing—thing about all this food is that it's quite delicious and doesn't seem "historical" at all; if the dates weren't appended to the dish names on the menu, I'm not sure I'd even realize that this food had ancient roots—which I suppose is a testament to the timelessness of good English cooking, whatever its age. But as Blumenthal asks, "Why do we think of creativity as being a modern thing? Think of all the imagination there was back then!"

MINCE AND TATTIES

There's a famous poem about this definitive Scottish comfort dish of ground beef and mashed potatoes by the late J. K. Annand that promises that if you "mash and mix the tatties / Wi mince into the mashin," your dinner will be voted "Smashin!" I like a Scottish street rhyme, collected on the electricscotland.com website, better: It warns "You canna shove your granny off a bus, / You canna shove your granny, / Cause she makes your mince n tatties." In her book *Broths to Bannocks*, Catherine Brown notes that "the best steak, cut from the rump and minced by the butcher, is how many Scottish housewives buy mince." This is an adaptation of her recipe.

1 tablespoon stone-ground Scottish oats (see
    Sources, page 316)
2 tablespoons corn or canola oil
1 large onion, finely chopped
1 pound (450 g) ground beef
1 large carrot, thinly sliced
1 (4 ounce / 115 g) black pudding, skin removed
    (optional)
Salt and freshly ground black pepper
1 recipe Mashed Potatoes (page 211)

Toast the oats in a small dry skillet over medium-high heat, shaking the pan frequently, until they turn golden brown, 4 to 6 minutes. Set aside.

Heat the oil in a large skillet over medium heat. Add the onion and cook, stirring frequently, until it browns, 10 to 12 minutes. Push it to one side of the skillet, then add the ground beef. Cook the beef, breaking it up into small pieces with a wooden spoon as it cooks, until it is well browned, stirring it frequently and mixing in the onions when the beef begins to change color, 12 to 15 minutes.

Add the carrot and the toasted oats, stirring them in well, then add the black pudding (if using), breaking it up with a wooden spoon so that it mixes well with the beef. Add enough water to just cover the ingredients, then season the mince generously with salt and pepper, reduce the heat to low, and simmer for about 15 minutes, or until the

carrots are soft. The finished mince should have the consistency of a thick stew. Serve with the mashed potatoes on the side.

SAUCERMEAT

Early one foggy morning, I was driving from Unst, at the very top of the Shetland Islands (and thus the very top of Great Britain) down to the first of two ferries that would eventually lead me to the road back to Lerwick, the islands' capital. I'd left my modest hotel before anyone was up, and this is one of the few corners of the world that Starbucks has not invaded, so I was fighting sleep as I passed through the harsh, treeless countryside. Then a vision appeared by the side of the road: a mobile coffee and snack trailer. I pulled over and got out to have a cup of something hot and some kind of breakfast. The coffee was, well, hot and not much else. For food, I was about to order a bacon sandwich, but then noticed that one of the offerings was something called saucermeat. I asked the proprietor—who, it turned out, was an Irishman who had married a local woman—what that was. "A local specialty," he replied. Of course I had to try it. What I got, sandwiched in a roll, was a slab of ground beef with an overload of aromatic sausage-y spices—peculiar, but not bad at all.

Saucermeat, also called *sassermaet* in the local dialect, may date back hundreds of years. The name apparently comes from the French word for "sausage," *saucisse*. It was once made in every local household, out of beef or lamb mixed with fat and half a dozen or so ground spices, and packed into earthenware crocks, where it could be stored for weeks, if not months, without refrigeration, thanks to its high salt content and the cool ambient temperature of the islands. Today, every butcher in Shetland makes his own version, always with a "secret" mixture of spices. It may be sold loose for making meat loaf or saucermeat bronies (page 114), but is more often offered the

recipe continues

way I encountered it, in the shape of square patties called Lorne sausages. (A popular breakfast meat not always made from saucermeat, Lorne sausages were named either for the region of Lorne in Argyll or for a 1920s-era Scottish comedian, Tommy Lorne.)

The standard recipe for saucermeat is that given by Margaret B. Stout in her *Cookery for Northern Wives*, published in 1925. "The poorer cuts of meat," she writes, "generally beef, minced and seasoned . . . may be made into bronies and fried, or into meat loaf and baked." She gives a recipe for twelve pounds of meat (enough to pack into a jar). Curiously, she calls for both allspice and Jamaica pepper, which are the same thing (*Pimenta dioica*). I reduced the spice quantities to suit a mere two pounds of ground beef, and then adjusted the quantities further by trial and error to come up with something not too aggressively flavored but still with a kick of spice. Interestingly, some bloggers who have tried commercially made saucermeat in Lerwick complain that it is rather flavorless. That is not the case here.

2 pounds (900 g) coarsely ground beef, preferably 30% fat
¼ teaspoon ground cloves
½ teaspoon ground allspice
½ teaspoon ground mace
½ teaspoon ground cinnamon
½ teaspoon finely ground white pepper
½ teaspoon finely ground black pepper
1 teaspoon ground ginger
1 tablespoon salt

With your hands, spread the ground beef across the bottom and around the sides of a medium bowl. Sprinkle in the cloves, allspice, mace, cinnamon, white and black pepper, ginger, and salt, distributing them as evenly as possible over the surface of the meat. With your hands, mix the spices into the meat thoroughly, but don't handle the meat more than necessary to incorporate them well. (Wash your hands thoroughly with soap and hot water before and after handling the meat.)

Form the saucermeat into 6 to 8 rectangular sausages about ¾ inch (2 cm) thick and cook as you would ordinary sausage patties, or use the saucermeat to make Saucermeat Bronies (see right).

SAUCERMEAT BRONIES

SERVES 6 TO 8

For those who find the aromatic spices in straight saucermeat overwhelming, this is a means of savoring some of the flavor with less pungency. The word *bronie*, probably a borrowing from the defunct Norn language once spoken by the Norse settlers in Shetland, is a modern synonym there for "hamburger." Alternately spelled "broonie" and "brunnie," the word is also used in Shetland and Orkney to mean anything small and cake-shaped, like a scone or oatcake. Like the preceding saucermeat recipe (page 113), this is adapted from Margaret B. Stout's small but definitive Shetland cookbook, *Cookery for Northern Wives*, originally published in 1925.

½ recipe (1 pound / 450 g) Saucermeat (page 113)
1 pound (450 g) ground beef
⅔ cup (65 g) fine bread crumbs
½ small onion, finely chopped
1 large egg, lightly beaten
Salt and freshly ground black pepper
3 tablespoons bacon fat or lard, or 1 tablespoon each butter and vegetable oil

With your hands, mix the saucermeat, ground beef, bread crumbs, onion, egg, a little salt, and plenty of pepper together in a medium bowl. Combine the ingredients thoroughly but don't overmix.

Melt the bacon fat (or melt the butter with the olive oil) in a large skillet over medium-high heat. Form the meat mixture into 6 to 8 patties about ¾ inch (2 cm) thick. Sear them for about 1 minute on each side, then reduce the heat to low and cook for 10 minutes more, turning once.

O'er Far Ben

The Shetlands, or Shetland Islands—often called just Shetland—are a subarctic archipelago forming part of the dividing line between the Atlantic Ocean and the North Sea. They are less than two hundred miles from Denmark's Faroe Islands and about two hundred miles closer to Bergen, Norway, than they are to Edinburgh, Scotland's capital. Remarkably, though, they were never attached to either Britain or the European land mass; they traveled on shifting tectonic plates from near the South Pole, and are now as close to the North Pole as Alaska is (though the North Atlantic Current keeps them warmer).

Not surprisingly, the Scandinavian influence here is strong. Place names like Skeld, Vidlin, Laxo, and Yell betray Nordic roots, and indeed the Vikings conquered the islands in the eighth and ninth centuries AD. Shetland remained a Norwegian province until 1468, when the Danes mortgaged it to the Scots as dowry for their Princess Margaret, who was marrying Scotland's James III. (The Danes later tried unsuccessfully to get it back.) The citizenry here used to speak a variation on the Norse language known as Norn, now extinct, but even today the official motto of Shetland is *Með Lögum Skal Land Byggja*—"the land shall be built by laws"—identical to the motto of the Icelandic national police.

The Shetland Museum & Archives on Hay's Dock in the islands' capital of Lerwick is a beautifully designed contemporary museum of local history and culture. (There's a remarkable audio art piece in the forecourt in which fragments of oral histories, Shetlands music, and sounds of nature blend and clash, driven by the patterns of the wind.) One of the displays inside the museum is a full-size "but'n'ben," or typical two-room crofter's cottage. These little houses had only one door, through the but, or outer room, which housed the kitchen; the ben was the inner room, the parlor and/or bedchamber. *Far ben* meant "far within," and metaphorically suggested intimacy; *o'er far ben* meant getting a little too intimate—presumably easy to do in so small a structure.

In the museum's but'n'ben, a dark, slightly shriveled looking mass hangs from the rafters over the peat fire in the hearth (there was no chimney in these houses, just a smoke hole, but not directly over the fire, lest the rain extinguish the smoldering peat). The hanging mass is a representation of one of the great, mysterious Shetland culinary specialties: reestit mutton. This is a large hunk of mutton brined in salt, saltpeter, and sugar for weeks, then hung above the fire to smoke and dry. (*Reestit* is related either to the Norwegian word for grilling or broiling or is a Scots variant on *roost*, referring to the rafters. Even the *Oxford English Dictionary* isn't sure.)

I never managed to try reestit mutton—though it is still made, it isn't the kind of thing that's served in restaurants, and if I'd bought it at a butcher shop, I would have had no way to prepare it (small pieces of it are commonly cut off and used in soups and stocks)—but the finished product is said to be salty (not surprisingly), firm, and dry; some people just think it tastes spoiled. It is unique to Shetland, which may be a good thing.

LANCASHIRE HOTPOT

SERVES 4

Lancashire—a county in northwestern England that historically encompassed the cities of Liverpool and Manchester, and that was a major center of trade and manufacturing in the nineteenth and early twentieth centuries—has a rich food culture. It produces one of England's great cheeses (called simply Lancashire) and is particularly known for baked goods, including both sweet and savory pies. The emblematic dish of the region, though, is hotpot, a long-cooked lamb (originally mutton) stew said to have been developed by factory workers during the Industrial Revolution because it could be left in a slow oven to cook all day while they labored. (There's a meatless version called "fatherless pie," perhaps because potatoes and onions were all a household could afford if there was no man bringing home the bacon.)

The Lancashire-born chef Nigel Haworth, who runs five traditional-style pubs around the region and oversees the kitchen at Northcote, a luxury country house hotel near Blackburn, has made a particular study of the dish and developed several versions of his own. He stresses that, as with any fairly simple dish, the quality of the ingredients is paramount. He specifies "preferably regional lamb, e.g., Bowland Lamb" (from the Forest of Bowland, an area known for its livestock) in one iteration of the recipe, and a rare heritage breed called Lonk in another, and for potatoes, calls specifically for King Edwards in one case and Maris Pipers in another, both floury heirlooms. Any good lamb may of course be substituted, and smallish russet potatoes work well for the spuds.

One version of Haworth's hotpot is fancied up with slices of roasted lamb loin. He has written that it is essential to cook a Lancashire hotpot in, well, a hotpot—a hand-thrown vessel of stoneware clay—but in the recipe he uses for his pubs, both the meat and potatoes are cooked in vacuum bags in a steam oven and then transferred to individual hotpots for serving. The version of Haworth's hotpot recipe I prefer and have adapted here, and certainly the one that works the best for home cooks, is an older one of his enshrined on the visitlancashire.com website. Unless you have authentic small Lancashire hotpots, I recommend using ceramic or terra-cotta baking dishes or onion soup bowls.

2¼ pounds (1 kg) boneless lamb shoulder, neck, and shin meat, cut into pieces about 1¼ to 1½ inches (3 to 4 cm) square
3 teaspoons salt
2 pinches of freshly ground white pepper
1 tablespoon raw sugar
3 tablespoons all-purpose flour
3 tablespoons (45 g) butter, melted
6 medium onions, thinly sliced
2¼ pounds (1 kg) russet or other floury potatoes, peeled
1 cup veal or beef stock, store-bought or homemade (page 314)
Pickled Red Cabbage (page 205), for serving (optional)

Preheat the oven to 350°F (175°C).

Put the lamb into a large bowl, season it with 1 teaspoon of the salt, a large pinch of white pepper, and the sugar, then dust it with the flour, making sure to coat all the pieces. Divide the lamb evenly between four hotpots or ceramic or terra-cotta baking dishes about 7 inches (18 cm) in diameter and 3½ inches (9 cm) deep.

Heat 1 tablespoon (15 g) of the butter in a large skillet with a lid over medium heat. Add the onions and about 1 teaspoon of the salt, cover the skillet, and cook without stirring for about 5 minutes.

Spread the onions evenly on top of the lamb, dividing it evenly between the four hotpots.

Slice the potatoes horizontally to a thickness of about 1/16 inch (2 mm). Put them into a medium bowl, add the remaining 2 tablespoons (30 g) butter, season with the remaining 1 teaspoon salt and pinch of white pepper, and toss well. Layer the potato slices on top of the onions in the four hotpots, dividing them evenly, then pour ¼ cup of the stock over each hotpot.

Bake, uncovered, for 30 minutes, then reduce the oven temperature to 275°F (135°C) and bake for 2½ hours more.

Serve with Pickled Red Cabbage (page 205), if you like.

SCOUSE

SERVES 4

Scouse—originally lobscouse—is a sailor's dish, a stew of meat and vegetables traditionally thickened with hardtack (ship's biscuit). It is eaten in North Wales and as far south as Staffordshire, but is so closely associated with the port city of Liverpool that *Scouse* is a slang name for a Liverpudlian and for the Liverpool dialect. The *Oxford English Dictionary* cites a derisive mention of the dish from 1707 ("He has sent the Fellow . . . to the Devil, that first invented Lobscouse") and Smollett refers to it as "lob's course" in 1751. The origin of the term is obscure, but it quite possibly derives from the Latvian *labs kausis*, "good cup or bowl," which also gave Norwegian its word for stew, *lapskaus*. On shipboard, the stew would have been made with salted meat (some recipes use corned beef today), as well as durable root vegetables, but today it usually involves mutton or a tougher cut of beef. A meatless version is called blind scouse. This recipe, which calls for thickening the stew with potatoes rather than hardtack, is adapted from the "secret" formula revealed by Christian Grall, chef at Liverpool Football Club's Boot Room Sports Café, in celebration of Global Scouse Day 2014—an event that celebrates local culture, with a focus on "Liverpool's finest culinary export."

¼ cup (60 ml) olive oil
1½ pounds (700 g) chuck steak or stewing lamb, diced
Salt and freshly ground black pepper
4 medium onions, diced
1 (500-ml) bottle good English or English-style bitter ale (for instance, Higsons Best, Young's Bitter, Newcastle Summer Ale, or Brooklyn Best Bitter)
2 large carrots, diced
1 small rutabaga, peeled and diced
1 pound (450 g) potatoes, peeled and diced
2 bay leaves
1 sprig thyme
5 cups (1.2 L) beef stock, store-bought or homemade (page 314)
Pickled Beets (page 205), for serving (optional)
Crusty bread, for serving (optional)

Heat the oil in a large, heavy-bottomed pot over medium heat for 1 to 2 minutes, then add the meat and cook, stirring frequently, for 5 to 7 minutes, or until it begins to brown on all sides. Season the meat generously with salt and pepper.

Add the onions and cook for 6 to 8 minutes more, or until they soften, then add the beer. Raise the heat to high, bringing the beer to a boil, and cook until it has reduced by about half.

Add the carrots, rutabaga, and half the potatoes, along with the bay leaves and thyme. Reduce the heat to low, cover the pot, and cook for 45 minutes.

Add the remaining potatoes and cook for about 1½ hours more, or until the meat is very tender. Adjust the seasoning if necessary.

Serve with Pickled Beets (page 205) and crusty bread, if you like.

British Pasta

The British have been eating pasta much longer than you think they have. Shortly before William the Conqueror and his Normans crossed the English Channel to change Anglo-Saxon life and language, a different bunch of Normans invaded Sicily and southern Italy, the Italian regions where pasta first became common fare, and they probably eventually introduced the idea of boiled dough into England and Wales. There is a thirteenth-century Anglo-Norman recipe for a dish called cressee, a latticework cake of pasta strips, some of them colored with saffron, that is boiled and then covered with cheese. Another recipe from around the same era describes "ravie-les," or ravioli, filled with cheese, herbs, and shallots. Several lasagna-like dishes appear in the seminal fourteenth-century English recipe collection *The Forme of Cury*.

Nonetheless, pasta as we think of it today became widely known in the British Isles only in the latter half of the twentieth century, thanks at least in part to the writings of Elizabeth David, who championed Italian and other Mediterranean food at a time when olive oil was sold only in tiny bottles at the pharmacist's, for medicinal purposes.

When the BBC broadcast an April Fool's Day "mock-umentary" in 1957 about spaghetti being harvested from trees in Italian-speaking Switzerland, a number of Britons apparently took it seriously, and wrote in asking how they could plant their own spaghetti trees.

SPAG BOL

SERVES 4

In a survey conducted in 2014, 23 percent of the Londoners polled named pasta as their favorite food, with only 21 percent opting for the traditional British roast dinner (and a mere 4 percent choosing fish and chips). Today, all over the U.K., chefs both indigenous and imported are cooking excellent Italian food, pasta included (the celebrated River Café in London has been hailed as "the best Italian restaurant in the world"—including Italy). For much of the latter twentieth century, however, pasta, to the average Briton, probably meant "spag bol"—an affectionate nickname, first used in 1970 (according to the *Oxford English Dictionary*), for spaghetti alla bolognese, or spaghetti with meat sauce. It should be noted that this dish is unknown in the eponymous Bologna, where the meat sauce, or ragù, commonly involves pork (ground meat or pancetta or both), red wine, and milk, but not tomatoes, and is served with fresh egg-dough pasta like fettuccine or tagliatelle, not dried pasta like spaghetti. But never mind. Spag bol is cheap and easy and filling, and it has fueled casual dinner parties, potlucks, student suppers, and solitary evenings at home with the telly for decades.

3 tablespoons olive oil
1 medium onion, finely chopped
1 to 2 cloves garlic, finely chopped
1 pound (450 g) ground beef
2 tablespoons tomato paste
1 (28-ounce / 794-g) can San Marzano or other
    good-quality Italian tomatoes, chopped,
    with juices
1 to 2 teaspoons red pepper flakes
Salt and freshly ground black pepper
1 pound (450 g) spaghetti
Grated Parmigiano-Reggiano cheese, for serving

Heat the olive oil in a large saucepan over medium heat, then add the onion and garlic and cook, stirring frequently, for about 5 minutes. Add the ground beef and cook, breaking it up with a spoon as it begins to brown and stirring it into the onion and garlic. Stir in the tomato paste, tomatoes with their juices, red pepper flakes, and salt and black pepper to taste, then reduce the heat to low and cook, uncovered, stirring occasionally, for 20 minutes.

Meanwhile, bring a large covered pot of salted water to a boil. Add the spaghetti, stirring it so that it doesn't stick together, and cook for 9 to 12 minutes, or until the pasta is done according to your taste.

Drain the spaghetti and put it into a large bowl, then stir in the sauce, making sure it coats all the noodles, and serve immediately, with the cheese on the side for sprinkling.

PORK CHOPS *WITH* CINNAMON AND APPLES

SERVES 4

When Sir Terence Conran opened the Butlers Wharf Chop House as part of his "gastrodome" complex on the south bank of the Thames, he said that he liked the term *chop house* because it was the only synonym for restaurant he could think of that didn't have Gallic origins. *Café*, *bistro*, *brasserie*, even *restaurant* itself are all French words. The term *chop house* is unmistakably British, as is the institution itself. The word first appeared in the late seventeenth century, when restaurants began cooking individual servings of meat instead of only roasting whole animals. (The oldest surviving chop house in London is Simpson's Tavern in Cornhill—not to be confused with Simpson's in the Strand—which opened in 1757.) The chops in question would most likely have been mutton or beef; pigs were still mostly roasted whole (see page 132), or turned into bacon or sausages. For us today, on the other hand, chops are usually pork, and applesauce—in Great Britain as well as America—is a frequent accompaniment to the cut. This recipe, from the Bodnant Welsh Food Centre in Wales, combines the meat and the fruit in a different way.

4 (¾- to 1-pound / 350- to 450-g) bone-in loin
    pork chops
Salt and freshly ground black pepper
4 tablespoons (½ stick / 55 g) butter
2 medium apples, peeled, cored, and thinly sliced
1 large white onion, thinly sliced
2 tablespoons brown sugar
1 teaspoon ground cinnamon
2 tablespoons apple cider vinegar
½ cup (120 ml) heavy cream

Season the pork chops generously on both sides with salt and pepper. Melt half the butter over medium-high heat in a heavy-bottomed skillet large enough to hold the chops without touching. Fry the chops for 4 to 5 minutes on each side, turning them once. Transfer the chops to a plate and set them aside.

Add the remaining butter to the skillet, then add the apples and onion and cook, stirring frequently, for 6 to 8 minutes, or until the onion is translucent. Stir in the brown sugar, cinnamon, vinegar, and cream, combining them well. Return the pork chops to the pan and cook for about 3 minutes on each side, turning once.

To serve, divide the pork chops between four plates and spoon the sauce over them, dividing it evenly.

BAKED HAM
with TREACLE GLAZE

SERVES 12 TO 20

Treacle was originally a salve or paste used to treat snakebites; molasses is a syrupy by-product of sugar production. The two terms were first conflated in the late seventeenth century. Today, treacle is simply the British name for dark or black molasses (light molasses is golden syrup). In the United States, ham is often glazed with honey; in the U.K., treacle is more prevalent and lends a richer, denser result. This preparation is properly made with gammon, or fresh (i.e., uncooked) ham. (Technically, it's gammon until it's baked, *then* it becomes ham.) Many cooks stud the ham with whole cloves, but I've seen so many examples of this preparation over the years, in person and in print, that I can hardly stand to look at one, so I include ground cloves in the glaze instead. This is a dish best prepared for cooking the night before serving and slow-baked overnight.

1 (8- to 10-pound / 3.65- to 4.5-kg) bone-in
    gammon (fresh or uncooked ham)
½ cup plus ⅓ cup (200 ml) black treacle or
    blackstrap molasses
⅓ cup (70 g) Demerara or muscovado sugar
1 tablespoon Colman's mustard
1 teaspoon ground cloves
½ teaspoon ground cinnamon
2 tablespoons dark rum
Freshly ground black pepper

Preheat the oven to 475°F (250°C).

Lay the gammon on two crossed pieces of aluminum foil large enough to completely enclose it. Drizzle ½ cup (120 ml) of the treacle over the top of the ham, letting it flow down the sides. Wrap the gammon in the foil so that it is completely sealed, adding another piece on top if necessary.

Place the foil-wrapped gammon on a rack in a large roasting pan and roast for 1 hour. Reduce the oven temperature to 200°F (95°C) and cook for 12 to 14 hours more.

Remove the ham from the oven and raise the oven temperature to 475°F (250°C).

Remove the ham from the rack and transfer it to a cutting board, reserving any pan juices and setting them aside.

Unwrap the ham, then, using kitchen shears, cut the tough skin, or rind, off the ham, leaving a thin layer of fat.

In a small bowl, mix together the remaining ⅓ cup (80 ml) treacle, the sugar, mustard, cloves, cinnamon, and rum. Add a few good grindings of black pepper. Drizzle the mixture over the ham, covering all surfaces.

Put the ham back on the rack in the roasting pan and roast for 20 minutes.

Remove the ham from the oven, reserving any pan juices and adding them to the juices reserved earlier. Transfer the ham to the cutting board. Let it rest for 30 minutes before carving.

Carve the ham and set the slices on a heated platter. Heat the reserved pan juices in a small saucepan over medium heat, and pour the liquid over the ham slices.

ROAST PRIME RIB OF BEEF

SERVES 8 TO 10

If there is any food associated with Great Britain more than "the full English" or fish and chips, it is surely roast beef (almost inevitably accompanied by Yorkshire pudding, page 179). We picture roast beef, probably not wholly inaccurately, as the centerpiece at medieval banquets; we recognize it as the heart of the Sunday dinner and thus of British domestic life. It still draws legions of diners—especially, but not always, on Sundays—to restaurants ranging from gastropubs and rural hotel dining rooms to London's Hawksmoor chain and the venerable Simpson's in the Strand. More than two million beef cattle are slaughtered every year in Great Britain (and more beef is imported from Brazil, New Zealand, Ireland, and elsewhere), and it certainly isn't all going into sliders.

1 (6- to 7-pound / 2.75- to 3.25-kg) prime rib of
    beef
1 tablespoon dry mustard
3 tablespoons all-purpose flour
Salt and freshly ground black pepper
1 cup (240 ml) dry red wine
Yorkshire Pudding (page 179), for serving
English mustard or Horseradish Sauce (page 277),
    for serving

Ask the butcher to remove the chine bone and short ribs from the prime rib. Save the chine bone for stock, if you like, and reserve the short ribs. Ask the butcher to tie the roast and weigh it without the chine bone and short ribs; remember the weight.

Preheat the oven to 450°F (230°C).

Combine the mustard, flour, and a generous amount of salt and pepper in a small bowl, mixing them together well. Rub the mixture all over the prime rib.

Make a bed of the short ribs in a large roasting pan, then place the prime rib on top of them, fat side up. Put the pan on the lowest rack in the oven and roast the meat for 30 minutes. Reduce the oven temperature to 325°F (160°C) and roast, basting the meat frequently with the pan juices, for 15 minutes more per pound (450 g).

After 1½ hours, pour the wine over the meat and roast for 15 minutes more. Insert a meat thermometer into the center of the roast. If it reads 120°F (50°C), the meat is done to medium-rare. If it hasn't reached this temperature, continue roasting, checking the temperature every 10 to 15 minutes.

When the meat is done, remove it from the oven and let it rest for 30 minutes before carving. Serve the short ribs alongside or reserve them for stock.

Serve with Yorkshire Pudding (page 179) and with English mustard or Horseradish Sauce (page 277).

The Roast Beef of Old England

The English have long accepted roast beef as a symbol of their nation's greatness, strength, and valor. The children's book author Mary Francis Ames, in her 1899 *An ABC for Baby Patriots*, offered this verse:

> *R is the Roast Beef*
> *That has made England great;*
> *You see it here pictured*
> *Each piece upon a plate.*

Henry Fielding, best known as the author of *Tom Jones*, anticipated Ames by more than a century and a half when he wrote this paean to roast beef for *The Grub-Street Opera*, which was supposed to debut in London in 1731 but was ultimately never produced. The song, however, set to music by the singer and composer Richard Leveridge and with several verses added by him, became immensely popular in the latter eighteenth and nineteenth centuries. As a measure of its renown, the melody was played by a bugler to summon first-class passengers to dinner on the *Titanic*.

> *When mighty Roast Beef was the Englishman's food,*
> *It ennobled our brains and enriched our blood.*
> *Our soldiers were brave and our courtiers were good*
> *O! the Roast Beef of Old England,*
> *And O! the old English Roast Beef!*

> *But since we have learnt from all-vapouring France*
> *To eat their ragouts as well as to dance,*
> *We're fed up with nothing but vain complaisance*
> *O! the Roast Beef of Old England,*
> *And O! the old English Roast Beef!*

> *Our fathers of old were robust, stout, and strong,*
> *And kept open house, with good cheer all day long,*
> *Which made their plump tenants rejoice in this song—*
> *O! the Roast Beef of Old England,*
> *And O! the old English Roast Beef!*

> *But now we are dwindled to, what shall I name?*
> *A sneaking poor race, half-begotten and tame,*
> *Who sully the honours that once shone in fame.*
> *O! the Roast Beef of Old England,*
> *And O! the old English Roast Beef!*

> *When good Queen Elizabeth sat on the throne,*
> *Ere coffee, or tea, or such slip-slops were known,*
> *The world was in terror if e'er she did frown.*
> *O! the Roast Beef of Old England,*
> *And O! the old English Roast Beef!*

> *In those days, if Fleets did presume on the Main,*
> *They seldom, or never, return'd back again,*
> *As witness, the Vaunting Armada of Spain.*
> *O! the Roast Beef of Old England,*
> *And O! the old English Roast Beef!*

> *Oh then we had stomachs to eat and to fight*
> *And when wrongs were cooking to do ourselves right.*
> *But now we're a . . . I could, but goodnight!*
> *O! the Roast Beef of Old England,*
> *And O! the old English Roast Beef!*

BRAISED BRISKET WITH PICKLED WALNUTS

SERVES 4

To the best of my knowledge, only the British have figured out that pickled walnuts are a perfect condiment for braised or roasted beef. You don't see the combination—or, for that matter, pickled walnuts in general—in France, Italy, or Spain. This is the estimable London-based chef-turned-writer-and-artist Simon Hopkinson's recipe marrying the two ingredients. It is possible to pickle your own walnuts if you have access to fresh young ones, still in their green outer skin, but it is a complicated process and walnut juices produce an indelible stain. Fortunately, commercially made pickled walnuts are easily obtainable. As with many long-cooked dishes, this one improves in flavor if it's made the day before serving and refrigerated overnight.

2 pounds (900 g) fresh beef brisket
Sea salt and freshly ground black pepper
3 to 4 tablespoons all-purpose flour
3 tablespoons lard
8 small yellow onions, quartered
1 medium leek, washed well and cut on an angle into thick pieces
3 stalks celery, with the fibrous "strings" shaved off with a vegetable peeler, cut on an angle into thick pieces
4 small turnips, peeled and quartered
1 tablespoon anchovy paste
1 tablespoon Lea & Perrins Worcestershire sauce
6 pickled walnuts, quartered lengthwise (see Sources, page 316)
3 tablespoons pickled-walnut brine
2 bay leaves
4 cups (960 ml) beef stock, store-bought or homemade (page 314)

Preheat the oven to 325°F (160°C).

Season the brisket generously with salt and pepper, then dredge it in the flour.

Melt the lard in a cast-iron pot over medium-high heat. Add the brisket to the pot and brown it well on both sides, turning it several times with tongs. Transfer the brisket to a plate and set it aside.

Reduce the heat to medium. Add the onions, leeks, celery, and turnips and cook, stirring frequently, until they just begin to brown, about 10 minutes. Add the anchovy paste, Worcestershire sauce, walnuts, walnut brine, bay leaves, and stock. Return the brisket and any accumulated juices to the pot.

Reduce the heat to low and bring the stock to a gentle simmer, skimming off any foam that forms on the top. Simmer for 10 minutes, uncovered. Cover the pot and put it into the oven. Bake until the brisket is very tender when poked with a fork, about 3 hours if you're going to serve it immediately, uncovering the pot for the final half hour. If you're going to refrigerate it overnight and serve it the next day, cook for about 2½ hours, uncovering the pot for the final half hour. Remove and discard the bay leaves.

If serving immediately, use two forks to pull the brisket apart in the pot into four pieces of about equal size. Transfer the meat to a warmed platter and spoon the vegetables and broth over it.

If you plan to serve it the next day, allow the brisket to cool to room temperature in the pot, then refrigerate it, still in the pot. To serve, preheat the oven to 325°F (160°C) and reheat the brisket, covered, for 30 minutes, then proceed as in the previous step.

FILET DE BOEUF À LA GELÉE

SERVES 6 TO 8

This is basically a variation on the traditional French pot roast called *boeuf à la mode* (which means, more or less, "fashionable beef"). It was probably an inspiration of the great French chef Marie-Antoine Carême (1784–1833), who moved to London after the fall of one of his French patrons, Napoleon Bonaparte, in 1815. There he served briefly as the chef to the Prince Regent, who was to become King George IV, and it is said that he cooked this dish for the future monarch in 1816. Carême apparently fancied up the dish by using Madeira, which is not traditional, and by substituting filet of beef for the tougher cut that would have been used in a classic *boeuf à la mode*. This is a time-consuming recipe, but the result yields a delicious dish and a beautiful presentation. Ask your butcher for a split calf's foot. It yields a more flavorful result than packaged gelatin.

1 (3-pound / 1.4-kg) filet of beef
1 calf's foot, split lengthwise
5 medium carrots
1 medium onion, halved
1 bouquet garni (4 sprigs parsley, 2 sprigs thyme, and 1 bay leaf, wrapped in cheesecloth or tied together with kitchen twine)
1 cup (240 ml) dry (Sercial or Rainwater) Madeira
½ cup (60 ml) cognac
4 quarts (3.75 L) veal or beef stock, store-bought or homemade (page 314)
12 whole black peppercorns
Salt

Put the beef, calf's foot, carrots, onion, bouquet garni, Madeira, cognac, stock, peppercorns, and a good couple of pinches of salt into a large pot. Cut a piece of parchment paper into a round about 2 inches (5 cm) larger than the diameter of the pot, then set it down into the pot, directly on top of the liquid. Cover the pot and bring the mixture to a boil over medium heat, then reduce the heat to medium-low and simmer for 30 to 40 minutes, or until the beef is just cooked through. (It should register about 130°F / 55°C on a meat thermometer.)

Let the meat cool for about 2 hours in the stock, then transfer it and the carrots to a platter, leaving the stock in the pot. Cover the beef and carrots with plastic wrap and refrigerate them.

Return the stock to a boil over high heat, then reduce the heat to medium-low and simmer, uncovered, until reduced by half (to about 8 cups / 1.9 L), about 4 hours.

Strain the stock through a colander lined with two layers of cheesecloth, discarding the solids, and refrigerate the stock.

Finely dice the carrots and scatter the pieces evenly over the bottom of a shallow roasting pan large enough to hold the beef comfortably.

Remove the stock from the refrigerator and skim off any fat that has solidified on the surface. Transfer it to a large pot and heat it over medium-low heat just until it liquefies. Transfer 2 cups (480 ml) of the stock to a medium bowl and refrigerate it. Stir it every 10 minutes until it becomes syrupy, about 1 hour.

Pour the remaining stock over the carrots and refrigerate until the aspic sets, about 2 hours.

Cut the beef into slices about ¾ inch (2 cm) thick and arrange them on an oval serving platter. Pour 1 cup of the syrupy stock over the meat and refrigerate it until the aspic sets, about 1 hour, then repeat the process with the other cup of syrupy stock. Refrigerate for 1 hour more.

Just before serving, spoon the carrots in aspic on either side of the beef.

CAWL

SERVES 4

Cawl, which literally means "broth" or "soup," but is more of a stew, is the Welsh version of the highly variable and forgiving meat-and-vegetable dish known to almost every culture. In her mini volume *A Book of Welsh Soups & Savouries Including Traditional Welsh Cawl*, the Welsh food writer and former restaurateur Bobby Freeman notes that "to the expatriate Welshman [cawl] is home, the hearth and everything he loves and yearns for of his roots in Wales." She adds that, however, "to those who lived through the hard times in rural Wales . . . it represents monotony and poverty which they do not want to recall." There were times, she says, when "poor, thin cawl" was eaten three times a day. The Bodnant Welsh Food Centre in Tal-y-Cafn in northern Wales makes a version to which this description certainly does not apply. This recipe for the dish is based on the cawl served there.

2 tablespoons bacon fat or lard, or 1 tablespoon
    each butter and vegetable oil, plus a little more
    if needed
1 pound (450 g) lamb or beef stew meat, cut into
    bite-size pieces
3 medium carrots, cut into pieces roughly ¾-inch
    (2-cm) square
2 medium onions, finely chopped
3 medium russet potatoes, peeled and cut into
    bite-size pieces
2 small leeks, thoroughly washed, white and green
    parts thinly sliced and kept separate
Salt and freshly ground black pepper
1 bay leaf
6 whole cloves
Leaves from 3 or 4 sprigs thyme

Melt the bacon fat (or melt the butter with the vegetable oil) in a large, heavy-bottomed pot with a lid or in a Dutch oven over medium heat. Add the meat and cook, stirring frequently, for about 5 minutes, or until it just begins to brown on all sides.

Add the carrots, onions, potatoes, and the white parts of the leeks, stir well, and cook, stirring frequently, for 6 to 8 minutes, or until the vegetables begin to soften. (Add a little more cooking fat if necessary.) Season the vegetables generously with salt and pepper, then add the bay leaf and cloves.

Add water to just cover the ingredients, cover the pot, reduce the heat to low, and cook for 1½ hours, or until the meat is tender. Half an hour before the cawl is done, uncover the pot and stir in the green parts of the leeks and the thyme.

Lamb on Pig

The writer Charles Lamb (1775–1834), a contemporary and friend of Wordsworth and Coleridge, is best remembered for *The Essays of Elia* and *Last Essays of Elia* ("Elia" was Lamb's nom de plume), two collections of delightful short pieces, originally published in the *London Magazine*, on topics ranging from "Witches and Other Night-Fears" to "Barrenness of the Imaginative Faculty in the Productions of Modern Art." That Lamb was an enthusiastic eater may be gleaned from his essay "Dissertation on Roast Pig," almost three thousand words of paean, exhortation, and something pretty much like poetry. This is an excerpt:

> Of all the delicacies in the whole mundus edibilis, I will maintain [pig] to be the most delicate. . . . I speak not of your grown porkers . . . but a young and tender suckling—under a moon old—guiltless as yet of the sty. . . .

> He must be roasted. I am not ignorant that our ancestors ate them seethed, or boiled—but what a sacrifice of the exterior tegument!

> There is no flavour comparable, I will contend, to that of the crisp, tawny, well-watched, not over-roasted, crackling, as it is well called—the very teeth are invited to their share of the pleasure at this banquet in overcoming the coy, brittle resistance—with the adhesive oleaginous—O call it not fat—but an indefinable sweetness growing up to it—the tender blossoming of fat—fat cropped in the bud—taken in the shoot—in the first innocence—the cream and quintessence of the child-pig's yet pure food—the lean, no lean, but a kind of animal manna—or, rather, fat and lean (if it must be so) so blended and running into each other, that both together make but one ambrosian result, or common substance.

> Pig—let me speak his praise—Is no less provocative of the appetite, than he is satisfactory to the criticalness of the palate. The strong man may batten on him, and the weakling refuseth not his mild juices.

> Hares, pheasants, partridges, snipes, barn-door chicken (those "tame villatic fowl"), capons, plovers, brawn, barrels of oysters, I dispense as freely as I receive them. I love to taste them, as it were, upon the tongue of my friend. But a stop must be put somewhere. . . . I make my stand upon pig.

LAMB CUTLETS REFORM

SERVES 4

The Reform Club, on Pall Mall in London, was founded in 1836 by Edward Ellice, a director of the Hudson's Bay Company and champion of the controversial Reform Act of 1832, which some scholars consider the genesis of modern British democracy. Its membership over the years has included Thackeray, Churchill, Henry James, Arnold Bennett, H. G. Wells, Arthur Conan Doyle, Jules Verne's fictional Phileas Fogg (whose bet that he could travel "around the world in eighty days" was made at the club), and, more recently (the first women having been admitted in 1981), Kiri Te Kanawa and the Duchess of Cornwall.

In earlier times, the club was also famous for its food, as well it might have been since two of the great culinary luminaries of the Victorian age, Alexis Soyer and Charles Francatelli, were chefs there. Francatelli is sometimes credited with having created this elaborate preparation, but it was certainly Soyer who invented it in the club's kitchens at some point in the 1830s. This is a slightly simplified version of his recipe, which he published in 1848 (six years before Francatelli took over his post at the Reform Club, incidentally) in his book *The Gastronomic Regenerator*.

FOR THE SAUCE:
⅓ cup (75 g) butter
1 medium onion, very thinly sliced
2 sprigs parsley
2 sprigs thyme
2 bay leaves
1 clove garlic, crushed
4 ounces (110 g) good-quality cooked ham, cut into thin strips about 2 inches long
2 tablespoons tarragon vinegar
Pinch of cayenne
1 tablespoon tomato paste
1¼ cups (300 ml) brown gravy (page 280)
½ cup (60 ml) beef or veal stock, store-bought or homemade (page 314)

1 tablespoon red currant jelly
Salt and freshly ground black pepper
1 large gherkin, cut lengthwise into thin strips
White of 1 large hard-boiled egg, cut lengthwise into thin strips
1 pickled green chile (not too spicy), cut lengthwise into thin strips

FOR THE CUTLETS:
4 ounces (110 g) good-quality cooked ham, very finely chopped
1 cup fresh bread crumbs
2 large eggs, beaten
¼ cup (55 g) clarified butter (page 312) or vegetable oil
12 thin lamb cutlets, frenched (with fat cut off)
Salt and freshly ground pepper

MAKE THE SAUCE:
Melt half the butter in a large saucepan over medium heat. Add the onion, parsley, thyme, bay leaves, garlic, and half the ham and cook, stirring occasionally, for 10 minutes. Add the vinegar, cayenne, tomato paste, gravy, and stock, stirring them in well, then bring the liquid to a boil. Reduce the heat to low and simmer the sauce, skimming off any foam that rises to the top, for about 20 minutes, or until it's thick enough to coat the back of a wooden spoon. Stir in the jelly and season with salt and pepper. Remove from the heat and set aside.

MAKE THE CUTLETS:
Mix the ham and bread crumbs together well in a large shallow bowl. Put the eggs in a separate shallow bowl. Heat the butter in a large skillet over medium heat. Season the cutlets generously on both sides with salt and pepper, then dip them into the beaten egg and dredge them in the bread crumb mixture. Working in batches, fry the cutlets, turning them once, until they're golden brown, 3 to 4 minutes on each side.

To finish the dish, arrange the cutlets on a warmed serving platter with the bones facing outward (Soyer suggests setting them "upon a thin border of mashed potatoes in a crown"). Strain the reserved sauce into a clean saucepan and warm it quickly over medium-high heat. Stir in the remaining butter, remaining ham, the gherkin, egg white, and green chile, then spoon the sauce over the cutlets.

ROAST LEG ᴼᶠ LAMB

SERVES 6 TO 8

In his book *Wild Wales* (1862), the English author and travel writer George Borrow rhapsodized over a leg of Welsh mutton he was served one evening. "It was truly wonderful;" he wrote. "Nothing so good had I ever tasted in the shape of a leg of mutton. . . . Certainly I shall never forget that first Welsh leg of mutton which I tasted, rich but delicate, replete with juices derived from the aromatic herbs of the noble Berwyn, cooked to a turn, and weighing just four pounds."

Welsh lamb is still highly regarded—but this is academic for the American cook. We get lamb from New Zealand and Australia (perhaps from New South Wales rather than the original Old North one), but not from the U.K. Nonetheless, there is plenty of good lamb raised around America, the best of it often from small producers who sell their wares at farmers' markets. Buy the best lamb you can for this simple, classic recipe.

1 (5- to 6-pound / 2.25- to 2.75-kg) leg of lamb, trimmed of excess fat
6 cloves garlic, quartered lengthwise
12 small sprigs thyme
4 tablespoons (½ stick / 55 g) butter, softened
Salt and freshly ground black pepper

Preheat the oven to 500ºF (260ºC).

With the tip of a sharp knife, make 24 small incisions all over the skin of the lamb. Push a quarter of a garlic clove into each of them. With the same knife, make 12 more incisions, distributed around the leg, and push a sprig of thyme into each of them. Brush butter all over the lamb leg and season it generously with salt and pepper.

Place the lamb on a rack in a roasting pan and roast for 15 minutes.

Reduce the oven temperature to 350ºF (175ºC) and roast for about 1 hour more for medium-rare lamb, basting occasionally. For medium lamb, roast for 20 minutes more.

Allow the lamb to rest for 15 to 20 minutes before carving. If possible, carve the meat on a board with grooves to collect the juices, then arrange the sliced lamb on a warm serving platter and drizzle the juices over it.

ROAST SADDLE OF LAMB

SERVES 8 TO 10

In her 1928 guidebook *The Restaurants of London*, Eileen Hooton-Smith noted that, at the venerable (and still thriving) London institution Simpson's in the Strand, the most popular dish was not the roast beef rib with which the restaurant's name is virtually synonymous, but roast saddle of Southdown lamb. (A saddle is the backbone of the animal with the loins still attached on both sides; the Southdown is a breed of small English sheep.) The meat was aged for ten to fourteen days, she reported, and the restaurant served thirty-five to forty saddles a night. She described the process thus: "The man who is in charge of the joints roasting on the jack [technically the device that keeps a spit turning, though Hooton-Smith seems to use the term to mean the spit itself] has a hot job; the jack is screened off from the main kitchen by a high iron screen and the roaster has to keep going behind this to look after the joints. There is a huge basting dish below them, slightly tilted to one end, and from there he keeps ladling up the hot fat and basting the meat. If a particular joint shows signs of cooking at all too quickly it has a wrapping of greased paper tied around it. Before a joint is served it is taken off the jack and placed on the basting pan, not where the fat is thickest, to give the outside a final crisping." Mere oven roasting may seem a poor substitute for this process, but it still produces a substantial quantity of juicy, flavorful meat.

4 tablespoons (½ stick / 55 g) butter, softened
1 (3- to 4-pound / 1.4- to 1.8-kg) boned lamb saddle (sometimes called a double loin), trimmed, rolled, and tied by your butcher
Leaves from 3 sprigs rosemary
Salt and freshly ground black pepper

Meat carvers and superintendents [managers] at Simpson's in the Strand, London, circa 1910

Preheat the oven to 350°F (175°C).

With your hands, spread the butter all over the exposed surfaces of the lamb, then sprinkle the rosemary over it, pressing the leaves down lightly so they stick to the butter. Season all the exposed surfaces of the lamb generously with salt and pepper.

Put the lamb saddle fat side up on a rack in a roasting pan and roast for 20 to 25 minutes per pound for medium-rare, or until a meat thermometer registers about 140°F (60°C).

Remove the lamb saddle from the oven, transfer it to a cutting board, and let it rest for 15 minutes.

To carve, cut along the outside of one side of the backbone, just through the fat, and peel the fat off one side of the meat. Cut the meat parallel to the backbone into thin slices and transfer them to a heated platter. Repeat the process on the other side. Turn the saddle over and cut off the tenderloin portions from each side. Cut these against the grain into slightly thicker slices. Cut off any remaining meat and slice it as thinly as possible against the grain. Drizzle any juices from the cutting board over the meat.

18-HOUR SLOW-BAKED SHOULDER OF LAMB

SERVES 4

One of the most pleasant surprises of a ramble I took through Scotland last fall was a meal at the curiously named Caddy Mann in Jedburgh, in the Scottish Borders, an area better known for golf courses than cuisine. The Caddy Mann looks like a tearoom, the kind of place you'd go for dainty sandwiches and cream-filled cakes. In fact, it's a serious restaurant with rich, flavorful, beautifully cooked food, like whisky-cured smoked venison on toasted wild garlic soda bread, rabbit and ham hock terrine with pickled cauliflower, local gray squirrel fricassee (!), chargrilled chicken breast stuffed with haggis and dry-cured bacon, steamed venison pudding (page 186), and this dish, one of the restaurant's most popular, made with excellent Borders lamb.

Chef Ross Horrocks, who owns the place with his wife, Lynne, explains that the Caddy Mann's name was bestowed upon it by its original owners, as a play on the name of their favorite restaurant and pub, the 1871-vintage Canny Man in Edinburgh. "In the beginning," says Horrocks, "we were a golf driving range with a small coffee shop/antique shop attached. I came to help the owners set it up, as they were friends of ours with no catering knowledge, on the understanding that it was only for a six-month period until they got on their feet. Seventeen years later, it has snowballed into the standalone restaurant that it is today and we are now the owners. It's been a very long six months!" He adds, "shoulder of lamb is one of the cheaper lamb cuts, and it has a high fat content. This method of cooking gently melts the fat through the meat, which leaves a mouth-watering, tender, and lean dish that grumbles at the mere sight of a fork. Do not be tempted to use a less fatty cut such as leg, as the meat will dry out."

1 (3- to 4-pound / 1.35- to 1.8-kg) boneless lamb
    shoulder, tied
Salt and freshly ground black pepper
1 tablespoon red currant jelly
1 tablespoon cornstarch
1 teaspoon chopped fresh mint leaves (optional)
1 recipe Mashed Potatoes (page 211; optional)

The night before you're going to serve the lamb, preheat the oven to 250°F (120°C).

Season the lamb shoulder generously on both sides with salt and pepper, then lay it skin side down on a large sheet of aluminum foil. Roll up the meat as tightly as possible in the foil and close both ends by twisting the foil.

Put the foil-wrapped lamb into a shallow baking dish and bake overnight, for about 18 hours in all.

Remove the lamb from the oven and let it cool for about 30 minutes, then cut open the foil and let the meat rest until it's cool enough to handle. Do not discard the juices in the foil or the pan.

When the lamb is cool enough to handle, carefully remove it from the foil and lay it skin side down on a large piece of plastic wrap. Roll up the meat as tightly as possible in the plastic wrap and close both ends by twisting the wrap, as you did with the foil.

Refrigerate the lamb for at least 2 hours, or until it is firm and set. Refrigerate the pan juices in a small bowl.

Preheat the oven to 350°F (175°C).

When the fat has set on top of the pan juices, skim it off and discard it. Heat about three-quarters of the juices in a small pan over medium heat, then stir in the jelly, cornstarch, and mint (if using). Turn off the heat and cover the sauce with the pan lid or foil to keep it warm.

Remove the lamb from the refrigerator and slice it with a sharp knife, through the plastic wrap, into pieces 1 to 1½ inches (2.5 to 4 cm) thick. Drizzle the remaining (unthickened) pan juices onto a baking sheet large enough to hold the lamb slices. Carefully pull the plastic wrap off the lamb slices, then lay the lamb slices over the juices and cover them loosely with foil. Cook until just heated through, about 10 minutes.

Divide about two-thirds of the mashed potatoes (if using) evenly between four warmed plates, smoothing them down with the back of a wooden spoon, and put the lamb slices on top of the potatoes. If not using the mashed potatoes, divide the lamb equally between four warmed plates. Reheat the sauce, if necessary, and spoon it over the lamb.

A Dream, a Vast Magic

The prolific English novelist and journalist Arnold Bennett (see page 29) wrote two novels set in and around hotels, *The Grand Hotel Babylon* (1902) and *Imperial Palace* (1930); both fictional institutions were modeled on The Savoy, the famed hotel overlooking the Thames opened in 1889 by the opera impresario Richard D'Oyly Carte. In a passage in *Imperial Palace*, Bennett vividly evokes the atmosphere of Smithfield Market, the wholesale meat market in the City of London. The heroine of the book, the young and beautiful Gracie Savott, is invited on an early-morning excursion to the market by the hotel manager. This is some of what she saw (and heard):

> *The illimitable interior had four chief colours: bright blue of the painted constructional ironwork, all columns and arches; red-pink-ivories of meat; white of the salesmen's long coats; and yellow of electricity. Hundreds of bays, which might or might not be called shops, lined with thousands of great steel hooks from each of which hung a carcass, salesmen standing at the front of every bay, and far at the back of every bay a sort of shanty-office in which lurked, crouching and peering forth, clerks pen in hand, like devilish accountants of some glittering, chill inferno. . . .*

> *One long avenue of bays stretched endless in front, and other on either hand, producing in the stranger a feeling of infinity. Many people in the avenues, loitering, chatting, chaffing, bickering! And at frequent intervals market-porters bearing carcasses on their leather-protected shoulders, or porters pushing trucks full of carcasses, sped with bent heads feverishly through the avenues, careless of whom they might throw down or maim or kill. An impression of intense, cheerful vitality, contrasting dramatically with the dark somnolence of the streets around! A dream, a vast magic, set in the midst of the prosaic reality of industrial sleep! . . .*

> *The hour was twenty minutes to five, and all was as customary as the pavement of Bond Street at twenty minutes to noon. And the badinage between acquaintances, between buyers and sellers, was more picturesque than that of Bond Street. Gracie caught fragments as she passed. "You dirty old tea-leaf!" "Go on, you son of an unmarried woman!" . . . Gracie was delighted.*

CHAPTER 6

WILD GAME AND OFFAL

"THEY HAVE LIKEWISE HERE ABUNDANCE OF WILD-FOWL, OF THE BEST SORTS; SUCH AS PHEASANT, PARTRIDGE, WOODCOCK, SNIPE, QUAILS, ALSO DUCK, MALLARD, TEAL, &C."

—DANIEL DEFOE, *A Tour Thro' the Whole Island of Great Britain* (1724–1727)

"FOR REASONS WE HAVE YET TO REASON ABOUT, TRIPE IS FUNNY."

—WILLIAM BLACK, *The Land That Thyme Forgot* (2005)

ngland, Wales, and especially Scotland abound with wild game, both furred and feathered, and there is a long tradition of British game cookery, from simply roasted grouse or haunch of venison to savory game pies to rich ragout-like preparations such as jugged hare. The king of game birds is the red grouse (*Lagopus lagopus scotica*), whose season runs each year from August 12 to December 10 and whose appearance is so eagerly anticipated that the season's first day is known as "the Glorious Twelfth" (see page 143). Gray and redlegged partridges, pheasant, woodcock, wood pigeon, several kinds of wild duck, and other birds are also shot (their season generally starts later and runs longer). Non-flying game includes hare and wild rabbit, as well as red, fallow, and roe deer (Scotland is particularly famous for its venison). Wild boar went extinct in Great Britain centuries ago and is only just now beginning to reappear, so most of the "wild" boar—and for that matter, a lot of the deer meat—sold today comes from animals that have been farm-raised.

Many other kinds of wild creatures used to be bagged for food in England, Scotland, and Wales. Seal meat was eaten in the Hebrides until the nineteenth century, and gannet, a seabird, is still considered a delicacy—and one with mythic import—on the Scottish island of Lewis (see page 155). Mrs. Leyel and Miss Hartley, in their early-twentieth-century book *The Gentle Art of Cookery*, note that "changes of taste are more marked among the fowl of the air than the fish of the sea"—and ponder why we no longer eat swans or peacocks, considered prized delicacies at important banquets from Roman times until the sixteenth century. Furthermore, they continue, "We no longer eat linnets and thrushes, and the art of serving four-and-twenty live blackbirds in a pie so that when the pie was opened the birds began to sing is forgotten so completely that the nursery rhyme that recalls it is taken as pure nonsense, instead of an interesting memory . . ."

Americans are at a major disadvantage when it comes to wild game. The laws in our country, for reasons of sup-posed health concerns as well as environmental issues, flat-out forbid the commercial sale of true wild game, shot by a hunter. That is presumably why such distinctly non-gamy foodstuffs as quail, "game hen," and rabbit are often listed on menus as "game"—though they're raised pretty much the way your average supermarket chicken is. If you are a hunter yourself, restaurants are usually permitted to prepare what you've bagged for you and your guests.

Chukar partridges in a London kitchen

Otherwise, the most common options are farm-raised versions of game animals. There are also, however, game ranches which let nonindigenous species of deer, boar, wild sheep, etc., range over huge areas, eating a natural diet, and then slaughter them in the field. And several firms import wild game birds, usually frozen but occasion-ally, for a brief seasonal window, fresh from Scotland and New Zealand (see Sources, page 316).

The animal organs known collectively as offal, on the other hand, are reasonably easy to come by, especially from certain farmers' markets, good butcher shops, and so-called ethnic markets—the ones patronized mostly by customers from other cultures, where economic con-ditions as well as considerations of flavor and tradition dictate that as much of a slaughtered animal as possible be turned into tasty food.

Like any agrarian society of earlier times, Britons of the past ate a good amount of offal, especially liver, kidneys, tripe (almost a heraldic symbol of old Lancashire), and miscellaneous mixes of organs, though less so sweet-breads or brains. With one key exception, heart has never been common on British tables, either, though Robert Kemp Philp's *Enquire Within Upon Everything*, dating from 1856, offers a recipe for heart stuffed with veal forcemeat and served with red currant jelly. "When prepared in this manner," he notes, "it is sometimes called 'Smithfield Hare,' on account of its flavour being something like that of a roast hare."

The exception is this: heart—in this case sheep's heart—is one of the traditional ingredients in that most notorious Scottish offal dish, haggis, along with the animal's liver

Sheep on the road on Lewis and Harris

and "lights" (lungs). It is this last ingredient that keeps true haggis out of the United States, though there are reasonable lungless equivalents made here. Haggis is a seasoned mixture of the minced organs, combined with oatmeal and (at least traditionally) stuffed into and cooked in a sheep's stomach. It admittedly sounds daunting, but is really delicious. Anyway, why should ground-up sheep parts stuffed into the animal's stomach cause us any more dismay then ground-up pig parts stuffed into the animal's intestine—i.e., sausage?

Haggis, in any case, was once eaten not just in Scotland but all over northern England. Today, with occasional exceptions (Lune Valley Smokehouse in Arkholme, in Lancashire, makes "laggis"—Lancashire haggis), this specialty is found almost exclusively in Scotland. There it is widely eaten in numerous forms—not just by itself as a kind of loose-knit meat loaf with the de rigueur accompaniments of "tatties and neeps" (mashed potatoes and mashed rutabaga), but also in the shape of croquettes or "bonbons," in savory tarts, in "burger" form, in place of ground meat in lasagna and tacos, and even, in some of Scotland's Indian restaurants, as a filling for samosas or pakoras. There is also a version based on venison instead of sheep parts, and even a vegetarian one, made with lentils, popularized and probably created by The Ubiquitous Chip in Glasgow (see page 209). Haggis's big day is the annual Burns Night, January 25, celebrating the birth (in 1759) of the great Scottish poet Robert Burns. Burns liked haggis so much that he wrote a poem, "Address to the Haggis," in its honor, hailing it as the "great chieftain o' the puddin race" and comparing French and Italian food unfavorably to it.

Another popular and versatile variety of offal, made not from an animal's internal organs but from its very blood, is

black pudding—blood sausage—which combines oatmeal (barley flour in some early recipes) and pork fat with congealed blood. It was originally flavored with pennyroyal, a potentially toxic herb with a minty flavor, also known as pudding grass—but this practice, thankfully, has long since died out. (*Pudding* was once a synonym for innards in general; it is for that sense of the word that Pudding Lane in the City of London, believed to be where the Great Fire of London started in 1666, is named.) Black pudding is sometimes a part of the full English breakfast, and more often included in the "full Scottish," but, like haggis, it is now found in croquettes and "bonbons," and in many other forms, including shepherd's pie, quiche, stuffing for roast birds, and, at one Glasgow restaurant, in the form of mushroom and black pudding pakora. The most celebrated black pudding in Great Britain is that from Stornoway, on the Scottish island of Lewis and Harris. It is compact and a little bland (I far prefer the more forcefully seasoned black puddings of Ireland).

A number of British chefs today include at least a bit of offal on their menus (crispy pig's head seems to be particularly popular) and, of course, old-style restaurants and hotel dining rooms are still likely to offer liver and onions or devilled kidneys, but the apostle of offal in Great Britain today is Fergus Henderson of St. John in London (see page 160). At his restaurant and its spinoffs and in his books—starting with the original *Nose to Tail Eating: A Kind of British Cooking* (he may well have coined the phrase "nose to tail")—he has explored the many oft-forgotten culinary possibilities offered by the pigs and sheep and cows and other beasts we kill for food. "It would seem disingenuous to the animal," he writes, "not to make the most of the whole beast: there is a set of delights, textural and flavorsome, which lie beyond the filet."

The Moorhen Is Not a Grinch

To grouse, meaning to complain, is nineteenth-century British army slang, probably derived by some circuitous route from the Greek word *gruzein*, "to grumble." *A* grouse, meaning a wild, jaunty-looking, and unfortunately (for it) delicious game bird, has no relationship at all to grumbling, at least not that I've been able to discover.

Grouse is a divisive bird. Its meat is rich and earthy, with a faint herbaceous flavor that probably reflects its diet, which is almost entirely heather; it does *not*, in other words, taste like chicken. Grouse is undeniably "gamy"—because, well, it's game. This effect is heightened by hanging—i.e., suspending the birds in a cool place until they begin to putrefy, or grow "high," a process that tenderizes their flesh and lends it a pungent, bitterish character much appreciated in some quarters and rather enthusiastically eschewed in others. My father-in-law, for instance, who once had an unfortunate digestive reaction to a well-hung grouse, grows pale at the very mention of the word. My wife is not a fan, either, though she acquitted herself admirably not long ago when a perfectly roasted—but, thankfully for her, not particularly high—grouse turned out to be the main event at lunch at Barton Court, Sir Terence Conran's country house.

The traditional accompaniments to grouse are rowan (sorb apple) or red currant jelly, "game chips" (potato chips to you), and that peculiar but somehow reassuring ancient British condiment called bread sauce, which is basically cream sauce thickened with bread crumbs. The grouse so favored by the British is the red grouse (*Lagopus lagopus scotica*), which exists today only in the British Isles and Ireland, and even

there mostly on the moors on Scotland and Northern England. This accounts for its alternate name, moorhen.

Each year, grouse hunters and stay-at-home gourmands alike await "the Glorious Twelfth"—the twelfth of August, which is the official start of grouse season (it extends until December tenth)—with all the giddy eagerness of five-year-olds counting down the days until Santa squeezes down the chimney. Why the twelfth? One common explanation is that this was the date on which Queen Victoria took up residence at Balmoral Castle in Scotland for her annual sporting holiday, and it would have been unseemly for anyone else to shoot grouse before she had the chance. Since she didn't inherit the throne until 1837, however, and grouse season was defined by the Game Act of 1831, that seems unlikely. (In the mid-1830s, the most famous French chef in London, Louis Eustache Ude, was sued by the Marquis of Queensberry for having served grouse at a private club called Crockford's a week before the official start of the season. He was found guilty and fined—but put grouse on the menu again the next day as *fruit défendu*, "forbidden fruit.")

It is not true that, as some grouse aficionados will tell you, there is no grouse in America; we just don't have red grouse. Ours is ruffed grouse (*Bonasa umbellus*), sometimes mistakenly identified as partridge, and anyone who has tasted both the British and the American species will tell you that the ruffed bird is a pretty sorry substitute for the red one. So sorry, in fact, that in Kentucky and Ohio, ruffed grouse is sometimes known as grinch.

ROAST GROUSE

SERVES 2 TO 4

There are at least twenty species of grouse in both the Old and New World, including some that go by the names of ptarmigan and capercaillie. The bird most often shot in England and (above all) Scotland (see page 143), between "the Glorious Twelfth" of August and the season's end on the tenth of December, is the red grouse (*Lagopus lagopus scotica*). Obtaining a couple of these very tasty birds in the United States is not easy, but they are possible to find, in season, probably frozen (see Sources, page 316). Roasting grouse is simple, but, like all simple processes, must be done precisely. This recipe, which is fairly traditional, comes from Jeremy Lee at Quo Vadis in London (see page 17). Since oven temperatures, and thus cooking times, will vary, Lee notes, "To check that the birds are done, tweak the grouse breasts with your thumb and forefinger. They should have the bouncy spring of a shelled hard-boiled egg." At that stage, he adds, they will end up with perfectly pink flesh once they've rested.

6 tablespoons (¾ stick / 85 g) butter, softened
2 red grouse, plucked and cleaned
Salt and freshly ground black pepper
Bread Sauce (page 280)
Game Chips (page 208)
Sherried Bread Crumbs (page 312)
Rowan or red currant jelly, for serving
Watercress, for garnish

Preheat the oven to 425°F (215°C).

Smear about 1 tablespoon (15 g) of the butter onto the bottom of a cast-iron skillet or heavy roasting pan. Put the grouse on top of the butter, then rub the remaining butter over their breasts and legs and season them generously with salt and pepper.

A grouse hunter, probably in Scotland, 1898

Roast the birds on the top rack of the oven for 7 minutes. Remove the pan from the oven and baste the birds generously with the butter. Roast for 7 minutes more, then baste again. Roast for 5 minutes more, then remove the pan from the oven.

Transfer the birds to a platter, loosely cover them with aluminum foil, and let them rest for 15 to 20 minutes before serving. If the birds are large enough or the grouse is being served as part of a multicourse dinner, cut each one in half lengthwise with a large, sharp knife or cleaver. Serve with Bread Sauce, Game Chips, Sherried Bread Crumbs, and rowan or red currant jelly, and garnish with watercress.

SALAD OF ROAST GROUSE, PURPLE FIGS, AND TOASTED COBNUTS

SERVES 4

When Sally Clarke opened her eponymous restaurant in Kensington Church Street in late 1984, she was widely accused of importing "California cuisine" to London. All that really meant was that, having worked for some years in several restaurants in Southern California and having been inspired by California chef-restaurateurs Alice Waters, Jonathan Waxman, and Michael McCarty, among others, she brought then-radical notions of seasonality, simplicity, and assiduous sourcing of ingredients to the city's restaurant scene. In the practicality, simplicity, and solidity of her recipes, there has never been any doubt that she is above all an English cook, using her homeland's wealth of raw materials to great advantage, and elegantly blending Mediterranean ideas into the mix—as with this splendid autumnal salad. Cobnuts are a species of hazelnuts, and the latter may be substituted.

3 ounces (85 g) shelled cobnuts or hazelnuts, halved

4 tablespoons (60 ml) extra-virgin olive oil

Salt and freshly ground black pepper

2 roast grouse (page 145), pan juices reserved, if possible

3 to 4 cups loosely packed small salad greens, such as landcress, escarole, frisée, castelfranco radicchio, etc.

8 ripe purple figs, washed

1 tablespoon balsamic vinegar

Preheat the oven to 350°F (175°C).

Toss the hazelnuts with 1 tablespoon of the olive oil and season them lightly with salt and pepper. Put them into a small baking dish or skillet and roast them for about 10 minutes, or until they're golden brown and crisp. Remove them from the oven and set them aside to cool.

Cut the wing tips from the grouse and reserve them for stock. Cut off the legs and set them aside, then carefully carve the breast meat from the carcass in one piece, reserving the carcass for stock. Cut the breast meat into two or three pieces on an angle. Cut the legs in half at the thigh joint.

In a large bowl, gently toss the salad greens with 1 tablespoon of the olive oil and season them with salt and pepper. Divide them among four plates. Tuck pieces of grouse in and around the leaves, dividing the meat evenly between the plates, then put four fig halves on each plate.

In a small bowl, whisk together the balsamic vinegar and the remaining 3 tablespoons olive oil, plus any pan juices reserved from roasting the grouse. Sprinkle the hazelnuts evenly over the salads, then drizzle the dressing over each serving.

POT-ROASTED PHEASANT WITH CIDER, APPLES, AND CELERIAC

SERVES 4

The Countryside Alliance—"The voice of the country-side"—is a London-based lobbying and promotional organization founded in 1997. It crusades against the closing of rural post offices and hunting and shooting bans, encourages the government to provide better broadband access outside of major towns and cities and reminds consumers that they should buy more British farm produce, runs special programs like one that teaches special needs children the joys of angling—and maintains a website called Game-to-Eat (gametoeat.co.uk), which is a rich source of information on the culinary pleasures of game, promoting wild-shot birds and animals as "a tasty and healthy alternative to lamb, chicken, beef or pork." The Game-to-Eat initiative "is a key part of the Countryside Alliance's campaigning work and is dedicated to promoting the produce of our shoots, game dealers, butchers and farm shops."

Included on the site is information about game butchery and cooking classes, tips for buying and handling game, reviews of game cookbooks, notes on wine and game matching, and a whole repertoire of recipes for pheasant, partridge, grouse, pigeon, wild duck, woodcock, wild rabbit, and venison. As noted on page 141, wild-shot game is difficult to find commercially, especially fresh, in the United States—unlike in Great Britain—but if you're not a hunter yourself, there are still some sources (see Sources, page 316). Using what I could find, I tested half a dozen Game-to-Eat recipes and had good luck in general. This was perhaps the most successful. Pheasant is a lean bird that dries out easily, but this method keeps the flesh moist, and the accompanying fruit and vegetables are very complementary to the mild flavor of the meat.

2 pheasants, about 2¾ pounds (1.25 kg) each, defrosted, if frozen, and dressed (see Sources, page 316)

Salt and freshly ground black pepper
2 tablespoons extra-virgin olive oil
6 ounces (175 g) thick-cut bacon, cut into 1-inch (2.5-cm) cubes
4¼ cups (1 L) Ross-on-Wye, Burrow Hill, Oliver's, or other good-quality British or American hard cider
4 sprigs thyme
2 bay leaves
2 Braeburn, Pink Lady, or other firm, juicy apples, peeled, cored, and quartered
½ medium bulb celeriac (about 8 ounces / 225 g), peeled and cut into ½-inch (1-cm) cubes
1 leek, white part only, washed well and sliced into very thin rings
2 stalks celery, cut into 1-inch (2-cm) pieces
1 onion, cut lengthwise into 8 wedges
4 tablespoons (½ stick / 55 g) butter

Preheat the oven to 325°F (160°C).

Season the pheasants generously inside and out with salt and pepper.

Heat the olive oil in a oven-proof casserole or Dutch oven large enough to hold the whole pheasants over medium heat, then add the bacon and cook it, stirring frequently, for 4 to 5 minutes, or until the cubes begin to brown. Add the pheasants and cook for 8 to 10 minutes, turning the pheasants several times with tongs, until they are golden brown on all sides and the bacon is dark brown.

Remove the pheasants and put them on a large plate or platter. Add the cider to the pot with the bacon. Increase the heat to high and deglaze the pan, scraping any brown bits from the bottom. Add the thyme, bay leaves, apples, leek, celery, and onion and cook, stirring occasionally, for 3 to 4 minutes.

Return the pheasants to the pot and spoon some of the cider and vegetables over them. Cover the pot tightly, transfer to the oven, and roast the pheasants for 40 minutes.

Remove the pot from the oven. Transfer the pheasants to a large plate or platter to rest. Return the pot to the stovetop over high heat and cook the cider, stirring occasionally, until it has reduced by about half. Stir in the butter and adjust the seasoning if necessary.

Carve the pheasant, allowing one leg and one breast per person, and spoon the sauce and vegetables over the meat.

ROAST VENISON with JUNIPER

SERVES 10 TO 12

Wild deer bound through forests and across meadows in much of England, all but a few parts of Wales, and most of Scotland, but it is Scottish deer—or, more specifically, Scottish venison—that is most famous of all. Two species, roe deer and red deer, are native to the country, and have been hunted there for probably ten thousand years. Fallow deer are a Mediterranean animal, brought into Britain around the twelfth century, while sika deer, from Japan, were introduced as decorative animals for nineteenth-century game parks, first escaping into the wild in large numbers in the 1920s. (A fifth species, the muntjac, from India, appeared in Wales around the same time, but is rarely if ever found in Scotland.) Many chefs and connoisseurs prefer the mild, sweet venison of the red deer over that of other kinds. Scotland was also the first place in Europe to farm deer for meat on a commercial scale, beginning in the early 1970s. What's raised today, more or less "free-range," is almost entirely red deer.

The aromatic juniper berry is a classic flavoring in many Old World countries for venison, as well as hare and wild boar meat. I've had venison with juniper sauce three or four times over the years in Scotland (I remember a nice one at Steayban in Lanarkshire and an even better one at Andrew Fairlie's Michelin two-star restaurant at the Gleneagles Hotel in Perthshire). This is my own version.

1 (4- to 5-pound / 1.8- to 2.25-kg) boneless loin (backstrap) of venison (see Sources, page 316), silverskin removed (ask your butcher, or see below) and halved crosswise
2 cloves garlic, peeled and finely chopped
20 juniper berries
20 black peppercorns
6 tablespoons (85 g) duck or goose fat (see Sources, page 316) or clarified butter (see page 312)
6 shallots, peeled and thinly sliced
½ cup (120 ml) ruby port or Bual or Malmsey Madeira
2 cups (480 ml) veal or beef stock, store-bought or homemade (page 314)
⅔ cup (165 ml) heavy cream
Salt

Preheat the oven to 425°F (220°C).

If the silverskin, the sinewy membrane on one side of the fillet, has not been removed, cut it off by inserting the tip of a sharp filleting knife under the skin at one end, then hold that end with one hand and work the knife at a slight upward angle toward the other end of the skin, as if you were filleting a fish.

Combine the garlic, juniper berries, and peppercorns in a small bowl, then use your hands to spread the mixture as evenly as possible over all surfaces of the meat. Wrap the meat in plastic wrap and set it aside at room temperature for 1 hour.

Melt the duck or goose fat or heat the clarified butter over medium-high heat in a heavy roasting pan just big enough to hold the two pieces of venison. Unwrap the meat, then use your hands to scrape off the juniper mixture; set the juniper mixture aside. Sear the meat on all sides, turning it with tongs, for about 2 minutes per side.

Transfer the pan to the oven and roast for 20 minutes, then reduce the heat to 300°F (150°C). Roast for about 10 minutes more per pound (450 g) for medium-rare. (A meat thermometer stuck into the thickest part of the roast should measure about 145°F/65°C.)

Remove the pan from the oven and remove the meat from the pan, setting it aside on a large dish and loosely tenting it with aluminum foil. Place the pan over 1 or 2 burners on the stovetop at medium heat. Stir the reserved juniper mixture and the shallots into the juices and cook, stirring constantly, for 2 to 3 minutes. Add the port or madeira and the stock, raise the heat to high, and cook, stirring constantly and scraping up any brown bits on the bottom of the pan, for 4 to 6 minutes, or until the mixture has reduced by half. Stir in the cream and let the liquid come just to a boil, then remove the pan from the heat. Season to taste with salt.

Strain the sauce through a sieve into a small bowl. Carve the meat into ½-inch (1.25-cm) thick slices, arrange them on a warmed platter, and drizzle the sauce over them.

The Great Eater of Kent

Long before the birth of the Nathan's Hot Dog Eating Contest at Coney Island (which was probably only in 1972, despite occasional efforts to give it a much earlier provenance) and the proliferation of other competitions around America and beyond involving the rapid consumption of huge amounts of food in an attempt to win prizes, there was Nicholas Wood—"the Great Eater of Kent."

Wood was born in the late sixteenth century, probably in Hollingbourne, near Maidstone in Kent, and lived most of his life in neighboring Harrietsham. He was employed as a gentleman's servant as a teenager, and later was able to buy a farm in the vicinity. The earliest references to his prodigious appetite date from the 1610s. One of his feats was consuming a dinner meant for eight people at Leeds Castle. On another occasion, he polished off seven dozen rabbits. On still another, he ate an entire roast pig, then had three pecks (six gallons) of damson plums for dessert.

As word of his abilities spread, Wood became a fixture at village fairs and festivals, taking bets and meeting most (if not quite all) of the challenges set to him. One clever adversary bet that he could satiate Wood for two shillings. He succeeded, by soaking a dozen loaves of bread in six large pots of ale. It is said that Wood managed to finish only half of this repast, and then went to sleep for nine hours.

John Taylor, "the Water Poet" (so called because he worked for much of his life as a ferryman on the Thames), became fascinated with Wood after witnessing him winning a bet at a country inn by eating everything the inn had in its larder: a leg of mutton, sixty eggs, a large black pudding, and three large meat pies. Apparently, after finishing, Wood claimed that he was still hungry, and the innkeep brought him a live duck, which Wood ripped apart with his bare hands and devoured.

It may be that Taylor's admiration for Wood was the latter's undoing. In 1630, he paid the Great Eater to come to London, where, it was promised to the citizenry of the capital, he would perform a succession of incredible feats, among them devouring a wheelbarrow full of tripe and dispatching twenty sets of sheep's innards.

Taylor even penned a tribute to Wood, part prose, part verse, "to be sold on London Bridge," as a kind of advertising vehicle for this exhibition of Wood's skills. Called *The Great Eater of Kent, or Part of the Admirable Teeth and Stomach Exploits of Nicholas Wood*, it was dedicated to its subject—"The Most Famous, Infamous, High and Mighty Feeder, Nicholas Wood, Great and Grand Gurmandizer of Harrisom [*sic*] in the County of Kent."

The poet may have overpromised, however, and shortly before Wood's first appearance in London, he apparently lost his nerve and fled the city. He died soon afterward, reportedly in poverty.

CREAMED SWEETBREADS

SERVES 4

At one point in my life, it apparently occurred to a number of my friends and family members independently that I shared a name with a popular brand of English mustard, and for four or five years, I seemed to receive at least a piece or two of memorabilia—plaques, reproduction posters, bowls and glassware, a little model vintage delivery truck—bearing the company's logo for Christmas or my birthday. Of course, I didn't say this at the time, but frankly, I found the Colman's mustard-yellow packaging a little garish, and anyway I've never cared much for mustard except as a subtle flavoring. Eventually (and I hope I'm not hurting anybody's feelings retroactively), all the Colman's swag filtered out of my life. With one exception—the one Colman's item that I actually liked, and used: a small book, published in 1980, called *Colman's Book of Traditional British Cookery* by one J. Audrey Ellison. The recipes were clearly written and the ones I tried all worked beautifully (I made my first potted shrimp from the book, and my first scones), and when I essayed to cook sweetbreads for the first time, it was Ellison's recipe I used. I was very happy with the results. This is my slight adaptation of what I suppose I might ambiguously call sweetbreads, Colman's style.

1 pound (450 g) calf's sweetbreads
Salt
1 tablespoon white wine vinegar
½ cup (1 stick / 115 g) butter
½ cup all-purpose flour
Freshly ground white pepper
1¼ cups (300 ml) chicken stock, store-bought or homemade (page 314)
1¼ cups (300 ml) whole milk
Juice of ½ lemon
2 teaspoons Colman's or other prepared English mustard
Leaves from 4 sprigs parsley, finely chopped
2 tablespoons Madeira or sherry
4 slices white Pullman bread, crusts removed, halved diagonally

Soak the sweetbreads in a large bowl of cold water for 1 hour, then drain and rinse them. Put them in a medium saucepan and add enough cold water to cover them completely. Season the water generously with salt, then add the vinegar. Bring the water to a boil over medium heat, then reduce the heat to low and simmer, uncovered, for 20 minutes. Drain and rinse the sweetbreads, then gently pull off and discard the membranes and fat. Set aside.

Melt half the butter in a large skillet over low heat. Stir in the flour and cook, stirring continuously, for about 3 minutes to form a roux. Season the roux with salt and white pepper, then remove it from the heat. Slowly stir in the stock, and then the milk, mixing well to form a sauce. Return the skillet to the heat and bring the sauce to a boil over medium heat, stirring continuously. Stir in the lemon juice, mustard, and about two-thirds of the parsley and cook for 5 minutes more.

Add the Madeira and the sweetbreads to the sauce and cook for 5 minutes more. Adjust the seasoning if necessary.

Meanwhile, melt the remaining butter in a large skillet over medium heat and fry each piece of bread until golden, turning once, about 2 minutes per side.

Spoon the sweetbreads into a warmed serving dish and garnish with the fried bread and remaining parsley.

LIVER WITH BACON AND ONIONS

SERVES 4

Calf's liver with onions or bacon, or both, was once a popular dish in American restaurants—though it seems to have pretty much disappeared in recent years—and liver with just the onions appears in numerous traditional cuisines (Italy's *fegato alla veneziana*, Catalonia's *fetge amb ceba*, the *higado encebollado* of Columbia and Peru, etc.). In England, bacon has long been the main accompaniment, with onions playing a minor role, if present at all. Perhaps the first mention of the dish by an Englishman comes courtesy of one William Wreathcock, an attorney of dubious moral character, who when accused of robbing a clergyman in 1735, offered as his alibi that on the evening of the crime, he had been dining with his clerk and a client at Symond's Inn on liver and bacon—no mention of onions—until the early hours of the morning. Onions aren't present, either, in Mrs. Beeton's recipe for calf's liver and bacon from 1861. Today, calf's or lamb's liver is often served with both accoutrements. I got this recipe in 1998, for an article I was writing for *Saveur* about London's Smithfield Market and the surrounding blocks. It comes from The Sirloin, the restaurant portion of the Victorian-era pub called The Hope.

1 tablespoon all-purpose flour
3 tablespoons (45 g) unsalted butter
1 tablespoon vegetable oil
8 slices back bacon or Irish bacon (see Sources, page 316)
2 medium onions, thinly sliced
1 pound (450 g) calf's liver, cut lengthwise into 4 thin slices of equal size
Salt and freshly ground black pepper
1 cup (240 ml) dry red wine
¾ cup (180 ml) veal or beef stock, store-bought or homemade (page 314)

Knead the flour and 1 tablespoon (15 g) of the butter together thoroughly, then wrap it in plastic wrap and refrigerate.

Preheat the oven to 200°F (95°C).

Heat the remaining 2 tablespoons (30 g) butter with the oil in a large skillet over medium-high heat. Fry the bacon for about 2 minutes on each side, turning it once, then use a fork or tongs to transfer it to a baking sheet and put it into the oven.

Reduce the heat to medium, add the onions, and cook, stirring occasionally, until they're very soft and golden, 25 to 30 minutes. Remove the onions from the skillet with a slotted spoon, put them into an oven-proof bowl, and put them in the oven.

Raise the heat to medium-high. Season the liver generously with salt and pepper, then fry it for about 2 minutes on each side, turning it once. Use tongs to transfer the liver to the baking sheet with the bacon in the oven.

Raise the heat to high and deglaze the skillet with the wine, scraping up the browned bits from the bottom with a wooden spoon. Cook until the wine has reduced by about half, about 5 minutes, then add the stock. Cook for 2 or 3 minutes, then stir in the butter and flour mixture. Continue stirring until the sauce is thick enough to coat the back of a spoon. Adjust the seasoning if necessary, then spoon the sauce onto a platter, arrange the bacon and calf's liver over it, and cover them with onions.

LIVER WITH BACON *AND* GREENS

SERVES 4

I discovered this curiously un-English-sounding recipe (which I've adapted slightly) in a book called *The Country Housewife and Lady's Director in the Management of a House, and the Delights and Profits of a Farm*, published in 1732 by Richard Bradley, an English naturalist (he was the first professor of botany at the University of Cambridge, and wrote important early works on the infectious nature of diseases and on what we now call ecology). It was one of a number of recipes given to him by one "Mrs. M. N." (others include formulas for "Orange or Lemon-Cakes" and "Crystal candy'd Sweet-meats"). She writes, "In Worcestershire and Shropshire, the following is in esteem, and I believe you will oblige several Gentlemen and Ladies of these Parts, if you would insert it in some of your Works."

8 slices back bacon or Irish bacon (see Sources, page 316), each cut into three pieces of equal size
1 pound (450 g) calf's liver, cut into 12 pieces of equal size
Salt and freshly ground black pepper
3 tablespoons (45 g) unsalted butter
1 medium onion, finely chopped
6 large leaves (not stems) Swiss chard, coarsely chopped
1 large bunch spinach, thoroughly washed, trimmed, and coarsely chopped
Juice of 1 lemon

Preheat the oven to 200°F (95°C).

Fry the bacon in a large skillet over medium heat for about 3 minutes on each side, turning it once, then transfer it to an oven-proof dish. Cover the dish lightly with aluminum foil and put it into the oven.

Season the calf's liver generously with salt and pepper, then raise the heat to medium-high and fry the calf's liver in the bacon fat in the same skillet for 3 to 4 minutes, turning it frequently so that it browns on all sides and is cooked rare (thicker pieces may take another minute or two). Remove the liver from the skillet and add it to the baking dish with the bacon.

Melt the butter in the same skillet and cook the onion, stirring frequently, for 3 to 4 minutes. Add the chard and spinach and cook, stirring frequently, until they have softened and begun to brown. Stir in the lemon juice.

To serve, transfer the bacon and liver to a warmed bowl and cover with the greens and any pan juices.

Duck That Tastes Like Fish

"Fin could still recall with mouth-watering clarity the oily flavour of the flesh on his tongue. Pickled in salt, and then boiled, it had the texture of duck and the taste of fish. . . . Two months before the men left for the rock, he would begin to anticipate the taste of it, just as he relished each year the rich flavour of the wild salmon during the poaching season."

That's a passage from the Glasgow-born novelist and screenwriter Peter May's novel *The Blackhouse*, the first volume of his *Lewis Trilogy*, a series of crime stories set on the northern (Lewis) portion of the island of Lewis and Harris in Scotland's Outer Hebrides. The meat imagined by May's hero, Detective Inspector Finlay MacLeod, is that of the creature that is by far the most exotic—and controversial—game bird in Great Britain: young gannet, a seabird of the genus *Morus*, known in these parts as *guga*.

Since at least the sixteenth century, and probably far longer, a complement of exactly ten men from the island's Ness district, on its far northern tip, have set off in a fishing boat every autumn to the islet of Sula Sgeir, thirty-eight miles to the north (*súla* is Old Norse for "gannet"). Here they camp in stone huts for two weeks, climbing up the islet's three-hundred-foot cliffs to snag the birds in their nests with spring-loaded jaws at the ends of poles, then killing them by striking their heads with rocks. The birds are then plucked (their feathers are treasured), singed over peat fires, cleaned, and brined.

Guga and other seabirds were once commonly eaten at banquets around Scotland and beyond, especially as whets (see page 245), or appetizers, but following the passage of the U.K.'s Sea Bird Preservation Act in 1869, the practice died out and today the consumption of guga on Lewis is virtually the only remnant of the practice.

As might be imagined, animal rights groups decry the bird hunt as inhumane, and similar practices would be banned anywhere else. Because of the deep cultural significance the Lewis guga hunt, though—participating in it is a rite of passage for the region's young men (a plot point in May's novel)—both the Protection of Birds Act of 1954 and the Wildlife and Countryside Act of 1981 permit continuation of the annual tradition. The men of Ness may take only two thousand of the birds each year, and the gannet population is considered to be sustainable.

Guga is served either boiled or roasted, usually with potatoes. The chances of an outsider like me having the opportunity to taste the delicacy are slim, and I'm not sure I would want to anyway. Descriptions of its flavor and aroma, unkinder than Fin MacLeod's, include "somewhere between rotten leather and fishy beef" and "like the worst thing you have ever smelt times one hundred thousand."

Hunting the Wild Haggis

The Scots have been known to occasionally have a bit of fun with visitors who are mystified by haggis. When asked what the stuff is, they sometimes reply that it's an animal that ranges the Highlands and the Hebrides; perhaps they are sometimes even believed (apparently a 2003 survey revealed that about a third of American visitors to Scotland indeed thought there was a haggis beast). The haggis maker Stahly Quality Foods devotes a long page on its website, thehaggis.com, to the "wild haggis (*Haggis scottii*)"—among other things noting that the animal has shorter legs on one side than the other, making it easier to negotiate the steep mountains in which it lives, and that there are two subspecies, *dexterous* and *sinistrous*, depending on which side the shorter legs grow. The two subspecies cannot mate, according to Stahly, "since in order for the male of one variety to mate with a female of the other, he must turn to face in the same direction as his intended mate, causing him to lose his balance before he can mount her."

Aberdeen author Chris Buswell, who runs a website called Traditional Scottish Recipes (scottishrecipes.co.uk), has helpfully offered his countrymen these tips for staging a haggis hunt for visitors:

1. Grab yourself a daft and gullible tourist.

2. Promise them a rare sighting of the Haggis animal (or Haggi, if they want to be greedy and see a herd) for £20 an hour.

3. Lock and load the shotgun and crossbow for effect. (Tell the worried tourists that [the Haggi] are wild and savage beasties.)

Savoy hotel chef François Latry receiving a shipment of haggis from Scotland, 1922

4. Don the Harris tweed and tam-o'-shanter, ensuring the bagpipes are visible on the back seat.

5. In a broad and thick accent, ensuring you roll your *rrr*s, ask if they want to see the three-legged species (three legs help the Haggis beast go round the hills faster) or the four-legged species.

6. Drive to a bonnie place where you can enjoy a spot of fishing whilst the numptees go off and hunt the Haggis.

7. Have a wee laugh as you pocket an easy £20!

8. Double your profits and sell them the fish you've just poached.

SCOTTISH PUMPKIN PIE

MAKES TWO 9-INCH (23-CM) SINGLE-CRUST PIES

You can't (legally) buy or make true haggis in the United States, because one of the essential ingredients, along with the lamb's heart and liver, is the animal's lungs—and the USDA unequivocally states that "Livestock lungs shall not be saved for use as human food." (The lungs are becoming an issue even in the U.K.: Apparently due to increased temperatures, blamed on global warming, a parasite called lungworm is infecting British sheep, rendering their lungs unfit for consumption; doomsayers predict that this may mean the end of traditional haggis even in Scotland.) Fortunately, several companies in the United States manufacture a lungless haggis, some in cans, some in a plastic skin (haggis in the traditional sheep's stomach is increasingly difficult to find even in Scotland); though connoisseurs claim that the lungs give the haggis a lightness that is missing in American versions, the ones I've tasted have been, to my palate, virtually indistinguishable from their Scottish counterparts.

One leading haggis maker that has a U.S. version, Stahly Quality Foods, headquartered in Glenrothes, in Fife, offers a complimentary downloadable recipe book on their website (thehaggis.com) called *A Flavour of Scotland: A Culinary Tribute to the Versatility of Haggis*. This unusual—and unlikely—recipe appears therein, and is used (with adaptations) with Stahly's kind permission. The recipe notes that the dish, which is quite delicious, may be served warm or cold, as a starter or a dessert.

1 recipe shortcrust pastry (page 313), or 2 premade shortcrust pie shells
All-purpose flour, for dusting
1 (15-ounce / 425-g) can haggis (see Sources, page 316)
3 large eggs
1¼ cups (300 ml) heavy cream
Grated zest of 1 lemon
1 teaspoon salt
1 (15-ounce / 425-g) can pure pumpkin puree

If making your own shortcrust pastry, remove the pastry disks from the refrigerator and let them come to room temperature, then roll each one out on a floured work surface to a diameter of about 11 inches (28 cm). Carefully press each crust into a 9-inch (23-cm) pie dish.

Preheat the oven to 350°F (175°C).

Divide the haggis equally between the pie shells, smoothing it down with the back of a wooden spoon.

In a large bowl, lightly beat the eggs, then whisk in the cream, lemon zest, and salt. Stir in the pumpkin puree, incorporating it thoroughly.

Spoon the pumpkin mixture over the haggis, smoothing it down with the back of a wooden spoon. Bake until the pumpkin is firmly set and the top is golden brown, about 1 hour.

DEVILLED KIDNEYS ᴏɴ TOAST

SERVES 4

Devilled means cooked in a piquant sauce, usually involving mustard and cayenne. The earliest reference to kidneys prepared in this manner, according to the *Oxford English Dictionary*, dates from 1800, but this preparation of lamb kidneys is a Victorian dish. It was originally a staple of gentlemen's breakfast menus, though it evolved into a late-night supper dish and is now sometimes seen as a main dish at dinnertime. This is an adaptation of a recipe by prolific chef-restaurateur Mark Hix. The biggest challenge for American readers will be finding lamb kidneys, especially those that haven't been frozen. Some Greek and other ethnic markets may be able to supply them, and they are sometimes available from old-style butcher shops or new "artisanal" ones.

2 tablespoons vegetable oil
20 lamb kidneys, halved and trimmed of gristle
Salt
Cayenne
2 tablespoons (30 g) butter, plus more for buttering toast
3 medium shallots, finely chopped
2 tablespoons apple cider vinegar
2 teaspoons English mustard
1 tablespoon tomato paste
1 recipe Brown Gravy (page 280)
Leaves from 2 or 3 sprigs curly parsley, finely chopped
4 thick slices white country-style bread, toasted and buttered

Heat the oil in a large skillet over high heat. Season the kidneys with salt and cayenne, then fry them, stirring continuously, for about 2 minutes, or until they begin to brown but are still pink inside. Reduce the heat to medium. Remove the kidneys from the skillet with a slotted spoon and set them aside.

Melt the butter in the same skillet, then add the shallots and cook, stirring frequently, for 3 to 4 minutes, or until they are soft but not browned. Stir in the vinegar, mustard, and tomato paste, then add the gravy and raise the heat to high. Cook, stirring frequently, until the sauce thickens enough to coat the back of a wooden spoon. Reduce the heat to low, return the kidneys to the pan, add the parsley, and cook for about 1 minute.

Divide the toast between four plates and spoon the kidneys and sauce over the toast, dividing it evenly.

TRIPE *AND* ONIONS

As lovers of offal—especially in England—understand, tripe is not one kind of meat but four. Tripe is the stomach lining of a cow, but the cow from which it comes has not one stomach but a quartet of them. (Sheep and pig tripe exist, but are far less common.) The most popular variety of tripe, in the United States and in Britain, is honeycomb tripe, which comes from the reticulum, or second stomach, of the animal. The tripe shops of England, and especially those of Lancashire—premier tripe country—also traditionally sold the first stomach, or rumen, a flat tripe cooked similarly, and the third stomach, or omasum (in Lancashire it was sometimes called "ladies' tripe"), said to be the best for frying. (The fourth stomach, or abomasum, also called reed tripe, is rarely used, though that's what you'll get if you brave a *lampredotto* sandwich in Florence, in which the tripe is simmered with onion in tomato broth and served on a crusty roll.)

Craig Bancroft, who runs the Lancashire luxury hotel Northcote with chef Nigel Haworth, told me once that one of his fondest childhood memories is of going to the market and eating pickled tripe with salt and pepper, washed down with sarsaparilla. Tripe faded from popularity in the region in the latter part of the twentieth century, but has been experiencing a revival there and elsewhere. Chefs like Haworth, Raymond Blanc, and even Gordon Ramsay have championed it, and the Lancashire-based Tripe Marketing Board (formerly the British Tripe Council) promotes it with recipes, publications, a Tripe Club, tripe swag (a fridge magnet, pens, an annual datebook, a T-shirt), and a jocular website whose FAQs include "Is tripe suitable for vegetarians?" with the answer "Not as such."

One popular traditional way of eating tripe in Lancashire, besides pickled, was in milk with onions. This is a variation on a slightly more modern recipe devised by Mark Hix.

3 tablespoons (45 g) butter
4 medium onions, thinly sliced
Leaves from 4 or 5 sprigs thyme
2 tablespoons all-purpose flour
¼ cup (60 ml) dry white wine
4½ cups (1 L) veal, beef, or chicken stock, store-bought or homemade (page 314)
2 pounds (900 g) honeycomb tripe, washed and cut into pieces about 3 inches (7.5 cm) square
Salt and freshly ground white pepper
2 tablespoons heavy cream

Melt the butter in a large skillet with a lid over medium-low heat, then add the onions and thyme, cover the skillet, and cook for 6 to 8 minutes, stirring occasionally, or until the onions are soft but not yet browned. (If they begin to brown, add a few tablespoons of water to the skillet.)

Reduce the heat to low, stir in the flour, and cook for about 1 minute more. Drizzle in the wine and then the stock, stirring continuously. Bring the liquid to a boil over high heat, then reduce the heat to low, add the tripe, and season with salt and white pepper. Cook, uncovered, stirring occasionally, for about 1 hour, or until the tripe is tender. If the sauce thickens too much, add a few tablespoons of water.

Stir in the cream and adjust the seasoning if necessary. Hix recommends serving the tripe with Mashed Potatoes (page 211).

An Offal Success

London-born and trained as an architect, Fergus Henderson is a self-taught chef who first attracted notice for the honest, ingredient-driven cooking he and his wife, Margot, offered at the French House Dining Room, upstairs from the historic pub of that name in Soho. In 1994, Henderson, in partnership with French House maître d'hôtel Jon Spiteri and restaurateur and wine merchant Trevor Gulliver, opened his own place: St. John, located on the street of the same name, in a former smokehouse near Smithfield, London's wholesale meat market. (Spiteri is no longer associated with the restaurant.)

From the beginning, St. John was a singular establishment. Skylit and minimalist, with whitewashed walls, wood plank floors, and neatly dressed tables in schoolboy rows, the restaurant staked out its territory immediately with a terse, uncompromising menu that became immediately famous for its array of offal, but that also offered plenty of smart, if usually uncommon, seafood and vegetable dishes. One of the first things I remember eating there, sometime in the late nineties, was described on the menu simply as "Radishes." Out came a plate of long, slender, mildly spicy breakfast radishes, still attached to their stems and leaves, which extended past the oval plate they were presented on, drooping audaciously onto the white tablecloth. With them was a crock of rich yellow butter and a little dish of sea salt. I couldn't have imagined a better beginning to my meal.

Other dishes I had in that era were similarly simple and not particularly challenging: thick asparagus in classic vinaigrette, fried ling cod with aïoli,

The bar menu at St. John, 1997

Gloucestershire Old Spot bacon chop. But the fun stuff was the fare that seemed to veer off into dangerous territory: a duck neck terrine inset with confit gizzards, a plate of pigs' tails braised and then roasted in a crust of mustard and bread crumbs, sautéed lambs' tongues, a slab of "blood cake" (black pudding in loaf

A pig splayed out for butchering is the St. John logo

form) topped with a fried egg . . . Clearly Henderson had a philosophy of food; he spoke of respecting the animals that died to feed us by using them—all of them—wisely and with respect. The first cookbook he published encapsulated his approach in its very title: *Nose to Tail Eating: A Kind of British Cooking*. Today, Henderson modestly says that he isn't really sure whether he coined the now-ubiquitous phrase that is the first part of his title, but I suspect he did—and that book and its 2007 sequel, *Beyond Nose to Tail* (the two were republished together in 2012 as *The Complete Nose to Tail*) certainly popularized the concept for younger chefs and influenced restaurant menus all over Britain and in America and beyond.

The menus at St. John circa 2016 are much the same as they have always been, though new dishes are

continually added. For lunch today, as I write this, for instance, a diner might choose rolled pig's spleen and bacon, rabbit offal and butterbean puree, pigeon and braised red cabbage, or devilled kidneys—or, for the less adventurous, grilled Jerusalem artichoke with red onions and olives, mussels with leeks and cider, brill with chicory and anchovy, or braised lamb with carrots and aïoli. Then there's one classic St. John dish that is almost never off the menu: Roast Bone Marrow and Parsley Salad (page 262).

"I do have leanings towards celebrating indigenous food," Henderson told me years ago when I wrote about him for *Saveur*. "It seems strange to me that 'modern British food' means using ingredients from all over the world and cooking them here. I'm not sure I see the point. Nor do I see the point of the Olde Worlde sticky toffee school of revival cooking. We're trying to glide through the middle with a sense of good food. Some things might sound daunting, but they're not meant to be. We do serve organ meats, but often when people try them, they discover they quite like them. And anyway, that seems like the sort of thing one ought to serve at Smithfield."

When I talked to him about this book, he added that he thought of his food as "simple but bountiful," and, while he doesn't dispute the critic Jay Rayner's contention that his cooking owes more to Marcella Hazan than to Mrs. Beeton, he does think that "if someone from a hundred years ago saw this food, they'd recognize it." He likes the fact that so many chefs today are now proudly cooking traditional dishes around the U.K., but adds, "A slight problem is that chefs have a hard time keeping it simple. Food like this loses its charms the more you touch it."

CHAPTER 7

—

SAVORY PIES
& PUDDINGS

"WE DINED AT THE BULLHEAD UPON THE BEST VENISON PASTY THAT EVER I EAT OF IN MY LIFE, AND WITH ONE DISH MORE, IT WAS THE BEST DINNER I EVER WAS AT."

—SAMUEL PEPYS, *The Diary of Samuel Pepys* (1660)

"SHALL I TELL YOU WHAT'LL BE THE MAIN DISH ON THE MENU IN THE CANTEEN? IT SHOULD BE STEAK-AND-KIDNEY PUDDING."

—JAMES BOND, QUOTED BY IAN FLEMING, *The Man with the Golden Gun* (1965)

When Americans think of "pie," it is nearly always sweet—a shortcrust shell filled with cooked apples, berries, peaches, or some other fruit and enclosed in a top crust or lattice-work of pastry, or else a pudding of some kind (chocolate, lemon) topped with meringue or whipped cream. We know shepherd's pie, of course, and chicken potpie, and those microwaveable frozen turnovers called Hot Pockets and their kin might be described as savory hand pies, but for most of us, most of the time, "pie" equals dessert.

In contrast, while there are certainly sweet fruit pies in British cuisine (many of them actually tarts, with little or no top crust), the term is more likely to evoke the image of something filled with meat or fish or vegetables. These include small, rounded pork hand pies, often leaden with shortening; crescent-shaped turnovers like the famous Cornish pasties; the oval-shaped beef pies, served with mashed potatoes and parsley-based green sauce, at famous old East End London shops like the 1902-vintage L. Manze (whose other specialty is jellied eels—a favorite dish of the poor in the eighteenth and nineteenth centuries); and monumental domed pastries in fancier places, filled with various ingredients that steam irresistible aromas when the crust is breached.

One theory about the development of what might be called savory pie culture in Great Britain is that the Romans introduced the technique (still sometimes used in Italy today) of braising or stewing meat, long and slow, in baking dishes sealed with a paste of flour and water. This was generally cut off and discarded when the dish was done, but doubtless at some point it occurred to somebody that this crust was edible, too—and it became even more so after somebody figured out that enriching the flour-and-water mixture with suet or lard gave it a more pleasing texture and richer flavor. After the potato belatedly achieved acceptance in Britain in the 1700s, mashed or pureed potatoes were introduced as a simpler substitute for a top crust on some pies.

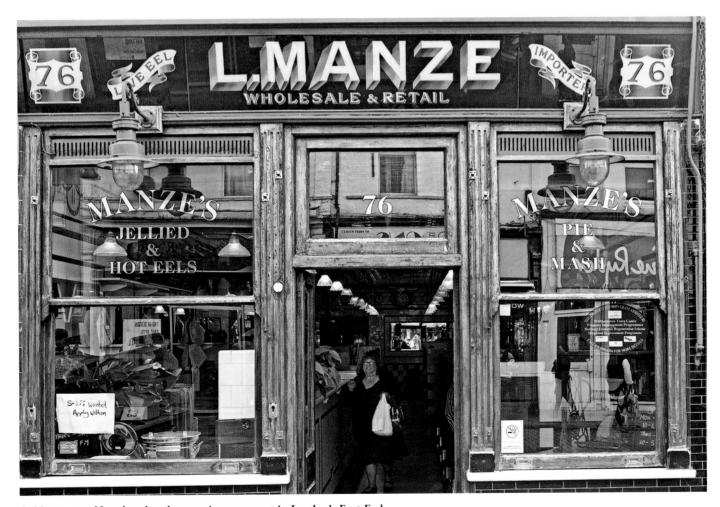

L. Manze, an old-style eel and meat pie restaurant in London's East End

A man advertising beefsteak puddings served at Pearce's Refreshment Rooms, London, 1891

Fish pies were particularly popular in medieval times and up through the Elizabethan era. Meat pies grew more complex and often included unlikely combinations of ingredients. Dr. Johnson's favorite dish was said to be a veal pie with plums and sugar added; it was also said that he liked to improve his plum pudding by draping it with lobster sauce. It was common to combine several kinds of meat or game in a pie, and beef was sometimes mixed with oysters—which were cheaper than meat and, as it were, beefed up the ingredients.

In marked contrast to these opulent concoctions was the much-maligned Woolton pie. During World War II, Frederick Marquis, the First Earl of Woolton, who was the government minister in charge of food policy, promoted this grim mixture of stewed potatoes, cauliflower, carrots, rutabagas, and onions mixed with oatmeal, flavored

with Marmite (see page 278), and baked under a potato crust. Despite the strictures of wartime rationing, the pie never became popular, and was quickly forgotten when a wider range of ingredients became available again. The Lancashire specialty called butter pie, simply onions and potatoes moistened with butter and baked in a crust, was similarly modest, but tasted much better.

The most unusual of British dishes baked in a crust is certainly stargazy pie, a specialty of the Cornish coastal town of Mousehole (pronounced "mau-zole"), near Penzance. First made in the sixteenth century, or the nineteenth, or perhaps the twentieth, this is a pie of whole small fish, traditionally the sardine relative called pilchards, but also sardines themselves or sometimes herring, whiting, or some other variety, mixed with hard-boiled eggs, bacon, bread crumbs, and other ingredients and usually vividly seasoned. What makes the pie unique is that the heads of the fish (and sometimes the tails) poke out of the crust—looking skyward, supposedly. It is an unsettling sight, though the flavor of the pie is in no way affected. According to legend, stargazy pie was first made by the citizens of Mousehole to honor one Tom Bowcock, who sailed bravely into a storm one December 23 in the 1500s to catch fish to feed the village. Never mind that the earliest reference to it dates from 1947. Mousehole celebrates Tom Bowcock's Eve every year, and the pie is eaten by all.

Unlike "pie," the British understanding of "pudding" is mostly as something sweet. The word is a common synonym for dessert in general, in fact—"pudding" in a British restaurant can mean actual pudding, but it can also be ice cream, cake, or a pastry chef's elaborate innovation. Savory puddings are old-fashioned and much less common than savory pies. These puddings have a kind of crust, too, but unlike pies they are baked "wet"—in effect steamed—in pudding bowls so the texture of the enclosing dough is moist rather than dry. One fabled savory pudding was "Ye Famous Rump Steak, Kidney, Lark and Oyster Pudding" served for centuries at the ancient London pub Ye Olde Cheshire Cheese (see page 174). A less famous and much less elaborate one is rag pudding, from the old Lancashire mill town of Oldham, consisting of minced beef and onions in suet pastry, boiled in a wrapping of cheesecloth. The most celebrated of savory puddings, however, is a batter pudding made with the drippings from roast beef or other meat, dating back to at least the early eighteenth century: Yorkshire pudding. This is a pudding whose dough encloses nothing but air.

Sweet, Firm, and Tough

Frederick T. Vine wrote a number of books for the baking and confectionary trade in the late nineteenth and early twentieth centuries—*Biscuits for Bakers, Cakes and How to Make Them, Ices: Plain and Decorated*, and so on. In his *Savoury Pastry: Savoury Dish and Raised Pies, Pork Pies, Patties, Vol-au-Vents, Mincemeats, and Pies, and Miscellaneous Savoury Pastries*, published in London in 1900 by *Baker and Confectioner* magazine, he offered this advice on the all-important subject of butter.

Butters suitable for puff paste are at all times to be purchased from the dealers, and each dealer has his own registered brand which he will recommend; but, for my part, when using pure butter for puff paste, I prefer the best I can get, which usually is "Kiel," and, for all practical purposes, it is hard to beat. It is tough and waxy to the feel and free from salt, of excellent flavour, and really a very ideal butter for pastry all the year round. Coming next are "Irish Firkins" and "Normandy," while during the winter you will be able to use "Danish Estates," "Jersey" and several brands of "Brittany." "Canadian Creamery" is not amiss, though sometimes it has to be avoided on account of its high and uncertain flavour, although of late years "Canadian," and even "Australian"—or, as it is more generally termed, "Colonials"—reach this country in much better condition than formerly.

No matter what brand or kind of butter you may select, the principal thing is to choose that which is sweet to the taste, and firm, tough, and waxy in the handling, avoiding all those butters which are short, crumbly, and rotten in the handling, as being useless for the purpose of puff paste.

FISH PIE

SERVES 6

This pie, as made by Mark Hix, is a homey, comforting dish with a "crust" of mashed potatoes, like that of cottage pie (page 176). Almost any combination of saltwater fish can be used (buy top quality—even though it's going into a pie). It adds considerable character to the pie, in any case, to use at least a bit of smoked fish, like cod or haddock. (I don't like using smoked salmon, as it tends to be too oily.) This dish can be made a day before serving, up to the point of adding the potatoes, and refrigerated overnight; just be sure to let it come to room temperature, then add the bread crumbs and cheddar and bake at 350°F (175°C) for 15 minutes.

2 cups court bouillon or fish stock, store-bought or
    homemade (page 315)
½ cup (120 ml) dry white wine
½ pound (225 g) boneless, skinless firm-fleshed
    white fish, such as cod, pollock, or halibut, cut
    into thick cubes about 1¼ inches (3 cm) square
½ pound (225 g) boneless, skinless salmon fillet,
    cut into thick cubes about 1¼ inches (3 cm)
    square
½ pound (225 g) boneless, skinless smoked
    whitefish, halibut, or smoked haddock or
    finnan haddie (see Sources, page 316), cut into
    thick cubes about 1¼ inches (3 cm) square
4 tablespoons (½ stick / 55 g) butter
½ cup (65 g) all-purpose flour
¾ cup (180 ml) heavy cream
2 teaspoons English mustard
1½ teaspoons Worcestershire sauce
1 teaspoon anchovy paste
Salt and freshly ground white pepper
Leaves from 3 or 4 sprigs parsley, chopped
½ cup (120 ml) whole milk
1½ recipes Mashed Potatoes (page 211)
½ cup fresh white bread crumbs
1½ ounces (40 g) cheddar cheese, grated

Bring the court bouillon and the wine to a boil in a large skillet over high heat. Reduce the heat to medium-low and add all the fish. Poach for about 2 minutes, then drain the fish in a colander over a bowl, reserving the poaching liquid. Leave the fish in the colander to cool.

Melt the butter in the same skillet over low heat. Slowly stir in the flour to make a roux, then slowly stir in the reserved stock. Bring the mixture to a boil over high heat, then reduce the heat to low and simmer for 30 minutes. Add the cream and cook for 10 minutes more. Stir in the mustard, Worcestershire sauce, and anchovy paste. Season generously with salt and white pepper, then let the sauce cool off the heat for 15 minutes.

Gently fold the fish and parsley into the sauce, then spoon it into six individual baking dishes or one large one, filling them to about 1½ inches (4 cm) from the top. Let the sauce set for about 30 minutes.

Preheat the oven to 350°F (175°C).

Stir the milk into the mashed potatoes, then carefully divide the potatoes evenly between the baking dishes, spreading it evenly over the fish with a spatula.

Bake the pies for 30 minutes, then scatter the bread crumbs evenly over them, followed by the cheese, and bake for 15 minutes more. Serve warm but not hot.

MUSSEL PIE

SERVES 4

One afternoon in May, back in the late 1990s, I found myself slogging through shallow salt water in green rubber Wellies at the edge of Loch Gruinart on the Scottish island of Islay, where some of the world's best whisky is made. I was with a man responsible for some of that whisky, Jim McEwan, then the master distiller for Bowmore (he went on to hold the titles of master distiller and production director for another Islay enterprise, Bruichladdich, until his retirement in 2015), and we were rummaging through clumps of seaweed and peering into fissures in the rocks looking for mussels.

The air was sharp with the sea smells of iodine and brine—Islay whisky translates those aromas into part of its weave of flavors—and there were black-faced lambs skittering across the grass-topped sand dunes above the beach and speckled gray-and-white harriers lofted by the breeze high above our heads. The loch was quiet, except for the soft plash of ripples against the rocks, the sloshing of our boots, and the clack of mussels dropping into our sacks. We must have collected five or six dozen of them, small, blue-black, bearded. That night, at the modest Bridgend Hotel, we ate those mussels, simply steamed in white wine, and of course they tasted better than any I had ever had. This mussel pie recipe is adapted from one in *An Islay Cookbook*, a small paperback book by Islay artist Carol Ogilvie.

2 cups (480 ml) dry white wine (optional)
2 pounds (900 g) blue (not New Zealand green-lipped) mussels, washed and bearded (do not soak in water)
Salt
1 pound (450 g) cod, skin removed, cut into 3 or 4 pieces
Zest of 1 orange
1 tablespoon good-quality Scotch whisky, preferably single malt from Islay
1 teaspoon freshly grated nutmeg
1 pound (450 g) puff pastry, store-bought (thawed, if frozen) or homemade (page 313)
Butter, for greasing
All-purpose flour, for dusting

Bring the wine or 2 cups (480 ml) water to a boil in a large pot over high heat. Add the mussels, cover the pot, and cook for 5 minutes, or until all or most of the shells have opened. Remove the mussels from the pot with a slotted spoon, discarding any that haven't opened, and set them aside in a large bowl until cool enough to handle. Remove the mussels from their shells, discarding the shells and reserving the meat in a large bowl.

Bring a small pot of generously salted water to a boil over high heat, then reduce the heat to medium and add the cod. Poach for about 10 minutes, or until just cooked through.

Preheat the oven to 375°F (190°C).

Drain the cod and let cool. When cool enough to handle, flake it into the bowl with the mussels. Stir in the orange zest, whisky, and nutmeg until well combined.

Lightly grease a 9- to 10-inch (23- to 25-cm) pie dish with butter.

Roll out half the puff pastry on a lightly floured board into a round about 12 inches (30 cm) in diameter, then carefully lay it into the pie dish, with the edges coming up the sides. Drain the cod and mussel mixture to remove excess moisture, then spoon it into the pie shell, gently flattening it and evening it out so it fills the shell evenly.

Roll out the remaining pastry into a slightly larger round to form a lid for the pie. Carefully place it over the filling and crimp the edges of the pastry inward. Cut four small vents in the pastry, evenly distributed over the surface, to allow steam to escape.

Bake for about 20 minutes, or until the top crust is golden brown. Serve warm but not hot.

VEGETARIAN BRIDIES WITH RED WINE SAUCE

SERVES 4

Having introduced the world to vegetarian haggis (see page 216), the late Ronnie Clydesdale, proprietor of the groundbreaking Ubiquitous Chip in Glasgow, applied his imagination to another traditional Scottish meat dish, the bridie. This is a kind of handheld meat pie said to have been invented in the town of Forfar, north of Dundee in eastern Scotland. The name may derive from "bride's pie," a larger meat pastry traditionally served to wedding guests. Here, as with Clydesdale's haggis, lentils fill in for ground meat.

FOR THE RED WINE SAUCE:
1 tablespoon corn or peanut oil
1 tablespoon (15 g) butter
1 small red onion, finely chopped
4 cloves garlic, crushed
1 sprig thyme
1 cup good-quality dry red wine

FOR THE BRIDIES:
1 tablespoon corn or peanut oil, plus more for greasing
1 tablespoon (15 g) butter
2 small red onions, finely chopped
2 cloves garlic, finely chopped
1 medium carrot, finely chopped
5 ounces (140 g) brown lentils, washed thoroughly
2 or 3 sprigs thyme
2 bay leaves
1 cup (240 ml) vegetable stock, store-bought or homemade (page 315)
Salt and freshly ground black pepper
12 ounces (340 g) puff pastry, store-bought (thawed, if frozen) or homemade (page 313)
1 large egg, beaten

MAKE THE RED WINE SAUCE:
Heat the oil and butter in a small skillet over low heat. Add the onion and garlic and cook, stirring occasionally, until they grow translucent but haven't begun to brown, about 5 minutes. Add the thyme and wine and bring to a boil over high heat. Immediately reduce the heat to low and simmer, uncovered, until the liquid has reduced by half, 10 to 15 minutes. Set the sauce aside without straining it.

MAKE THE BRIDIES:
Heat the oil and butter in a medium skillet with a lid over low heat. Add the onions and garlic and cook, stirring occasionally, until they grow translucent but haven't begun to brown, about 5 minutes. Add the carrot, lentils, thyme, bay leaves, and vegetable stock and season with salt and pepper. Simmer, partially covered, for 30 minutes. Set the vegetable mixture aside to cool, then remove and discard the thyme and bay leaves.

Roll out the puff pastry to a thickness of about ⅛ inch (3 mm). With the rim of a bowl or a sharp knife, cut the pastry into four 6-inch (15-cm) rounds. Lightly sprinkle a baking sheet with water, put the pastry rounds on it, and refrigerate them for 30 minutes.

Preheat the oven to 400ºF (200ºC). Lightly grease a baking sheet.

Remove the pastry from the refrigerator and divide the vegetable mixture evenly between the pastry rounds, spooning it onto one half of the dough and gently spreading it with a dinner knife or the back of a spoon so that it forms a semicircle, with about 1 inch (2.5 cm) of pastry around the rim. Dampen the edges of each circle with water and fold them over to make a semicircle. Crimp the edges of each bridie with the tines of a fork and cut a small hole in the top of each to vent steam. Brush the tops of the bridies with the beaten egg, then transfer them to the prepared baking sheet. Bake for 10 to 15 minutes, or until they're golden brown.

When the bridies are almost done, strain the red wine sauce and reheat it in a small pan over medium heat. Serve it alongside the bridies, to be spooned over them.

CHEESE AND ONION PIE

SERVES 4

Lancashire, in northwestern England, is particularly good food country—famous, among other things, for its repertoire of savory pies. The residents of one municipality, Wigan, a part of Greater Manchester, are jocularly known as "Pie-Eaters" and the community hosts the annual World Pie Eating Championship. (One theory holds that the residents' sobriquet doesn't refer to their appetite for pies at all, but to the fact that striking miners in the region in 1926 gave up their protest and were forced to "eat humble pie.") The most famous pie in Lancashire is probably butter pie, which is simply onions and potatoes baked beneath a simple crust. This was the dish most commonly eaten by local Catholics on Fridays, when meat was forbidden. Paul and Linda McCartney made reference to the specialty in their song "Uncle Albert/Admiral Halsey" ("I had a cup of tea and butter pie"). This pie substitutes Lancashire cheese for the potatoes, but is similar in spirit. The recipe is adapted from one used at The Three Fishes in Mitton, one of five gastropubs in the Ribble Valley Inns Group, overseen by chef Nigel Haworth, whose main bailiwick is the upscale Northcote country house hotel. At the gastropubs, the rims of the pies are elaborately crimped, but this is hardly necessary.

1 recipe shortcrust pastry (page 313)
1 large onion, finely chopped
Salt and freshly ground white pepper
3 ounces (85 g) cream cheese
1 pound (450 g) Lancashire cheese (see Sources, page 316), grated
All-purpose flour, for dusting
1 large egg, beaten

Divide the dough into eight equal portions and wrap each one separately in plastic wrap. Press each dough ball into a disk and refrigerate for at least 1 hour before using.

Put the onion in a small saucepan and add enough water to cover. Bring the water to a boil over high heat, then season the onion generously with salt and white pepper. Reduce the heat to low and simmer, stirring occasionally, until the onion is soft, about 10 minutes. Set aside to

An old cast-iron stove at The Three Fishes in Lancashire

cool, then drain the onion, transfer it to a medium bowl, and mix in the cream cheese, then the grated Lancashire cheese. Adjust the seasoning.

Preheat the oven to 350°F (175°C).

Unwrap the pastry disks and roll them out on a floured work surface into disks just large enough to fit into four baking dishes 5 to 6 inches (13 to 15 cm) in diameter. Lightly press one disk into each of the baking dishes. Divide the onion mixture evenly among the baking dishes.

Lay the remaining pastry disks on top of the pies, pushing the edges down into the baking dishes lightly. Brush the tops of the pies with the egg wash, then bake for 25 to 30 minutes, or until the top crusts are golden brown and the cheese is well melted. Serve the pies in their baking dishes.

Pudding at Ye Olde Cheshire Cheese

For generations, if not longer, the most celebrated savory pudding in London was probably "Ye Famous Rump Steak, Kidney, Lark and Oyster Pudding," served from October to April every year at the venerable Fleet Street pub called Ye Olde Cheshire Cheese. A public house was first opened on the site of the Cheshire Cheese in the 1530s, then rebuilt after the block was destroyed in the Great Fire of London in 1666. A vaulted ceiling in the cellar may have been part of a monastery. In the nineteenth and early twentieth centuries, the pub became a literary hangout, whose habitués included Dickens, Goldsmith, Thackeray, Tennyson, Conrad, Sir Arthur Conan Doyle, G. K. Chesterson, and Max Beerbohm. Yeats and his friend Ernest Rhys founded The Rhymers' Club at the pub, where poets read their works over tankards of ale (Yeats began his poem "The Grey Rock" by hailing "Poets with whom I learned my trade, / Companions of the Cheshire Cheese").

Around the turn of the twentieth century, the gourmet-about-London who wrote under the byline Lieutenant Colonel Newnham-Davis noted that, at the Cheshire Cheese, "The pudding in its great earthenware bowl stands on a little table in the middle of the room. It is a triumph of old British cookery. In it are larks, kidneys, oysters, mushrooms, steak, and there are ingredients in the gravy which are a secret of the house." The pudding was indeed a large thing; one account says that a single one could feed sixty or seventy diners, and a newspaper story from 1887 claimed that each pudding weighed anywhere from fifty to eighty pounds, that it was boiled for sixteen to twenty hours—and that "the smell on a windy day has been known to reach as far as the Stock Exchange" (about half a mile away).

An American stockbroker liked the pudding so much that he had one shipped to himself in New York (it was held up in customs for a week, not for health reasons but over a tariff dispute). On one occasion, a waiter bringing in a new pudding tripped and dropped the treasured concoction. Eileen Hooten, in her 1928 book *The Restaurants of London*, reports that when that happened, the pub's proprietor wept openly and disappeared, and that "the customers sadly took their hats and left."

The Cheshire Cheese is owned today by the Samuel Smith Brewery and serves "the best of British pub food." The menu offers Ye Famous Steak & Kidney Pudding (the larks and oysters have been phased out), but also includes chicken wings, burgers, and something called "Mexican-style stuffed pasta boats." Poets are seldom in residence.

HOMITY PIE

MAKES ONE 9- TO 10-INCH (23- TO 25-CM) PIE

An open-top potato tart—sort of comparatively eggless quiche, if you will—homity pie was apparently invented during World War II, probably in Devon, as an efficient way to utilize the sparse ingredients that were available under the country's rationing program. Some sources trace the dish to the so-called Land Girls, female civilians who volunteered to take over agricultural work around Great Britain to replace farmworkers who were off at war. Homity pie might have drifted into obscurity, but it was discovered and revived in the 1960s by David and Kay Canter at their pioneering London vegetarian restaurant Cranks, where it became one of their most popular dishes. What does *homity* mean? Nobody seems to know; the best guess is that it's just a made-up word that sounded good to the people who ate the pie. The Cranks version uses wholemeal (whole-wheat) pastry, but white-flour pastry was probably used in the original. This recipe is an amalgam of several different versions of the pie.

10 ounces (300 g) shortcrust pastry (page 313)
2 large white potatoes, unpeeled
3 tablespoons vegetable oil
2 tablespoons (30 g) butter
1 medium onion, coarsely chopped
1 medium leek, washed well and chopped
Leaves from 6 to 8 sprigs parsley, chopped
Leaves from 2 large sprigs thyme
2 large eggs, lightly beaten
8 ounces (225 g) grated cheddar cheese
Salt and freshly ground black pepper

Roll out the pastry to a round about 1½ inches (4 cm) larger than a 9- to 10-inch (23- to 25-cm) pie or tart tin or shallow baking dish, then gently press the dough into the bottom and sides of the tin. Cover the dough with plastic wrap and refrigerate it.

Put the potatoes in a medium pot and add 2 quarts (1.9 L) cold water. Bring the water to a boil over high heat, then reduce the heat to medium-high and cook, uncovered, for 25 to 30 minutes, or until the potatoes are soft when pierced with the tines of a fork. Drain them, pat them dry with a clean dish towel, and set them aside to cool to room temperature. When the potatoes are cool enough to handle, peel them and cut them into cubes roughly 1 inch (2.5 cm) square, then coarsely crush them with the tines of a fork.

Preheat the oven to 425°F (220°C).

Heat the oil and butter in a large skillet over medium heat. Add the onion and leek and cook, stirring frequently, until they're translucent and just beginning to brown, about 10 minutes. Stir in the potatoes, parsley, thyme, eggs, and half the cheese, and season with salt and pepper. Mix the ingredients together thoroughly, then remove the skillet from the heat and let cool for about 5 minutes.

Remove the pie shell from the refrigerator and fill it with the vegetable mixture, lightly tamping it down with the back of a wooden spoon. Sprinkle the pie evenly with the remaining cheese and bake for 35 to 40 minutes, until the top is golden brown.

COTTAGE PIE

SERVES 6

"Pies" with a crust of mashed potatoes instead of pastry appear to have developed in Britain in the second half of the eighteenth century. Though potatoes were known in England by the late 1500s, they weren't widely cultivated for another two hundred years—but once they were, they supplanted barley and wheat as a field crop in many regions, as they were easier to grow. The impoverished farmworkers and other rural folk of the time who lived in modest dwellings, or cottages, would have planted potatoes but probably not wheat (and wheat would have been expensive to buy), so potatoes became their piecrust—sometimes, in early recipes, lining the pie dish as well as topping the pie. The term *shepherd's pie*, often used as a synonym for *cottage pie*, dates only from the late nineteenth century. Purists maintain that shepherd's pie must be made with lamb (since shepherds keep sheep); however, cottiers—the old term for those who lived in cottages—didn't raise cattle, so the distinction is probably meaningless.

4 tablespoons (½ stick / 55 g) butter
1 tablespoon vegetable or olive oil
1 onion, finely chopped
1 stalk celery, finely chopped
1½ pounds (680 g) finely minced or ground beef
1 tablespoon tomato paste
1 cup (240 ml) beef stock, store-bought or
    homemade (page 314)
Salt and freshly ground black pepper
1 recipe freshly made Mashed Potatoes (page 211)

Preheat the oven to 350°F (175°C).

Melt half the butter with the vegetable oil in a large skillet over medium heat. Add the onion and celery and cook, stirring frequently, for 8 to 10 minutes, or until they are soft but not browned.

Raise the heat to high, add the beef, and cook, stirring frequently, until it is well browned. Stir in the tomato paste and the stock and bring the liquid to a boil. Reduce the heat to low, season the meat generously with salt and pepper, and simmer for 15 to 20 minutes, or until stock is almost evaporated.

Melt the remaining butter in a small saucepan over low heat.

Spoon the meat into a 3-quart (3-L) round or oblong baking dish, smoothing it down with the back of a spoon. Spoon the mashed potatoes onto the meat, then flatten them down with a dinner knife. Lightly drag a fork across the top of the potatoes to make a crosshatch pattern, then brush the potatoes with the melted butter. Bake for 45 minutes, or until the potato crust is golden brown and crisp around the edges.

Tossing Pennies with the Pie Man

In her 1932 classic *Good Things in England*, Florence White, who founded and ran the English Folk Cookery Association, published this description of a street pie merchant in Bath, based on what she describes as "interesting particulars supplied by an old Bathonian."

> The "Pie Man" stood on the Boro' Walls, between Cater's and Ship and Teagles, close to the pavement by Cater's.
>
> He had a brightly polished case of stout tin standing on 4 legs and fitted with three drawers.
>
> In one he kept meat pies, the other mince pies, the third had a small charcoal fire arrangement which kept the pies hot.
>
> He announced his presence by fairly quietly repeating quickly, "All 'ot all 'ot all 'ot," about five times very rapidly. (Try it and you get the effect.)
>
> He sold them at the recognized price of the day— one penny each. But with boys, who tossed with him (halfpennies) or with men who tossed (pennies); if they lost he took the money, if they won they had a pie. I think the meat pies were 2d. as the men generally took meat pies, but if they did not choose they had mince pies.
>
> But, as I have said, you could also buy.
>
> I should not like to say how many halfpennies of mine he had. . . .
>
> He disappeared, I think about 1893. I remember him from 1880. As I told Mr. Taylor, he bought the "stale pies" from Fisher's. By "stale" is meant pies more than a day old. I do not think confectioners are so particular to-day, but in my youth all confectionery was half price the day after the buns, tarts, and pies were made. . . .

YORKSHIRE PUDDING

SERVES 6 TO 8

Yorkshire pudding, that light, handsomely inflated egg-batter concoction—related to the popover—considered essential with traditional Sunday-dinner-style roast beef (and sometimes lamb), was originally called "dripping pudding," not only because it is flavored with drippings from the roast but because in its original form, the meat juices actually dripped onto it. In the eighteenth century, meat would have been roasted on a spit or suspended in front of an open fire, instead of being cooked in an enclosed oven. What is quite possibly the earliest published recipe for "A Dripping Pudding," in the novelist and satirist William Kenrick's 1737 household manual, *The Whole Duty of a Woman*, calls for frying a "Batter as for Pancakes . . . a little" in a pan and then putting the pan "under a Shoulder of Mutton instead of a Dripping-pan" and shaking it frequently. The name of Yorkshire was first applied to the pudding by Hannah Glasse a decade later. Today, there are two common ways of making Yorkshire pudding. The more traditional is to pour the batter into the drippings in the roasting pan from which the meat has just been extracted and returning the pan to the oven; also acceptable is baking the puddings in individual muffin tins. Both methods are described here.

1 cup (125 g) all-purpose flour
Pinch of salt
2 large eggs
1 cup (240 ml) whole milk
¼ cup (60 ml) vegetable oil or bacon fat (optional)

If you have just cooked a roast, remove the roasting pan from the oven, lift the roast out of the roasting pan, and raise the oven temperature to 450°F (230°C).

Sift together the flour and salt into a medium bowl. In another bowl, beat the eggs and milk together, then make a well in the middle of the flour and slowly pour in the egg mixture, whisking it until the ingredients are just combined (do not overmix).

Pour the batter into the roasting pan and bake until the pudding has risen and browned, 20 to 25 minutes.

If you have not just cooked a roast, preheat the oven to 450°F (230°C), then divide the vegetable oil evenly between the wells of an 8- or 12-cup muffin tin. Put the tin into the oven for 5 minutes, then divide the batter evenly between the cups and bake until the puddings have risen and browned, 20 to 25 minutes. Serve immediately.

TOAD *in* THE HOLE

SERVES 4

Inevitably mentioned in those "funny English food names" articles, toad in the hole is a batter pudding into which sausages (or pieces of sausage) are baked. The name was in use at least by the late eighteenth century. The *Oxford English Dictionary*'s earliest citation dates from 1787, when it is mentioned in English lexicographer Francis Grose's *A Provincial Glossary* as a synonym for a Norfolk specialty that is essentially the same dish, pudding-pye-doll. Grose defines this simply as "meat in a crust," and indeed early recipes don't use sausages at all. The novelist and diarist Fanny Burney, writing in 1797, reacting to the news that the celebrated tragedienne Sarah Siddons had bought the Sadler's Wells Theatre, cracked that the pairing "seems to me as ill-fitted as the dish they call a toad in a hole; which I never saw, but always think of with anger,—putting a noble sirloin of beef into a poor, paltry batter-pudding!" Sausages apparently first intrude into the dish in the 1920s, but today the dish is always made with them. Toad in the hole is typically served with mashed potatoes (page 211) and gravy (page 280).

1 cup (125 g) all-purpose flour
½ teaspoon salt
2 large eggs, beaten
1¼ cups (300 ml) whole milk
1 tablespoon lard, bacon fat, or clarified butter (page 312)
6 bangers (see Sources, page 316) or other mild pork sausages, each cut into 3 or 4 pieces

Sift the flour and salt together into a large bowl, then make a well in the middle of the flour. Add the eggs and about ¼ cup (60 ml) of the milk and stir to make a thick, smooth batter. Gradually whisk in the rest of the milk until the mixture has the consistency of thick cream. Cover the bowl and set the batter aside to rest for 1 hour.

Preheat the oven to 425ºF (220ºC).

Put the lard in a 6 x 8-inch (16 x 20-cm) baking dish, then put it in the oven for about 5 minutes. Remove the baking dish from the oven and arrange the sausage pieces in the baking dish, distributing them evenly, then return the dish to the oven for 15 minutes.

Remove the baking dish from the oven again and carefully pour the batter around the sausage pieces, then bake for 30 to 40 minutes, or until the batter is well set and the top is golden brown. Serve immediately.

CORNISH PASTIES

MAKES 6

The Cornish pasty, often called the national dish of Cornwall, was the traditional lunch for miners and other workingmen. It was durable (sometimes the pastry in which it is enclosed can be very durable indeed) and contained the makings of a nutritious meal—meat and vegetables—in a form that could be easily carried and eaten with one hand. Some versions had the savory filling at one end and strawberry preserves or stewed apples at the other, making them a main dish and dessert all in one.

Florence White, in her *Good Things in England* (1932) quoted a Mr. John Pollock as saying "In my youth every knowing man and boy put a meat pasty in his pocket when going for a day's tramp or hunt on Dartmoor." He adds that the shape of the thing, "like a quarter moon with somewhat blunted horns," suggested "the emblem of Astarte, goddess of the Phoenicians."

An old legend says that the devil never crossed the Tamar into Cornwall because Cornish women are known for putting anything in a pasty, and he was afraid that's how he'd end up.

FOR THE PASTRY:
Pinch of salt
4 cups (540 g) bread flour, plus more for dusting
½ cup (1 stick / 115 g) cold butter, cut into small
    pieces
½ cup (115 g) lard, cut into small pieces

FOR THE FILLING:
1 medium russet potato, peeled and cut into
    ½-inch (1.25-cm) pieces
½ pound (225 g) piece of rutabaga, peeled and cut
    into ½-inch (1.25-cm) pieces
1 small onion, finely chopped
Salt and freshly ground black pepper
1 pound (450 g) beef round or chuck steak, cut into
    ½-inch (1.25-cm) pieces

1 large egg, lightly beaten
2 tablespoons milk

MAKE THE PASTRY:
Mix the salt into the flour in a large bowl, then rub in the butter and lard with your hands until the mixture resembles coarse meal. Stir in 1 cup water, then knead the dough for about 10 minutes, or until it becomes elastic. Cover the bowl with plastic wrap and refrigerate for 3 to 4 hours.

Cut the dough into six equal pieces, then roll one piece at a time out on a board lightly dusted with flour into disks about 8 inches (20 cm) in diameter. Put the first disk on a sheet of waxed paper just big enough to hold it, then cover it with a piece of waxed paper of the same size. Repeat the process with all the disks.

Preheat the oven to 375°F (190°C). Line a baking sheet large enough to hold all the pasties in a single layer with parchment paper.

MAKE THE FILLING:
Mix the potato, rutabaga, and onion together in a medium bowl and season the mixture generously with salt and pepper.

Lay one pastry disk on a board lightly dusted with flour and spread about one-sixth of the vegetable mixture evenly over it, stopping about 2 inches (5 cm) from the edges. Scatter about one-sixth of the meat over the vegetables, and season it lightly with salt and pepper.

Fold the pastry over into a half-moon shape and pinch the edges together with your fingers. With your thumb and forefinger, twist the edges about every ½ inch (1.25 cm) to crimp them. Repeat the process with the remaining five pastry disks and the rest of the filling ingredients.

In a small bowl, lightly beat together the egg and milk. Brush the pasties on both sides with the egg and milk mixture, then put them on the prepared baking sheet and bake for 1 hour, or until they are golden brown, turning them once.

VENISON & BEEF PIE

SERVES 4

The best wild-shot venison comes from Scotland, so it's not surprising that Scottish-born chefs, like Jeremy Lee of Quo Vadis in London, like to use the meat in their savory pies, as in this recipe. American cooks don't have access to domestically shot wild venison unless they hunt it themselves. The alternatives are meat from Asian deer species raised and slaughtered by Broken Arrow Ranch (see Sources, page 316), a huge game preserve in Texas, or that imported from New Zealand and sometimes Scotland, usually frozen but occasionally fresh in season.

3 tablespoons sunflower or vegetable oil
1¾ pounds (800 g) venison (see Sources, page 316), cut into large pieces
⅔ pound (300 g) beef brisket, cut into large chunks
2 red onions, sliced
1 large carrot, halved lengthwise and cut into 10 to 12 pieces
1 (4-ounce / 120-g) piece thick-cut bacon, cut into ½-inch (1.25-cm) cubes
1 clove garlic, crushed
Salt and freshly ground black pepper
1 bay leaf
1 tablespoon red currant jelly
2½ cups (600 ml) good-quality red wine
12 ounces (340 g) puff pastry, store-bought (thawed, if frozen) or homemade (page 313)
1 large egg, beaten

Heat half the oil in a Dutch oven or large skillet with a cover over medium-high heat. Working in batches, brown the venison and the brisket, turning the pieces frequently with tongs until they are well browned on all sides, 6 to 8 minutes. Set the meat aside as it is done.

Add the rest of the oil to the pot, reduce the heat to medium, and add the onions and carrot. Cook for 5 minutes, until they begin to soften. Add the bacon and garlic and cook for 2 to 3 minutes more. Season generously with salt and pepper, then add the bay leaf and stir in the red currant jelly and the wine.

Bring the liquid to a boil over high heat, then reduce the heat to low, return the meat to the pot, cover, and simmer for about 45 minutes, or until the meat is tender. Set aside to cool.

Preheat the oven to 400°F (200°C).

Spoon the meat into four individual baking dishes or one large one.

If using individual dishes, divide the puff pastry into four equal parts and roll out each part to form a round just large enough to fit over the top of a baking dish. If using one large baking dish, roll out the puff pastry to form a round just large enough to fit over its top. Gently lay to pastry over the top of each baking dish. Decorate the pastry with any trimmings, if you like. Make a small hole in the middle of the pastry to allow steam to escape, then brush the beaten egg over the top.

Bake the pies or pie for 20 minutes, then reduce the oven temperature to 350°F (175°C) and bake for 30 minutes more, or until the pastry has risen and turned golden brown.

A Gosling's Christmas in Wales

One of the more curious and daunting-sounding traditional Welsh dishes is goose blood tart, a specialty of Montgomeryshire in central Wales. While goose in rural Britain is strongly identified with Michaelmas, September 29 (see page 98), the bird, fattened between that date and the year-end holidays, was the usual main course at Christmas dinner. A large number of geese were thus always slaughtered around that time of year, and a tart flavored with their blood became associated with the Christmas menu.

The Welsh historian of domestic culture S. Minwel Tibbott writes in her book *Welsh Fare* that "there is no evidence to show that it was prepared in any other county in Wales" beyond Montgomeryshire—though a contributor to an online discussion of the dish remembered a neighbor in Porthmadog, in the county of Gwynedd, northwest of that region, talking about it as having been a dish served at sheep-shearing time there. (This would have been considerably earlier in the year than Christmastime.) Apparently, the practice died out after World War II when sheep-shearing became a mechanized process and the task lost its aspect of social collaboration.

The recipe for goose blood pudding—*cacen waed gwyddau* in Welsh—that Tibbott offers, from the Montgomeryshire village of Trefeglwys, calls for the "blood from a number of geese" as well as currants, brown sugar, shredded suet, salt and spices, and "four wooden spoonfuls golden syrup," baked in a short-crust pastry with both top and bottom crusts.

The Welsh food writer and former restaurateur Bobby Freeman, in her book *First Catch Your Peacock*, observes that the blood is used in this recipe "in exactly the same way as beef once was for mincemeat." Both the meat in mincemeat and the blood in this tart "all but disappear" in the cooking, she adds. The goose blood tart itself has all but disappeared from Wales, according to most sources. It is certainly no longer traditional at Christmastime, and if there's some nose-to-tail Welsh restaurant reproducing it, I haven't found it. Early in 2014, however, the American-born, Welsh-based food writer Annie Levy wrote an account on her *Kitchen Counter Culture* blog of making the tart by following instructions found on the National Museum Wales website (museumwales.ac.uk). Getting the goose blood wasn't easy, but a friend with a small farm eventually supplied her with the blood of two birds. She followed the recipe as closely as possible, but using her cook's instincts to improvise where she thought it necessary (she added a bit of flour and a bit of butter, and substituted raisins for currants). The result, she reports, was "custardy, spicy, smooth and very chocolatey." Goose blood tart, she decided, was "truly—and not in any bizarre or challenging way—truly delicious."

STEAK *and* KIDNEY PUDDING

SERVES 6

As long ago as 1899, the man-about-London Lieutenant Colonel Newnham-Davis was able to describe Simpson's in the Strand—the onetime coffee house and chess club turned traditional English dining room, next to the Savoy—as an "old-fashioned eating-place." (He reports dining there with an old friend who had fallen upon hard times; the two, with another friend of Newnham-Davis's, dispatched turbot in sauce, fried sole, stewed eels, whitebait, salmon, and cheese and celery, washed down with Liebfraumilch.) Dickens, Shaw, Disraeli, and Sir Arthur Conan Doyle (and Sherlock Holmes) were among the habitués of this institution, whose origins date to 1828. The main dining room, called the Grand Divan, looks more like an old-style library or turn-of-the-last-century boardroom than a restaurant—or would, if it weren't for the formally dressed waitstaff and the antique silver-domed gueridons that ply the room.

The food at Simpson's is mostly traditional British (the occasional baked goat's cheese or monkfish with pancetta aside), but the specialties have long been aged roast beef, roast lamb saddle, and both steak and kidney pie and steak and kidney pudding—the primary difference between the two being that the former is baked, the latter is steamed. Simpson's is not a place I've been to often (it's nearly impossible to entice any of my food-savvy British friends to accompany me there), but I do appreciate their continued commitment to the old ways, and I do like that pudding. The restaurant was kind enough to share the recipe with me, and I've adapted it only slightly here.

There's no guarantee that the restaurant will continue in the same vein, unfortunately. As I write this, Savoy Hotels, which owns the lease on the property (Simpson's, like the Savoy itself, is now managed by the Fairmont Hotels and Resorts group), is looking for a new operator—perhaps a celebrity chef of some description. Whoever takes it over, apparently, would be free to rename Simpson's, or to keep the name and expand the brand.

You'll need a pudding bowl or steaming basin for this recipe.

4 tablespoons (½ stick / 55 g) butter, plus more for greasing
2 pounds (900 grams) lean chuck steak, cut into 1-inch (2.5-cm) cubes
½ pound (225 grams) beef kidney, cut into 1-inch (2.5-cm) cubes
1 large onion, chopped
¾ pound (350 g) portobello mushrooms, halved and sliced
4 tablespoons (30 g) all-purpose flour
1 cup (240 ml) good-quality English ale
1 cup (240 ml) veal or beef stock, store-bought or homemade (page 314)
2 tablespoons Worcestershire sauce
Bouquet garni (2 sprigs parsley, 2 sprigs thyme, and 1 bay leaf, wrapped and tied in cheesecloth)
Salt and freshly ground black pepper
2⅓ cups (290 g) self-rising flour, plus more for dusting
1 teaspoon baking powder
6 ounces (175 g) suet (see Sources, page 316), shredded, or chilled lard, chopped into very small pieces
2 tablespoons chopped fresh parsley
Ice water

Melt the butter in a Dutch oven or large skillet over medium-high heat and cook the steak and kidney pieces, in batches if necessary, stirring frequently, for 4 to 5 minutes or until browned on all sides. Stir in the onion and mushrooms, lower the heat to medium, and cook for 4 to 5 minutes more. Sprinkle the all-purpose flour over the mixture, stir it in well, and cook for 2 minutes more.

Add the ale, stock, Worcestershire sauce, and bouquet garni, then season generously with salt and pepper. Bring the liquid to a boil over high heat, then reduce the heat to low, cover the Dutch oven or skillet, and cook for 1½ hours, or until the meats are very tender.

Set the mixture aside to cool, removing and discarding the bouquet garni.

Meanwhile, sift the self-rising flour and baking powder together in a large bowl and season with 1 teaspoon salt. Add the suet and parsley and mix into the flour well with your hands until the consistency resembles that of coarse bread crumbs. Stir in enough ice water (¾ to 1¼

recipe continues

cups) to form a soft dough. Cover the dough and let it rest for 30 minutes.

Lightly grease a 3-pint (1.3-L) pudding basin with butter. Turn out the dough onto a floured work surface and form it into a ball. Knead the dough lightly, then roll out about 80 percent (four-fifths) of it into a disk about half an inch (1.25 cm) thick. Drape the dough loosely over the rolling pin, then unroll it over the pudding basin. Push and pat it down into the bowl, letting about ¾ of an inch (2 cm) hang over the edge.

Fill the dough-lined pudding bowl with the cooled meat mixture. Roll the remaining pastry out on a floured work surface into a disk just large enough to fit into the pudding bowl, completely covering the venison. Dampen the dough with cold water and set it down into the bowl, then fold the overhanging pastry over it to seal it and pat the pastry down gently.

Bring a large pot of water to a boil over high heat.

Cover the pudding bowl with a double layer of greased aluminum foil or parchment paper, pleating it in the middle (as the pudding will rise). Tie kitchen twine securely about the bottom of the basin and knot it on the top, so that you can easily lift the basin out of the water it steams in.

Put the bowl into a stockpot or other large, deep pot or roasting pan and pour the boiling water around it to a height of about 1½ inches (4 cm). Cover the pot and steam the pudding over low heat for 2 hours, checking the water level periodically and keeping it constant.

Carefully lift the pudding basin out of the pot, remove the string and foil or parchment, and let it rest for 10 minutes. To serve, either spoon it directly out of the basin or shake the pudding out gently onto a warmed serving platter. Present the whole pudding at the table, then portion out six servings with a large serving spoon.

STEAMED VENISON PUDDING

SERVES 6

Chef Ross Horrocks, who, with his wife, Lynne, owns an excellent restaurant called The Caddy Mann in the Scottish Borders, serves this extraordinary old-style steamed pudding as part of his menu of hearty, meaty fare (see his recipe for eighteen-hour slow-baked shoulder of lamb on page 136). He likes to make it with venison from local roe deer, rather than the considerably larger Highland red deer. He finds the meat milder and sweeter—"far superior." Americans can't get either kind, but free-range farmed axis deer venison from Texas works well in this dish, as does farmed New Zealand venison, and both are readily available in the United States. Anyway, as Horrocks says, "Any meat can be used for this pudding, from beef to reindeer!" You'll need a pudding bowl or steaming basin for this recipe.

2 tablespoons extra-virgin olive oil
4 tablespoons (½ stick / 55g) butter, plus more
    for greasing
2 carrots, halved
2 onions, quartered lengthwise
3 stalks celery
1 clove garlic, crushed
5 tablespoons (35 g) all-purpose flour
Salt and freshly ground black pepper
2 pounds (900 g) boneless leg or shoulder of
    venison (see Sources, page 316), cut into large chunks
2 tablespoons red currant jelly
2 cups (480 ml) good-quality red wine
Dash of Worcestershire sauce
2 cups (480 ml) beef stock, store-bought or
    homemade (page 314)
2 sprigs rosemary
1 bay leaf
2 cups (500 g) self-rising flour, plus more
    for dusting
4 ounces (115 g) suet (see Sources, page 316), shredded, or chilled lard, chopped into very small pieces
Ice water

Preheat the oven to 325°F (160°C).

Heat half the olive oil and half the butter together in an oven-proof casserole or Dutch oven over medium heat. Add the carrots, onions, and celery and cook, stirring occasionally, for 4 to 5 minutes, or until they soften. Add the garlic and cook for another minute, then set the casserole aside.

Season the all-purpose flour generously with salt and pepper, then put it into a paper or plastic bag large enough to hold the venison with room to spare. Add the venison to the bag and shake it well to coat the meat with the flour.

Heat the remaining olive oil and butter together in a large skillet over medium-high heat. Working in batches if necessary, cook the venison for 8 to 10 minutes, stirring occasionally, until it is well browned on all sides.

Remove the venison from the skillet and add it to the casserole with the vegetables. Add the red currant jelly, wine, and Worcestershire sauce to the skillet. Increase the heat to high and deglaze the skillet, scraping up any brown bits from the bottom. Pour the contents of the skillet into the casserole with the vegetables and venison. Add the stock, rosemary, and bay leaf and bring the liquid to a boil over high heat.

Cover the casserole tightly and bake for at least 2 hours, or until the venison is very tender. When it is very tender, remove the casserole from the oven, adjust the seasoning if necessary, and set it aside to cool. Increase the oven temperature to 350°F (175°C).

When the casserole is cool, remove the carrots, onions, celery, rosemary, and bay leaf and discard them.

While the casserole is cooling, combine the self-rising flour and the suet in a large bowl and mix them together well with your hands until the consistency resembles that of coarse bread crumbs. Stir in enough ice water (about ½ cup / 120 ml) to form a soft dough.

Grease the bottom and sides of a 1½-quart (1.4-L) pudding basin. Turn out the dough onto a floured work surface and form it into a ball. Knead the dough lightly, then roll out about 80 percent (four-fifths) of it into a disk about ½ inch (1.25 cm) thick. Drape the dough loosely over the rolling pin, then unroll it over the pudding basin. Push and pat it down into the bowl, letting about ¾ inch (2 cm) hang over the edge.

Bring a kettle full of water to a boil over high heat.

Fill the dough-lined pudding bowl with the cooled venison and sauce from the casserole, reserving about 1 cup of the sauce. Roll out the remaining pastry on a floured work surface to a disk just large enough to fit into the pudding bowl, completely covering the venison. Dampen it with cold water and set it down into the bowl, then fold the overhanging pastry over to seal it and gently pat down the pastry.

Cover the pudding bowl with parchment paper and two layers of aluminum foil crimped tightly around the edges of the bowl to form a seal. Put the bowl into a deep roasting pan and pour boiling water from the kettle around the bowl to a depth of about 1½ inches (4 cm). Bake the pudding for 1½ hours.

When the pudding is almost done, warm the reserved sauce in a small saucepan over medium heat.

Uncover the pudding and shake it out gently onto a warmed serving platter. Present the whole pudding at the table, then portion out six servings with a large serving spoon. Serve the warmed sauce on the side.

CHAPTER 8

VEGETABLES

———

"AS TO THE QUALITY OF VEGETABLES, THE MIDDLE SIZE ARE PREFERABLE TO THE LARGEST OR THE SMALLEST; THEY ARE MORE TENDER, JUICY, AND FULL OF FLAVOUR, JUST BEFORE THEY ARE QUITE FULL-GROWN: FRESHNESS IS THEIR CHIEF VALUE AND EXCELLENCE."

—ROBERT KEMP PHILP, *Enquire Within Upon Everything* (1856)

———

"GOOD VEGETABLES ARE (OR SHOULD BE) AT THE HEART OF EVERY KITCHEN AND IT IS IMPORTANT TO REMEMBER THE GENERALLY ACCEPTED ADVICE TO EAT 'FIVE PORTIONS A DAY.'"

—J. C. JEREMY HOBSON AND PHILIP WATTS, *The New Country Cook* (2009)

For decades, if not longer, the most common libel against British cooking was that "they boil their vegetables to death," or some variation thereon. Vegetables in Great Britain were soggy and flavorless, an insult to the fields that grew them. Any life—any flavor—they may have had dissolved in the cooking pot. Variety was lacking, too, as suggested by an old wisecrack of indeterminate origin that "The British have three vegetables and two of them are cabbage." The authors of *The Gentle Art of Cookery*, early in the twentieth century, proposed that "the repugnance of many English children for green vegetables is explained by the dishes of stringy, watery, tasteless, tough green leaves that were sent up for the nursery dinner, a relic of the Victorian days when . . . butter was regarded as a superfluous luxury for children."

And yet a cornucopia of vegetables has long been grown around the nation, and especially in parts of England and in southern Wales where a milder climate proved hospitable to a wider range of plants than would thrive in Scotland and northern Britain. (The nineteenth-century American writer and Cambrophile Wirt Sikes recorded that "Welsh market-women deal in everything salable, from toys to butcher's meat, but most often their line is vegetarian.")

The earliest Britons were hunter-gatherers, but more the latter than the former; historian Colin Spencer estimates that about 85 percent of the prehistoric British diet was made up of plants. The Romans and later the Normans cultivated all manner of new vegetables in Britain, and there are many medieval British recipes built around beans, field peas (dried and reconstituted, like the

An Englishwoman buying vegetables—but not potatoes—during World War II shortages, 1941

marrowfat peas eaten "mushy" with fish and chips or the black or parched peas of Lancashire), lentils (also considered good fodder for animals), squash, celery, cucumbers, onions, turnips, carrots, fennel, salad greens, and more. Spinach was eaten by itself but also added to soups for color. It might surprise some to learn that the British have also long been fond of garlic; garlic-sellers worked the streets of London and Oxford as early as the thirteenth century, and Glastonbury Abbey was said to use eighty thousand garlic bulbs a year.

Onions stewed in cream and butter were once a favored supper dish in Scotland, and were thought to have medicinal value as well. The onion's thick-stemmed relation, the leek, became the emblematic vegetable of Wales—either, tradition holds, as a tribute to the country's patron, Saint David, who once fasted on nothing but leeks, or because the soldiers of seventh-century King Cadwallon ap Cadfan affixed leeks to their helmets to identify themselves when they battled the Saxons in a leek field. (Another symbol of Wales is the daffodil, which Welsh author Gilli Davies says was eaten by the Romans in Wales "as a stimulating pudding with beaten green figs"; today it is thought to be poisonous, so much so that the government warns supermarkets not to display the flower or its bulbs near edible produce.)

The potato seems not to have reached Britain until fifty years or so after the Irish first planted it. John Evelyn, in his *Acetaria: A Discourse of Sallets* (1699), describes the tuber as a "small green Fruit" and advises roasting it in the embers of a fire, cutting it open, buttering it, and seasoning it with salt and pepper (though he also notes that "Some eat them with Sugar together in the Skin . . ."). The earliest mention of potatoes in Scotland comes two years later, in the Duchess of Buccleuch's household accounts, which mention a peck of them brought over from Ireland.

Wild mushrooms abound in Britain, including the cep, the chanterelle, and the questionably edible shaggy milk cap (*Lactarius torminosus*), as well the common field mushroom, but until cultivated button mushrooms became an essential part of the full English breakfast (see page 36) in the mid-twentieth century, they didn't figure substantially in the British diet. Mrs. Raffald, writing in 1769, reported that there were said to be nearly five hundred kinds of mushrooms in England alone, but "there are not ten sorts ascertained to be fit for human food." She recommends eating only cultivated ones, though the flavor is inferior, as "so many fatal accidents happen every season from the use of poisonous mushrooms. . . ."

Fear of being poisoned may have accounted for the notion that vegetables needed to be cooked for forty minutes or an hour, too. The scientific consensus in Britain in the nineteenth century, like the folk wisdom of the Middle Ages, seemed to be that raw vegetables were poisonous and that boiling them well lessened any risk of illness. (This may have been true, in fact, in the days before good practices of hygiene and sanitation were understood.)

On my early trips to London in the 1960s and '70s, I don't think I ever encountered a firm or crisp vegetable outside of salads. I remember honey-glazed carrots that disintegrated when they met a fork, and hunks of turnip that oozed water as they sat on the plate. By the 1980s, though, things had changed. Chefs like Simon Hopkinson at Bibendum, Sally Clarke at Clarke's, Prue Leith at Leith's, Alastair Little at the restaurant of the same name, Rowley Leigh at Kensington Place, and Ruth Rogers and Rose Gray at The River Café—their inspirations variously French, Californian, Italian—were serving bright, vivid-tasting vegetables, mostly U.K.-grown, that still had flavor and texture.

Today, at least in better restaurants, vegetables are treated with considerably more respect than they used to be. There are some vegetable dishes that *need* to be cooked long, of course; nobody wants firm baked beans or fibrous rutabagas.

The Noncarnivorous Briton

Great Britain—that bastion of roast beef—has a long vegetarian tradition. Perhaps this is precisely because meat eating has always been so prevalent; I know a prominent vegetarian cookbook writer who claims that she gave up meat only because her arriviste father insisted on crowding every dinner table with roasts and steaks.

Even before the founding of the Vegetarian Society in Cheshire in 1847, the country was known as one of the most hospitable in Europe for those who eschewed meat. Percy Bysshe Shelley was a vegetarian, as was his wife, Mary (author of *Frankenstein*); George Bernard Shaw was one, too, often fulminating about the immorality of eating meat. One prominent vegetarian, Sir W. E. Cooper, in a pamphlet called *Is Meat-Eating Sanctioned by Divine Authority?* wrote that "Man is not of the order of carnivorous animals, and no amount of sophisticated jugglery can prove him to be so." Even the nonvegetarian novelist and critic Ford Madox Ford proposed in his book *Provence* that "If you eat too much bleeding beef you become eventually ashamed of yourself." (In the same book, though, he wrote that he had always found it curious "that the four fiercest of all animals—the bull, the stallion that is more terrible than the bull, the rhinoceros that is a charging castle, and M. Hitler—should all be vegetarians.")

Vegetarianism is more prevalent in the north and south of Great Britain than in the middle of the country, and twice as many women as men follow a vegetarian diet, or claim to. An estimated one in eight British adults, it has been computed, is vegetarian or vegan today. But, as a book called the *Cultural Encyclopedia of Vegetarianism* notes, in contemporary Britain "the idea of calling oneself a vegetarian is attractive and confers some form of imagined status or interest to one's personal identity . . ." but also that "there is a weak relationship between the act of calling oneself a vegetarian and the more difficult task of actually living a vegetarian life."

BEETROOT AND A SOFT-BOILED EGG

SERVES 4

This is, as chef Jeremy Lee of Quo Vadis in London says, "a cheery salad" and seeking out a farmer or vegetable purveyor who grows or sells a wide variety of beets is worth the trouble, he adds, "to jolly up this salad even more." (I've always liked the sound of the word *beetroot*—but of course it's just the synonym in the U.K. for *beet*.)

2¾ pounds (1.25 kg) small beets, preferably of assorted colors, trimmed and washed
⅔ cup (135 g) plus 1¼ tablespoons sugar
⅔ cup (165 ml) good-quality red wine vinegar
4 large eggs
1⅓ tablespoons white wine vinegar
1⅓ teaspoons Dijon mustard
¼ cup (60 ml) heavy cream
1 fresh horseradish root, about 6 inches (15 cm) long
3 to 4 cups loosely packed baby spinach and other small salad greens
2 ripe medium tomatoes, each cut into 8 segments
8 to 10 fresh chives, finely chopped

Bring about 3 inches (7.5 cm) of water to a boil in a large pot with a steamer basket and lid over high heat. Arrange the beets in a single layer in the basket. Reduce the heat to low and steam the beets until very tender, 45 minutes to 1 hour, depending on the size of the beets. When the beets are cooked, transfer them to a large bowl, let them cool to room temperature, then rub or peel off the skins. Cut the beets into large pieces of about the same size, then set them aside in a bowl big enough to hold them comfortably.

In a small bowl, whisk ⅔ cup (135 g) of the sugar into the red wine vinegar until it is well dissolved. Stir in 1 cup (240 ml) water, then pour the mixture over the beets, cover the bowl with plastic wrap, and refrigerate.

Bring a pot of water to a rolling boil over high heat. Add the eggs, return the water to a boil, then cook for 3 minutes. Transfer the eggs carefully with a slotted spoon to a bowl of ice water. When they're cool enough to handle, carefully peel them, then transfer them to another bowl of ice water and set them aside.

Dissolve the remaining sugar in the white wine vinegar in a small bowl, then stir in the mustard, followed by the cream. Refrigerate the dressing.

Peel the horseradish and cover it with a clean kitchen towel.

Divide the salad leaves evenly between four plates, then arrange the tomato segments and the lightly pickled beets under and around them. Halve the eggs and lay two halves on each plate. Season them lightly with salt and pepper. Spoon the dressing over the salads, including the eggs, then quickly grate the horseradish over the salads, dividing it evenly between them. Scatter the chives evenly over the salads.

*Braised Peas with Lettuce,
Spring Onions, and Mint*

BRAISED PEAS WITH LETTUCE, SPRING ONIONS, AND MINT

SERVES 4

"Green peas," wrote Robert Kemp Philp in the mid-nineteenth century in his anonymously published *Enquire Within Upon Everything*, "unless sent to us from warmer latitudes than our own, are seldom worth eating before Midsummer." These days, however, peas are considered a quintessential springtime treat in Great Britain and this is one way they are enjoyed. This preparation is French in origin, but has been popular in England, especially, for at least a century.

1 cup (240 ml) chicken stock, store-bought or
    homemade (page 314)
2 tablespoons (30 g) butter
6 scallions, finely chopped
6 to 8 large leaves romaine lettuce, cut into ribbons
2½ cups shelled fresh peas (about 2 pounds / 900 g
    in the pod)
Juice of ½ large lemon
Leaves from 6 to 8 sprigs mint, cut into chiffonade
Salt and freshly ground black pepper

Bring the stock to a boil in a large saucepan over high heat. Stir in the butter until it melts. Reduce the heat to medium-low and add the scallions, lettuce, and peas.

Cover the saucepan and cook for 5 to 6 minutes, or until the peas are just tender.

Stir in the lemon juice and mint and season with salt and pepper.

BUTTERED CARROTS

SERVES 4

The carrot, whose wild ancestors probably came from ancient Persia, was first cultivated in Asia Minor around AD 900, but wasn't grown in any quantity in Britain until the early 1500s. Even then, it wasn't the vivid orange root vegetable we know today. The earliest carrots were purple or yellow, and later varieties emerged from the soil in red or white. The orange carrot seems to have been developed in the Netherlands in the mid-seventeenth century. Somewhat earlier than that, though, Queen Elizabeth I, who reigned from 1558 to 1603, became a big fan of the carrot—so much so that, according to one tale, a Dutch admirer once presented her with a wreath of young carrots studded with diamonds, with a pot of butter in the middle. She is said to have removed the diamonds, then sent the carrots and butter to the royal kitchen. Her chef cooked the former in the latter, returning the combination to her as buttered carrots.

1 pound (450 g) carrots, cut into batons about 3
    inches (7.5 cm) long and ½ inch (1.25 cm) wide
4 tablespoons (½ stick / 55 g) butter
Pinch of sugar
Salt

Put the carrots, butter, sugar, and salt to taste in a medium skillet with a lid. Add about ½ cup (120 ml) water. Cover the pan, bring the water to a boil over high heat, then uncover, reduce the heat to low, and cook for 6 to 8 minutes, or until the water has evaporated. Shake the skillet to make sure the butter glazes all the carrots.

Vegetarian London

In *Dinners and Diners* (1899), the retired army officer, author, and man-about-town Lieutenant Colonel Newnham-Davis writes that he resolved one day to dine in a vegetarian restaurant—not at all his usual sort of thing—because "Whenever I come across a Philistine who has eaten a vegetarian dinner, he always professes that he narrowly escaped with his life," and he is curious to see if the experience can be as bad as all that. He plans to have dinner at one such establishment, St. George's Café in St. Martin's Lane.

That afternoon, Newnham-Davis is part of a committee meeting to discuss a benefit theatrical performance and takes advantage of the occasion to ask his fellow committee members if one would like to join him for dinner that evening.

> One man had to go to a Masonic banquet; another was dining at a farewell feast to a coming Benedick [a man about to get married]; another had promised his dear old aunt to spend the evening with her . . . I went on to my Service club and found there a subaltern who, in old days, had been in my company, and who would have followed me, or preceded me, into any danger of battle without the tremble of an eyelid. Him I urged to come with me,

> telling him that a man can only die once, and other such inspiriting phrases, and had nearly persuaded him when old General Bundobust joined in the conversation and told how Joe Buggins, of the Madras Fusiliers, once ate a vegetarian dinner and swelled up afterwards till he was as big as a balloon. That finished the subaltern, and he refused to go.

Our intrepid culinary explorer goes on alone. His menu for the evening includes hors d'oeuvres (in fact a small plate of olives), carrot soup, flageolets with cream and spinach, a fried duck's egg with green peas, a mixed salad (he refuses the proffered stewed fruit), and a slice of Gruyère. The soup, he notes, "was quite hot and was satisfying." He only gets halfway through the spinach ("not up to club form") and flageolets (which "did not look inviting"), but enjoys the well-fried duck's egg, though the peas are "a trifle hard." The wine list offers not the Rhine wines or clarets he was used to, but a choice of "orange wine, rich raisin wine, ginger wine, black currant wine, red currant wine, raspberry wine, elderberry wine." Newnham-Davis settles for ginger beer, and writes that he left the place feeling "rather empty" but that Joe Buggins's fate was not his.

BAKED BEANS

SERVES 4 (AS A SUPPER DISH) TO 8 (AS PART
OF A FULL ENGLISH BREAKFAST)

Baked beans, which are navy beans (usually) long-cooked in a sweetened tomato sauce, are an essential part of the full English breakfast—a pork-heavy meal enjoyed, with regional variations, all over the U.K. (see page 36)—and are also eaten as a lunch or supper dish, spooned over toast. The beans are nearly always out of a can, and probably Heinz brand, even in upscale cafés and hotel dining rooms. Beans prepared in this manner are apparently American in origin (the famous Boston baked beans are an antecedent), and cans were first imported into the U.K. in the 1880s, as something of a delicacy, by Fortnum & Mason. There's nothing wrong with canned baked beans, and indeed they have a "comfort food" quality that many find irresistible, but such beans are also easy enough to make at home and I think taste much better to those whose palates aren't affected by nostalgia.

1 pound (450 g) dried navy beans or other small
    white or brown beans, washed and picked over
1 small onion, finely chopped
½ cup dark brown sugar
⅓ cup (80 ml) blackstrap molasses or treacle
1 teaspoon Worcestershire sauce
2 tablespoons apple cider vinegar
2 cups chopped canned tomatoes, with their juices
½ teaspoon dry mustard
Salt

Put the beans in a large bowl and cover them with water to twice their height. Soak for at least 8 hours, or overnight.

Drain the beans and put them in a large pot with enough water to cover by about 2 inches (5 cm). Bring the water to a boil over high heat, then reduce the heat to low and simmer, adding more water if necessary to keep the beans just covered, for 1 to 1½ hours, or until the beans are soft but not beginning to split.

Strain the beans, reserving the cooking water, then set both the cooking water and the beans aside.

Preheat the oven to 275°F (135°C).

Put the beans, onion, sugar, molasses, Worcestershire sauce, vinegar, tomatoes, mustard, and several generous pinches of salt into a bean pot or deep baking dish. Add the reserved bean cooking water and a little more water, if necessary, to just cover the beans. Bake, uncovered, for 4 to 5 hours. The top should get brown and crusty, but if it starts to get too dark, cover the pot with a lid or aluminum foil.

BROWN BEANS with DATES, ONIONS, AND ANCHOVIES

SERVES 4 TO 6

I'm pretty sure that the first really good London-English—as opposed to Indian, French, or suchlike—restaurant I ever dined in was Chanterelle on the Old Brompton Road. It was a cozy, woody bistro in a freestanding little brick building with cathedral windows; Terence Conran did the decor "with his inimitable lack of decorator's chi-chi," as Robin McDouall put it in his 1969 restaurant guide *The Gourmet's London*. I used to stay at Blakes Hotel, just around the corner, and I'd wander into Chanterelle in the evening sometimes, alone, and order something adventurous—scallops in sea urchin sauce, calf's liver—and a few glasses of wine, and feel very sophisticated. Chanterelle, I later learned, had been opened in 1953 by Walter Baxter, a somewhat notorious author who had published two controversial novels, one dealing with a sexual relationship between two English soldiers in Asia during World War II, the other about a sexually active widow who takes a lover in India. He retired from the restaurant in 1978, which must have been just about when I first encountered the place (Blakes opened that year), and his longtime romantic partner, chef Fergus Provan, took over and ran it for a few years more.

Since it closed, the site has hosted a number of other places, including Shaw's, Lundum's, and Ambassade, and is now occupied by a Japanese "head to tail" fish restaurant called Yashin Ocean House. One dish I don't remember ever seeing at Chanterelle is an appetizer Robin McDouall mentions of brown beans, dates, onions, and anchovies, a very curious combination—McDouall calls it "delicious!"—that sounded so intriguing, I had to try to reproduce it. I have no idea if my end result is anything like what the restaurant served, but I thought it was pretty good, and am including it here as a small homage to the London restaurant scene of almost forty years ago. Serve as an appetizer or a side dish with simply grilled or roasted pork or chicken.

8 ounces (450 g) dried pinto beans
½ small red onion, very finely chopped
6 to 8 Medjool dates, stoned and finely chopped
6 to 8 anchovy fillets, chopped
Salt and freshly ground black pepper
Juice of ½ lemon
2 tablespoons (30 ml) extra-virgin olive oil

Pick any stones out of the beans, rinse them well, then put them into a large bowl and cover them with at least 4 inches (10 cm) of water. Let the beans soak overnight.

Drain the beans and rinse them again, then put them into a large pot and again cover them with at least 4 inches (10 cm) of water. Cover the pot and bring the water to a boil over high heat, then reduce the heat to low and simmer, partially covered, until the beans are very tender but not disintegrating. This may take anywhere from 1 to 2½ hours, depending on the age of the beans; sample them for texture every 15 minutes after the first hour.

Drain the beans and put them into a large salad bowl. Stir in the onion, dates, and anchovies, mixing the ingredients together well. Season lightly with salt and generously with black pepper, then stir in the lemon juice and olive oil. Serve at room temperature.

MUSHY PEAS

SERVES 4

Mushy peas are an almost canonical accompaniment to fish and chips (page 67), and are also frequently served alongside various kinds of meat pies (see chapter 7). Marrowfat peas are conventional large green peas harvested late, after they've dried out in the fields. Some cooks today make this dish with fresh peas, but that's like making salade niçoise with fresh tuna—a needless refinement that alters the basic nature of the dish.

8 ounces (225 g) marrowfat peas (see Sources, page 316), soaked overnight
2 tablespoons (30 g) butter
Pinch of sugar
Salt and freshly ground black pepper

Drain the peas and put them in a large saucepan with a lid. Add enough water to come about 2 inches (5 cm) above them. Bring the water to a boil over high heat, then reduce the heat to low, cover the pan loosely, and simmer, stirring occasionally, for 1½ to 2 hours, or until the peas are very soft. (If the peas begin to dry out, add enough water to just cover them and continue cooking.)

Drain the peas, then return them to the saucepan. Add the butter and stir the peas until it has melted completely, then stir in the sugar and season the peas generously with salt and pepper. Mash them with a wooden spoon into a coarse puree.

PEASE PUDDING

SERVES 4 TO 6

Pease pudding, a popular traditional dish in northern England, is neither a dessert pudding nor a steamed savory one. It is perhaps better described as "pease porridge" (as in the nursery rhyme that starts "Pease porridge hot, pease porridge cold, / Pease porridge in the pot, nine days old") or "pease pottage." *Pease*, derived from the Latin word for the vegetable, *pisum*, was originally a collective noun, first used in English as early as the fifteenth century. The *Oxford English Dictionary* finds the first reference to "pease pudding" in 1725. Surprisingly similar to the Greek dish *fava* (made from yellow split peas like this pudding, and not from fava beans), it is often served with pork, and is considered a particularly appropriate accompaniment to roast ham.

1 pound (450 g) split yellow peas
1 ham hock (approximately 1 pound / 450 g)
1 small onion, coarsely chopped
1 small potato, peeled and coarsely chopped
Pinch ground nutmeg
2 tablespoons (30 g) butter
Salt and freshly ground black pepper

Put the peas into a large bowl and cover them with at least 4 inches (10 cm) of water. Let the peas soak overnight.

Drain the peas and put them into a large pot. Add the ham hock, onion, and potato, and cover everything with at least 4 inches (10 cm) of water. Cover the pot and bring the water to a boil over high heat, then uncover the pot, reduce the heat to low, and simmer the peas for about 1 hour, or until most of the liquid has cooked off.

Stir in the nutmeg and butter and season generously with salt and pepper.

Transfer the ingredients to a large bowl and mash them together into a coarse puree with a fork or potato masher.

DRESSED KALE

SERVES 4

It's amusing to wonder what the Scots of an earlier time would have made of the kale mania that has swept the United States in recent years. This slightly bitter, leafy relative of cabbage was one of the most important vegetables in medieval Britain, but in Scotland most of all. In the eighteenth century, Dr. Johnson reported that he was told in Aberdeen "that the people learned from Cromwell's soldiers to make shoes and to plant kail. How they lived without kail, it is not easy to guess. They cultivate hardly any other plant for common tables; and when they had not kail, they probably had nothing." Having a "gude kail yaird" was as vital to the Scottish cotter, or peasant farmer, as a potato patch was to his Irish counterpart. The word *kail* came to signify dinner as a whole ("Will you tak' your kail wi' me?") and the kitchen garden, even if it grew other crops, was called the kailyard. There was even a Kailyard School of fiction in the 1890s—J. M. Barrie of *Peter Pan* fame was a member—specializing in tales that chronicled the difficulties of Scottish rural life.

Kale was a food of Lowland Scotland, though. The Highlanders were great meat eaters (they were sometimes said to consume animal flesh raw and dripping blood), and when they ate greens, it was more likely to be wild nettles than cultivated kale. Highlanders considered the consumption of kale to be a sign of effeminacy, in fact. The Grant clan was apparently particularly fond of the vegetable, and Highlanders were known to denounce them as "soft kail-eating Grants."

The typical Scottish ways of eating kale are in soup or mixed with mashed potatoes (a variation on Rumbledethumps, page 212), but this side dish goes well with haggis (alongside tatties and neeps; page 211) or any kind of simply cooked meat or poultry.

4 tablespoons (½ stick / 55 g) butter
1 teaspoon vegetable oil
1½ pounds (680 g) curly kale, thoroughly rinsed
    and coarsely chopped

Herb garden of The Pig-near Bath in Somerset

½ cup (120 ml) vegetable stock, store-bought or
    homemade (page 315)
Salt and pepper
2 tablespoons red wine vinegar

Melt the butter with the olive oil in a large skillet with a lid over medium heat. Add the kale and cook, stirring frequently, for about 5 minutes, then stir in the stock, cover the skillet, and cook for 6 to 8 minutes, or until the kale is tender.

Cook, uncovered, for 2 to 3 minutes more, or until the liquid has evaporated. Season generously with salt and pepper. Remove the kale from the heat, then stir in the vinegar.

Olive Oil in London

The English naturalist Richard Bradley (1688–1732) wrote on topics ranging from garden design, plant reproduction, and animal husbandry to the development of mold in fruit, the growth rate of trees, and the value of birds in controlling the insect population on farms. He was also an early proponent of the germ theory of disease, in his study of the spread of the plague in Marseilles in 1721. Bradley was elected a fellow of the Royal Society at the age of twenty-four, and a decade later became the first professor of botany at the University of Cambridge, near which he had been born. He was also interested in food (he is said to have been the first author to publish recipes for pineapple in English), and, in the year of his death, he produced a book called *The Country Housewife and Lady's Director in the Management of a House, and the Delights and Profits of a Farm*, in which he offered both recipes and general advice about cooking and other aspects of running a household and a farm. At one point, in celebrating the foods of springtime, he offers this digression on salads, including an appreciation of a Mediterranean ingredient not generally associated with English cooking.

Sallads should yet partake of some warm Herbs, as I have directed in my New Improvement of Planting and Gardening. The Method which I most approve of for dressing a Sallad, is, after we have duly proportion'd the Herbs, to take two thirds Oil Olive, one third true Vinegar, some hard Eggs cut small, both the Whites and Yolks, a little Salt and some Mustard, all which must be well mix'd and pour'd over the Sallad, having first cut the large Herbs, such as Sallery, Endive, or Cabbage-Lettuce, but none of the small ones: then mix all these well together, that it may be ready just when you want to use it, for the Oil will make it presently soften, and lose its briskness. Onions should always be kept in reserve, because it is not every one that like their relish, nor is Oil agreeable to every one; but where Oil is not liked, the Yolks of hard Eggs, bruis'd and mix'd with the Vinegar, may be used as above. The difficulty of getting good Oil in England, is, I suppose, the reason why every one does not admire it; for I was once of opinion I could never like it: but when I was once persuaded to taste such as was of the best sort, I could never after like a Sallad without it. The best Oil that I have met with in England, is at Mr. Crosse's, a Genouese Merchant, at the Genouese Arms in Katherine-Street, in the Strand, London.

The Welshman's Caviar

Any country with a long seacoast has access to a lot of seaweed, and Great Britain is no exception. Some seven hundred varieties are said to slosh around off the shores of England, Scotland, and Wales, the vast majority of them edible—though with one exception they have never been much eaten here. So-called Irish moss, or carrageen (*Chondrus crispus*), is common; it contains a gelatinous substance widely employed commercially as a thickener and stabilizer in products ranging from luncheon meats to ice cream—but the British have traditionally used it much less in home cooking than the Irish. Dulse (*Palmaria palmata*), which has a faintly metallic character, was some-times served as a vegetable in coastal communities, but only in recent years have cookery writers begun to acknowledge it. The young leaves of badderlocks (*Alaria esculenta*) can be eaten as a salad green, but seldom are.

The gathering and processing of kelp—a generic term for a number of species of large brown algae—became a major industry in Scotland's Outer Heb-rides in the late eighteenth and early nineteenth centuries, but it was not for gastronomic purposes. The mineral-rich seaweed was used as a fertilizer and burned to form soda ash, a source of alkali in chemical manufacturing. Though not seaweeds, rock samphire (*Crithmum maritimum*), which grows on rocks and cliffs near the sea, and marsh samphire (*Salicornia bigelovii*), which grows in salt marshes and was also burned for soda ash (a synonymn for marsh samphire is *glasswort*), are often described as "sea vegetables." On menus, "samphire" usually means rock samphire, but both plants are pickled and served as a condiment.

The one variety of seaweed that has a prominent place in culinary tradition—specifically Welsh culinary tradition—is purple laver (*Porphyra unbilicalis*). There are records of its consumption at least as early as 1607, and laver was an important source of nutrients for miners and the rural poor throughout the 1800s. Back in 1932, Florence White wrote in her book *Good Things in England* that laver was eaten in Devonshire and Somerset as well, and that "before the invasion of French chefs in 1848 it was common enough in London," but it is only in Wales that it is seen (and consumed) today.

The Welsh eat laver primarily in the form of laverbread (*bara lawr* in Welsh), which is not bread at all but a sort of gelatinous paste made by drying and then boiling it, after which it is pureed or finely chopped. It is eaten in various ways: formed into patties, rolled in oatmeal, and fried (in which form it is eaten for break-fast along with bacon and cockles); as a sauce for lamb or fish; as a spread on toast; as a flavoring and thickener for soup . . . and so on. In her book *Lamb, Leeks & Laverbread* (the title of which suggests that the substance is indeed one of the heraldic foods of Wales), Gilli Davies gives recipes, too, for laverbread and crab parcels and mussel-and-tomato tart with laverbread. Richard Burton is said to have called it "the Welshman's caviar." Having tasted laverbread once, and caviar many times, I can only say that for this reason alone I'm glad I'm not Welsh.

PICKLED RED CABBAGE

MAKES ABOUT 1 PINT (475 ML)

"*Cabbages* are thought to allay Fumes, and prevent Intoxication . . ." wrote the seventeenth-century English writer and gardener John Evelyn in his *Acetaria: A Discourse on Sallets*. Today, we'd probably be more likely to say that cabbages *cause* fumes—but that aside, in its pickled form, red cabbage is considered an essential accompaniment to Lancashire Hotpot (page 117). It goes well with other meats, too. This recipe is based on one from chef-restaurateur Mark Hix.

2 cups (480 ml) red wine vinegar
1 tablespoon pickling salt (see Sources, page 316)
    or sea salt
1 tablespoon sugar
1 tablespoon pickling spice
1 teaspoon freshly ground black pepper
1 small head red cabbage, quartered, cored, and
    very thinly sliced

Combine the vinegar, salt, sugar, pickling spice, and pepper in a nonreactive medium saucepan, then bring the mixture to a boil over high heat. Remove it from the heat and set it aside to cool.

Mix the cabbage with the pickling liquid in a nonreactive medium bowl. Cover and refrigerate overnight.

Spoon the cabbage into a sterilized 1-pint (475-ml) jar, still hot from the oven (see page 283), filling it to within 1 inch (2.5 cm) of the top. Top off the cabbage with some of the pickling liquid, filling it to about ½ inch (1.25 cm) from the top, then seal the jar. Let the cabbage rest for at least 2 weeks before eating. Pickled cabbage will last up to 3 months if stored in the refrigerator or, unopened, in a cool, dark place.

PICKLED BEETS

MAKES ABOUT 1 PINT

When the British talk about the taproot portion of the plant whose Latin name is *Beta vulgaris*, they call it *beetroot*. In the United States, it's just *beets*. The former actually makes more sense, because the leaves or greens of the vegetable are edible too, and it might on occasion be useful to distinguish between root and leaf. Whatever they're called, the plant's roots have long been pickled in many cultures. In England, they are known in that form as, among other things, the perfect condiment for the thick Liverpudlian stew called scouse (page 118). It isn't necessary to use pickling salt in this recipe, but regular sea salt may cloud the pickling liquid.

2 medium beets, scrubbed but not peeled
2 cups (480 ml) white wine vinegar
1 tablespoon pickling salt (see Sources, page 316)
    or sea salt
1 tablespoon sugar
½ teaspoon celery seed
½ teaspoon freshly ground black pepper

Preheat the oven to 400°F (200°C).

Wrap the beets tightly in aluminum foil, then roast them for 35 minutes or until tender but not too soft.

Unwrap the beets. When they're cool enough to handle, peel them and slice them very thinly. Combine the vinegar, salt, sugar, celery seed, and pepper in a medium nonreactive saucepan, then bring the mixture to a boil over high heat. Stir in the sliced beets, then remove the saucepan from the heat and set the beets aside to cool.

Spoon the beets into a sterilized 1-pint (475-ml) jar, still hot from the oven (see page 283), filling it to within 1 inch (2.5 cm) of the top. Top off the beets with some of the pickling liquid, filling the jar to about ½ inch (1.25 cm) from the top, then seal the jar. Let the beets rest for at least 2 weeks before eating. Pickled beets will last for about 2 months if stored in the refrigerator, or, unopened, in a cool, dark place.

GLAMORGAN SAUSAGES

SERVES 2 TO 4

The earliest reference anyone has been able to find to these Welsh vegetable croquettes is apparently a line by the nineteenth-century English author, translator, and traveler George Borrow in his book *Wild Wales: Its People, Language and Scenery*, vintage 1862. After spending the night at a raucous inn at "Gutter Vawr" (the Welsh mining town formerly called Y Gwter Fawr and since renamed Brynamman), he descends from his room for a morning meal. "The breakfast was delicious," he reports, "consisting of excellent tea, buttered toast, and Glamorgan sausages, which I really think are not a whit inferior to those of Epping." Interestingly, he doesn't mention that they contain no meat (Epping sausages are pork sausages flavored with assorted herbs, often cooked without casings). Glamorgan, in far southern Wales, is one of the thirteen original Welsh counties, and was once a small kingdom of its own. These sausages—which were originally a farm family's meat substitute—are said to have been named not for the county but for the cheese made from the milk of Glamorgan cattle, an old Welsh breed now almost extinct.

4 tablespoons (½ stick / 55 g) butter
1 medium leek, white part only, very thoroughly washed and very finely chopped
1 scallion, trimmed and very finely chopped
2 cups coarse bread crumbs
8 ounces (225 g) Caerphilly or Welsh cheddar, grated
Leaves from 2 to 3 sprigs fresh thyme
2 tablespoons finely chopped parsley
1 teaspoon dry mustard
Salt and freshly ground black pepper
2 large eggs, separated
1 tablespoon whole milk
¼ cup (55 g) clarified butter (page 312)
½ cup (65 g) all-purpose flour

Melt the butter in a small skillet over medium heat, then add the leek and scallion. Cook, stirring frequently, for 4 to 5 minutes, or until the vegetables are beginning to soften. Let cool to room temperature.

In a large bowl, combine the leek and scallion mixture, about three-quarters of the bread crumbs, the cheese, the thyme, the parsley, and the mustard. Season generously with salt and pepper, then stir in the egg yolks and the milk and mix the ingredients together thoroughly.

Cover the bowl with plastic wrap and refrigerate it for about 1 hour.

Shape the mixture into 8 to 12 sausage shapes, about 2 inches (5 cm) thick and 4 inches (10 cm) long.

Heat the clarified butter in a large skillet over medium heat. Sift the flour onto a plate and spread the remaining bread crumbs out on another plate. Roll each sausage in flour, dip it in the egg whites, then roll it in bread crumbs.

Fry the sausages for 8 to 10 minutes, turning them occasionally, until they are golden-brown on all sides. The sausages may be served hot or at room temperature.

CHIPS

SERVES 4

Chips in the U.K. (as in fish and chips, page 67), of course are what we call French fries in the United States (and what Americans call chips, in turn, are "crisps" across the Atlantic). Much has been written about chips, and countless "perfect" or "ultimate" or "best ever" recipes have been published. Chips are typically fried twice, but Heston Blumenthal discovered some years back that frying them three times left them crisper, without the steamy insides, and "thrice-cooked chips" are now common on menus. I appreciate all the thought and even science that various chefs and amateurs alike have put into the matter (and

recipe continues

Glamorgan Sausages

Blumenthal's chips are really pretty memorable), but ultimately, I can't help thinking that we're just talking about fried potatoes here and those probably aren't a matter that should be worried to death. This is a pretty simple way to make good chips, and that's all we're after, right?

6 medium russet potatoes (about 2 pounds /
    900 g), scrubbed and cut into strips about
    3 inches (7.5 cm) long and ¾ inch (2 cm) thick
    (peel them before slicing, if you prefer)
4 to 6 cups (960 ml to 1.4 L) sunflower or peanut
    oil, for frying
Salt
Malt vinegar, for serving

Soak the potatoes in a large bowl of cold water for 30 minutes, then rinse them in a colander and dry them very thoroughly with paper towels.

Pour the oil into a deep-fryer or large, deep, heavy-bottomed saucepan to a depth of 3 to 4 inches (7.5 to 10 cm) and heat it over high heat until it registers 350°F (175°C) on a deep-fry thermometer. Fry the potatoes in small batches for 5 to 8 minutes per batch, or until they're light brown, stirring them occasionally with a slotted spoon. Remove them with the slotted spoon as they're done and drain them on paper towels.

After you've finished the initial round of frying, heat the oil until it registers 375°F (190°C), then repeat the frying process, this time frying the potatoes for 2 to 3 minutes per batch, or until they're golden brown, stirring them occasionally with a slotted spoon. Remove them with the slotted spoon as they're done and drain them again on paper towels.

Salt the chips generously and sprinkle them lightly with malt vinegar.

GAME CHIPS

SERVES 2 TO 4

Why and when the British first conceived of serving thin fried potato rounds with game birds is not recorded, as far as I can tell (the *Oxford English Dictionary*'s oldest citation of the usage dates back only to 1921), but they have long been considered an essential accompaniment for roast grouse and other wild fowl. (Curiously, the name is an exception to the usual British terminology; it seems as though these ought to be called "game crisps.")

1 very large or 2 medium russet potatoes,
    unpeeled, scrubbed well
Salt
4 to 5 cups (960 ml to 1.2 L) vegetable oil,
    for frying

Cut a small slice from each end of the potato to remove the rounded ends.

Put 4 to 5 cups (960 ml to 1.2 L) water into a large bowl and stir in about 2 teaspoons of salt. Using a mandoline or slicer, cut the potatoes into slices about 1⁄16 inch (2 mm) thick, then add them to the water.

Heat the oil in a deep-fryer or deep, heavy-bottomed pan until it registers 375°F (190°C) on a deep-fry thermometer.

Drain the potatoes, rinse them thoroughly with cold water, and dry them very thoroughly with paper towels.

Working in batches, fry the potatoes for about 2 minutes per batch, or until they're golden brown. Drain them on paper towels and season them lightly with salt as they're done.

He Just Did It

The Ubiquitous Chip opened in Glasgow in 1971, the same year that Chez Panisse opened in Berkeley. In its own way, it was every bit as revolutionary; the difference was that this gritty Scottish city wasn't fertile ground for culinary upheaval in the way that that Northern California university town was, and the Chip's influence was thus milder and took far longer to percolate down to other restaurants.

The man behind the Chip was Glasgow-born Ronnie Clydesdale. He had spent the 1960s working in the whisky trade, for Long John Distilleries, which bottled such prestigious single malts as Ardbeg and Laphroaig from Islay as well as its own blended scotch. "Working in that industry," Clydesdale told me years ago, "I dined out a lot, and I loved it. You know . . . callow youth . . . flambéed cooking . . . prawns wrapped in smoked salmon . . . isn't this wonderful? Then there was a crisis in the company and I was offered a promotion that I didn't want, so I decided to leave. Now, essentially I thought I could cook. I'd do parties for friends and things like that. So I thought I might open a little restaurant." The name was a joke, inspired by Angry Young Man playwright Arnold Wesker's hit 1962 comedy-drama *Chips with Everything*.

Clydesdale did two things that nobody in Scotland had ever done before: He refined traditional Scottish dishes—cock-a-leekie, cullen skink, haggis, and more—to make them suitable for a restaurant table, and he called out the sources of his ingredients. ("People used to look at me like I was crazy," he told me, "when I put something like 'Oban-landed monkfish' on the menu. '*Landed*? What does that mean?' they'd ask. 'Why *Oban*?'")

In 2008, Clydesdale suffered spinal injuries in a fall at home, and died two years later. His son Colin, who had been running a restaurant of his own called Stravaigin, took on the Chip as well. "I think I can say that my father really started the renaissance in Scottish cooking," he told me recently. "He didn't know what he was doing; he just did it."

The menu at the Chip today continues to dress up traditional cooking, and to site provenance. Typical items: Laphroaig and Dill Marinaded Orkney Organic Salmon; Ritchie's of Rothesay Peat Smoked Finnan Haddie and Hen's Egg Poached in Milk and Onions with Ayrshire Bacon and Mash; Ardnamurchan Venison Sausage, Marag Gheal (white pudding), Soused Red Cabbage and Gin and Juniper Sauce; Roasted Quail Stuffed with Tartan Purry (savory oatmeal porridge), Roast Crushed Paprika Potatoes, Wilted Spinach and a Rich Wine Sauce; Bread Pudding with Fruit Fattened in Rutherglen Muscat and Double Cream . . .

"People come to the Chip to have a great time," says Colin. "They fill restaurants like this. We're a different beast from Edinburgh. Glasgow doesn't need that contemplative hushed reverence. Gordon Ramsay didn't make it here. Michael Caines didn't make it here. To make it, you have to have humanity about you."

Mashed Rutabagas (top)
Vegetarian Haggis (middle, page 216)
and Mashed Potatoes (bottom)

MASHED POTATOES (TATTIES)

SERVES 4 TO 6

"Mash" is a common accompaniment around Great Britain for simply cooked meats, sausages (as in the iconic bangers and mash), and sometimes sauced dishes. Some cooks peel and halve or quarter their potatoes, then boil them in salted water before mashing, but in my experience, the potatoes have better flavor and are less watery if you steam them in their jackets.

5 to 6 medium russet potatoes (about 2 pounds / 900 g), unpeeled, scrubbed
1 cup (240 ml) heavy cream
6 to 8 tablespoons (¾ to 1 stick / 85 to 115 g) butter, softened
Salt and pepper

Put the potatoes into a pot large enough to hold them in a single layer and fill the pot halfway with cold water. Cover the pot and bring the water to a boil over high heat. When the water begins to boil, carefully drain off all but about ½ inch (1.25 cm) of it, then return the pot to the heat, cover, reduce the heat to low, and let the potatoes steam until tender, about 40 minutes. Add a little more water if the pot begins to go dry. Reserve 2 tablespoons of the cooking water, then transfer the potatoes to a bowl, cover them with a clean dish towel, and set them aside for 15 minutes to cool slightly.

Meanwhile, put the cream, butter, and reserved cooking water into a small pot and bring the mixture to a simmer over medium-high heat, then reduce the heat to low and simmer until the potatoes have cooled.

Drain and carefully slip the peels off the potatoes, then return them to the large pot and mash them well while slowly pouring in the cream mixture. Generously season the potatoes with salt and pepper, then whisk them vigorously with a large whisk to dissolve any large lumps (potatoes will not be completely smooth).

MASHED RUTABAGAS (NEEPS)

SERVES 6

The traditional accompaniment to haggis (even the vegetarian kind; see page 216) is "tatties and neeps"—mashed potatoes and mashed rutabagas, served side by side. *Neep* is the Scots word for "turnip" (compare the Spanish *nabo*, the Catalan *nap*, or even the second half of the English word for the vegetable). In Scotland, however, a turnip is understood to be a yellow turnip, or swede, or rutabaga.

2 pounds (900 g) rutabagas, peeled and diced
6 to 8 tablespoons (¾ to 1 stick / 85 to 115 g) butter, softened
Salt and freshly ground black pepper

Put the rutabagas in a medium pot and add cold water to cover. Bring the water to a boil over high heat. Reduce the heat to medium and cook until the rutabagas are very soft, 15 to 20 minutes

Drain the rutabagas and return them to the pot, then add the butter and mash them coarsely until well incorporated. Season with salt and pepper.

CLAPSHOT

SERVES 4 TO 6

In her book *A Caledonian Feast*, Annette Hope quotes the twentieth-century Scots poet and author George Mackay Brown, a native of the islands of Orkney, as calling clapshot "one of the best things to come out of Orkney, together with Highland Park [whisky] and Orkney fudge and Atlantic crabs. . . . It goes with nearly everything. . . ." Indeed it does. It's a natural with haggis, but also a good accompaniment for any roasted or grilled meat, sausages, or almost any other hearty fare.

Clapshot is nothing more than those two key Scottish vegetables, tatties and neeps (page 211)—potatoes and "turnips," which in Scotland are what we call rutabagas—boiled and mashed together with butter and a bit of milk. The addition of onion is not traditional, but Brown describes making the dish with onion included and calls it "about the best I've ever had," and the estimable haggis-maker Jo Macsween also likes to add onion, so I've included it here as an optional addition.

4 tablespoons (½ stick / 55 g) butter
1 small onion, finely chopped (optional)
1 pound (450 g) russet potatoes, peeled and
    coarsely chopped
1 pound (450 g) rutabaga, peeled and coarsely
    chopped
¼ cup (60 ml) whole milk
Salt and freshly ground black pepper
15 to 20 fresh chives, finely chopped

If using the onion, melt half the butter in a small skillet over low heat. Add the onion and cook, stirring frequently, for 15 to 20 minutes, or until it is very soft. Set the onion and the butter it cooked in aside.

Bring a large pot of water to a boil over high heat, then add the potatoes and rutabaga, reduce the heat to medium-high, and cook for 15 to 20 minutes, or until the vegetables are very soft.

Drain the vegetables, return them to the pot, and mash them coarsely. Stir in the onion and the butter it cooked in, if using the onion, and the remaining butter, or stir in all 4 tablespoons (55 g) of the butter. Stir in the milk and season the clapshot generously with salt and pepper. Stir in the chives just before serving.

RUMBLEDETHUMPS

SERVES 4 TO 6

This old Scottish vegetable dish is worth making, in my opinion, not only because it tastes good but because its name is so much fun to say out loud. It comes from the Scottish Borders, dating back at least a couple hundred years: The *Oxford English Dictionary* cites a reference to "rumblety thump" from circa 1800. It appears elsewhere as "rummble-te-thumps," "rumley thump," and "rumelty-thump," among others. The name is thought to derive from the rumble of the boiling water used to cook the potatoes and the thump of the wooden dowel that would have been used to mash them when they were done.

Rumbledethumps is obviously a close relation of Ireland's colcannon, and it is quite possible that the Irish brought the idea to Scotland; the dish is known as kailkenny, in fact, in Aberdeenshire and other portions of northeastern Scotland—and F. Marian McNeill, in *The Scottish Kitchen*, offers a recipe for "a Highland dish" actually called colcannon, involving potatoes, cabbage, carrots, turnips (rutabagas), brown sauce, and sauce mignonette. Clapshot (see left), from the Orkneys, England's bubble and squeak, and the punchnep of Wales (in which the potatoes are combined with small white turnips) are also clearly in the same family.

The addition of cheese melted over the dish is not traditional, though F. Marian MacNeill did suggest it back in 1929, and I think it makes a good dish even better.

4 tablespoons (½ stick / 55 g) butter
1 tablespoon vegetable oil
½ savoy cabbage, shredded (4 to 5 cups)
1 small onion, finely chopped
1 recipe Mashed Potatoes (page 211), prepared
    without the heavy cream
Salt and freshly ground black pepper (optional)
6 ounces (175 g) good-quality cheddar cheese,
    shredded (optional)

Melt the butter with the oil in a large skillet over low heat. Add the cabbage and onion and cook, stirring occasionally, until the vegetables are very soft, about 30 minutes.

Meanwhile, if using the cheese, preheat the oven to 400°F (200°C).

Stir the mashed potatoes into the cabbage and onion mixture, mixing them in thoroughly.

Season with salt and pepper, if necessary (keeping in mind that the potatoes have been seasoned already).

If using the cheese, transfer the rumbledethumps to a baking dish just large enough to hold them and scatter the cheese evenly over the top. Bake for about 15 minutes, or until the cheese is golden brown.

SMOKED HADDOCK MASH

SERVES 6

Plas Bodegroes is a Georgian country house in Pwllheli in northwestern Wales (*plas* is Welsh for "mansion"), repurposed as a "restaurant with rooms," which in this case means a sort of boutique-hotel B&B with a serious dining room. (It was the first Welsh restaurant to earn a Michelin star, back in 1991.) The menu is full of local or near local products—Nefyn Bay scallops, Carmarthen ham, Welsh

Mountain lamb, Welsh whisky (made into ice cream)—and the cooking is solid, in a style that might be called elaboration without pretension. One excellent dish I've enjoyed there was a piece of perfectly done crisp-skinned local cod with an accompaniment of smoked haddock mash. As good as the fish was, the mash made the dish. Chef Chris Chown, who owns Plas Bodegroes with his wife, Chunna (as I write this, the property is up for sale), shared his recipe with me, noting that "It's just a nod to kedgeree—as I'm sure you know, a dish we stole from the Raj." That presumably explains the presence of a hint of the Indian spice mixture called garam masala. These potatoes are a wonderful accompaniment to simply broiled or grilled fish.

½ cup (120 ml) whole milk
7 tablespoons (100 g) butter
Pinch of garam masala or curry powder
6 ounces (170 g) smoked haddock or finnan
    haddie (see Sources, page 316), skin and bones
    removed
1 recipe Mashed Potatoes (page 211)
1 small bunch scallions, finely chopped
2 teaspoons finely chopped fresh parsley
1 teaspoon finely chopped fresh tarragon
1 teaspoon finely chopped fresh lovage (optional)
Salt and freshly ground black pepper

Heat the milk and butter together in a large saucepan over low heat until the butter melts. Stir in the garam masala, then add the haddock and cook, stirring two or three times, for about 2 minutes.

Stir the potatoes into the finnan haddie, then stir in the scallions, parsley, tarragon, and lovage (if using).

Taste the potatoes, add salt to taste if necessary (the finnan haddie will be salty), and season lightly with pepper.

A Farm Shop and a Steak Barn

In late September 2010, hoping to find a local market for the meats and produce they raised on their Strathtyrum Estate on the edge of St. Andrews, the famous golfing destination on the eastern coastline of Fife, the Cheape family opened a farm shop called Balgove Larder ("Balgove," a name borrowed from a neighboring farm, was reckoned easier to spell and pronounce than "Strathtyrum"). The enterprise, launched with the assistance of a grant from the Scottish Rural Development Programme, was set up in an old farm building just off the A91 highway, across the street from the Old Course Hotel.

The shop is a treasure trove for lovers of local food products. Meat is a specialty, especially heritage-breed beef, raised on the estate and butchered on the property, then hung for a minimum of twenty-eight days. There's local pork and lamb, as well, and shop-made sausages, haggis, black pudding, and more. A deli section offers premade meals (the shepherd's pie is popular). The bins and shelves of produce vary in color and content with the seasons, as they should, but even in winter are full, with huge green cabbages, shiny dark brown–skinned onions, bundles of fat leeks, and more. The cheese case is irresistible. Some 90 percent of what the shop sells comes from Scotland, a lot of it from Fife, if not from the farm itself

(wine is one obvious exception). Along with The Brig Larder in Kirkwall, in Orkney (see page 284), this is a model of what locally focused food shops should be.

Balgove Larder has grown since its birth, adding a home and garden store and a bustling café serving breakfast (featuring free-range Fife eggs and its own scones, sausages, and black pudding, among other things), along with soups and sandwiches and a few main dishes (beef stew, smoked haddock and salmon fishcakes, etc.)

The showpiece of the complex, however, beyond the farmshop, is The Steak Barn. This is a former saw-mill next to the shop, its walls lined with weathered potato-shipping crates, its floors dirt, its communal picnic tables made of rough-hewn beech by an onsite carpenter. There are a few starters (crab and squat lobster fishcakes with whisky-infused tartare sauce, for instance), but the main attractions here are the burgers, sausages, and above all steaks—four different cuts—cooked on live-fire grills on one side of the room. These come with salad and very good twice-fried chips, but the best side dish by far are the onion rings (see opposite), cooked in a batter made with red ale from the Eden Mill brewery—a local product, of course.

STEAK BARN ONION RINGS

SERVES 4 TO 6

Deep-fried onion rings aren't thought of as typically British, but the first time I had an example that I found truly memorable was in the 1970s at the famous Mirabelle in London (later taken over by Marco Pierre White and subsequently shuttered). These, I recall, were very thin, perfectly crisp though light in color, wonderfully sweet, and served in a tangle. And the best onion rings I've had in recent years were those served at the unpretentious Steak Barn, part of the Balgove Larder farmshop complex in St. Andrews, Scotland. These were very different from Mirabelle's—big, rich, golden brown, almost crunchy rather than merely crisp, and not at all tangled.

One key to their success is doubtless the locally brewed Eden Mill Clock Ale, made in a former Haig family distillery, that goes into the batter. I haven't been able to locate it in the U.S. (though I may have missed it, or it may ultimately find an importer); any good Scottish red ale (or an American interpretation of same, like Mckulick Scottish Red Ale from Pennsylvania or Old Bisbee Scottish Red Ale from Arizona) may be substituted.

In sharing the Steak Barn's recipe with me—I've tweaked it slightly—Balgove's assistant manager, Liana Nickel, notes that the onion rings "are definitely a point of pride on the Steak Barn menu," and adds that, once cooked, they should be served immediately "preferably with a massive steak!"

2 large yellow onions (about 2 pounds [900 g] total), peeled and sliced into ½-inch (1.25-cm) rounds
3 cups all-purpose flour
2 cups (480 ml) Eden Mill Clock Ale or other Scottish or Scottish-style red ale
1 cup (240 ml) soda water
Salt and freshly ground black pepper
4 to 6 cups (960 ml to 1.4 L) vegetable oil, for frying

Carefully separate the onion rounds into rings, reserving the smallest ones for another purpose. Put about a third of the flour into a large bowl and add the onions, then toss them with your hands so that they're all covered in flour.

In a separate large bowl, mix together the ale, soda water, and salt and pepper to taste. Slowly sprinkle in the remaining flour, stirring the mixture with a whisk, until the batter has the consistency of a thick pureed soup. Add a bit more soda water if necessary.

Pour the oil into a deep-fryer or large, deep, heavy-bottomed saucepan to a depth of 3 to 4 inches (7.5 to 10 cm) and heat it over high heat until it registers 375°F (190°C) on a deep-fry thermometer.

Dip the onion rings in the batter, letting the excess drip off, then fry them in batches for about 2½ minutes. Turn them over with tongs and fry for 2½ minutes more, or until they are very crisp and golden brown.

Drain the onion rings on paper towels and season them with salt and pepper.

VEGETARIAN HAGGIS

One of the things the late Ronnie Clydesdale, who opened the game-changing Scottish restaurant The Ubiquitous Chip in Glasgow in 1972, did was to make his own haggis. "Nobody does that," says his son, Colin, who now runs the place. Butchers make haggis, not chefs or restaurateurs. Clydesdale senior not only made his own haggis, but he made it from venison—as it would have been made in the Highlands in earlier times—instead of the traditional lamb. Colin Clydesdale still serves it at the Chip, and it's delicious. But what was really revolutionary was that the restaurant also served a "haggis" made from vegetables. "I'm not sure if my father invented vegetarian haggis," says Clydesdale, "but nobody had ever heard of anyone else making it when he started." (The big haggis producer Macsween's developed their own vegetarian haggis for the opening of the Scottish Poetry Library in Edinburgh in 1984.) Not all his father's innovations were a success, Clydesdale admits. "We once dabbled in fish haggis. It was damned near awful." (In fact, there *is* a kind of fish haggis in the Shetlands, called hakka muggies, made with the fish stomach stuffed with cod or ling liver and oatmeal.)

¾ cup (1½ sticks / 170 g) butter

2 medium yellow onions, finely chopped

8 ounces (225 g) brown lentils, rinsed well and picked over

2 tablespoons finely chopped fresh parsley

1 teaspoon fresh thyme leaves

1 bay leaf

1 tablespoon ground allspice

2 cups (480 ml) vegetable stock, store-bought or homemade (page 315)

1 tablespoon fresh lemon juice

1¼ cups (100 g) stone-ground Scottish oats (see Sources, page 316)

Salt and freshly ground black pepper

4 to 6 sprigs watercress

Melt half the butter in a medium pot over medium heat. Add the onions and cook, stirring occasionally, for 8 to 10 minutes, then add the remaining butter, the lentils, parsley, thyme, bay leaf, and allspice. When the butter has melted, stir in the stock and lemon juice, then raise the heat to medium-high and bring the stock to a boil.

Reduce the heat to medium-low and simmer, uncovered, until the lentils are soft but not mushy and the liquid has evaporated, about 45 minutes.

Meanwhile, put the oats into a large, dry skillet and toast them over medium heat, stirring frequently, until they turn golden brown, about 10 minutes.

Remove the bay leaf from the lentils, then stir all but about ¼ cup (20 g) of the oatmeal into the lentils. Season generously with salt and pepper.

Serve the haggis in a large bowl, garnished with the remaining toasted oats and the watercress. Accompany the haggis with "tatties and neeps"—Mashed Potatoes (page 211) and Mashed Rutabagas (page 211).

The Innkeeper and the Novelist

The prolific and influential Scottish novelist, poet, playwright, and essayist Sir Walter Scott (author of *Ivanhoe*, *Rob Roy*, and *The Lady of the Lake*, among many other classics) lived for the last seven years of his life at Abbotsford House in Galashiels, in the Scottish Borders (he died in 1832). Visitors to the house today can see Scott's library—said to be one of the few early-nineteenth-century libraries preserved intact anywhere in the world—and his little armory, a remarkable collection of pistols, rifles, knives, swords, hatchets, and other weaponry spanning hundreds of years and at least three continents, in whose company Scott apparently felt particularly comfortable. The author's kitchen is not open to the public, but his dining room is. Here, looking out on the River Tweed, he ate meals with his family and entertained friends—sometimes lavish feasts full of rich soups, roasted meats, wild game, and the inevitable haggis, accompanied by plenty of good wine (Scott is said to have popularized Champagne in Scotland).

Scott was serious about food, and his books are full of it. In *Waverley*, he describes a breakfast that included smoked salmon, reindeer ham, roast beef and mutton, and many kinds of bread. In *The Tale of Old Morality*, he writes of another morning meal of "No tea, no coffee, no variety of rolls, but solid and substantial viands—the priestly ham, the knightly sirloin, the noble baron of beef, the princely venison pasty . . ." In *Guy Mannering*, Scott's characters dig into a game stew, "cooked by a gypsy girl," including hare, partridge, and "moor-game, boiled in a large mess with potatoes, onions, and leeks. . . ." And in *St. Ronan's Well*, there is cooking lore galore, along with a few recipes. (An essay called "A Highlander and his Books: The Gastronomic World of Sir Walter Scott" by Kay Shaw Nelson, author of *The Art of Scottish-American Cooking*, delves deeply into Scott's descriptions of the table.)

St. Ronan's Well is a fictional spa town, apparently modeled after Innerleithen in Tweeddale (which in real life was said to have been founded in AD 737 by one of several Saint Ronans). The center of activity in the novel is the Cleikum Inn, presided over by an eccentric innkeeper and no-nonsense but extremely capable cook named Meg Dods. (She is said to have been based on one Miss Marian Ritchie, "the termagant landlady" of the Cross Keys inn in Peebles.)

Dods turned out to have a life of her own when "she" published a near-encyclopedic collection of authentic Scottish recipes under the title *The Cook and Housewife's Manual* in 1826. In fact, the author of this volume was Christian Isobel Johnstone (1781–1857), a liberal activist and protofeminist, an editor and publisher, and the author of numerous novels and works of nonfiction. The introduction to the book is a lively and humorous interchange between members of the Cleikum Club, a group of gourmands who meet regularly at Dods's inn. The writing is so energetic—and so similar in places to passages in *St. Ronan's Well*—that Scott himself was rumored to have ghostwritten the book, or at least the introductory passages. A contemporary review of *The Cook and Housewife's Manual* says, "We have no hesitation in saying that if the humorous introduction is not written by Sir Walter Scott, the author of it possesses a singular talent of mimicking his best comic manner. . . ."

CHAPTER 9

DESSERTS AND CONFECTIONS

"I WILL PICK OUT FOR SPECIAL MENTION CHRISTMAS PUDDING, TREACLE TART AND APPLE DUMPLINGS."

—GEORGE ORWELL, "In Defence of English Cooking" (1945)

"I THINK WE DO OURSELVES A GREAT DISSERVICE IF WE DISMISS THE RECIPES OF THE PAST. THE SHEER SOPHISTICATION OF THE BAKING OVER THE LAST 400 YEARS IS SOMETHING WE SHOULD CELEBRATE."

—MARY-ANNE BOERMANS, *Great British Bakes: Forgotten Treasures for Modern Bakers* (2014)

British cakes, pies, sweet puddings, and the like are among the country's best-loved and most distinctive dishes. Visitors often smile at their colorful names—tipsy laird, spotted dick, apple goody, queen of puddings, lardy cake, batty cake, black-eyed Susan, whim-wham, maids of honour tart—and keep on smiling when they take a bite. Today, restaurants both old-fashioned and modern offer Eton mess, Bakewell tart, bread-and-butter pudding, sticky toffee pudding, trifle, assorted crumbles and fools, and other classic confections on their dessert menus. These sweet finales sometimes seem to pull restaurants back into British tradition even when their other dishes may roam the world.

Sugar may have first reached Britain in the baggage of Crusaders returning from adventures in Sicily or North Africa or from the Holy Land, where caravans sold sugar from Yemen and even India. It is first mentioned in England, in the Royal Rolls, in 1203. Initially considered a kind of "sweet salt" and used commonly in savory dishes, it long remained a luxury product, as expensive as the rarest spices.

One of the earliest of English-language cookbooks, the late-fourteenth-century recipe collection *The Forme of Cury*, notes that "Honey was the great and universal sweetner in remote antiquity, and particularly in this island. . . ." but that "Sugar, or Sugur, was now beginning here to take place of honey. . . ." It is, in any case, used sparingly in the book's recipes, not many of which would qualify as dessert. One that does is "ryse of fische daye," which is to say, rice to be served on "fish days"—those when not just meat but all animal products were to be eschewed for religious reasons. It calls for rice cooked in almond milk with almonds, sugar, and salt. There is also a recipe for cryspels (crêpes) dressed with honey, and one for confit pears.

After the Dutch imported sugarcane to the Caribbean in the mid-seventeenth century and it spread to islands owned by the British, French, and Spanish (who all enslaved the local citizenry and brought in slaves from Africa to harvest it), it became more widely available. By the eighteenth century, it was being used at almost every level of British society. It became something of a fad, in fact; it is said that sugar consumption in England alone increased fivefold between 1710 and 1770.

Puddings filled with ground offal and other meats are ancient; sweet ones probably evolved out of them in the seventeenth century, when pudding bags were introduced, meaning that the filling no longer had to be packed into animal intestines or paunches. Tarts and pies were popular in that era, too. What may well be the first published recipe for pumpkin pie appeared (as "pompion pye") in an anonymous volume called *The Compleat Cook*, published in London in 1658. Chocolate reached Britain in 1530, originally as a beverage—it was served in the coffee houses (or chocolate houses) of early seventeenth-century London—and chocolate dessert recipes began appearing in the latter 1700s. (It was a British firm, incidentally, that produced the first chocolate bar; in 1847, J. S. Fry & Sons, Ltd. of Bristol combined cocoa powder with sugar and cocoa fat in a form that could be molded into what they described as "*chocolat délicieux à manger.*")

The nineteenth-century cookbook writer and entrepreneur Agnes Marshall, dubbed "Queen of Ices," helped popularize ice cream and its cousins. She was probably the first person to suggest serving ice cream in a cone; she invented a machine that could freeze ice cream in five minutes; and she suggested that ice cream could be made with liquid oxygen—roughly a century before Heston Blumenthal and Ferran Adrià started doing it with liquid nitrogen—though she apparently never actually tried it.

Fruit has long been important in the British diet. Most nontropical varieties grow superbly in one part of Great Britain or another, and historian Colin Spencer reports that archeologists have found traces of apples, pears, plums, cherries, grapes, damson plums, gooseberries, strawberries, and blackberries, among other fruits, in fossil remains from medieval times. Many classic English and Scottish desserts are fruit-based, including Eton mess (strawberries), cranahan (raspberries), Bakewell tart (cherries), gooseberry fool, and apple dumpling. (The apple seems somehow the most English of fruits, despite its central Asian origins, and English heirloom varieties today are some of the finest eating apples anywhere; the flavor of a perfect Cox's Orange Pippin pretty much defines "apple" to me.)

One great champion of old-style British desserts has been The Pudding Club, founded in Mickleton, in the Cotswolds, in 1985 by "a small but dedicated group of pudding lovers." The club has grown into an international organization that holds regular meetings, including dinners that are concluded with a parade of seven different puddings, produces its own line of packaged puddings, and runs a hotel with pudding-themed guestrooms. The Spotted Dick and Custard Room awaits you.

Gooseberry Fool

GOOSEBERRY FOOL

SERVES 4 TO 6

The estimable cookbook editor and author Judith Jones once called gooseberries "the north country's answer to the lemon," for its ability to heighten flavors with its acidity. In this simple, iconic English dessert, the tartness of the fruit—which is related to the currant—offsets the richness of the cream and the sweetness of the sugar. A fool is no more than crushed or pureed fruit folded into sweetened whipped cream. (The fruit is usually cooked, though Mark Hix says that "sweet, soft fruits that don't need to be cooked can simply be mashed and folded through the whipped cream.") Fools are made with summer berries, peaches, plums, and other fruits, but gooseberry fool is classic. The word *fool* in this context, incidentally, is often said to derive from the French *fouler*, "to crush"—I've written that myself—but the *Oxford English Dictionary* calls that derivation baseless, and suggests that it's actually related to the more common use of the word.

1 cup (200 g) sugar
1 pound (500 g) fresh gooseberries, trimmed
2 cups (480 ml) heavy cream, lightly whipped
1 tablespoon fresh lemon juice

Stir the sugar into 1 cup (240 ml) warm water in a medium saucepan and bring to a boil over medium-high heat, stirring continuously. Immediately reduce the heat to low and cook, stirring continuously, for 2 minutes more to form a syrup.

Add the gooseberries and bring the syrup to a boil over medium-high heat. Reduce the heat to medium and cook, stirring occasionally, for 6 to 8 minutes, or until the gooseberries begin to crack.

Puree the fruit and syrup coarsely in a blender or food processor, then set aside to cool. When the fruit has cooled to room temperature, gently stir in the cream. Refrigerate for 1 to 2 hours before serving.

STEWED RHUBARB

SERVES 4 TO 6

Rhubarb is a curious plant. Its stalks, called petioles, look like pinkish-red celery; its leaves, high in oxalic acid, are toxic; its roots have been used in traditional medicine, primarily as a laxative and cathartic agent and for diseases of the lungs and liver, for thousands of years in China and the Middle East. In mid-seventeenth-century England, medicinal rhubarb was three times as expensive as opium. When people started eating the petioles, it was most likely in the hopes of assimilating some of the plant's therapeutic value. It was probably first consumed for purely gastronomic reasons in England in the seventeenth century. The sweetest, tenderest rhubarb is forced rhubarb, which is not grown outside—where it is one of the earliest ripening plants of the spring—but in dark sheds, in winter. Today, the so-called Rhubarb Triangle in West Yorkshire produces about 90 percent of the world's forced rhubarb. Sweet though it may sometimes be, rhubarb retains a significant sour character, and is virtually always prepared with plenty of sugar, as in this simple recipe.

4 to 6 stalks rhubarb, trimmed and cut into 3- to 4-inch (7.5- to 10-cm) pieces
1½ cups (300 g) plus 2 tablespoons sugar
Zest of 1 orange
1 cup (240 ml) fresh ricotta cheese

Preheat the oven to 325ºF (160ºC).

Put the rhubarb in a baking dish large enough to hold it in one layer. Sprinkle 1½ cups (300 g) of the sugar evenly over it, then scatter the orange zest across the top.

Add enough water to the baking dish to barely cover the rhubarb, then bake, uncovered, until the rhubarb is very tender, about 1 hour.

Strain the juices from the baking dish into a small saucepan, then return the rhubarb to the baking dish and set it aside. Boil the rhubarb juices over medium-high heat until they are thick and syrupy, 15 to 20 minutes.

recipe continues

Divide the rhubarb evenly between four to six bowls. Pour the syrup over each serving, dividing it evenly, then add a scoop of ricotta to each bowl. Sprinkle a bit of the remaining sugar over each bowl.

SUMMER PUDDING

SERVES 6 TO 8

What we now call summer pudding, according to Sarah Edington in her encyclopedic *Complete Traditional Recipe Book*, produced for the United Kingdom's National Trust, "was known as Hydropathic Pudding in the 19th century, when it was served at health resorts where pastry was forbidden." (Hydropathy was the nineteenth-century medical treatment popularly known as "the water-cure.") Well, yes and no. Fruit encased in slices of bread and formed into a pudding basin dates back at least to the eighteenth century—Dr. Johnson made his with rhubarb—but until the mid-1900s, the fruit used in this manner was always well stewed. Raw fruit had previously been considered unhealthy, and certainly wouldn't have been served at a health spa. Confusingly, the *Oxford English Dictionary* defines summer pudding as one "made of stewed fruit (freq. raspberries and red currants) . . ." and its earliest citation of the term, from 1933, specifies stewed fruit, too. In the U.K. today, though, summer pudding is commonly understood to use fresh fruit that has been no more than slightly warmed to encourage it to release its juices, and as such to symbolize the season's bounty.

16 to 20 slices dry (but not too hard) good-quality white bread, crusts removed

2½ pounds (1.2 kg) assorted summer fruit, such as strawberries, raspberries, blackberries, blueberries, red currants, and/or black currants, at least two kinds, larger fruits halved or quartered

¼ to ¾ cup (50 to 150 g) sugar, depending on sweetness of the fruit

Clotted or whipped cream, for serving (optional; see Sources, page 316)

Women picking fruit in Kent to be made into jam for British troops during World War I, 1916

Line a 1-quart (1-L) bowl or pudding basin with the bread slices, overlapping them slightly and cutting them as necessary to fit the bottom and sides. Reserve enough slices to completely cover the top.

Put the fruit, sugar, and ½ to 1 cup (120 to 240 ml) water (depending on the juiciness of the fruit) into a medium pan over medium heat. Bring the mixture to a slow boil, stirring continuously and crushing the berries slightly with a wooden spoon, then quickly remove the pan from the heat and set the fruit aside to cool for 10 to 15 minutes.

Spoon the fruit mixture into the prepared bowl, then fit the remaining bread slices on top. Cut waxed paper to exactly cover the top layer of bread, then weigh the pudding down with a plate or pie pan that fits the space exactly, with one or two cans of canned food set on top.

Refrigerate the pudding overnight, then remove the weights and plate and invert the pudding onto a serving platter.

Serve with clotted or whipped cream, if you like.

Summer Pudding

Eton Mess

ETON MESS

SERVES 4 TO 6

This rather exuberant-looking dessert takes the first half of its name from Eton College in Berkshire—the famous public school (in the English sense) founded in 1440 by King Henry VI, which counts among its graduates some nineteen British prime ministers as well as Princes William and Harry, Percy Bysshe Shelley, John Maynard Keynes, Ian Fleming, Hugh Laurie, and (according to J. M. Barrie) Captain Hook. The source of the second half of its name should be self-explanatory. It apparently dates from the late nineteenth century (the *Oxford English Dictionary*'s oldest citation is from 1896), and by the early years of the twentieth century was being served at the famous annual Eton–Harrow cricket match. Strawberries are the traditional fruit for the dish, though some recipes call for raspberries or even bananas.

10 egg whites
2 cups (400 g) sugar
¾ cup (70 g) ground almonds
12 ounces (340 g) fresh raspberries, rinsed
1 teaspoon fresh lemon juice
1¼ cups (300 ml) heavy cream
8 ounces (225 g) fresh strawberries, rinsed
    and hulled
¼ cup (30 g) slivered almonds

Preheat the oven to 325°F (160°C). Line a baking sheet with nonstick parchment paper.

Beat the egg whites in a large, very clean bowl until stiff peaks form. Pour in about half the sugar, then beat again until stiff peaks form again. With a metal spoon, fold in the rest of the sugar and the ground almonds. Spoon the meringue onto the prepared baking sheet and spread it out without smoothing it down. Bake for 20 minutes, then reduce the heat to 275°F (135°C) and bake for 40 minutes more, or until the meringue is pale and slightly crisp. Remove the baking sheet from the oven and set it aside to cool and dry for at least 3 hours.

Press about half the raspberries through a sieve into a small bowl, then stir in the lemon juice.

Whip the cream in a large bowl until soft peaks form. Break the meringue into irregular bite-size pieces with your hands, then stir the meringue, the remaining raspberries, and the strawberries into the cream.

Divide the mixture evenly among four to six dessert bowls. Drizzle the raspberry juice evenly over the servings, then scatter the slivered almonds evenly over them.

APPLE DUMPLINGS

SERVES 6

According to Charles Lamb in *The Essays of Elia*, Samuel Taylor Coleridge "holds that a man cannot have a pure mind who refuses apple-dumplings." I tested several recipes for this classic English dessert and the best one I found, for "Old Fashioned Apple Dumplings," came from a blog called "The English Kitchen" (theenglishkitchen. blogspot.com)—whose motto is "De-bunking the myths of English Cookery one recipe at a time." The blog's author, Marie Rayner—a Canadian happily expatriated to Chester, just south of Liverpool—was kind enough to let me share her method for making this delicious dessert.

FOR THE DUMPLINGS:
1 recipe shortcrust pastry (page 313), left in 1 piece
All-purpose flour, for dusting
½ cup (100 g) granulated sugar
1 teaspoon ground cinnamon
2 tablespoons fresh lemon juice
6 medium Granny Smith or other firm cooking apples
¾ cup (165 g) packed light brown sugar
2 tablespoons (30 g) unsalted butter, plus more for
    greasing

recipe continues

FOR THE SAUCE:
¾ cup (150 g) granulated sugar
2 tablespoons (30 g) butter
1 teaspoon pure vanilla extract
⅛ teaspoon ground cardamom
⅛ teaspoon freshly grated nutmeg
Heavy cream, for serving (optional)

MAKE THE DUMPLINGS:
Preheat the oven to 375°F (190°C). Lightly grease a baking pan large enough to hold the dumplings without touching.

Roll out the pastry dough on a lightly floured work surface to a rectangle measuring 14 by 21 inches (35 by 55 cm). Cut the dough into six even squares.

In a medium bowl, whisk together the granulated sugar and the cinnamon. Put the lemon juice in a separate medium bowl.

Peel and core the apples, leaving them whole, then roll the apples first in the lemon juice, then in the cinnamon sugar. Put each apple into the center of one pastry square. Fill the cavity of each apple with 2 tablespoons of the brown sugar and 1 teaspoon of the butter. Pull up the sides of the pastry squares to cover each apple, crimping the edges tightly shut.

Put the apples in the prepared pan. Bake for 30 minutes.

MAKE THE SAUCE:
In the meantime, in a medium saucepan, combine the sugar, butter, vanilla, cardamom, nutmeg, and 2 cups (480 ml) water. Bring the mixture to a boil over medium-high heat and boil for about 1 minute. After the apples have baked for 30 minutes, drizzle the sauce over them, dividing it evenly between them, then return the apples to the oven and bake for 30 minutes more, basting the dumplings occasionally with the sauce.

Serve warm with a pitcher of heavy cream, if you like.

DEVONSHIRE IN AND OUT PUDDING

SERVES 6

Devonshire is famous for its apples, and the traditional cooking of the region uses them in a number of desserts, including apple dumplings and the apple dappy, a kind of rolled apple tart, typically sliced and served with lemon sauce. I've been unable to discover why this particular dessert is described as "in and out," though perhaps the name is a reference to the extreme simplicity of the recipe—into the pie dish, then out of the oven. A recipe for in and out pudding in the 1898-vintage manual *The Housewife's Referee* calls for no sugar, but seasons the pudding with salt and pepper—then boils it, presumably in cheesecloth—which would make it more of an actual pudding than this recipe yields. Some versions of the dish add blueberries, which doesn't seem like a bad idea—except that, at least in the American Northeast, blueberries and apples are rarely at their seasonal peak simultaneously.

Butter, for greasing
1¾ cups (220 g) self-rising flour
4 ounces (100 g) suet (see Sources, page 316) or unsalted butter
½ cup (105 g) Demerara sugar
4 to 5 tablespoons (60 to 75 ml) apple juice
4 medium cooking apples, preferably Bramley, Granny Smith, or Northern Spy, peeled, cored, and thinly sliced
½ cup (120 ml) heavy cream

Preheat the oven to 350°F (175°C). Grease a pie pan or shallow baking dish.

In a large bowl, combine the flour, suet, and sugar and mix together well, working in the suet thoroughly with your fingers. Slowly drizzle in enough apple juice, mixing it well, to make a soft dough, then stir in the apples.

Put the mixture into the prepared pan or dish and bake for 45 minutes, or until the top is golden brown. Drizzle the cream over the top just before serving.

The Great Pudding Riot

For centuries, the people of Paignton, a seaside town in Devon, on what is now known as the English Riviera, were called either Flat-polls or Pudden-eaters. Flat poll is a type of white drumhead cabbage, often used for cattle feed, which was once grown abundantly in the area. "Pudden" means pudding, and came to be applied to the local citizenry because, in 1295, they contrived to bake a gigantic version of the confection known as a white-pot or bag-pudding as a thank-you to the king for having granted them a civic charter. The massive concoction was said in jest to have taken seven years to make, seven years to bake, and seven years to eat.

For several centuries after the original was prepared, a pudding of similarly massive proportions was baked every fifty years. The practice eventually died out, but was revived in 1819. On that occasion, it was reported that the recipe called for 400 pounds of flour, 170 pounds of suet, 140 pounds of raisins, and 20 dozen eggs. This mixture was boiled for four days in a copper brewer's vat; apparently this wasn't long enough, as the resulting pudding, according to contemporary reports, was dry and crumbly on the outside but still raw in the middle.

The good people of Paignton tried again in 1859, when it was decided that a huge pudding should be part of the celebrations marking the extension of the railway line to the town. A splendid feast of bread and meat and the famous Devon cider was offered to locals and to visitors who came from all over the region—some eighteen thousand of them in all. Everything went well until the Paignton pudding was brought out, displayed behind a fence. When a town official began breaking off pieces and offering them to the people closest to the fence, the rest of the assemblage, perhaps feeling the effects of the cider, apparently feared there wouldn't be enough to go around and surged forward, knocking down the barrier and descending on the pudding like carrion birds. Soon nothing but crumbs remained.

Not surprisingly, Paignton seems to have forgotten about the pudding for more than a century after that, reviving the idea only in 1968. It was subsequently made again in 2006, 2009, and 2015, without incident—and, in 2014, it was featured on an episode of the popular television program *The Great British Bake Off* (see page 239).

At the time, Helen Hallett of Hallett's The Bakers in Paignton, who made a version of the pudding for the show, noted that in the thirteenth century, when it was created, there weren't many ingredients available, so she enhanced the recipe. "When I made an original to the original recipe," she added, "it was revolting! Nobody would eat it now."

BAKEWELL TART

MAKES ONE 10-INCH (25-CM) TART

The name of this cherry and frangipane (sweet almond paste) confection has nothing to do with baking. It's named for the market town of Bakewell in the Derbyshire Dales, in the East Midlands of England, where it was probably invented. Bakewell in turn draws its name from that of a man named Badeca or Beadeca, and the spring—*wellwill* or *wiell* in Old English—on the spot that he apparently owned.

A different local specialty, called Bakewell pudding—a kind of jam tart topped with a mixture of egg, butter, sugar, and ground almonds—may be older than Bakewell tart; it is said in town lore to have been invented by one Mrs. Greaves at a local hotel in 1859, though it is mentioned by Eliza Acton in her book *Modern Cookery, in All Its Branches*, which was published in 1845. (In Ireland, the tart and the pudding are sometimes the same: Some people call it a tart if it's cold, a pudding if it's hot.)

Bakewell tart, which is a somewhat more sophisticated concoction, probably dates from the early twentieth century. Jeremy Lee at London's Quo Vadis restaurant notes that the tart is "quite luxurious" and adds that both the pastry and the frangipane are better if they're made the night before the tart is assembled—and that the tart improves as it sits, so he likes to make plenty. Serve with whipped cream if desired. (At Quo Vadis, Lee adds heavy cream and custard sauce as well.)

FOR THE PASTRY:
2 cups (250 g) all-purpose flour, plus more
    for dusting
½ cup (65 g) confectioners' sugar
Pinch of salt
⅔ cup (150 g) butter
1 large egg

FOR THE FRANGIPANE:
9 ounces (250 g) granulated sugar, plus more
    for dusting
9 ounces (250 g) butter, softened
2 large eggs, lightly stirred with a fork
9 ounces (250 g) whole almonds, coarsely ground

FOR THE JAM:
18 ounces (500 g) fresh cherries, pitted
3½ ounces (100 g) granulated sugar

MAKE THE PASTRY:
Sift together the flour, confectioners' sugar, and salt into a large bowl. Cut the butter into small pieces and work it into the flour mixture with your hands until fine crumbs are formed. Add the egg and 1 teaspoon water and knead lightly but well until a dough forms. Wrap the dough in plastic wrap and refrigerate it.

MAKE THE FRANGIPANE:
Using a stand mixer or a hand mixer, beat the granulated sugar into the butter until pale. Pour the eggs into the butter and sugar and beat them together well, then stir in the almonds. Cover the bowl and refrigerate it.

MAKE THE JAM:
Combine the cherries and granulated sugar in a saucepan and cook over medium-high heat, stirring continuously, for about 5 minutes, or until the mixture forms a thick jam.

Roll out the pastry on a lightly floured work surface to a round about 14 inches (36 cm) in diameter, then carefully lift it into a 10-inch (25-cm) tart or pie pan, smoothing over any small holes or tears.

If you are preparing the tart up to this point the night before baking it, refrigerate the tart shell and the jam overnight.

Preheat the oven to 375°F (190°C).

Spread the cherry jam over the bottom of the tart shell, then gently spread the frangipane over the jam.

Put the tart on a rack in the middle of the oven and put a baking sheet on the rack below it to catch any juices that might overflow. Bake the tart for 45 minutes, then reduce the oven temperature to 300°F (150°C) and bake for 15 to 20 minutes more.

Remove the tart from the oven and scatter a little sugar over the top. Let the tart rest for at least 1 hour before serving.

WHISKY-SOAKED-RAISIN AND ORANGE MARMALADE BREAD ᴀɴᴅ BUTTER PUDDING

SERVES 6 TO 8

One evening in Ambleside, in England's Lake District, we checked into very much the wrong hotel: There was a karaoke setup in the lobby bar, the room decor looked like something out of a 1960s sci-fi film, and, worst of all, the Wi-Fi was out of order. We quickly decamped and drove around the area, finally finding a nice berth about five miles down the road in Windermere. Then the question was where to eat. It was on the late side (for that part of the world) and we wanted something within walking distance.

There wasn't much that looked attractive until we turned down Crescent Road into Windermere village and saw a modest-looking storefront place, called Wild & Co, with a couple of empty tables. We took a chance, and were very glad we did. Instead of the standard tourist fare common in the Lake District, we found an appealing menu of first-rate modern British food—things like Scottish scallops with spiced pig cheek and burnt apple puree, fish pie with Isle of Mull Cheddar crust, roast wild duck with preserved cherries and wilted Little Gem lettuce, and for dessert this memorable variation on bread pudding. Wild & Co. chef Dylan Evans and his partner, Caterina Giannotti, kindly shared the recipe for this homey dessert with me.

1 cup (145 g) sultanas (golden raisins)
½ cup (60 ml) good quality Scotch whisky, plus more if needed
1¼ cups (300 ml) whole milk
1¼ cups (300 ml) heavy cream
Pinch of salt
2 vanilla beans, split lengthwise
5 large eggs
4 tablespoons (50 g) sugar
½ cup (90 g) mixed candied citrus peel
1 large loaf brioche bread or challah, cut into 1-inch (2.5-cm) slices

1¼ cups (2½ sticks / 285 g) butter, softened
2 cups (480 ml) orange marmalade, store-bought or homemade (page 282 or 285)
Vanilla ice cream, for serving (optional)

Put the sultanas in a small bowl and cover them with the whisky (add a little more if necessary to completely cover them). Soak for at least 2 hours, then drain them and set them aside (reserve the whisky for cocktails, if you like).

Preheat the oven to 300°F (150°C).

Combine the milk, cream, salt, and vanilla beans in a medium pot. Bring the liquid to a boil, then take the pot off the heat and set it aside to infuse for at least 15 minutes.

Whisk the eggs and sugar together in a medium bowl, then strain the milk mixture into the eggs and stir well.

Mix the sultanas and the citrus peel together, then spread them evenly over the bottom of a 4.8-quart (4.5-L) baking dish.

Butter each slice of brioche or challah on one side, then cut each one on an angle into two triangles each. Arrange the slices, overlapping, on top of the sultanas and citrus peel. Pour the custard mixture evenly over the bread, then bake the pudding, uncovered, for 30 minutes.

Just before the pudding has finished baking, put the marmalade into a small saucepan and heat it over low heat, stirring occasionally.

Remove the pudding from the oven and spread the heated marmalade over the top. Bake for 10 minutes more.

Serve warm or at room temperature, with vanilla ice cream, if you like.

CAMBRIDGE BURNT CREAM

SERVES 4 TO 6

The earliest extant recipe for this dessert of custard topped with a crust of caramelized sugar dates from 1691, when it appeared in the famed French chef François Massialot's book *Le cuisinier royal et bourgeois*—though interestingly he called it *crème à l'anglaise*, "cream in the English manner." The first English-language recipe for burnt cream appeared, under that name, in a confectioner's dictionary in 1723. (In Catalonia, where the preparation is called *crema catalana*, locals say it dates back to medieval times, but to the best of my knowledge nobody has found a Catalan recipe for it that dates from earlier than the latter part of the nineteenth century.)

The association between burnt cream and Cambridge University—and specifically the institution's Trinity College—derives from the fact that in the late 1800s it became popular to brand the top of the dessert with the college arms. Trinity's own website acknowledges that "The story that crème brûlée itself was invented at the College almost certainly has no basis in fact." Nonetheless, its identification with the university persists, so I have given it the school's name.

6 egg yolks
1 teaspoon all-purpose flour
3 cups (720 ml) heavy cream
Pinch of ground cinnamon
6 tablespoons (75 g) sugar

Put the egg yolks into a medium bowl, then whisk the flour into them, combining them well. Add the cream and cinnamon and whisk until well combined.

Pour the mixture into a heavy-bottomed pot and bring it to a boil over medium-high heat. Stir in 3 tablespoons of the sugar as it boils, then remove the pot from the heat and strain the custard through a sieve into a medium bowl, then carefully ladle it into four to six glass or ceramic ramekins. Let the custard cool to room temperature, then refrigerate it until it sets.

Sprinkle the remaining sugar over the tops of the custards, adding a bit more if necessary, then caramelize it with a kitchen torch. Alternatively, in a small pot, melt the remaining sugar with 1 teaspoon water and cook the mixture over low heat until the sugar caramelizes. Pour the caramelized sugar onto a sheet of aluminum foil and allow it to cool and harden, then break it into pieces and scatter them over the custards.

CALEDONIAN OATMEAL ICE CREAM wɪᴛʜ BERRIES

SERVES 8

One of the most famous and widely copied "modern Scottish" innovations dreamed up by the late Ronnie Clydesdale at his Ubiquitous Chip in Glasgow, this delicious ice cream was perhaps inspired by the traditional dessert called cranachan—a mixture of toasted oats soaked in whisky, whipped cream, and berries. The dish has remained on the menu at the Chip for decades with various accompaniments (it is currently served with white wine jelly and caramelized plums), but I think all it needs is some sweetened berries. There's no whisky in this recipe; I suggest adding it yourself, in a glass, on the side.

2½ cups (500 g) sugar
½ cup stone-ground Scottish oats (see Sources, page 316)
1 tablespoon vegetable oil
3 cups (720 ml) heavy cream
1 cup (240 ml) milk
2 cups (about 300 g) assorted fresh berries, such as blueberries, blackberries, raspberries, etc.
1½ tablespoons (22 g) butter
1½ cups (150 g) dry bread crumbs

Combine 1 cup (200 g) of the sugar with 1 cup (240 ml) water in a small saucepan. Bring the water to a boil over medium-high heat, stirring to dissolve the sugar. Reduce the heat to medium and cook, stirring occasionally, until the syrup has reduced by half, about 20 minutes. Set the syrup aside to cool.

Heat a nonstick skillet over medium-high heat, then add the oats and toast them, shaking the pan and stirring the oats occasionally, for about 6 minutes, or until they are golden brown. Set the oats aside.

Lightly grease a baking sheet with the vegetable oil.

Combine 1 cup (200 g) of the sugar with 3 tablespoons water in a small saucepan. Bring the water to a boil over medium-high heat, stirring to dissolve the sugar. Reduce the heat to medium and cook for 8 to 10 minutes, or until the syrup has caramelized and reached 325ºF (160ºC) on a candy thermometer. Remove the pan from the heat, stir in the toasted oats, then pour the mixture out onto the prepared baking sheet and let it cool.

When the oat mixture has cooled, crush it into small pieces with a rolling pin and set it aside.

Put the reserved syrup into a large bowl, then beat it with a hand mixer on medium speed until it thickens slightly. Add the cream and milk and continue beating until soft peaks form. Fold in the oatmeal pieces, mixing them in well, then cover the bowl with plastic wrap and freeze for about 1 hour. Remove the mixture from the freezer and beat it again for about a minute. Transfer the ice cream to a 5-cup (1.1-L) loaf pan, cover with plastic wrap, and freeze until firm, at least 3 hours.

Combine the remaining ½ cup (100 g) sugar and ½ cup (120 ml) water in a small pan. Bring the water to a boil over medium-high heat, stirring to dissolve the sugar. Reduce the heat to medium and cook until the syrup has reduced by half, about 10 minutes. Stir in the berries and cook for about 15 seconds. Transfer the berries to a small bowl and set them aside to cool.

Melt the butter in a large skillet over medium heat. Add the bread crumbs and toast them, stirring frequently, until they're golden brown, 5 to 7 minutes. Transfer the bread crumbs to a wide, shallow dish large enough to hold the ice cream loaf.

Unmold the ice cream loaf by briefly dipping the base of the pan into a bowl of hot water to loosen it from the edges, then tip the loaf out into the dish of bread crumbs and coat all sides with the crumbs. Slice the loaf into eight pieces about 1 inch (2.5 cm) thick, then cut each slice in half lengthwise. Arrange two pieces of ice cream on each of eight chilled plates, then spoon some of the berries next to each serving, dividing them between the plates.

Meditation on a Pudding

Traveling in the Scottish Highlands in October 1773, Dr. Johnson and his amanuensis, James Boswell, lodged at an inn where Johnson asked if there were any books to be read in the house. The only one that could be turned up was the formidably titled *Meditations and Contemplations: Containing Meditations Among the Tombs; Reflections on a Flower-Garden; A Descant up on Creation; Contemplations on the Night; Contemplations on the Starry Heavens and A Winter Piece*—a then-popular collection of essays by the clergyman James Hervey. Johnson, says Boswell, "thought slightingly of this admired book . . . [and] treated it with ridicule." After mocking the author's meditation on the moon, and spontaneously composing a countermeditation portraying the moon as treacherous to mankind, he "indulged a playful fancy, in making a Meditation on a Pudding." This is Johnson's improvisation:

> *Let us seriously reflect of what a pudding is composed. It is composed of flour that once waved in the golden grain, and drank the dews of the morning; of milk pressed from the swelling udder by the gentle hand of the beauteous milk-maid, whose beauty and innocence might have recommended a worse draught; who, while she stroked the udder, indulged no ambitious thoughts of wandering in palaces, formed no plans for the destruction of her fellow-creatures: milk, which is drawn from the cow, that useful animal, that eats the grass of the field, and supplies us with that which made the greatest part of the food of mankind in the age which the poets have agreed to call golden. It is made with an egg, that miracle of nature, which the theoretical Burnet has compared to creation. An egg contains water within its beautiful smooth surface; and an unformed mass, by the incubation of the parent, becomes a regular animal, furnished with bones and sinews, and covered with feathers. Let us consider; can there be more wanting to complete the Meditation on a Pudding? If more is wanting, more may be found. It contains salt, which keeps the sea from putrefaction: salt, which is made the image of intellectual excellence, contributes to the formation of a pudding.*

HONEY *AND* WHISKY PARFAIT WITH BUTTERSCOTCH SAUCE

SERVES 4

In the 1990s, I made several extended trips around Scotland to research articles on the country's underrated and largely misunderstood culinary traditions and modern cooking for the *Los Angeles Times* and the regrettably short-lived U.K. edition of *Metropolitan Home*. One of my stops was a hostelry called Farleyer House in Aberfeldy, a town that's also the home of the top-flight Aberfeldy distillery. This sixteenth-century property, originally part of the 90,000-acre Menzies Estate, was one of Scotland's first (and best) country house hotels. (It closed not long after my visit but was reopened in 2002 as the more modest Farleyer Lodge.) The chef at the time was Frances Atkins—now chef-proprietor of the Michelin-starred Yorke Arms in Ramsgill-in-Nidderdale, Yorkshire—and this was one of her excellent desserts. Since the Aberfeldy distillery is owned by Dewar's, that firm's eight-year-old White Label scotch would be a good choice for this recipe, though any good blended Scotch will do.

8 ounces (235 ml) heather honey (see Sources, page 316)
1¼ cups (300 ml) plus 2 tablespoons good-quality blended Scotch whisky
12 medium egg yolks
2 cups (480 ml) heavy cream
1 cup stone-ground Scottish oats (see Sources, page 316)
6 tablespoons (¾ stick / 85 g) butter, plus more for greasing
2 tablespoons golden syrup (see Sources, page 316)
2 tablespoons brown sugar

Combine the honey and 1¼ cups (300 ml) of the whisky in a small saucepan and bring the mixture to a boil over medium-high heat. Remove the pan from the heat and set it aside.

Beat the egg yolks in a food processor, then, with the motor running, pour in the whisky-honey mixture through the feed tube in a slow, steady stream. Continue processing until the mixture thickens slightly, then transfer it to a bowl and set it aside to cool to room temperature.

Stir the cream into the cooled egg yolk mixture, then process the mixture in an ice cream maker according to the manufacturer's instructions.

Meanwhile, preheat the oven to 350°F (175°C). Spread the oats out evenly on a baking sheet and toast them in the oven until they're golden brown, 5 to 7 minutes. Set the oats aside to cool.

While the oats are cooling, line a 1½-quart (1.4-L) terrine with buttered waxed paper, then sprinkle the toasted oats evenly around the terrine so that they stick to the sides and bottom. Spoon the parfait mixture into the terrine and tamp it down lightly. Cover the terrine and freeze the parfait overnight.

About 40 minutes before serving the parfait, combine the butter, golden syrup, and brown sugar with ¼ cup (60 ml) water in a small saucepan. Heat the mixture over low heat, stirring continuously, until the butter and sugar have melted. Remove the pan from the heat and set it aside to let the sauce cool to room temperature. When it has cooled, stir in the remaining 2 tablespoons whisky.

About 15 minutes before serving the parfait, carefully unmold it and peel off the buttered waxed paper. Run a knife under hot water and use it to cut the parfait into eight to twelve thick slices. Divide the slices evenly between four chilled dessert plates, then spoon some syrup over each serving.

LANCASHIRE CHEESE ICE CREAM

MAKES ABOUT 1 QUART (1 L)

The technique for producing Lancashire cheese was developed in the late nineteenth century. Because the region's dairy farms tended to be small, with little milk produced daily, the local tradition was to blend the curd from several days' milkings. At Mrs. Kirkham's, the premier producer of the cheese today, a two-day curd is used, and the result has what the makers call "a rich creamy 'buttery crumble' texture." This is in contrast to the more modern style of the cheese, which is lighter in color, with a texture more like that of Caerphilly, which might be called "unbuttery crumble." Lancashire wasn't considered a major cheese until the latter twentieth century—*Cheddar Gorge: A Book of English Cheeses* (1937) mentions it only glancingly, while devoting a chapter to the now obscure Blue Vinny—and Ruth Kirkham, who started making her cheese in 1978, is largely responsible for the reputation it enjoys today.

Lancashire chef Nigel Haworth is a great champion of Mrs. Kirkham's cheese, and uses it in a number of recipes, including his cheese and onion pie (page 172) and this unusual ice cream—which he serves at the luxury hotel Northcote with an apple crumble soufflé.

7 ounces (210 ml) heavy cream
7 ounces (210 ml) whole milk
½ cup (100 g) sugar
6 large egg yolks
⅔ cup cream cheese
¾ cup grated Lancashire cheese

Combine the cream and milk in a medium saucepan, then bring them to a boil over medium-high heat, stirring frequently. Remove the mixture from the heat and set it aside.

In a large bowl, whisk the sugar into the egg yolks, then stir in half the cream mixture. When it is well incorporated, stir in the remaining cream mixture, then return the mixture to the saucepan and cook over low heat, stirring continuously, until it thickens slightly, about 5 minutes.

Allow the mixture to cool slightly, then transfer it to the bowl of a stand mixer fitted with the paddle attachment. Running the mixer on medium speed, slowly add the cream cheese and Lancashire cheese, processing until they are completely incorporated.

Pass the mixture through a fine sieve, allow it to cool, then process in an ice cream maker according to the manufacturer's instructions.

Strictly Come Baking

When Americans tune into competition food shows on television, they're apt to see a clutch of hapless young junior chefs with facial jewelry and tattoos challenged to make edible food from a basket of ingredients that includes canned tuna, cherimoya, Hershey bars, and chia seeds (for a $10,000 grand prize), or else expected to cook dishes inspired by their astrological sign or the name of their first pet for a group of B-list celebrities on the rim of a volcano (where the payoff might be as much as $125,000).

When Britons tune into competition food shows on television, they will very likely be watching a miscellaneous collection of men and women of various ages, some young and slim but others plump and a little frumpy, and rarely pierced or inked, nervously watching ovens at cooking stations in a large tent on the grounds of a country manor house (for no prize money at all, just an engraved plate). This is the program called *The Great British Bake Off*, which is by far the most watched food program in Great Britain, and for that matter the most-watched TV show of any kind. And it eats American food shows for dessert.

The Great British Bake Off's 2015 season averaged 12.3 million viewers per episode, with its October 7 show scoring 15 million; back in the United States, *Top Chef* usually draws around two million viewers, and the 2016 season of *Hell's Kitchen* came in at 3.4 million. And America, remember, has roughly five times the population of Great Britain. (The second most popular show in the U.K. is *Strictly Come Dancing*, the British version of *Dancing with the Stars*. It finished 2015 with an average viewership of almost 9 million, with a high of 12.5 million for one show.)

What's so appealing about the show? It's nice. It's genuine. Probably because there is no prize money at stake—just bragging rights—there is no posturing, no insulting or sabotaging of fellow contestants (well,

there *were* accusations of some funny business with a baked Alaska in season five, but they were apparently unfounded). The pace is slow—watching bread rise is at least distantly related to watching paint dry—but the show becomes genuinely engaging, not only through its interspersed portraits of the personalities participating but also through its video vignettes of baking history and illustrator Tom Hovey's signature graphic depictions of the baked goods being made. Even the slightly loopy humor of hosts Sue Perkins and Mel Giedroyc helps.

The contestants on *The Great British Bake Off* are amateur bakers—an accountant, a schoolteacher, a child welfare officer, a stay-at-home dad. To be chosen, they have to undergo an interview and screen test in London, then serve a couple of their baked goods to the show's two judges, the veteran English food writer Mary Berry, who looks like the proper but approachable headmistress at a very fine girls' school, and baker Paul Hollywood, who could play the part of Guy Fieri's lost English uncle. In each episode, contestants have to produce a "signature" item; a test of technique, for which each baker uses the same recipe; and a "showstopper," involving a technically difficult classic. Each episode is themed—cakes, bread, pastry, etc. One episode of season six had a Victorian theme, in which the signature theme was "raised game pie" (savory baked goods show up occasionally). At the end of each episode, a "star baker" is named, and one unfortunate soul is sent home.

CBS tried to launch an American spinoff of *The Great British Bake Off* a few years back, called *The American Baking Competition*. It lasted for six weeks. PBS, though, has started airing the original, under the title *The Great British Baking Show* (is it assumed we colonials won't know what a "bake off" is?), and has racked up a viewership of as many as 2.5 million.

MARMALADE ICE CREAM

SERVES 4

Nick Clarke's restaurant Nick's Diner was a "Swinging London" hotspot in the 1960s, a modest Anglo-French bistro once described as "the ultimate gourmet experience in the Fulham Road for young London," where the clientele included Princess Margaret, Mick Jagger, and Ursula Andress and the influential English folk and jazz guitarist Davey Graham played almost nightly. A scene from Joseph Losey's dark role-reversal classic *The Servant* was filmed there, and the celebrated anthropologist Lionel Tiger made special mention of the garlic potatoes in his book *The Pursuit of Pleasure*. This recipe is adapted from one given by Clarke to the writer and editor Robin McDouall for his book *The Gourmet's London*. Clarke recommends serving it with the long, flat cookies called *langues de chat*, "cat's tongues"—or, curiously but intriguingly, with hot buttered toast.

1 cup coarse-cut orange marmalade, store-bought or homemade (page 282 or 285)
2 egg yolks
½ cup (100 g) superfine sugar
2½ cups (600 ml) half-and-half or light cream
⅔ cup (160 ml) heavy cream

Put the marmalade into a small bowl, then set the bowl into a large bowl filled with hot water for about 10 minutes to soften (be careful that the water doesn't come over the sides of the smaller bowl).

Whisk the egg yolks and sugar together in the top of a double-boiler. Bring the half-and-half to a boil over medium heat in a small pot. Meanwhile, bring the water in the double-boiler to a boil over high heat, then slowly pour the cream into the egg mixture, whisking continuously, and cook until the custard thickens.

Remove the custard from the heat and stir in the marmalade, then set it aside to cool to room temperature.

Meanwhile, in a metal bowl, with a whisk or a hand mixer, whip the heavy cream until stiff peaks form.

When the marmalade custard has cooled, stir in the whipped cream, then process in an ice cream maker according to the manufacturer's instructions.

STICKY TOFFEE PUDDING

SERVES 4 TO 6

The origins of this most indulgent of British desserts—a date-filled sponge cake drenched in toffee sauce—are a little complicated. It seems to have been first served in the 1970s by Francis Coulson at his Sharrow Bay Country House near Pooley Bridge, in the Lake District of Cumbria—sometimes said to have been the first "country house hotel" in Great Britain. According to the estimable chef-turned-writer Simon Hopkinson, Coulson said he got the basic recipe from another hotelier, Patricia Martin of the Old Rectory Hotel in Claughton, Lancashire—who in turn got it from two Canadian Air Force officers who stayed there. Today, the Cartmel Village Shop in the pretty little town of Cartmel on Morecambe Bay, 25 miles or so south of Pooley Bridge, calls Cartmel "the home of sticky toffee pudding," and notes that the shop has been serving it since 1995. Along with a number of variations (including sticky banana pudding, sticky ginger pudding, and sticky chocolate pudding), it's available in various sizes at the shop, and it's also possible to buy a single serving, with or without ice cream, in a plastic bowl. (Simon Hopkinson, who claims to be so obsessed with "STP" that he "can bore for England over it," says definitively that it should never be served with ice cream, as it is already far too sweet.) Tourists wander all over Cartmel with these bowls in hand, usually with smiles on their faces; it really is a delicious dessert. I tried a number of recipes from various sources (chef Mark Hix's was the most useful), and came up with this as a reasonable approximation of the Cartmel version.

FOR THE PUDDING:

1 cup (125 g) pitted dates
⅓ cup (75 g) butter, plus more for greasing
¾ cup (165 g) packed dark brown sugar
2 large eggs, lightly beaten
2 cups (250 g) self-rising flour

FOR THE SAUCE:

2 cups (480 ml) heavy cream
1¾ cups (350 g) granulated sugar
⅓ cup (75 g) butter

MAKE THE PUDDING:

Put the dates into a small saucepan and add water to cover. Bring the water to a boil over high heat, then reduce the heat to low and simmer the dates for 20 minutes, or until the water has almost evaporated. Transfer the dates with any remaining cooking liquid to a blender or food processor, puree, and set aside.

Preheat the oven to 325ºF (175ºC). Grease a 4-cup (1-L) loaf pan lightly with butter, then line it with parchment paper.

In a food processor or the bowl of a stand mixer fitted with the paddle attachment, cream the butter and brown sugar together until creamy, then slowly add the beaten eggs. Transfer the mixture to a large bowl and gradually stir in the flour with a large spoon. Fold in the pureed dates.

Transfer the mixture to the prepared baking pan and bake for 1 hour or until the pudding is firm. Remove it from the oven, leaving the oven on, and allow it to cool.

MAKE THE SAUCE:

While the pudding is baking, put half the cream into a heavy-bottomed medium saucepan, then stir in the sugar and butter. Bring the mixture to a boil over medium-high heat, stirring continuously. Boil, stirring continuously for about 10 minutes, or until a golden-brown caramel sauce has formed. Remove the sauce from the heat and cool for about 10 minutes, then whisk in the remaining cream.

Turn the pudding out of the baking pan, then turn it on its side and, with a sharp knife, carefully cut it into four even horizontal slices.

Line the baking pan with a new piece of parchment paper, then put one layer of the cake on the bottom of the pan. Remove about one-third of the sauce from the pan and set it aside. Pour about a quarter of the remaining sauce over the first layer of the pudding, then put another layer on top. Repeat the process to use all four layers and all the sauce except for what has been set aside.

Return the pudding to the oven for about 15 minutes, or until heated through.

Meanwhile, heat the remaining sauce over low heat, stirring occasionally.

To serve, cut the pudding into four to six vertical slices and divide them among four to six warmed bowls. Pour the warmed sauce over the pudding slices, dividing it evenly between the bowls. Serve with ice cream, if you like (banana is a popular flavor, but vanilla is traditional), or with dollops of crème fraîche.

CHAPTER 10

WHETS AND SAVOURIES

"HE . . . SWALLOWED HIS TWO DOZEN GREEN OYSTERS AS A WHET, AND PROCEEDED TO DINE."

—WILLIAM JERDAN, *The Autobiography of William Jerdan* (1852)

"THOSE WITH A KEEN INTEREST IN AFFAIRS OF THE GUT NEED NO INTRODUCTION TO THE SAVOURY, THAT CROWNING GLORY OF VICTORIAN AND EDWARDIAN EATING."

—TOM PARKER BOWLES, *Let's Eat: Recipes from My Kitchen Notebook* (2012)

"*H*ors d'oeuvres are not, as some think, a nineteenth-century innovation from France," wrote the prolific English author Thomas Burke in his book *Dinner Is Served! Or, Eating Round the World in London*, published in 1937. "They were in use in the Elizabethan and Stuart ale-houses, and in the drinking-rooms of taverns. . . . They were known as 'whets', 'shoe-horns', 'gloves'; and as their purpose was to provoke thirst, they were well spiced." Among them, Burke says, were salted manchets (a kind of bread roll), anchovies, slices of ham, cod's roe, prawns, "powdered beef" (which is not beef in the form of powder, but beef that has been powdered with salt—that is, corned or salt beef), toasted cheese, and pickled herring.

The term *whet* is seldom, if ever, used today, but I like it, in a British context, because it's an English word (derived from the proto-German *hwatjan*, "to incite or encourage") and not inherited from the French, like *apéritif*—though both words can mean either food or drink. The two earliest citations for *whet* in the *Oxford English Dictionary*, in fact—not from the Elizabethan era, Burke notwithstanding, but from the late seventeenth century, the age of the Stuarts—refer specifically to wine. The sense of whets as food appears soon afterward, however, and the term was in common use with that meaning by the mid-1700s (Mrs. Raffald, in 1771, writes that bread slices fried in butter "make a nice Whet before Dinner.") Modest in size and generally fairly salty, whets, as I'm defining them here, are basically the kinds of things that appear increasingly on modern menus as "snacks"—nibbles meant to be ordered before "small plates," as appetizers are now becoming known—though they may often serve as appetizers themselves.

Another term sometimes applied to such delicacies is *kickshaws*. This word does have French origins; it's a corruption of *quelque chose*, "something"—and "little somethings" isn't a bad definition. It was first used somewhat scornfully to mean something dainty or unsubstantial, i.e., something French, as opposed to hearty English fare. Shakespeare's Justice Shallow suggests this contrast in *Henry IV, Part II*, when he sends his servant, Davy, for "Some pigeons . . . ; a couple of short-legged hens; a joint of mutton; and any pretty little tiny kickshaws . . ." Roughly two hundred and fifty years later, in writing about one of George Cruikshank's satirical "Sunday in London" etchings, Thackeray describes "Monsieur the Chef . . .

The thoroughly British Quo Vadis in London

instructing a kitchen-maid how to compound some rascally French kickshaw or other." George Augustus Sala, in *The Thorough Good Cook*, published in 1896, gives a recipe for what I'm tempted to call rascally rabbit kickshaws (with "Italian Sauce"), in effect steamed rabbit-meat custards. The twentieth-century English food writer Jane Grigson included fruit- or preserve-filled kickshaws in several of her books, and today the term—and the idea—is being kept alive by Jeremy Lee at Quo Vadis in London. His menu always includes a kickshaw, which in his interpretation is usually minced chicken or veal in a packet of deep-fried shortcrust pastry.

In many cases, a preparation that could be served as a whet (or a kickshaw) would function equally well as a savoury, which is why I'm grouping these bookends of a meal into one chapter. The savoury is a peculiarly British innovation from the Victorian era (it is first mentioned in print by Eliza Acton in 1845)—a salty tidbit served after dessert. Especially popular in the dining rooms at men's clubs, it is said to have been invented as an accompaniment to any wine left over from the main dish, or as something to eat with the port, or maybe as an excuse to order another bottle or two. "Savouries, the passion of the average Englishman . . . ," wrote Ambrose Heath in *Good Savouries*, back in 1934, "make an admirable ending to a meal, like some unexpected witticism or amusing epigram at the close of a pleasant conversation. . . ." George Sala, on the other hand, thought that "When you have consumed a well-cooked dinner . . . it is in a sense monstrous to indulge in a savoury. . ." and, if such things were to be consumed at all, it should be before dinner (as a whet, he might have said).

One of the most famous of savouries is angels on horseback, an arrangement—the provenance of its name unknown—of shucked oysters wrapped in bacon and roasted or fried, then served on skewers or on toast. Other savouries depend heavily on anchovies or other cured fish or on cheese, and a hint of spice is frequently involved. A curiosity called fairy butter consists of a layered mold of cayenne butter, anchovy-and-sardine butter, and parsley butter, served with dry toast to which it is to be applied. Another one, which I discovered in an early twentieth-century Scottish cookbook, is called luxette. This is a formidable-sounding mixture of ham, tongue, finnan haddie, kippers, and bloaters, plus "a few anchovies" and some anchovy sauce, all pounded together in a mortar and passed through a sieve, then potted under a layer of solidified melted butter. (Bloaters are herring that are smoked whole, rather than being butterflied like kippers. They're generally not as salty or smoky as their kin; they're also more typically English—they're associated with the port of Great Yarmouth in Norfolk, where an old name for them is "Yarmouth capon"—while kippers are more likely to be Scottish or Manx.)

A savoury even more renowned—and certainly more widespread throughout the world—than angels on horseback is Welsh rarebit, that irresistible, if not necessarily Welsh, concoction of spiced melted cheese on toast. This dish and the tradition of Stilton with port aside, the cheese course is not a British institution, but I consider cheese in its unmelted, even unadorned, state to come under the heading of savouries. The prolific London restaurateur (and now hotelier) Jeremy King told me once that he would always remember the cheese he was served after a meal by the chef Simon Hopkinson in his pre-Bibendum days at the now defunct Hilaire in Kensington. "In those days," said King, "any English restaurant that served cheese would offer little cut-up pieces arranged on a plate with chutney, walnuts, celery, and so on. I ordered some Cheshire, and it came out just as a beautiful slab on a plate. That was a revelation to me. It revolutionized the way I thought about food."

While whets, at least under that name, are unknown today, savouries are experiencing something of a revival. They're on the menus at King's Colony Grill Room and The Wolseley, at Fergus Henderson's St. John, at some of Mark Hix's restaurants, and, not surprisingly, at old-school establishments like Simpson's in the Strand and Wilton's. I often order one in place of dessert—and I doubt that anyone would mind if you asked for one at the beginning, instead of the finish, of your meal.

ARBROATH SMOKIE PÂTÉ

SERVES 10 TO 12

Like smoked mackerel, Arbroath Smokies (see page 52) make an excellent pâté, though one that's generally milder in flavor than the mackerel version. Everyone who makes or sells Smokies seems to have his or her own recipe; this is an amalgam of several.

1 pair (about 1 pound or 450 g) Arbroath Smokies (see Sources, page 316), skin and bones removed, flesh flaked
1 8-ounce (227-g) package cream cheese
¼ cup (60 ml) crème fraîche or sour cream
Juice of 1 lemon
Salt
Crackers, oatcakes (see page 27), or toast, for serving

Pulse the Arbroath Smokies in a food processor until they are just coarsely pureed (don't overprocess; the texture should not be smooth).

Transfer the Smokie puree to a bowl. Process the cream cheese and crème fraîche in the food processor (no need to clean it first) until they are mixed together thoroughly.

With a rubber spatula, fold the cream cheese mixture into the Smokie puree and mix thoroughly. Stir in the lemon juice and season with salt.

Serve the pâté with crackers, oatcakes, or toast.

A woman smoking haddock at Auchmithie, circa 1895

KIPPER PÂTÉ

SERVES 8 TO 10

Before they were unfortunately (in the minds of traditionalists like me, at any rate) ceded to Gordon Ramsay and his crew for some years, the restaurant and the grill at the Connaught Hotel in Mayfair served exquisite, old-style French cuisine along with a handful of English dishes prepared with classical precision. Michel Bourdin, the estimable chef in charge of the Connaught kitchens for twenty-six years, once showed me the recipe for one of these English specialties, kipper pâté, which his predecessor, Daniel Dunas, had scrawled on the back of a piece of decorative tissue in which an orange from Provence had been wrapped.

I had asked Bourdin about it because I found this smoky, salty, full-flavored paste of cured herring so addictive that for several years I could never persuade myself to order any other appetizer at the Connaught. "I don't do it quite the same way Daniel did," Bourdin told me. "There used to be soft herring roe in it, for instance." But he was proud of the fact that the Connaught had been buying its kippers from the same source, J. Curtis, on the Isle of Man, since 1902, and he undeniably brought Gallic grace to this preparation. (It is more typically made by merely mashing kippers with butter and sour cream—delicious, too, but without the finesse of this version.) Bourdin retired from the hotel in 2001, incidentally, and is now director of the Musée Escoffier de l'Art Culinaire in Villeneuve-Loubet, near Nice. This is his recipe.

8 ounces (225 g) fatty back bacon or Irish bacon
    (see Sources, page 316), diced
1 large onion, thinly sliced, and 1 small onion,
    thinly sliced, kept apart
Pinch of quatre-épices (French four-spice powder;
    see Sources, page 316)
4 large kippers
1 medium russet potato, boiled or steamed, peeled,
    and cut into large pieces
1 large egg, lightly beaten
1 tablespoon Drambuie
1 tablespoon good quality Scotch whisky

Salt and freshly ground black pepper
1 cup leaf lard (see Sources, page 316)
1 clove garlic, crushed
1 bay leaf
1 sprig fresh thyme
Melba toast, for serving

Cook the bacon and sliced large onion in a medium skillet over medium-low heat, stirring frequently, until the onion is very soft, about 1 hour. Stir in the quatre-épices and set aside.

Preheat the oven to 350°F (175°C).

Lay the kippers out on a baking sheet, skin side down, in a single layer and bake until pliable, 6 to 8 minutes. Leave the oven on. With your fingers, remove the meat from the bones, gently flaking it and removing any small, soft bones. Set the boned fish aside in a medium bowl and discard the bones, heads, tails, and skin.

Add the onion and bacon mixture and the potatoes to the bowl with the kippers, mixing them together well. Transfer the mixture to a food processor and process until fairly smooth, then turn it out into a large bowl. Stir in the egg, Drambuie, and Scotch until thoroughly combined, then season the mixture generously with salt and pepper.

Pack the pâté into a 5-cup (8½ x 4½ x 2½-inch / 22 x 11 x 6-cm) terrine or glass or ceramic loaf pan. Gently tap the terrine on a tabletop to settle the pâté. Cover the terrine with aluminum foil and set it in a small roasting pan. Add enough water to the pan to reach two-thirds of the way up the sides of the terrine, then bake for 1 hour.

Remove the terrine from the baking pan, remove and discard the foil, and set the terrine aside to cool.

Meanwhile, combine the lard, garlic, bay leaf, and sliced small onion in a small pan over low heat. Cook until the lard has completely melted, 6 to 8 minutes, then remove the pan from the heat and set aside for 1 hour.

Remove and discard the solids from the lard with a slotted spoon, then pour the seasoned fat over the pâté. Cover the terrine with foil and refrigerate the pâté overnight. Serve the pâté directly from the terrine, with Melba toast on the side.

POTTED SHRIMP

The eminent British food scholar Colin Spencer says that this dish was invented in the sixteenth century for the officers' table on shipboard. Before refrigeration, potting under a seal of butter was a method of preserving fresh shrimp. The success of this dish depends, of course, on the quality of the shrimp. In England, some of the most famous, particularly associated with this preparation, are the tiny brown shrimp taken in nets from shore in Morecambe Bay—in fact, not a bay but the combined estuaries of five rivers—just south of the Lake District. Shrimping has been an industry there since 1799. The estuaries form extensive mudflats, and fishing for the shrimp can be arduous and, because of quicksand and the speed with which rising tides rush in, dangerous (in 2004, twenty-three Chinese workers digging for cockles were drowned when the tides cut them off from the mainland).

The best American shrimp for this recipe are the small pink Maine shrimp that theoretically come into season briefly each winter, though in 2014 and 2015, the season was canceled after rising water temperatures decimated the stock. California spot prawns, available in spring and summer, are larger but work well here, too. If you can find any other fresh American shrimp, use them, chopping them into smaller pieces if necessary. Those ubiquitous little supermarket "bay shrimp" are flavorless and will make sorry potted shrimp.

½ cup (115 g) clarified butter (see page 312)
1 cup peeled small shrimp
2 teaspoons fresh lemon juice
½ teaspoon cayenne
Pinch of ground mace
Salt and white pepper
8 slices white or whole-grain toast, crusts removed, quartered on the diagonal

In a medium pot, bring the butter to a boil over medium heat, then reduce the heat to low, add the shrimp, and simmer them for about 5 minutes. Set the shrimp aside to cool in the butter.

Stir the lemon juice into the shrimp and season with the cayenne, mace, salt, and a touch of white pepper.

Spoon the shrimp into four small ramekins with a slotted spoon, dividing equally between them, then pour the remaining butter on top of each ramekin, again dividing it evenly. Refrigerate the potted shrimp immediately.

When the butter has solidified, serve the potted shrimp with the toast.

FINNAN HADDIE TOASTS

Finnan haddie—smoked haddock—turns out to be surprisingly versatile, finding its way into soups, omelets, salads, and more. This simple Scottish savoury can be combined with a tossed green salad as a light lunch.

4 thick slices good-quality white bread, crusts removed
4 ounces (110 g) finnan haddie (see Sources, page 316)
2 tablespoons (30 g) unsalted butter, softened
2 tablespoons heavy cream
Freshly ground white pepper
1 tablespoon fine bread crumbs
1 tablespoon grated Gruyère cheese

Preheat the broiler. Lightly toast the bread under the broiler on one side. Leave the broiler on.

In a medium bowl, mash together the finnan haddie, butter, and cream and season with white pepper.

Spread the finnan haddie mixture on the untoasted side of the bread slices, dividing it evenly. Sprinkle a fine film of bread crumbs over the toasts, then divide the cheese evenly over them. Return the toasts to the broiler and cook until they're golden brown but not dark.

Slice each toast on an angle into two triangles before serving.

The Best Cheese in All Europe?

The county of Cheshire, abutting northern Wales, has been famous for its dairy cattle at least since the early twelfth century, and Cheshire cheese is first mentioned in print as early as the 1580s. It is quite possibly, in fact, the oldest named English cheese. The Cheshire-born cartographer and historian John Speed in the early seventeenth century called it "the best cheese in all Europe."

Not everyone agreed. When Dr. Johnson visited the Hebrides in 1773, he was served some and wasn't happy about it. "They pollute the tea-table," he wrote, "by plates piled with large slices of Cheshire cheese, which mingles its less grateful odours with the fragrance of the tea." And the English author George Borrow, who made a point of ordering it when he visited Chester, Cheshire's main city, in the early 1860s, reacted thus to a taste of it:

> To my horror the cheese had much the appearance of soap of the commonest kind, which indeed I found it much resembled in taste, on putting a small portion into my mouth. "Ah," said I, after I had opened the window and ejected the half-masticated morsel into the street, "those who wish to regale on good Cheshire cheese must not come to Chester, no more than those who wish to drink first-rate coffee must go to Mocha."

In a fascinating book from 1937 called *Cheddar Gorge: A Book of English Cheeses*, Vyvyan Holland—Oscar Wilde's second son, and himself an author and translator—contributes a chapter on Cheshire. He describes it as a slow-ripening cheese, a characteristic he believes is encouraged by the high degree of salinity in the milk of cows grazing over the region's subterranean salt springs. He describes three varieties of the cheese, red (dyed with annatto; historically, carrot juice was used instead), white, and blue. Only the red one was ever melted on toast, he says, while the white "is served with radishes or watercress or celery when in season."

In the 1930s, there were at least four hundred farms producing genuine Cheshire cheese, unpasteurized, wrapped in calico cloth. Today, there is only one: Appleby's, started by Lucy Appleby and her husband, Lance, in 1952 in the stables at their Hawkstone Abbey Farm, actually about ten miles outside the limits of Cheshire, in Shropshire, but still on the salty Cheshire Plain. The cheese, made today by the Applebys' grandchildren, is rich, buttery, and, yes, salty, with a hint of pungency but an aftertaste that is mellow rather than sharp. Its name is probably known today mostly thanks to the centuries-old London institution Ye Olde Cheshire Cheese (see page 174), but it deserves to be known, and enjoyed, for itself.

Driving to Caerffili

The road to Caws Cenarth in Carmarthenshire, in southwestern Wales, is the narrowest I have ever negotiated in an automobile. Six-foot-high hedgerows hug the lane on both sides; they brush both sides of the car as we go along. Caws Cenarth is one of the best-known Welsh cheese producers, and one of the best (*caws* is Welsh for "cheese"; Cenarth is a village nearby, on the banks of the River Teifi). It is also the site of a small farmhouse cheese museum, which draws visitors by motor coach. (I thought about that as we drove away, back down that narrow road.)

Caws Cenarth was a dairy farm, producing milk and cream and not much more, when, in 1984, the European Union imposed milk production quotas on member nations. The owners of the farm, Thelma and Gwynfor Adams, in common with other dairy farmers, suddenly found themselves with a surplus of milk that they were not allowed to sell, at least not in its natural form. Thelma decided to try making cheese. "I started with four pounds on the kitchen table," she told me, "and gave it away to friends." The friends were impressed and asked for more, and in 1987, the Adamses went into the cheese business on a serious basis.

The one Welsh cheese people tend to know all over the world is Caerphilly—properly spelled Caerffili. Caws Cenarth produces one of the best, very much in a traditional style, creamy and mild but with a tang of citrus. (They also make smoked and garlic-and-herb versions.) Another famous Welsh cheese is the farm's Perl Las, a forthright blue with a long, earthy finish. One of their newer efforts, Golden Cenarth, a semisoft cheese with a cider-washed rind, was named Supreme Champion at the British Cheese Awards one year.

The Adamses' son, Carwyn, has joined the family business, and works with his mother to develop other new products. We tasted a cheese called Llain, sold only at the farm, an almost fruity cheese with a tart finish, inspired by Parmigiano-Reggiano. We also sampled a new blue cheese Thelma was working on, very soft but pungent. "I think we need to lessen the salt," she said.

DEVILLED BISCUITS

MAKES 40 TO 48

In his best-selling early-nineteenth-century cookbook *Apicius Redivivus: or, The Cook's Oracle*, the optician and serious amateur cook William Kitchiner called this anchovy spread the "*ne plus ultra* of highly spiced relishes" and noted that devilled biscuits often make their appearance "at the fag end of a tavern dinner, when the votaries of Bacchus are determined to vie with each other in sacrificing to the jolly god, and to celebrate his festive rites, 'com furore.'" In addition to flour, egg, and milk, Kitchiner's recipe for the biscuits calls for arrowroot and four drachms (an old apothecary measure equaling an eighth of an ounce or just under 4 grams) of carbonate of ammonia and recommends that the dough be "[beaten] . . . well with a rolling-pin for half an hour." This is a simpler version of the recipe. Kitchiner notes that the spread may also be served on toast (I'd say crustless, cut into 2-inch squares) fried in butter.

FOR THE BISCUITS:
2 cups (250 g) all-purpose flour, plus more for
    dusting
½ cup (1 stick / 115 g) butter, cut into ½-inch
    (1.25-cm) cubes
1 large egg plus 1 large egg yolk, beaten together
½ cup (120 ml) whole milk
2 teaspoons salt
¾ teaspoon sugar

FOR THE ANCHOVY SPREAD:
4 ounces (125 g) oil-packed boneless, skinless
    anchovies
4 tablespoons (½ stick / 55 g) unsalted butter,
    softened but not melted
¼ teaspoon dry mustard
¼ teaspoon cayenne, or more to taste
¼ teaspoon finely ground black pepper
½ teaspoon curry powder
Zest of 1 lemon

MAKE THE BISCUITS:
Preheat the oven to 400°F (200°C).

Put the flour into a medium bowl, then add the butter and work the mixture with your fingers until it resembles coarse crumbs. Stir in the egg and enough of the milk to make a stiff dough. Stir in the salt and sugar.

Roll out the dough on a lightly floured work surface to a thickness of about ¼ inch (6 mm), then use a cookie cutter or the rim of a shot glass to cut out disks about 2 inches (5 cm) in diameter.

MAKE THE ANCHOVY SPREAD:
Pound the anchovies and butter together with a mortar and pestle until they form a smooth paste. Alternately, puree them in a food processor. Add the mustard, cayenne, black pepper, and curry powder and stir until thoroughly combined.

Put the biscuits on an ungreased baking sheet, making sure they don't touch, and bake for 12 to 15 minutes, or until the tops are light brown.

Allow the biscuits to cool slightly, then spread the top of each with the anchovy mixture, dividing it equally between them. Sprinkle a bit of lemon zest over the top of each one. Serve slightly warm.

COCKLE POPCORN

SERVES 4

To the best of my knowledge, the first person to use the term *popcorn* to describe crunchy deep-fried food that had nothing to do with actual corn was the late Paul Prudhomme, who served "Cajun popcorn"—deep-fried crawfish tails—at his seminal New Orleans restaurant K-Paul's Louisiana Kitchen. The usage is now fairly universal around the United States (you can buy frozen popcorn shrimp at any supermarket) and increasingly in the U.K. At his Hix Oyster and Fish House in Lyme Regis, Mark Hix adapts the concept to cockles, tiny saltwater clams, today widely available fresh at better fish markets and also canned and frozen (the latter are preferable if you can't find them fresh). "I must admit," confesses Hix, "that I stole this dish from one of our local fish merchants, Samways, who served these at a local food festival."

Vegetable or corn oil, for deep-frying
⅔ cup (70 g) self-rising gluten-free or all-purpose flour
1 teaspoon cayenne
Salt
7 ounces (200 ml) whole milk
6 ounces (175 g) raw fresh cockle meat or frozen cooked cockle meat, thawed
Good-quality malt vinegar, for serving

Heat 3 to 4 inches (7½ to 10 cm) of oil in an electric deep-fryer or large, heavy-bottomed saucepan to a temperature of 350°F (175°C).

Put the flour into a shallow medium bowl and stir in the cayenne and salt to taste. Put the milk in another shallow medium bowl, and put out a third (empty) shallow medium bowl.

Toss the cockles in the flour, then shake off any excess and put them in the milk. Pass them back through the flour, then put them in the empty bowl as they're ready.

Deep-fry the cockles in batches, stirring them continuously with a slotted spoon, for 2 to 3 minutes or until golden brown, then transfer them with the slotted spoon to paper towels to drain. Serve immediately, accompanied by good-quality malt vinegar.

CRISPY PRAWN SHELLS

SERVES 4

At his sun-flooded little Hix Oyster and Fish House over-looking the beach at Lyme Regis, Mark Hix serves these addictive treats as a snack before meals. They're not exactly British in origin: "I first had these at a tiny restaurant in Tokyo called Sushi Ken," Hix told me. "The dish was called 'dancing prawns,' where live prawns were hooked out of the tank in front of you and peeled. Once you had eaten the peeled live prawns, they brought the shells back crisply fried and simply scattered with sea salt. In Lyme Regis, when the local prawns are in season, we do exactly the same with the shells—occasionally getting an odd customer reaction, but once you tuck into them, they are like a prawn cracker you've never tasted before." Though we sometimes use the term *prawn* in the United States to mean a kind of large shrimp, in the U.K., *prawn* and *shrimp* are synonymous. If you're serving shrimp, of whatever size, save the shells and heads for this purpose.

Vegetable or corn oil, for deep-frying
2 large handfuls cooked or raw shrimp shells,
**   heads included**
Maldon or other flaky sea salt

Heat 3 to 4 inches (7½ to 10 cm) of oil in an electric deep-fryer or large, heavy-bottomed saucepan to a temperature of 350°F (175°C). Add the shrimp shells and fry them, stirring them continuously with a slotted spoon, for about 2 minutes, or until they're crisp but not brown. Transfer the shells with the slotted spoon to paper towels to drain and scatter them with sea salt.

Serve immediately.

POTTED STILTON

SERVES 4

Stilton, dating from the early eighteenth century and produced only in the counties of Derbyshire, Leicestershire, and Nottinghamshire, is one of the world's great cheeses, best served spooned straight out of the tall, cylindrical wheel in which it is made. At its best, it needs no help—but when the cheese has been mostly scooped out of its wheel and what remains starts to get dry around the edges, this is a great way to turn it into a savoury.

12 ounces (340 g) Stilton cheese
3 ounces (85 g) butter, softened
Pinch of ground mace
¼ teaspoon cayenne
3 tablespoons ruby, late-bottled vintage,
**   or vintage port**
2 ounces (50 g) clarified butter (page 312), melted
Crackers, for serving

Combine the Stilton, softened butter, mace, cayenne, and port in a medium bowl, then mash all the ingredients together well with a fork to form a paste.

Gently pack the paste into a 16-ounce (450-g) glass or earthenware bowl or crock, or into four smaller ones.

Pour the clarified butter over the top of the Stilton, then refrigerate it for at least 2 hours before serving with crackers.

Saving British Cheese

Folklore has it that Monty Python's famous cheese shop sketch was inspired by a visit paid to Neal's Yard Dairy in Covent Garden by Python's John Cleese and Graham Chapman. In the sketch, a man comes into the shop to buy cheese, but none seems to be available; he asks for roughly forty varieties in turn, receiving answers ranging from "Never at the end of the week, sir" to simply "No" (repeated many times). The original Dairy sold cheesemaking supplies and made its own fresh cheese, crème fraîche, and yogurt, and thus might very well not have had any Wensleydale or suchlike on offer when the Pythons stopped by—and stopped by they surely did, as their studio was upstairs from the neighboring Neal's Yard Remedies shop from 1976 to 1987.

Unfortunately, Cleese tells a very different story of the sketch's origin, involving a conversation with Chapman about whether one could buy cheese in a chemist's shop—a pharmacy—as the two were on the road returning from Folkestone Harbour to London. In any case, the cheese shop routine was first broadcast in 1972, before either the Pythons or the Dairy had taken up residence at Neal's Yard.

Neal's Yard Dairy is significant for other reasons, though. Like Remedies (which sells organic health and beauty products), it grew out of a food shop opened in 1976 by Nicholas Saunders, a colorful character best known as publisher of the *Alternative London* guides and later as an articulate apostle of the recreational drug MDMA (ecstasy). Saunders opened the Dairy in 1979 as an extension of the food shop, together with a young man with a degree in food science named Randolph Hodgson. Hodgson, and Neal's Yard, went on to revolutionize—or at least revive and reanimate—the British farmhouse cheese industry.

Neal's Yard wasn't the first purveyor of good British cheese. The venerable Paxton & Whitfield in Jermyn Street, among others, carried some fine examples, along with plenty of French and other imported cheeses. But Hodgson realized what a wealth of good cheese there was—or had been—in Great Britain itself. According to the British Cheese Board, there are more than seven hundred named cheeses made in the U.K., fifteen of them considered unique enough to have been granted a Protected Designation of Origin (PDO) by the European Union in the 1990s. Hodgson thought the Dairy should focus on what his own country produced.

He also quickly realized, though, that the state of traditional small-scale cheesemaking in the U.K. was dire. "When I started," Hodgson told the writer John Whitley in *Saveur* in 1996, " . . . there were really only a handful of farmers left. Everyone else had either given up or changed to making commercial products with pasteurized milk and wax coatings. The tradition was close to being lost." (Over half those PDO cheeses named in the 1990s are no longer being produced.)

He was having none of that, and set out to discover and help expand the market for those authentic farmhouse cheeses that were still being made and to encourage other farmers to revive or initiate cheesemaking programs of their own. One of the first cheeses the Dairy sold was Duckett's Caerphilly from Somerset (it's still one of the shop's most popular cheeses). Thanks to Hodgson and his crew, Duckett's gained a measure of celebrity in the food community. So did Mrs. Kirkham's Lancashire, Mrs. Appleby's Cheshire, Mrs. Montgomery's cheddar, cheeses with names like Lincolnshire Poacher and Stinking Bishop, classics like Colston Bassett Stilton and Cornish Yarg,

A milk truck at the Colston Bassett Dairy in Nottingham, producers of Stilton cheese, 1923

and many more. Today, cheese shops and upscale markets all over England, Scotland, and Wales offer British cheeses, as do many restaurants.

In 1989—on the same day that the British minister of agriculture announced that he was seeking a ban on the sale of all unpasteurized cheeses in the U.K.—Hodgson founded the Specialist Cheesemakers Association, bringing together cheesemakers, retailers and wholesalers, and just plain cheese lovers to help promote British cheeses, lobby against unfair legislation, exchange information and ideas, and in general encourage excellence in cheesemaking. In the late 1990s, Hodgson was instrumental in transforming London's Borough Market in Central London from a strictly wholesale enterprise into a major retail food emporium and culinary tourist attraction. In 2005,

dismayed by the disappearance of raw-milk Stilton (due to EU regulation), he cofounded Stichelton Dairy to make a cheese that recalls the Stilton of old, but doesn't qualifiy for the Stilton PDO because it's based on unpasteurized milk.

Today, in addition to the original shop, Neal's Yard Dairy has outposts at Borough Market and nearby in Bermondsey. Hodgson is no longer actively involved. According to Jason Hinds, sales director and co-owner of this now celebrated institution, "Randolph is now farming in Herefordshire and is also cheesemaking on an R & D basis at his farm. He is rarely in London and is never in the business. It is fair to say that he is very 'withdrawn' from it." He didn't withdraw before his mission was accomplished.

A World of Oysters

The Romans loved shellfish, and particularly enjoyed the wild oysters they found along the coast of Britannia—so much so that they even packed them up in barrels and shipped them home. Some historians have suggested that they made Camulodunum (modern-day Colchester, in Essex) their British capital for a time, in fact, precisely because they were so fond of the oysters that grew there. The bivalves fell out of fashion after the Romans left the island in the early fifth century AD, but interest had revived by the tenth century. They were plentiful and thus very cheap—historian Colin Spencer notes that they went for twopence a gallon in 1298, much less than a comparable quantity of fish—and by Elizabethan times, they were common food for both rich and poor, served as street snacks and as a part of formal dinners and everything in between.

The so-called native oyster, the flat European *Ostrea edulis*, was, and remains, the most prized species. Pollution around the turn of the last century effectively killed the British oyster industry, but it began to revive in the latter twentieth century. Natives still show up on menus, but the gully-shelled Portuguese (*Crassostrea angulata*) and the more recently imported dimple-shelled Pacific oyster (*Crassostrea giga*) are widely cultivated today.

England's most famous oyster town is Whitstable, in Kent. There are also excellent oysters grown around Falmouth, on the Cornish coast; Colchester and nearby Mersea Island; Whitby in Yorkshire; several parts of the Suffolk coast; Swansea Bay and the Menai Strait in Wales; and Loch Ryan and Loch Fyne in Scotland, among other places.

In his *Apicius Redivivus; or, The Cook's Oracle* from 1817, William Kitchiner suggests how seriously some nineteenth-century diners took oysters. "Those who wish to enjoy this delicious restorative in its utmost perfection," he wrote, "must eat it the moment it is opened, with its own gravy in the under shell: If not eaten while absolutely alive, its flavour and spirit is lost. The true lover of an oyster will have more regard for the feelings of his little favourite, than to abandon it to the mercy of a bungling operator, but will always open it himself, and contrive to detach the fish from the shell so dexterously, that the oyster is hardly conscious he has been ejected from his lodging, till he feels the teeth of the *gourmand* tickling him to death." Not quite a decade later, writing as Meg Dods, Christian Isobel Johnstone had another suggestion: "Let the [oyster] opener stand behind the eater's chair, who should make a quick and clean conveyance."

That oysters in that era weren't the preserve of gourmandise alone may be gleaned from this famous passage from Charles Dickens' *The Posthumous Papers of the Pickwick Club*, published the same year as Johnstone's book, *The Cook and Housewife's Manual*:

> "Not a very nice neighbourhood this, sir," said Sam, with a touch of the hat, which always preceded his entering into conversation with his master.
>
> "It is not indeed, Sam," replied Mr Pickwick, surveying the crowded and filthy street through which they were passing.
>
> "It's a very remarkable circumstance, sir," said Sam, "that poverty and oysters always seems to go together."
>
> "I don't understand, Sam," said Mr. Pickwick.
>
> "What I mean, sir," said Sam, "is, that the poorer a place is, the greater call there seems to be for oysters. Look here, sir; here's a oyster stall to every half dozen houses. The streets lined vith 'em. Blessed if I don't think that ven a man's wery poor, he rushes out of his lodgings and eats oysters in reg'lar desperation."

ANGELS ON HORSEBACK

SERVES 4

"It seems a shame to cook the oyster," proposed the pseudonymous London restaurant writer "Diner-Out" in 1924. "It is almost like mulling Port. Still I must admit in fairness the virtues of 'an angel on horseback.'" Angels on horseback are simply shucked oysters wrapped in bacon and fried or roasted, then served on toothpicks or placed on small pieces of toast as canapés. Mrs. Beeton mentions them in the 1888 edition of her famous *Book of Household Management*, noting their French translation (*anges à cheval*)—though whether the preparation existed previously in France isn't clear. Neither is any metaphorical connection between oysters and angels, or bacon and horses. (Almost as old is a variation called devils on horseback, in which the oysters are replaced by pitted prunes—or, more often these days, pitted dates.)

8 slices American-style bacon
16 small oysters, shucked
1 lemon quarter
4 pieces white sandwich bread, crusts removed,
    toasted and quartered (optional)

Cook the bacon in a medium skillet over medium heat for about 5 minutes, or until softened but not browned, turning it once.

Remove the bacon from the skillet and let it cool slightly, then cut each piece in half crosswise. Wrap each oyster in a piece of bacon, overlapping the edges, and skewer each piece, through the bacon, with a toothpick. Return the bacon-wrapped oysters to the same skillet and cook over medium heat, turning frequently, until the bacon is crisp on all sides.

Squeeze a few drops of lemon juice over each "angel," then serve them on the toothpicks, or transfer each one to a square of toast.

CREAMED MUSHROOMS ON TOAST

SERVES 4

Sliced, sautéed button mushrooms (page 39) are generally considered an essential part of the full English breakfast (see page 36)—but mushrooms in other forms were comparatively uncommon on traditional British tables in earlier eras. One preparation that has long been appreciated, though, is this one, which may be served as an appetizer or a savoury.

4 tablespoons (½ stick / 55 g) butter, plus more for
    buttering toast
1½ pounds (675 g) button mushrooms or assorted
    wild and/or cultivated mushrooms, brushed
    clean and quartered (for button mushrooms) or
    cut into small pieces of approximately equal size
¾ cup (180 ml) heavy cream
Juice of ½ lemon
Dash of fino sherry (optional)
Leaves from 3 or 4 sprigs parsley, finely chopped
Salt
4 thick slices country-style white or sourdough
    bread, crusts removed, toasted

Melt the butter in a large skillet over medium-low heat. Add the mushrooms and cook, stirring frequently, for about 20 minutes, or until they have released their liquid and reabsorbed some of it.

Stir in the cream, lemon juice, sherry (if using), and half the parsley, reduce the heat to low, and cook, stirring occasionally, for 8 to 10 minutes more, or until the sauce thickens. Season the mushrooms with salt.

Lightly butter the toast, then divide it between four plates. Spoon the mushrooms over the toast, dividing them equally. Garnish with the rest of the parsley.

ROAST BONE MARROW & PARSLEY SALAD

SERVES 4

Fergus Henderson became one of the most influential chefs in modern Britain, at his restaurant St. John (see page 160) and its spinoffs, not through lapidary elaboration of technique or fantastical culinary conceptions but through the daring of confident simplicity. I've already mentioned the simple presentation of radishes I once encountered on an early visit to St. John (see page 160). I couldn't believe a restaurant would serve something that apparently offhanded, but somehow so perfect.

I had the same feeling about another dish I ordered, probably on the same occasion—this presentation of marrow bones, standing tall, elemental, unapologetic. It was like nothing I'd ever seen before, and somehow the boldness of the presentation, with just a few slightly pungent parsley leaves on the side, seemed to intensify the marrow's subtle but earthy flavor.

The easiest way to extract the marrow from the bones is with a marrow spoon or seafood pick; these are readily available at cookware stores and online, at prices ranging from about $5 to $75 each.

4 pieces veal marrow bone, 5 to 6 inches (13 to 15 cm) long, or 8 pieces veal marrow bone, 3 to 4 inches (7.5 to 10 cm) long (ask your butcher to cut them)
1 cup loosely packed fresh flat-leaf parsley leaves, coarsely chopped
2 small shallots, very thinly sliced
1 tablespoon capers, drained
2 tablespoons extra-virgin olive oil
Juice of ½ lemon
Maldon or other flaky sea salt and freshly ground black pepper
8 to 12 small pieces country-style bread, toasted

Preheat the oven to 450°F (230ºC).

Put the bones upright, with the wide side down, in a heavy-bottomed roasting pan, and roast for about 20 minutes, or until the marrow is soft but not melting.

Meanwhile, combine the parsley, shallots, capers, olive oil, and lemon juice in a medium bowl and toss well, then season the salad generously with salt and pepper.

Divide the marrow bones between four plates, wide side up, then add a small amount of the salad to each plate, dividing it evenly among them. Garnish each plate with a teaspoon or two of salt. Serve with the toast on the side.

POTTED RABBIT

SERVES 8 TO 12

Returning to London after a driving trip through Wales, my wife and I decided to drop our rented car at Heathrow and take a taxi into town instead of braving the capital's traffic (and congestion charges). It was lunchtime, though, so we thought we'd stop for a meal before we got to the airport. One of our guidebooks recommended The Royal Oak in Littlefield Green, just outside the ancient Berkshire town of Maidenhead. We pulled up to an unassuming-looking whitewashed building (unassuming except for the sign reading PARKING FOR FERRARIS ONLY near the entrance), obviously a former pub, and walked in and sat down to the best meals of our trip—unpretentious, full of flavor, skillfully cooked.

We later learned that The Royal Oak has a Michelin star, that the owner is longtime food and beverage professional Nick Parkinson (son of the celebrated erstwhile BBC radio host Michael Parkinson), and that the chef, Michael Chapman, is a South African who worked under Marcus Wareing at Pétrus in London.

The dish that got our meal off to a delicious start was potted rabbit, and Chapman generously shared his recipe. Potted meats are essentially what the French call *rillettes*, meats cooked and preserved in fat. In France, rillettes are traditionally made with pork, duck, or goose—which have enough fat of their own for the process—but also with leaner meats, like wild game, rabbit, and even salmon or trout, in which case fat must be added. This recipe relies on pork belly and duck fat for moisture and richness. Specialty purveyors sell rabbit legs (buy the meaty hind legs only, which are generally all that is sold; the forelegs are sinewy and meager).

1¾ cups Maldon sea salt (see page 82)
1 head garlic, cloves peeled and finely chopped
¼ cup fresh rosemary leaves
¼ cup fresh thyme leaves
12 whole black peppercorns
6 bone-in rabbit legs (about 3.3 pounds / 1.5 kg;
    see Sources, page 316)

1 (1-pound / 450-kg) pork belly, cut into 4 pieces
4 cups duck fat, at room temperature
Table salt and freshly ground black pepper
2 teaspoons cognac or Armagnac
Cornichons, for serving
Sourdough or other rustic bread, toasted,
    for serving

Prepare the meat a day ahead: In a large bowl, mix the Maldon salt, garlic, rosemary, thyme, and peppercorns. Add the rabbit legs and pork belly to the bowl and, with your hands, dredge them in the salt mixture until it covers all surfaces. Cover the bowl with plastic wrap and refrigerate for 24 hours.

Remove the rabbit legs and pork belly from the salt mixture, discarding the mixture and thoroughly rinsing out the bowl, and rinse the meats well in a colander. Return the meats to the bowl and set the bowl under cold, slowly running water, turning them several times, for 20 minutes.

Pat the rabbit legs and pork belly dry, then put them into a heavy-bottomed lidded pot large enough to hold them several inches below the rim. Melt the duck fat and pour in enough to completely cover the meats. Cover the pot and heat the fat over medium heat for about 5 minutes, then reduce the heat to low and poach the meats until they are very tender and the rabbit meat easily falls off the bone, about 1½ hours.

Allow the meats to cool to room temperature in the fat. Transfer them to a large bowl, discarding the bones, and shred the meats with two forks. Work in just enough duck fat so that the mixture can be spread easily on toast, reserving the rest of the fat. Season the mixture generously with table salt and pepper and stir in the cognac.

Immediately pack the mixture into ramekins or small hermetic jars and pour about ½ inch (1.25 cm) of duck fat over the top of each. Refrigerate the potted rabbit for at least 2 to 3 hours, or overnight. Remove it from the refrigerator about 1 hour before serving.

Serve with cornichons and quartered slices of toasted sourdough or other rustic bread.

The Walnut Tree

Like a surprisingly large portion of Great Britain, Wales—at least the part that isn't slate scarps and coal tips—feels rural, pastoral, agrarian. The landscapes are vast and often stunning, defined by meadows and leas, copses and woods, all green and yellowing green; black-and-white-splotched cows mosey over the highway on a metal bridge near Keele in the afternoon sun. It looks like a country that would produce an abundance of good culinary raw materials, and be rich enough to enjoy what they're turned into.

Indeed, the nineteenth-century American author and journalist Wirt Sikes, who became a specialist in Welsh customs and traditions, wrote in his book *Rambles and Studies in Old South Wales* (1881) that "The most magnificent banquet I ever attended was a private dinner, in a certain Welsh castle that shall here be nameless . . . It was an expression of the limits of civilization in this direction—a dinner not merely provided by vast wealth, quite careless of cost, but adorned with luxurious piles of the rarest exotics, grown in my host's conservatory, and including pheasants shot on the estate, and great pine-apples, oranges, peaches, the most luscious grapes, fruit of the rarest perfection and in profuse abundance, all reared in the hot-houses belonging to the castle. . . ."

That was probably the exception, though. "It's very recent that there has been good food here," says Shaun Hill, the Irish-born chef who runs The Walnut Tree, just outside Abergavenny in Monmouthshire, in southeastern Wales. "Most of the food trades in Wales disappeared with the Industrial Revolution. There's a great nostalgia here for a food culture that didn't exist. What Wales has to offer is not all the horseshit the tourist board will tell you; it's good producers, good people, a blank slate. The reality is that there is a national taste in Wales, if not a cuisine, per se. It fits in with the climate, the sensibility."

The Walnut Tree was a small rural pub when Franco Taruschio, an Italian from the Marche who had been sent to England to study local cooking and the English language, took it over in 1963 after meeting the Englishwoman who was to become his wife. "When we bought the place," he told me, "you couldn't get ingredients. We used to grow our own vegetables and herbs and beg the local farmers for chickens and rabbits. The idea of 'no food miles' was forced on me. We had no choice." Taruschio started cooking the dishes of his home region in Italy, with some Welsh touches and of course based on Welsh ingredients. The influential restaurant guide publishers Egon Ronay and Raymond Postgate discovered the place and, Taruschio said, "People started driving here from England, and the Welsh actually started to believe that there could be good food here."

After thirty-seven years of running the place, and earning it a reputation as one of the best rural restaurants in the U.K., Taruschio sold The Walnut Tree to concentrate on writing cookbooks. The subsequent owner had problems—the restaurant won a Michelin star in 2002 but lost it two years later; it also was featured on Gordon Ramsay's *Kitchen Nightmares*—and the place closed, remaining shuttered for two years. Shaun Hill, who had been chef and managing director at the highly rated Gidleigh Park, a luxury country house hotel in Devon, took over the place in 2007, and in 2010 got its Michelin star back. Based on a meal my wife and I had there of silken chicken liver parfait with buttery brioche, tender rabbit fricassee with fresh peas, a slab of monkfish in a dense tomato reduction flavored with ginger and chiles, and a piece of light-as-air pistachio cake with apricot ice cream obviously made with fresh fruit, it deserves it. "I look for nice stuff to eat and try not to screw it up," says Hill. He seems to succeed.

WELSH RAREBIT

SERVES 6

The original Welsh rarebit—the definitive savoury—was nothing more than cheese melted on toast (see page 268). As the dish has evolved over the years, however, other ingredients have found their way into the recipe, and today it is more often a kind of fondue or fonduta, liquid enough to be poured over the bread instead of just placed on top of it—usually courtesy of a good dose of ale. At his groundbreaking St. John in London's Smithfield neighborhood, Fergus Henderson uses Guinness stout, and spices the cheese up with mustard, chili powder, and Worcestershire sauce. If you increase the quantities in this recipe—which is an adaptation of Henderson's—or decrease the audience, you'll have a nice breakfast dish (some crisp bacon laid across the cheese, while hardly traditional, wouldn't be amiss) or a light lunch, best accompanied by a simple green salad.

5 tablespoons (75 g) butter
¾ cup (95 g) all-purpose flour
1 tablespoon dry mustard
1 teaspoon chili powder or cayenne
Pinch of salt
Pinch of finely ground black pepper
½ cup (120 ml) Worcestershire sauce
1 cup (240 ml) Guinness stout or good English ale
1½ pounds (680 g) good English farmhouse
 cheddar or Cheshire cheese, grated
6 slices good white bread, about 1 inch thick, from
 a large loaf, crusts removed

Melt the butter in a large skillet over low heat. Stir in the flour, mustard, chili powder, salt, and pepper, then add the Worcestershire sauce and stout. Slowly whisk in the cheese until a thick, smooth paste forms (don't let the mixture boil).

Pour the cheese mixture out onto a rimmed baking sheet and set it aside to cool completely and set. (This may take as long as 4 hours.)

When the cheese is almost set, preheat the broiler.

Put the bread on a baking sheet and toast it under the broiler on one side only, until it's just beginning to brown. Divide the set cheese into six equal pieces. Flip the bread untoasted side up and set one portion of cheese on each one, pressing it down lightly with your fingers so that it completely covers the bread.

Broil for 2 to 3 minutes, or until the cheese bubbles and browns. Serve immediately.

Rabbit and Rarebit

The Welsh rarebit—surely the most famous dish with which the Welsh are associated around the world—was originally a Welsh "rabbit," of course. Why a rabbit? The name may have originally been a joke, suggesting that the Welsh, due either to poverty or some innate lack of hunting skill (or a prohibition against taking rabbit from near the noble estates), were more likely to sup on bread and cheese than an actual roasted lagomorph. There are parallels in dish names from other cultures. For instance, Scotch woodcock is a savoury of eggs scrambled with anchovy paste on toast in lieu of the savory game bird its name invokes. In parts of Italy, veal rolls filled with pancetta or prosciutto are called *ucceli scappati*, "escaped birds," presumably in the same spirit. In Catalan, the same word, *truita*, means both "omelet" and "trout"—perhaps because the former might end up being dinner if the fish aren't biting.

The substitution of *rarebit*—which is, as far as anybody knows, simply a portmanteau joining of *rare* and *bit* (as in morsel), suggesting an uncommon delicacy—for *rabbit* goes back some time, in any case. The *Oxford English Dictionary* cites a usage as early as 1781. Curiously, there appears to be no other use of the term except to describe this cheese dish.

The question of rabbit versus rarebit was tackled by Ambrose Bierce in *The Devil's Dictionary* back in 1911. His definition of rarebit was as follows: "n. A Welsh rabbit, in the speech of the humorless, who point out that it is not a rabbit. To whom it may solemnly be explained that the comestible known as toad in the hole is not really a toad and that *ris de veau à la financière* is not the smile of a calf prepared after the recipe of a she-banker."

Whether rarebit or rabbit, was the dish really invented in Wales? Perhaps not. Some scholars suggest that

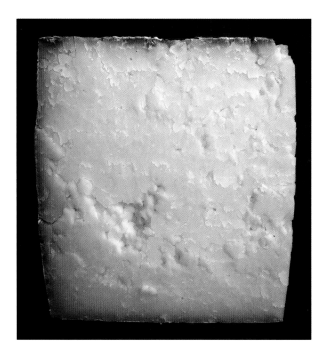

English farmhouse cheddar

the term *Welsh* was first applied not as a geographical or cultural indicator but as a pejorative: In Old English, the word could mean "foreign" or "alien," and perhaps some English diners found the preparation to be strange or un-English—though that's hard to imagine. Or the term may have been applied to the dish not because the Welsh invented it but because they had long had a reputation for being particularly fond of cheese. An old (as in, sixteenth-century) joke holds that God grew tired of the ruckus the Welsh were raising in heaven, so St. Peter stood outside the Pearly Gates and shouted, "There's roasted cheese here!" When all the Welsh rushed out, he slammed the door on them. On the other hand, Hannah Glasse, in *The Art of Cookery Made Plain and Easy* (1747), seems to be ascribing national origins to the recipes she gives for four different "rabbits"—Scotch, Welch [*sic*], and English (two different versions).

Considerably later, in 1943, the English journalist and food writer Ambrose Heath, in a little volume called *Good Cheese Dishes*, gives recipes for ten different "cheese rabbits," including variations made with anchovies, celery, haddock, sardines, and tomatoes, plus an "Irish rabbit," enhanced with "a dessertspoonful of coarsely chopped pickled gherkin." The formula for what Heath calls simply Welsh rabbit, though, calls for nothing more than "a slice of crisp, dry toast, less than a quarter of an inch thick," with a piece of cheese of slightly smaller dimensions "toasted" on both sides and laid across it. There is similar simplicity in the recipe collected by S. Minwel Tibbott, a historian of Welsh domestic culture who worked with the Welsh Folk Museum (now the St. Fagans National History Museum) outside Cardiff. It calls for "cheese" and "a slice of bread" and the instructions read in full: "Toast a slice of bread. Bake a large slice of cheese and place on top of the toast." She gives it the Welsh name *caws wedi'i bobi*, which means simply "baked cheese."

The dish has evolved over the years to include ale, mustard, cayenne, sometimes milk or cream, sometimes flour, sometimes an egg—and as such it is sometimes considered hard to digest. The American cartoonist Winsor McCay, whose *Little Nemo* was one of the most famous of early comic strips, capitalized on this feature of the dish with a strip called *Dream of the Rarebit Fiend*, which ran from 1904 to 1911 (with some later rebirths). In these strips, a character would eat Welsh rarebit before retiring for the evening and then have weird dreams or nightmares as a result of his rich repast. The strip was made into a short film by the Edison Company in 1906, in which the hapless "fiend" is whisked through the air by demons and left dangling on a church steeple.

Strawberry Preserves (page 285)

CHAPTER 11

—

SAUCES, CONDIMENTS, AND PRESERVES

"SAUCES ARE TO FOOD WHAT ACTION IS TO ORATORY."

—ANONYMOUS, "Transcendental Cookery," *The New Monthly Magazine*, Vol. 138 (1866)

"PRESERVING EVOKES DEEP-ROOTED, ALMOST PRIMEVAL FEELINGS OF SELF-SUFFICIENCY AND SURVIVAL, OF GATHERER AND HUNTER, FOR THIS IS HOW OUR ANCESTORS STAYED ALIVE."

—PAM CORBIN, *The River Cottage Preserves Handbook* (2010)

S auces are one of the great glories of French cuisine, perhaps the defining refinement, a way of enhancing and elevating ingredients from mere fodder to gastronomy; the *chef saucier* is considered the most exalted member of the classical French kitchen brigade.

Sauces are not one of the glories of English cuisine. You may have heard the "satirical allocution" (as one nineteenth-century writer called it), variously attributed to Voltaire and to the Neapolitan diplomat Domenico Caracciolo, that the English have sixty—or a hundred—religions and only one sauce. That one sauce, according to *The New Monthly Magazine* in 1866, was melted butter. "Melted butter," wrote an anonymous commentator, "is to English sauces what stock is to French soups—melted butter and eggs, melted butter and parsley, melted butter and capers, melted butter and anchovies—it is always melted butter."

While this assessment is more amusing than accurate, a good many traditional British sauces are indeed based on melted butter, or rather on white sauce made from melted butter and flour, thinned with milk or cream—a sauce used by itself or enhanced with cheese, parsley, mustard, or other additions. Other sauces are simple preparations like the pan gravy (sometimes with onions added) that accompanies roasts; tartar sauce for fish; mint sauce and horseradish sauce for various meats; apple sauce for pork; and the much-maligned Marie Rose sauce, basically a cocktail-sauce mixture of tomatoes or tomato ketchup and mayonnaise with Worcestershire sauce and various seasonings. Steamed or boiled shrimp (prawns) served with this sauce were a cliché of late twentieth-century British restaurant fare. Then there is the world-famous Worcestershire sauce itself, widely used in Britain, both alone and as an ingredient in countless other sauces and prepared dishes. (The pseudonymous restaurant writer "Diner-Out," in the mid-1920s, recommended it as an "admirable appetizer," noting that "You can take a spoonful of it neat, or better still, in a cup of clear consommé.")

A case could be made that the most definitive of British sauces are those condiments that come commercially prepared, in bottles—principally Worcestershire and HP Sauce and other brown sauces (see page 25), but also the anchovy-based Gentleman's Relish (also called Patum Peperium), the legendary Marmite (see page 278), Major Grey's Chutney, and piccalilli and the closely related Branston Pickle. Simple malt vinegar, widely considered an essential condiment for fish and chips, might be added—and of course there's always good English mustard, Colman's or otherwise.

Perhaps the most interesting noncommercial British sauce, in terms of provenance if not flavor, is bread sauce. This essential accoutrement to roast grouse and other game birds and to chicken and turkey is a survivor of the medieval British kitchen, where dried bread was crushed or grated to thicken sauces. In this case, bread crumbs are mixed with milk flavored with cloves, mace, and other spices, producing a sauce both stodgy and comforting.

Then there's Cumberland sauce. I discovered this once popular accompaniment to game and to sausages under unlikely circumstances: I was having lunch at the long-defunct Scandia in Los Angeles many years ago with my friend Jock Livingston, then proprietor of a local institution called Ports. We had ordered venison, and when it arrived, he asked the waiter for some mustard and some red currant preserves. These he mixed together at the table, adding a few drops of whatever red wine we were drinking. "Cumberland sauce," he announced. Well, it wasn't quite, though it leaned in the right direction. It was lacking the requisite citrus zest and/or orange marmalade; the red wine should have been port; and a hint of ginger and maybe cayenne should have been stirred in.

Given the abundance of excellent fruit grown around England, Scotland, and Wales, and the respect for seasonality imposed by the climate, it's hardly surprising that jellies, jams, and preserves have long been a part of the British larder. ("To preserve fruits that are in common use . . . is justly considered a point of good housewifery," notes Meg Dods.) What is surprising is that the most celebrated of the country's preserves, found on tables all over the world, is made from a fruit grown not in Great Britain (outside, perhaps, of the odd greenhouse) but in Spain: bitter oranges. There are many myths around the creation of orange marmalade (see page 282), but by the latter part of the eighteenth century, it had become a familiar condiment on breakfast tables all over the country. And the morning meal specifically was its preserve, if you will: George Orwell wrote in 1946 that a proper English breakfast included toast with butter and orange marmalade, and that "other kinds of jam are seldom eaten at breakfast, and marmalade does not often appear at other times of [the] day." This is perhaps because, as the late Chicago-born writer and editor Jeanine Larmoth once remarked, "Marmalade in the morning has the same effect on the taste buds that a cold shower does on the body."

MAYONNAISE

MAKES ABOUT 2 CUPS (480 ML)

This classic, now ubiquitous French condiment is sometimes said to have a faint British connection: According to some sources, it was invented by the duc de Richelieu's chef after the French army captured Port Mahon, a British outpost in Spain's Balearic Islands, in 1756, and originally called *sauce mahonnaise*. The *Oxford English Dictionary* considers this unlikely, however, as today's spelling was recorded in French earlier than that version. The term first appears in English in 1815.

1 large egg
1 egg yolk
Juice of 1 lemon
1 teaspoon Dijon mustard
1 teaspoon salt
1 cup (240 ml) canola oil
1 cup (240 ml) mild extra-virgin olive oil

In a medium bowl, whisk the egg and the yolk together slowly, then add the lemon juice, followed by the mustard and the salt. Whisk until thoroughly combined.

In a separate medium bowl, combine the canola and olive oils, then, while whisking continuously, drizzle the oils very slowly into the egg mixture.

Cover the mayonnaise and refrigerate it for at least 2 hours before using. It should last, covered and refrigerated, for at least 1 week; some sources say that it will last until the use-by date of the eggs you made it with.

MINT SAUCE

MAKES ½ CUP (120 ML)

In the fancy restaurants of my youth, lamb was inevitably served with a little bowl of mint jelly (I'm sure this practice hasn't completely died out). Mint complements lamb superbly, but the jelly is too cloying. This tart-edged mint sauce is, I think, a better condiment. Simon Hopkinson told me not long ago that he "couldn't live without roast lamb with mint sauce." It was, he added, "the epitome of English flavors, along with the roast potatoes that you squash down into the gravy and the congealing lamb fat."

12 to 15 leaves fresh mint, cut into very fine chiffonade
1 tablespoon sugar
1 teaspoon salt
2 tablespoons white wine vinegar

Bring a very small pot or pan of water to a boil.

Combine the mint, sugar, salt, and vinegar in a small bowl. Pour in ¼ cup (60 ml) of the boiling water and stir until the sugar has dissolved.

Serve in a small bowl or sauceboat with a spoon so that diners may stir the sauce before using.

Mint Sauce

ESSENCE OF CELERY

MAKES ½ CUP (120 ML)

In 1996, in observation of its fiftieth birthday, the great Parisian restaurant Taillevent closed down briefly and brought its chefs to New York City, where they prepared an extraordinary dinner at Gramercy Tavern. Ruth Reichl, who was then writing for the *New York Times*, interviewed the chefs after the event and, among other things, came away with a superbly simple but useful *truc*, or little trick, habitually employed by the kitchen: When they cleaned and trimmed black truffles for use in various dishes, they'd macerate the scraps in Armagnac. A few drops of the resulting elixir, added to sauces, improved their flavor in an indefinable but undeniable way. I thought of that when I came across this recipe (if you can call it that) in the nineteenth-century omnibus *Enquire Within Upon Everything*. The flavoring element this time is not truffles but celery seed. According to studies made by Japanese scientists in 2008, celery contains compounds called phthalides, which give the condensed vapors of boiled celery the ability to noticeably improve the flavor of soups—more so than the vegetable itself. A few drops of this simple preparation (to make not vapors but flavored brandy) will, according to *Enquire Within*, "flavour a pint of soup or broth equal to a head of celery."

3 to 4 tablespoons celery seed (not ground)
½ cup (120 ml) V.S. cognac or other good brandy

Combine the celery seed and brandy in a small hermetic jar or other glass container. Let macerate for 2 weeks, then strain out the celery seeds, reserving the brandy in a tightly covered bowl or bottle. The essence will keep indefinitely.

To use, add a few drops to consommé or broth, Scotch Broth (page 58), Cock-a-Leekie (page 57), or other broth-based soups.

PARSLEY BUTTER

MAKES ½ CUP (115 G)

This is a simple but flavorful condiment for grilled or broiled fish or simply cooked chicken or veal.

Juice of 1 lemon
Leaves from 2 to 3 sprigs parsley, finely chopped
½ cup (1 stick / 115 g) butter, softened
Salt and freshly ground white pepper

In a bowl, mix the lemon juice and parsley into the butter, then season it with salt and a little white pepper.

Refrigerate the butter until it begins to harden, then spoon it into the middle of a piece of plastic wrap. Roll the plastic wrap around the butter to form it into the shape of a thick sausage, sealing the ends tightly by twisting the plastic wrap. Freeze the butter until you're ready to use it, then unwrap it, run a knife under hot water, and use it to thinly slice the butter. Put rounds of it on top of fish, chicken, or veal.

TARTAR SAUCE

MAKES ABOUT 1¼ CUPS (300 ML)

This familiar condiment is considered essential with fish and chips, and goes well with any fish or shellfish, especially when they are deep-fried. I think tartar sauce is best when freshly made, but it may be kept in the refrigerator, covered, for up to three days.

1 cup (240 ml) mayonnaise, store-bought or
**   homemade (page 274)**
1 teaspoon Colman's or other prepared English
**   mustard**

3 to 4 cornichons, minced
2 tablespoons capers, drained and minced
Leaves from 3 or 4 fresh chives, snipped into small
   pieces
Leaves from 2 or 3 sprigs parsley, minced
1 tablespoon fresh lemon juice

Put the mayonnaise in a small bowl, then stir in the mustard, cornichons, capers, chives, parsley, and lemon juice and mix well.

HORSERADISH SAUCE

MAKES ABOUT 1 CUP (240 ML)

Along with good English mustard, horseradish is a favorite British condiment for roast beef and other meats. There are good bottled versions available (Colman's is the standard), but it's easy to make your own, especially these days when fresh horseradish root is increasingly available at farmers' markets. Be careful, though, when peeling and grating the root: It's extremely pungent, thanks to a compound called sinigrin, which can irritate the skin and cause eyes to water. There's no particular secret to minimizing these effects; just work quickly, with your head turned partially away. The results are worth the trouble.

½ cup (120 ml) heavy cream
½ cup (120 ml) crème fraîche
1 teaspoon sugar
1 teaspoon fresh lemon juice
2 tablespoons grated peeled fresh horseradish root

Whisk the cream, crème fraîche, and sugar together in a small bowl, then stir in the lemon juice and fold in the horseradish root.

WHITE SAUCE

MAKES ABOUT 1¼ CUPS (300 ML)

This is a very dense sauce. For a lighter version, substitute half-and-half or whole milk for the cream.

2 whole cloves
1 small onion
1 cup (240 ml) heavy cream
1 small bay leaf
2 tablespoons (30 g) butter
2 tablespoons all-purpose flour

Stick the cloves into the onion, then combine the cream, onion, and bay leaf in a small pan. Bring the cream to a boil over medium heat, then remove the pan from the heat and set it aside for 15 to 20 minutes to steep.

Strain the cream into a small bowl, discarding the onion and the bay leaf, and wipe out the pan. Melt the butter in the pan over low heat, then whisk in the flour, stirring for about 1 minute to make a roux. Slowly pour the cream into the roux and cook, stirring, for another minute or so.

The Mysterious Yeast

"I'm in a great mood tonight," the English comedian Peter Kay once said, "because the other day I entered a competition and I won a year's supply of Marmite . . . one jar."

Marmite, to the uninitiated, is a curious British condiment made from a secret recipe involving an extract of brewer's yeast flavored with various spices, heavily salted, and enriched with vitamins and minerals; this last fact has occasioned a Marmite ban in Canada and Denmark, which control the sale of food products thus augmented. It has more or less the consistency of molasses, and has been described (by the BBC America website, but probably echoing the opinions of many thousands of others who have sampled it) as tasting like "salty beefy fermented soy sauce" and "the flavor packet that comes with beef-flavored ramen if you moistened it." As the manufacturers of Marmite, now the multinational food company Unilever, plainly put it in an ad campaign in the 1990s: "Love it or hate it."

A good many Britons come down on the side of love. Some eat it daily, typically in the form of a thin layer spread on lightly buttered toast—as a joke, the uninitiated are sometimes exhorted to spread it on as heavily as jam; they generally only do that once—or as a dressing on sandwiches (Starbucks stores in the U.K. sometimes sell a cheddar and Marmite panini). Marmite is also used in many kinds of recipes, from barbecue sauce to desserts; Nigella Lawson has a recipe for Marmite spaghetti sauce. (*Marmite*, after all, is French for a kind of earthenware cooking pot, a larger version of the pot in which the product was originally packaged.) There are also Marmite-flavored potato chips, Marmite-flavored nuts, even Marmite-flavored rice cakes.

The funny thing about Marmite is that its origins aren't British at all. It grew out of the discovery by the nineteenth-century German chemist Justus von Liebig that yeast extract could be concentrated into an edible substance high in the meaty flavor characteristics we now call umami. (Von Liebig also developed the meat extract that became the Oxo bouillon cube. Another Unilever product, Bovril, has some of the same characteristics as Marmite, but is actually made with beef.) The idea of turning the extract into a commercial product came from two entrepreneurs, Swiss-born Frederick Wissler and German-born George Huth, who set up a factory to produce the product in Burton upon Trent in East Staffordshire in 1902, with an English partner, Alexander Vale. Originally, the yeast used in producing Marmite came from the Bass Brewery, long a Burton landmark.

Special-edition Marmites are regularly released (a 2007 edition was made with Guinness yeast; a Valentine's Day version produced in 2008 for the Selfridges department store in London was spiked with champagne), and there is a slightly different product sold under the same name by the Sanitarium Health and Wellbeing Company in New Zealand. This version is sweeter than its British counterpart but lower in calories, carbohydrates, and protein, slightly higher in sodium, and lower in fat. New Zealanders generally don't like the British Marmite, and vice versa. The same is true of Australians with their own yeast extract, Vegemite.

In the event that you, like Peter Kay, should win a "year's supply" of Marmite and find that you have trouble using it up, it is apparently an effective mosquito repellent. Using it for that purpose, however, would presumably entail spreading it over your skin, which may make you repellent to more than just flying insects.

Opposite: Marmite ad, 1929

MARMITE

For Health and Good Cooking

Carried Unanimously

WOOLLEY

BREAD SAUCE

In medieval European cookery, chunks or crumbs from stale bread were often used to thicken sauces. This traditional accompaniment to roasted game birds, and sometimes turkey and other domestic fowl, is an obvious descendent of those sauces. It first became a popular condiment in the mid-eighteenth century.

2 cups (480 ml) whole milk
6 whole cloves
1 medium onion
Pinch of ground mace
6 whole black peppercorns
1 bay leaf
1¼ cups coarse white bread crumbs
1 tablespoon (15 g) butter, softened
Salt and freshly ground white pepper

Stick the cloves into the onion and put it in a medium saucepan, then add the milk, mace, peppercorns, and bay leaf. Bring the milk to a rapid boil, then remove the pan from the heat, cover with a lid or aluminum foil, and let steep for 30 minutes.

Strain the milk into a small saucepan and heat it over low heat for about 3 minutes, then stir in the bread crumbs and butter and season the sauce with salt and white pepper. Serve it in a small ceramic jug or bowl. Excess sauce may be cooled to room temperature, then stored, covered, in the refrigerator for up to 1 week or the freezer for up to 1 month.

BROWN GRAVY

MAKES ABOUT 1¼ CUPS (300 ML)

The best brown gravy is that made by mixing a bit of flour into the pan drippings from a roast, then diluting the resulting roux slightly with stock or wine. For recipes that call for brown gravy without a roast, this is a good substitute.

2 cups (480 ml) veal or beef stock, store-bought or homemade (page 314)
3 tablespoons (45 g) butter
3 tablespoons all-purpose flour
2 teaspoons tomato paste
Dash of Worcestershire sauce
Salt (optional)

Bring the stock to a boil in a small saucepan over high heat. Reduce the heat to medium-high and boil until it is reduced by half.

When the stock is reduced, melt the butter in another saucepan over low heat, then whisk the flour into the butter, stirring for about a minute to make a roux. Slowly pour in the stock, whisking continuously to form a sauce.

Stir in the tomato paste and the Worcestershire sauce, then season lightly with salt if you're using unsalted homemade stock.

WOW-WOW SAUCE

MAKES ABOUT 1 CUP (240 ML)

The name of this pungent nineteenth-century creation suggests the astonishment with which it might have been greeted initially (the exclamation "Wow!", expressing admiration or wonderment, dates from Scotland in the early sixteenth century). It made its debut appearance in the optician and cook William Kitchiner's *Apicius Redivivus: or, The Cook's Oracle*, first published in 1817. His original recipe for wow-wow sauce reads:

> *Chop parsley leaves fine; take two or three pickled cucumbers, or walnuts, and divide into small squares, and set them by in readiness; put into a saucepan a piece of butter as big as an egg; when it is melted, stir into it a tablespoonful of fine flour, and half a pint of the broth of the beef; add a tablespoonful of vinegar, one of mushroom ketchup, or port wine, or both, and a tablespoonful of made mustard; simmer together till it is as thick as you wish, put in the parsley and pickles to get warm, and pour it over the beef, or send it up in a sauce-tureen. This is excellent for stewed or boiled beef.*

In a footnote, Kitchiner adds that for increased piquancy, the cook may enhance the sauce with capers, minced shallots or shallot wine, essence of anchovy, basil, elder or tarragon or horseradish, or burnet vinegar, among other things. The late Terry Pratchett, author of the many Discworld comic fantasy novels, appropriated the sauce, making a version of it favored by some of his characters. The Discworld recipe ramps up the piquancy with asafoetida, sulfur, saltpeter, and the imaginary ingredients wahoonie and scumble; it is described as highly volatile and capable of dissolving tree roots. This is a rather gentler modern adaptation of Kitchiner's original formula.

3 tablespoons (45 g) unsalted butter
1 tablespoon all-purpose flour
1 cup (240 ml) beef stock, store-bought or homemade (page 314)
1 tablespoon white wine vinegar
2 tablespoons ruby port
1 tablespoon spicy mustard
3 sprigs parsley, minced
3 small gherkins or cornichons, or 2 pickled walnuts (see Sources, page 316), finely chopped

Melt the butter in a small saucepan over low heat. Stir in the flour to make a thin roux, about the consistency of a cream soup, then slowly stir in the beef stock.

Stir in the vinegar, port, and mustard and simmer, stirring frequently, until the liquid has reduced by about a third.

Stir in the parsley and gherkins and cook for about 2 minutes more.

Serve at room temperature with cold roast beef or lamb, or with pot roast, corned beef, or boiled brisket.

TRADITIONAL ORANGE MARMALADE

MAKES 6 TO 8 PINTS (2.8 TO 3.8 L)

The story goes that James Keiller, an eighteenth-century grocer in the Scottish port town of Dundee, on the Firth of Tay, invented orange marmalade. This came about, supposedly, when a cargo of oranges he had ordered from Spain turned out to be the bitter Seville variety instead of the sweet ones from Valencia—or, according to another version of the story, when a ship full of Seville oranges took shelter from a storm in Dundee harbor and, having to dispose of the fruit before it spoiled, sold the lot to Keiller at a Scotsman's price. In either case, his wife, Janet, is supposed to have then had the bright idea of creating a bittersweet preserve from the oranges. The truth is that Keiller was a bachelor in the late 1700s, when this supposedly occurred (Janet may have been his mother); that large shipments of fruit of any kind were uncommon in that era, so if there were oranges brought into Dundee by boat it probably wasn't more than a few barrels' worth; and that marmalade already existed.

The word comes from the Portuguese *marmelo*, "quince," and the original *marmelada* was quince paste. The term first appears in English, as *marmelate*, in 1480, and subsequently is used to describe preserves made not only from quince but from plums, apricots, and dates. A reference to "Orange Marmalett" appears in 1714, and Hannah Glasse (1747) gives a recipe for orange marmalade. When James Keiller established his marmalade company in 1795, then, the preserve was well-known in the British Isles. Keiller, though, might be said to have invented marmalade as we know it today: His innovation was to include pieces of the peel or rind in the preserve, and he was the first to commercialize marmalade on any significant scale. Though many companies now produce orange marmalade, it remains virtually synonymous with James Keiller & Son.

Note that in order to have its familiar characteristic bitterness, it must be made from Seville oranges, which are available seasonally (some are grown in the United States, but they are also imported from Spain). This is a traditional recipe, for which you'll need canning jars, a canning rack, and a pot large enough to hold the rack; instructions for a much easier and less time-consuming Quick Marmalade follow on page 285.

2 pounds (900 g) Seville oranges, halved crosswise (see Sources, page 316)
8 cups (1.6 kg) sugar

Squeeze the juice from the oranges into a large glass bowl or other nonreactive bowl, then use a sharp spoon to scrape out and discard the flesh, seeds, and pith, leaving only the peels.

Slice the peels into thin strips, 1½ to 2 inches (4 to 5 cm) long, and add them to the bowl with the juice. Stir in 4 cups water, then cover the bowl and refrigerate it overnight.

Pour the contents of the bowl into a large nonreactive pot and bring to a boil over high heat. Reduce the heat and simmer, uncovered, until the liquid has reduced by half and the orange peels are very soft.

Put a small saucer in the refrigerator to chill.

Stir the sugar into the pot a little at a time, making sure that it dissolves completely. Increase the heat to medium-high and bring the liquid to a gentle boil. Let it boil slowly for 15 to 20 minutes, or until the temperature registers 220°F (105°C) on a candy thermometer. Skim off any foam that rises to the surface as the marmalade cooks.

Reduce the heat to low, then spoon a teaspoon of the marmalade onto the chilled saucer. Allow it to cool for a minute, then tip the saucer to one side. If the marmalade remains in place, it's ready; otherwise, cook it for 5 minutes more and test it again.

Bring a pot of water large enough to hold a canning rack to a boil over high heat, then reduce the heat slightly to keep the water at a rolling boil. Divide the marmalade evenly between six to eight sterilized 1-pint (475-ml) jars (see opposite), then seal them with sterilized rings and lids. Transfer the jars to a canning rack and submerge it carefully in the pot, making sure that the jars are covered by at least 1 inch (2.5 cm) of water. Boil for 5 minutes, then carefully lift the jars from the water and put them on a dish towel to cool, undisturbed, for 24 hours.

To Sterilize Jars

If you're planning to keep marmalade, preserves, or chutneys for longer than a week or so, the jars they're stored in must be sterilized. The easy way to do this is in the oven. Use new glass canning jars with two-part metal lids with rubber seals. Preheat the oven to 200ºF (95ºC). Wash the jars and lids thoroughly with hot water and detergent, rinsing them very well. Arrange them with their open sides facing upward, without touching their interior surfaces, in a baking pan large enough to hold them, along with the lids. Leave them in the oven for 30 minutes. When they are almost done, bring a small pot of water to a boil. When you remove the baking pan from the oven, dip the ends of a pair of tongs into the boiling water, then use the tongs to lift the jars and lids out. Hot preserves should be canned in hot jars to avoid shattering.

The Brig Larder

When I told him that I was planning a trip to Orkney, Michael McCuish, who works for VisitScotland, that country's national tourism organization, told me to be sure to visit The Brig Larder in Kirkwall, the islands' capital. I dutifully found the place on a town map and walked over from my hotel, expecting some quaint little corner shop stocked with canned goods and a few wheels of local cheese. Instead, I found a big, sleekly furnished, nicely lit food (and drink) shop that would have looked at home in Greenwich Village or Berkeley.

The Brig Larder was opened in 2014 by two couples with long experience in the food business in Orkney, Thorfinn and Katherine Craigie (his name an obvious reminder, incidentally, of the Viking heritage in these islands) and George and Anne Stout. "We opened it," Thorfinn told me as we sipped an unpeated Bruichladdich single malt made from bere barley (see page 27), "because we saw a place in the market here for a butchery and fishmonger on the street, and a shop to supply good Orkney products from ice cream to beremeal. Then the chance came up for an off-license side [to sell wine and spirits], which complements the whole shop well."

The Craigies and the Stouts have other enterprises in town: Craigie Butchers, a wholesaler that sells locally farmed lamb, beef, and pork both on the island and to top restaurants around Scotland; a shop called Jollys of Orkney, where the specialty is fresh and smoked fish (they have their own kiln), along with meats, cheeses, and food to go; and a whisky specialist called John Scott & Miller Ltd., whose inventory includes limited-edition private-label bottlings from Orkney's two distilleries, Highland Park and Scapa.

With my glass of a non-Orkney whisky (made, however, with Orkney bere) in hand, I wandered around, looking at the beautiful meats, including house-made sausages and bacon; the selection of Orkney and other Scottish cheeses; the section of fresh and frozen premade dinners; the shelves full of preserves and oatcakes and pickled vegetables and other foods that you'd expect a larder to have. All I could think was that I was happy (if a bit surprised) that a town this size (the population is just over nine thousand) could support a store like this, and that the look and feel of the place and its commitment to local products were just so right that I wished every small town could have a food shop like it.

QUICK ORANGE MARMALADE

MAKES ABOUT 2 PINTS

"There are almost as many ways of making marmalade as there are varieties of jam," wrote F. Marian McNeill in *The Scots Kitchen*. This is a particularly easy method, not for making large quantities to can, but good for producing a small amount for use in recipes—for instance, the Whisky-Soaked-Raisin and Orange Marmalade Bread and Butter Pudding (page 232) served at Wild & Co in Windermere, in England's Lake District. This is the recipe the restaurant's chef and co-owner, Dylan Evans, uses for that dessert, though it also goes very nicely on buttered toast or oatcakes (page 27). Use only Seville oranges for this recipe.

1½ cups (300 g) sugar
2 Seville oranges (see Sources, page 316),
    unpeeled, thinly sliced and seeded
Juice of 2 Seville oranges

Bring 1¼ cups (300 ml) water to a boil in a medium saucepan over high heat, then add the sugar and stir until it has dissolved. Reduce the heat to low, add the sliced oranges and the orange juice, and cook, covered, for 2 to 2½ hours, or until mixture has thickened and the orange slices are very soft. This marmalade will keep in ordinary jars or bowls, covered, in the refrigerator for at least 1 week.

STRAWBERRY PRESERVES

MAKES ABOUT 2 PINTS (900 ML)

Strawberries are sweet (good ones, anyway), but they don't have much acidity, and strawberry preserves won't set without added pectin. If your strawberries are very sweet, you can probably get away with 1 cup of sugar in this recipe.

3 cups (450 g) quartered hulled fresh strawberries
2 cups (400 g) sugar
1 (1.75-ounce / 175-g) box or package pectin
1 tablespoon (15 g) butter

Put the strawberries into a large bowl and crush them lightly with a potato masher or wooden spoon. Stir in the sugar and set aside for 30 minutes.

Combine the pectin with 1 cup (240 ml) water in a small saucepan, then bring the mixture to a boil over high heat. Add the butter and boil, stirring continuously, for 1 minute, then add the mixture to the bowl with the strawberries and stir well to thoroughly combine and melt the sugar.

Pour the mixture into two sterilized 1-pint (475-ml) jars, still hot from the oven (see page 283), filling them to within ½ inch (1.25 cm) of the top. Seal the jars and let the preserves cool overnight before refrigerating them.

APPLE CHUTNEY

MAKES 1½ TO 2 PINTS (710 TO 900 ML)

In India, the word *chutney* (or *chatni* in Hindi) traditionally refers to a whole class of side dishes or condiments, but in Anglo-Indian cooking and in the U.K. in general, the term is used to describe tart-sweet spiced fruit preserves—most famously Major Grey's, a kind of mango and raisin chutney made by several manufacturers from a recipe said to have been (but probably not) developed by a British Army officer in India in the nineteenth century. Imported chutneys may have reached England and Scotland as early as the early eighteenth century, and by later in the 1700s recipes for some approximation of the Indian relish began appearing in recipe manuscripts and cookbooks. Chutney became a popular accompaniment around Great Britain to cold meats, cheddar cheese, and other foodstuffs as well as to Anglo-Indian curries and curry-flavored dishes. Indian food, or some approximation of it, has been popular in Scotland since the days of the Raj, when many Scottish soldiers and officers served in India. This recipe, based on the apple, that most English of fruits, comes from *The Edinburgh Book of Plain Cookery Recipes*, published in 1932 by the Edinburgh College of Domestic Science.

2 small apples, peeled, cored, and chopped
½ cup (75 g) sultanas (golden raisins)
½ small onion, chopped
¼ cup (35 g) raw almonds, chopped
2 teaspoons salt
1 teaspoon ground ginger
1 teaspoon cayenne
1 teaspoon whole white peppercorns and
    ½ teaspoon coriander seeds, tied securely
    in cheesecloth
1½ cups (360 ml) apple cider vinegar
2 or 4 whole red serrano, cayenne, or other chiles

Combine the apples, sultanas, onion, almonds, salt, ginger, cayenne, peppercorns and coriander seeds, and vinegar in a medium saucepan with a lid. Bring the vinegar just to a boil over medium-high heat, then reduce the heat to low, cover the pan, and cook for 2 hours.

Remove and discard the cheesecloth bundle. Pour the mixture into 2 sterilized 1-pint (475-ml) jars, still hot from the oven (see page 283), filling them to within ½ inch (1.25 cm) of the top. Push 1 or 2 chiles down into each jar. Seal the jars and let the preserves cool overnight before refrigerating them.

RUM BUTTER

MAKES ABOUT 1 PINT (475 ML)

One of the first things I ever made in a kitchen, as a young lad, was what my half sister Deidre called "hard sauce." This was simply softened butter mixed up with confectioners' sugar. We'd make batches when Mom and Dad weren't home and spread it on toasted cinnamon-raisin bread—wonderful—or, around Christmastime, on slices of fruitcake warmed in the oven. I rediscovered hard sauce, under the name rum butter (a name reflecting an ingredient we didn't add to the mix when I was seven or eight years old), many years later in the Lake District, where it is sometimes served at teatime with scones or crackers. Rum flowed into this part of England in the eighteenth and nineteenth centuries, legally and illegally, through the West Cumbria ports of Workington, Whitehaven, and Maryport. West Indian sugar came through, too. The combination of these ingredients with rich local butter became a local specialty. There were even pottery butter bowls to hold it. Most recipes today call for unsalted butter, softened to room temperature, but I found one dating from 1867 that called for clarified butter. Deidre would have never gone to the trouble, but I liked the effect a lot.

2 cups (420 g) Demerara or muscovado sugar
1 recipe clarified butter (page 312), or 1¾ cups
   (3½ sticks / 400 g) butter, softened to room
   temperature
¾ cup (180 ml) dark rum
Pinch of ground or freshly grated nutmeg

In a medium bowl, mix the sugar into the butter with a wooden spoon, combining them thoroughly. While stirring, drizzle in the rum, then add the nutmeg and stir until it is well distributed.

Transfer the rum butter to a bowl or crock, cover it, and refrigerate it for at least 2 hours before serving. Serve with toast, crackers, scones, or—why not?—slices of fruitcake warmed in the oven. Rum butter will keep, covered, in the refrigerator for at least 2 weeks.

Welsh butter

CHAPTER 12

TEATIME

"ALAS, FOR THE EFFECTS OF BAD TEA AND
BAD TEMPER!"

—EMILY BRONTË, *Wuthering Heights* (1847)

"THE BRITISH REALLY ARE THE ONLY PEOPLE
IN THE WORLD WHO BECOME GENUINELY
EXCITED WHEN PRESENTED WITH A HOT
BEVERAGE AND A SMALL PLAIN BISCUIT."

—BILL BRYSON, *The Road to Little Dribbling* (2016)

Tea first reached Europe in 1610, imported from China into Holland by the Dutch East India Company. It probably got to England around 1650. In 1660, according to Thomas Rugge's seventeenth-century journal *Mercurius Politicus Redivivus*, "That excellent and by all Physicians, approved, China drink, called by the Chineans Tcha, by other nations Tay alias Tee, is sold at the Sultaness Head Coffee-House, in Sweetings Rents, by the Royal Exchange, London." Also in 1660, Samuel Pepys records that after a meeting with the merchant and politician Sir Richard Ford and other concerned parties about war and peace in Europe, "I did send for a cup of tee, a China drink, of which I never had drank before." He does not record his impressions of it.

Tea got a boost when Charles II married the Portuguese princess Catherine of Braganza in 1662. The beverage was already popular in Portugal, especially among the nobility, and Catherine promoted it in her adopted country. As sugar became more readily available in the eighteenth century, the British started sweetening their tea with it, and adding milk. By the late 1700s, tea had become so commonplace that Samuel Johnson was able to proclaim, "I am a hardened and shameless tea drinker, who for twenty years diluted his meals with only the infusion of the fascinating plant; who with tea amused the evening, with tea solaced the midnight, and with tea welcomed the morning."

Virtually all the tea brought into Britain came from China, until the first half of the nineteenth century when the British East India Company began establishing tea plantations in India, and especially in Assam—which became the world's largest tea-producing region. The overwhelming majority of what the British drink today is black tea, most of it Assam or Darjeeling from India, Ceylon from Sri Lanka, or Keemun from Anhui Province in eastern China.

Originally a habit of the upper classes, tea drinking became increasingly popular with the citizenry as a whole as prices fell and availability increased. (Factory owners liked the fact that their workers drank tea: The perception was that it gave them added energy to work harder and longer.) Interestingly, the addition of that once rare ingredient, sugar, declined among the well-to-do, and drinking unsweetened tea (though still with milk) came to be thought of as a mark of sophistication. George Orwell once proposed that "If one made a list of the people in Britain who prefer wine to beer, one would probably find that it included most of the people who prefer tea without sugar."

Tea evolved into "tea," as an afternoon or evening meal, in the mid-nineteenth century, when British society, emulating Anna Maria Russell, the Duchess of Bedford (see page 295), began taking light meals with their Darjeeling or Earl Grey. Institutions like Fortnum & Mason and its neighbor The Ritz hotel, as well as innumerable other hotels and tearooms throughout England, Scotland, and Wales, continue to offer traditional afternoon teas (tea in The Ritz's Palm Court—ties and jackets for the gentlemen, please, and no denim on anyone—includes an array of sandwiches and pastries, a choice of sixteen brews, and music by a harpist or string quartet).

There is innovation afoot, though, welcome or not, in the afternoon tea scene, especially in certain London hotels. The Lanesborough offers gluten-free scones and trendy sandwiches like smashed avocados with chiles, in addition to more conventional fare. The Halkin, home of Ametsa with Arzak Instruction, a modern Basque restaurant overseen by the legendary Arzaks of San Sebastián, has blended afternoon tea with a tapas crawl, and serves churros as well as scones. The Milestone Hotel apparently wants to rescue afternoon tea from its image as the preserve of proper ladies with raised pinkies: It hosts a "gentleman's" tea, where the fare includes bacon scones and mini Cornish pasties and where, in addition to tea, an assortment of whisky is available.

Builder's Tea

Though British construction workers and other blue-collar laborers have long had a tradition of drinking strong tea, from a mug instead of a teacup, during their breaks, the *Oxford English Dictionary*—which defines builder's tea as "a robust, full-bodied blend of black tea, brewed very strong, and usually drunk with milk"—traces the phrase back only to 1996.

The typical builder's tea is tannic and high in caffeine, and generally mixed with not only milk but a fair amount of sugar. One enterprising company has even started marketing a product called Builders British Tea, whose package describes it as "The Full Flavoured British Cuppa / Tested & approved by real builders." The tea is a mixture of leaves from Tanzania, Malawi, Kenya, and Uganda, "taste-tested by real master builders until the perfect thirst-quenching blend was developed."

Ah, but traditions evolve. Tea purchases in Great Britain in general have declined about two-thirds over the past forty years, and a survey conducted in 2013 by a major building materials chain revealed that some 44 percent of the workers polled prefer coffee—often a latte or Americano—to a mug of tea.

A GOOD POT of TEA

SERVES 1

Nothing is simpler than tea: It's nothing more than hot water in which some dried leaves, in a bag or a tea ball or just loose, have been steeped. And yet . . . we know the care and ritual with which the Japanese and Chinese make tea, and I learned myself many years ago, not the easy way, that the English (and presumably the Scots and the Welsh) take the brewing process pretty seriously themselves, if without quite the same degree of reverence. There are countless fine points and variations, of course, and I'm sure plenty of people would disagree, but the way I learned to make a good pot of tea, English-style, was in a small ceramic teapot, just big enough to hold one cup at a time, and of course using loose tea.

2 cups (480 ml) cold, fresh filtered water
1 heaping teaspoon good-quality loose Darjeeling, Ceylon, Assam, or other black tea
Whole milk, for serving
Sugar, for serving

Bring the water to a rolling boil over high heat, then pour half into a teapot. Let it sit for about 30 seconds, swirl it around, then pour it into the teacup.

Add the tea leaves to the pot. Return the remaining water to a boil, then pour it into the pot. Wrap a tea towel around the pot to keep it warm as the tea steeps. Steep for 3 to 5 minutes, depending on how strong you like your tea.

Pour the water out of the teacup and dab the interior dry with a paper towel. Put as much milk as you like into the teacup, then pour the tea into the cup through a tea strainer. If you like sugar in your tea, stir in 1 or 2 teaspoons. Drink as soon as it's just cool enough not to burn your lips.

CUCUMBER SANDWICHES

MAKES 12 SMALL SANDWICHES

Sometimes a sandwich is just a sandwich, but these dainty little concoctions are fraught with social significance. The cucumber is native to India, and it may have been there that the British first thought of putting it into a sandwich, perhaps as a way of keeping cool (at their annual meeting in 2012, the American Chemical Society identified the cucumber sandwich and a cup of hot tea as being an excellent means of regulating body temperature and avoiding dehydration in tropical weather). Back home, once the Duchess of Bedford had invented the concept of afternoon tea (see page 295), cucumber sandwiches were widely adopted as a teatime snack—not just because they were tiny and refined but also because their consumption was a marker of class: Being mostly water, cucumbers have very little nutritive value, meaning that the working class wouldn't bother with them; if you ate cucumber sandwiches, you were a person of leisure (and had a serious dinner coming later).

It has been said that Oscar Wilde "consecrated the cucumber sandwich as the bite-sized symbol of the British upper class" by making it the centerpiece of a scene in *The Importance of Being Earnest*. The sandwiches became even more popular during the Edwardian era, when the cultivation of cucumbers in hothouses became something of a fad. Cucumber sandwiches, often with extraneous elements added these days, are still de rigueur at any proper English tea. (Other tea sandwiches may be constructed by following the instructions below but, in place of the cucumber, using leaves and stalks of tender young watercress, thin-sliced roast beef, or thin-sliced smoked salmon.)

8 slices white Pullman bread, crusts removed
4 tablespoons (½ stick / 55 g) salted butter, softened
½ seedless cucumber, peeled and sliced paper-thin on a mandoline

recipe continues

Butter the bread slices generously on one side, then lay the cucumber slices across four slices, dividing them equally. Form sandwiches with the remaining bread, pressing down very lightly on them. Cut each sandwich on an angle into four triangular pieces. Serve with a good pot of tea (page 293).

SCONES

MAKES 10 TO 12

Scones are an essential feature of afternoon tea—and especially of the cream teas of Devonshire and Cornwall, at which they are spread generously with clotted cream, the heat-thickened cream indigenous to the region. The word itself, first used in English in the sixteenth century, probably derives from the Middle Low German *schon-brot*, "fine bread"—though scones more closely resemble sweetened American biscuits than bread. How *scone* should be pronounced—whether to rhyme with *Joan* or *John*—is a matter of some dispute. An anonymous verse encapsulates the controversy: "I asked the maid in dulcet tone / To order me a buttered scone; / The silly girl had been and gone / And ordered me a buttered scone."

7 cups (875 g) self-rising flour, plus more
    for dusting
½ cup (100 g) sugar
1 pound (4 sticks / 450 g) cold butter, cut into
    25 to 30 pieces
1 large egg
1 cup (240 ml) whole milk
Salt
Butter or clotted cream (see Sources, page 316)
    and jam, for serving

Preheat the oven to 400°F (200°C).

Mix the flour and sugar together well in a large bowl, then add the butter and, with your fingers or a pastry cutter, work it into the flour mixture until it resembles coarse meal.

Whisk the egg and milk together in a small bowl, then add 1 cup of the mixture to the flour mixture, working it in with your fingers until a soft dough forms. Add another tablespoon of the milk mixture if the dough is too dry. Set the remaining milk mixture aside.

Turn the dough out onto a lightly floured work surface, sprinkle a pinch or two of salt over it, then pat the dough gently into a large disk about 1 inch (2.5 cm) thick. Using a round cookie cutter or the rim of a glass about 3 inches (7.5 cm) in diameter, cut out the scones. Press leftover dough scraps together lightly, then cut out more scones, making 10 to 12 in all.

Put the scones on a lightly floured baking sheet, leaving at least ½ inch (1.25 cm) between them. Brush the tops of the scones with the remaining milk mixture.

Bake the scones for 20 to 25 minutes, or until golden brown. (Tent them loosely with aluminum foil if they brown too quickly.) Cool the scones on a wire rack and serve at room temperature with butter or clotted cream (see Sources, page 316) and jam.

The Truth About High Tea

"High tea" isn't what most Americans think it is. Today, the term evokes images of proper ladies (mostly) whiling away the afternoon sipping Earl Grey or Darjeeling from bone china cups while discreetly nibbling scones, slices of sponge cake, or cucumber sandwiches on crustless bread, and indiscreetly gossiping. The "high" might well be taken to describe their extended pinkies.

In fact, that sort of affair is more properly called simply afternoon tea. The custom of taking a light meal, with tea, around four in the afternoon is said to have originated in the 1840s with Anna Maria Russell, the Duchess of Bedford, who complained of hunger pangs between lunch and dinner and figured out something to do about it. The custom was quickly adopted by the upper class in general, and later filtered down the social ladder, so that eventually even working men and women enjoyed it, though with more modest menus than those of their more exalted counterparts. Today, most of the grand hotels around the British Isles and the Commonwealth serve afternoon tea, with varying degrees of ceremony and culinary complexity, as do countless teashops and restaurants.

A subset of afternoon tea is cream tea, in effect an afternoon tea at which the main food consumed is scones with clotted cream—so dense and rich that it's practically butter—and jam. Cream tea is also

Fashionably dressed women in a London teashop, 1927

called Devonshire tea, and is enjoyed mostly in Devon and neighboring Cornwall, in southwestern England, where the cows produce high-butterfat cream that lends itself well to clotting.

High tea, in contrast, means an old-style working-class supper, usually eaten between five and seven in the evening, and consisting of reasonably substantial dishes, hot or cold—sliced meats, steak and kidney pie, various casseroles (in Ireland, high tea is sometimes called "meat tea")—along with baked goods of various kinds. In its original sense, at least, high tea is more family dinner than social diversion.

BARA BRITH

SERVES 10 TO 15

Bara brith means "speckled bread" in Welsh (it's a close relation to the barn brack of Ireland, whose name derives from the Irish *bairin breac*—which means exactly the same thing). The speckles, of course, are the bits of dried fruit. The late Welsh food writer Gareth Jones warned me that "Bara brith is a recipe closely guarded by traditional Welsh families. To ask for the recipe is a faux pas."

I believe Jones, but I ate bara brith, a popular confection to accompany tea in Wales, from a bakery in Abergavenny, at my hotel in Cardiff, and at the Bodnant Welsh Food Centre in Tal-y-Cafn, in far northern Wales, and I have to say that they all looked and tasted pretty similar. Perhaps there is a standard formula used commercially and it's only in private homes that the uniqueness and exclusivity exists. If that's the case, I wouldn't be surprised if the standard formula were the one published in Gillie Davies's book *Lamb, Leeks & Laverbread*. This is my version of it.

12 ounces (350 g) mixed black currants and
    sultanas (golden raisins)
1 cup (220 g) packed dark brown sugar
1 cup (240 ml) warm black tea (page 292), strained
Butter, for greasing
½ teaspoon ground cinnamon
½ teaspoon freshly grated nutmeg
1 large egg, beaten
1 pound (450 g) self-rising flour

Mix the currants, sultanas, and brown sugar together in a large bowl, then pour in the tea. Cover the bowl and let it sit at room temperature for at least 6 hours or overnight.

Preheat the oven the 325ºF (175ºC).

Line a 2-pound (900-g) loaf pan with parchment paper and lightly butter the parchment.

Stir the cinnamon and nutmeg into the fruit, then add the egg and stir it in. Slowly stir in the flour with a wooden spoon to form a medium-thick batter, then spoon the batter into the prepared loaf pan.

Bake for 1½ hours, or until a toothpick inserted into the center of the loaf comes out clean. If the top begins to brown to a dark color, cover the pan with aluminum foil.

Let the bara brith rest for 10 minutes, then tip it out of the loaf pan onto a cooling rack. Serve slightly warm with good butter or Caerphilly cheese.

CHAPTER 13

WHISKY, CIDER, BEER, AND WINE

"COME ALL YOU GOOD FELLOWS,
GIVE EAR TO ME, COME! / I'LL SING IN THE
PRAISE OF GOOD BRANDY AND RUM. /
OLD ALE AND GOOD CYDER 'O'ER ENGLAND
DO ROLL, / GIVE ME THE PUNCH-LADLE,
I'LL FATHOM THE BOWL!"

—OLD SUSSEX DRINKING SONG

"PUB. BOOZER. TAVERN. LOCAL.
RUB-A-DUB. PUBLIC BAR. VILLAGE INN.
GIN PALACE. HOME FROM HOME."

—ADRIAN TIERNEY-JONES, *Great British Pubs* (2012)

The British have been drinking fermented liquids for at least five thousand years—traces of ale have been found on Neolithic pottery from Orkney and beyond—and distilled spirits for at least five hundred, and along the way they have created or refined some of the world's great alcoholic beverages.

The relationship of the populace to strong drink has been varied. Theirs is not the thirstiest of cultures (the United Kingdom ranks somewhere between twentieth and twenty-fifth in the world in per capita alcohol consumption), but the British have long had a reputation for alcoholic excess—from the drunkeness of English soldiers (noted by their Norman foes) at the Battle of Hastings to the gin craze of the early eighteenth century (when a population of less than seven million downed eighteen million gallons of gin annually, and "Mother's Ruin" decimated the urban poor), and from the Friday night binge drinking that became part of twentieth-century pub culture to the beer-fueled soccer hooliganism of recent times.

On the other hand, British taste and craft and mercantile concerns have shaped some of the most refined of European wines: The English revived a moribund Bordeaux trade following the marriage in 1152 of Eleanor of Aquitaine to Henry Plantagenet (the English or Anglo-Irish names attached to the châteaux and négociants of the region even today—Palmer, Barton, Clarke, Lynch, Brown, and Boyd, among others—are a reminder of their influence); they also in effect invented Port, Sherry, and Madeira as we now know them (hence labels like Cockburns, Taylor, Dow, Grahams, Sandeman, Osborne, Leacock, and Cossart Gordon on the fortified wines of Portugal and Spain). At home, meanwhile, they developed styles and standards of beer that are appreciated (and copied) all over the world, and, in Scotland, perfected the art of distillation to such a degree that . . . well, let's just say that distillers in Japan, Australia, and just about everywhere else outside the U.S. are imitating Scotch, not Bourbon.

If the British have been notorious tosspots, they have also been skilled artisans in the production of alcoholic beverages—beer, cider, mead, whisky, gin, even (now) wine—and revered connoisseurs of the fermented and the distilled, whether homemade or imported. Alcohol in some form or another—perhaps in moderation, but not necessarily bridled by restraint—belongs on the British table.

SCOTCH WHISKY: Iodine & Smoke

The Scottish secret agent, diplomat, and author Sir Robert Bruce Lockhart proposed, in his *Scotch: The Whisky of Scotland in Fact and Story* (1951), that "the history of malt whisky lies shrouded in the mists of the Celtic dawn." That sounds very romantic, but in fact, it's not particularly shrouded at all. Whisky—the word derives from its original name, uisge beatha, or "water of life"—has been made in Scotland since the late fifteenth century; even the Scots admit that they learned the art of distillation from the Irish, who were at it in the *early* fifteenth century. Whisky soon became an indispensible part of life in Scotland, as it had been across the Irish Sea. As Dr. Johnson put it in 1775, speaking of the inhabitants of one part of the country, "A man of the Hebrides. . . . as soon as he appears in the morning, swallows a glass of whiskey [*sic*] . . . No man is so abstemious as to refuse the morning dram, which they call a *skalk*."

A Ross & Cameron's whisky advertisement, featuring a Scot in full Highland dress, circa 1890

For hundreds of years, all Scotch was malt whisky—meaning that it was made from a fermented mash of malted barley—and distilled in copper pot stills. The invention of the more efficient column still (patented by an Irishman, Aeneas Coffey, in 1830) led to the increased distillation of unmalted grain, producing so-called grain whisky, which took less time to make than malt and cost less. Soon, distillers (or the merchants who bought their raw material and bottled it) were combining malt and grain into blended whisky—a category that today encompasses all those famous whisky names like Johnnie Walker, Dewar's, Chivas Regal, and Cutty Sark, and that still accounts for about ninety percent of whisky sales worldwide.

The iconic Laphroaig distillery on the island of Islay

Single malt whisky, the malt whisky from a single distillery, unblended, was all but unknown outside Scotland until the early 1960s, when a bottler and distiller called Gordon & MacPhail tried marketing it internationally and found tentative interest among consumers. Now-famous distilleries like Glenfiddich and The Glenlivet had early success with their single malts, and beginning in the 1970s, such whiskies became something of a craze among discerning drinkers, or those who wanted to appear as such. Today there are more than a hundred named distilleries bottling single malt.

The Scotch whisky map is divided into five parts: Highland (the largest region by far, covering most of northern and western Scotland, including all the whisky-producing islands but Islay), Speyside (geographically a big bite of the north-central Highlands, but considered separately, and home to about half of all the country's distilleries), Lowland (with only a handful of distilleries), Campbeltown

(likewise), and Islay—pronounced "eye-la"—a 239-square-mile island in southwestern Scotland, which boasts eight or nine distilleries (depending on how you're counting) and produces whiskies that are, to me, the apotheosis of the distiller's art.

With the occasional exception of the sensuous Springbank (see pages 298–299), from Campbeltown, full of spice and dried-fruit savor, and the complex, elegant Highland Park from Orkney (which whisky specialist Paul Pacult once called "the best spirit in the world"), Islay whiskies are what I always order if I have the chance. They are not subtle. Whisky novices (and bourbon lovers) tend to loathe them. They have what the artist Ralph Steadman, in his book *Still Life with Bottle: Whisky According to Ralph Steadman*, called "a strong salt-sprayed, aye, aye, Cap'n, seaweedy flavour." They're salty indeed, and tinged with iodine. Some, like Ardbeg, are very heavily peated, meaning that the malted barley they're based on is slowly dried with the smoke from peat fires, lending the finished product a smoky, earthy, vaguely acrid character. Others are peated more lightly, or, like modern-day Bruichladdich, not peated at all, but they all taste, to a greater or lesser degree, like they come from the sea.

The definitive Islay whisky is probably the forthright but deftly balanced Laphroaig—talk about iodine and smoke—which once ran an advertising campaign stressing the love-it-or-hate-it reaction first-time drinkers tend to have to it. Laphroaig's neighbor, Lagavulin, produces whisky that is possibly even smokier. Bowmore produces an unusually wide range of malts of impeccable quality. My friend Jim McEwan, who started working at Bowmore when he was fifteen and ended up running the place, defected in 2000 to take over Bruichladdich, which had closed in 1995 but was being revived. Until his retirement fifteen years later, he consistently produced some of the best, and sometimes most unusual, whisky in the world—not just the unpeated Bruichladdich but a heavily peated range bearing the name of the long-defunct Port Charlotte distillery and an even more heavily peated bottling named for the ruined nineteenth-century Octomore distillery. Aggressive, impossibly intense, bracing, almost bewilderingly complex, there is nothing else like these spirits anywhere in the world.

The Load of Mischief 🎗 The Swan With Two Necks

That hallowed British institution the pub (or public house, meaning a place where the public can come to drink) has long been a center of social and cultural life in England, Scotland, and Wales (and beyond) for the local citizenry, whether in a tiny village or a bustling London neighborhood (a pub is also called a local)—and also a great lure for tourists. One of the characteristics that distinguishes pubs from their counterparts elsewhere is the variety and sometimes apparent whimsy (or eccentricity) with which they have been named.

Some pub names have roots in British history. Pubs called The Royal George, of which there are many, were christened in honor of the eighteenth-century warship of that name, which fought in the battles of St. Vincent and the Dardanelles (some sources say the name refers to King George III); London's celebrated "haunted" pub The Grenadier was named that in honor of the Grenadier Guards who contributed to the defeat of Napoleon at Waterloo. Other names are apparent corruptions: The George and Cannon may have been named originally for Tory statesman and (briefly) prime minister George Canning; The Bag o' Nails might have been The Bacchanal.

The most popular pub name in Great Britain today is said to be The Red Lion (there were more than 750 places with that moniker in 2013). The Royal Oak and The White Hart are also common. Back in 1922, one G. A. Tomlin published a book listing hundreds of hotel, inn, and tavern (or pub) names. Below is a list of a few of the more unusual ones recorded by Tomlin, with the addition of a few that I've noticed myself over the years (some of these pub names, like The Swan with Two Necks, are shared by more than one institution). Several of these pubs are no longer in business. While attrition over the course of almost a century is

to be expected, at least a handful of the defunct pubs below, including some which had endured for a century or more, have closed in the past twenty or thirty years. This is part of an unfortunate trend. There were about sixty-nine thousand pubs throughout the United Kingdom in 1980; today it is estimated that there are closer to forty-five thousand.

I Am the Only Running Footman, London
St. Peter's Finger, Lychett Minster
The Ass in a Bandbox, Nidd (defunct)
The Bell and Mackerel, London (defunct)
The Bull and Spectacles, Blithbury
The Cart Overthrown, Edmonton
The Case Is Altered, Pinner
The Cottage of Content, Alcester
The Cow and Snuffers, Cardiff (defunct)
The Craven Heifer, Skipton
The Eel's Foot, Leiston
The Gate Hangs Well, Syston
The Hog in the Pound, London (defunct)
The Horseshoe and Magpie, London (defunct)
The Hung Drawn and Quartered, London
The Jolly Taxpayer, Portsmouth
The Legend of Oily Johnnies, Winscales
The Lion and French Horn, London (defunct)
The Load of Mischief, Blewbury (defunct)
The Old Industrious Bee, Blackburn (defunct)
The Pyrotechnists Arms, London
The Queen's Head and Artichoke, London
The Roaring Donkey, Swindon
The Salmon and Compass, London (defunct)
The Sun and Whalebone, Harlow (defunct)
The Swan with Two Necks, Longdon
The Tippling Philosopher, Milborne Port
The Wheelbarrow and Castle, Radford
The Who'd Have Thought It, Milton Combe

Viking Brews

Sonny Priest, of Unst—the northernmost of Scotland's Shetland Islands and thus the northernmost land mass in Great Britain—makes six ales, including one, called White Wife, named for a ghost said to sometimes appear in the cars of lone males driving near the brewery, and two involving the ancient barley called bere (see page 27). He got started in the brewing business, Priest told me when I visited him at his Valhalla Brewery near the Unst hamlet of Haroldswick (which is, not surprisingly, the northernmost brewery in the U.K.), after an evening of, well, beer. "I'd never even been inside a brewery when I got the idea to do this," he said.

After the discovery of new oilfields in the North Sea in the 1960s, the Chevron Corporation established a large base on Unst, and an airport was built at Baltasound to transport workers back and forth to the offshore oilfields. Priest got a job in the control tower there and worked at the airport for sixteen years. When Chevron relocated farther south in Shetland, the airport was mothballed, and Priest and thirty-eight of his fellow workers were laid off. The Shetland Islands Council offered some financing to the laid-off workers to generate new jobs, and Priest was considering opening a laundromat, which Unst didn't have.

Then, one night, in 1997, Priest and some of his out-of-work friends went to the firehouse to have a few beers. "In fact, we had quite a few," he confessed.

A folk art "pub scene" on the roadside on the island of Unst on Shetland

"There were three steps coming out of the firehouse and the doorframe was low, and you had to duck your head down. I went out through the door and one of my friends came right after me, but he forgot to duck and he went sprawling and skinned his elbow. Just like that the idea came to me, and I said, 'I'm going to set up a brewery to keep you all drinking.'"

He got in touch with one of Scotland's best-known beer experts, Graham Stewart, professor emeritus of brewing and distilling at Heriot-Watt University in Edinburgh, for advice, and hired a graduate brewer from the university for six months, and in 1997 opened Valhalla Brewery—named in reference to Shetland's strong Viking roots. "I learned everything I could and then took over," said Priest. "Since then, I've trained half a dozen brewers myself."

CIDER: Good Health ⚖ the Apple Trees

There is increasingly good wine produced in England and to a lesser extent Wales, and of course English ales are famous worldwide, but the most definitively British alcoholic beverage made today—outside of whisky, of course—is quite possibly cider, made from that most emblematic of British fruits: the apple.

To Americans, "cider" means apple juice, not alcoholic unless modified by the adjective "hard" (the non-alcoholic juice is generally pasteurized, so no longer contains the yeasts necessary for fermentation). In the U.K., cider always packs a kick—at a legal strength of anywhere from 1.2 to 7.5 percent alcohol by volume. The word itself comes ultimately from the Hebrew shēkār, meaning "strong drink." Good English cider is delicious: it tastes of apples, of course, but with the fruit's sweetness tempered by acidity and softened by a faintly earthy character, and then enlivened by a carbonation that ranges from pinpoint to effervescent.

Wild apples have grown in Britain since Neolithic times, and their juice has probably been expressed for drinking for thousands of years—and may well have been actively fermented for nearly that long. The Romans reported in 55 B.C. that the people of Kent made an alcoholic beverage from local crabapples. The art of proper cider-making, though, was probably brought to England by the Normans; they certainly introduced many new varieties of apples and refined the fermentation process.

The seventeenth and eighteenth centuries were cider's golden age in Britain. In the 1630s, the Viscount Scudamore, a prominent politician, diplomat, and landowner, planted so many apple trees in Herefordshire, primarily a bittersweet variety called the Redstreak, that the county was said to resemble one gigantic orchard. Scudamore had been the British ambassador to France, and, tasting Normandy cider there, thought he could make something as good back home. The bottle-fermenting of cider, Champagne style, became common in the late 1600s, after coal-fired kilns began producing stronger glass than had previously been available. (Spontaneous explosion had been a constant danger with cider, as with Champagne, when weaker glass was used.) The eighteenth-century poet John Philips took cider as the putative subject of

Wassailing apple trees with hot cider in Devonshire on Twelfth Night, 1861

his imitation of Virgil's *Georgics*, a fifty-page masterwork called *Cyder: A Poem, in Two Books*, in the course of which he proclaims that "my mill / Now grinds choice apples, and the British vats / O'erflow with generous Cyder," and later concludes that cider "Shall please all tastes, and triumph o'er the vine."

The practice of wassailing, which we now associate with Christmas caroling, was a popular eighteenth-century tradition (*wassail* derives from the Old English *wes hál*, "be in good health" or "be fortunate") aimed at insuring the well-being of the apple orchards. Farmers and their families would gather around the trees, sing a wassailing song, pour cider on the roots, make loud noises (banging pots and pans, shooting off rifles), and then make an appropriate toast. (A cider bar called Wassail opened in New York City in 2015—on, appropriately enough, Orchard Street.) There was a good reason, beyond the cash value of the crop, for this concern for the health of the apple trees: Until legislation forbade the practice in 1887, agricultural workers received a portion of their salary in cider, which didn't seem to bother them at all.

The traditional cider-apple varieties are hard, sweet but tart, and almost always ugly—mottled and shriveled. Cider can be made from cooking and eating apples too, though, and as planting of these increased in the nineteenth and early twentieth centuries, the number of cider-apple trees decreased; why not grow fruit that can serve two purposes? Today, cider apples are classified as sweet (comparatively bland varieties like Sweet Coppin, used mostly for blending), bittersweet (Dabinett, Ellis Bitter, Somerset Redstreak, etc., considered to yield the astringent fruitiness that defines British ciders), sharp (particularly high in acid, like Bramley's Seedling and Crimson King), and bittersharp (Stoke Red and Yarlington Mill, for example, with high levels of tannin and acid). In general, ciders from the West Country of Gloucestershire, Herefordshire, Somerset, Devon, Dorset, and Cornwall are based on classic cider varieties, and so tend to be keener, drier, and more astringent, with a lingering mouthfeel, while those from Kent and East Anglia, usually based in whole or large part on eating and/or cooking apples, are sweeter and lighter. (Perry is a cider made from pears, mostly in Gloucestershire, Herefordshire, and Worcestershire.)

Cider sales tapered off in the latter nineteenth century and throughout the twentieth, for various reasons, but have revived in force in recent years. Today, the British bottle and consume more cider than anybody else, with annual sales close to £1 billion (about $1.4 billion). Large-scale producers like Bulmers and Aston Manor account for most of this, of course, but there are plenty of small producers doing interesting things. Among the many good brands to look for are Severn from Glouscester-shire, Dunkertons from Herefordshire, Fowey Valley from Cornwall, and Perry's, Worley's, Hecks, and Ham Hill from Somerset. The Kent Cider Company produces a particularly good example of the sweeter style. Like craft beers and wines from small producers, these and other artisanal ciders can be difficult to find, but they're worth the trouble for anyone who wants a true taste of Britain.

A glass of cider at Perry's Cider Mill, Dowlish Wake, Ilminster, Somerset

BEER: The Bitter AND the Stout

Cider, whisky, wine—these are all wonderful beverages, made well in various corners of England, Scotland, and Wales—but what Britons really drink is beer. There are about 1,500 breweries in the U.K.—the highest number per capita of any country in the world—producing more than ten thousand different beers annually, counting seasonal and other specialty offerings. For every ten drinks sold in pubs, seven are beer. That said, between 2008 and 2013, the last year for which complete statistics are available as this is written, beer consumption fell by 16 percent in Britain, and more than 7,000 pubs closed.

Beer of some description was first brewed as long ago as 10,000 BC, probably in the Fertile Crescent, and beer based on barley, by far the brewer's most common grain today, dates from around 3500 BC It probably first reached Britain roughly five hundred years later, and quickly took hold. After the Roman invasion in the first century AD, pro-Roman tribes minted coins bearing the image of a grapevine; the coins of loyal Britons bore instead an ear of barley. The first British beer producer mentioned by name was one "Atrectus the brewer," whose name is found on account tablets dating from the early second century AD, unearthed at the old Roman garrison of Vindolanda, in modern-day Northumbria.

Though grapevines were cultivated in medieval Britain, they never thrived to the extent that barley and other grains did, and ale became one of the most common beverages of the period. (Like tea in Asia—it had not yet reached Britain—beer was far safer to consume than water, the brewing process having destroyed malevolent bacteria.) The term *beer* was first used in English around 1000 AD, as *béor*, from a proto-Germanic word for barley. *Ale*, originally *eala*, may be even older, but its etymology is uncertain.

For centuries, beer was flavored with various herbs and sometimes sweetened with honey. Pepys, writing in the latter 1600s, makes numerous references to combining beer with, of all things, wine ("half a pint of Rhenish wine at the Still-yard, mixed with beer"), and when he developed an ulcer, his Dr. Burnett prescribes a spoonful of herbal syrup—made with cinnamon, nutmeg, comfrey, and rose petals, among other things, macerated in old wine and clarified with an egg white—"in every draught of Ale or beer you drink."

Hops were first planted on British soil in the early sixteenth century, in Suffolk, Kent, Surrey, and Essex. An anonymous street rhyme held that "Hops, Reformation, bays [i.e., the coarse cloth we call baize], and beer / Came to England all in one year." Beer is included in that verse because, as hops began to be added to it, that was the term used to describe hopped ale; from that time until the eighteenth century, it was understood that beer was hopped and ale wasn't.

Today, of course, *beer* is the generic term for all beverages brewed from grain. The common British beer types today—and these categories are broad and contain subsets—are brown ale, which tends to be sweetish, with a malty flavor; pale ale, popularly called "bitter," which grew in popularity in the 1960s and which has a sharp and, yes, bitter bite though often a fruity character, too; and the richer, darker, usually strongly hopped porter and stout. (The two styles are very similar and the terms are sometimes used interchangeably, but porter is usually made with malted barley, while the barley used for stout is roasted but unmalted.) All are fermented with the common yeast strain *Saccharomyces cerevisiae* (also used in winemaking and to raise bread dough), which rises to the surface of the beer. The other main variety of beer, which really took hold in Great Britain only in the 1960s, is the lighter, crisper, usually paler style called lager, which is fermented at colder temperatures with *Saccharomyces pastorianus* (also called *Saccharomyces uvarum*), a yeast that sinks to the bottom of the beer.

There are, as noted, many thousands of British beers (though many imports are also sold in the U.K. today, about 85 percent of the beer Britons drink is made on home ground). The various brands from large concerns like the massive Bass (now owned by the Molson Coors Brewing Company), Fuller's, and Samuel Smith's are easy to find. Fuller's creamy, mocha-flavored London Porter and Samuel Smith's appropriately nutty Nut Brown Ale are classics. A handful of other British brews worth looking for are WEST's St. Mungo lager, citrusy and clean; HSB (Horndean Special Bitter), a very nicely rounded beer with a good balance of malt and hop flavors; the coffee-and-molasses-tinged Belhaven Scottish Stout; and Hook Norton Double Stout, toasty, with a hint of chocolate flavor.

WINE: Côtes-de-Yorkshire? Vin de Wales?

The Romans may or may not have introduced winemaking to Britain—they certainly imported a lot of wine, but Tacitus (whose father-in-law had helped conquer Britain) called the climate ""unpleasant and unsuited to the growing of vines"—but the Saxons and the Angles and then the Normans definitely cultivated grapes and fermented their juice. The *Domesday Book*, a mere twenty years after the Norman Invasion of 1066, lists 46 vineyard sites around the south of England, and by the early sixteenth century, there were almost 150 sizeable plots of grapes in England and Wales, about a third of them attached to monasteries or other ecclesiastical properties. "Wine, in both England and Scotland," writes historian Charles Ludington in his book *The Politics of Wine in Britain: A New Cultural History*, "was a symbol of political power and legitimacy because it had long represented the court, the aristocracy, and the Church."

This was an early high point in English wine history. In subsequent centuries, probably due at least in part to a cooling of the climate (the so-called Little Ice Age that lasted worldwide from the sixteenth through the nineteenth centuries), vineyard acreage shrank dramatically. In the late 1800s, John Patrick Crichton-Stuart, the Marquess of Bute, began making wine on a commercial basis at his Castell Coch in South Wales—but during World War I and afterwards, both vines and winemaking effectively disappeared from Britain.

The modern British wine industry dates its origins to the years following World War II. The chemist and amateur orchardist Ray Barrington Brock established a research station at Oxted in Surrey in 1945, where he grew about 600 different varieties of table and wine grapes over a period of twenty-five years, attempting to determine which ones did best on English soil. The socialist historian and amateur fruit-grower Edward Hyams, who had planted his own vines in Kent, collaborated with Brock and in 1949 published a seminal book called *The Grape Vine in England*. The entomologist and economist George Ordish and the Wiltshire farmer John Edginton also experimented with assorted varieties (hybrids Edginton planted in 1962 may be the oldest surviving cultivated grapevines in the U.K.).

Harvesting grapes from the royal grapevines at Hampton Court, early 1930s

The first real commercial vineyards and winery in Britain since the days of Castell Coch were the work of Major General Guy Salisbury-Jones, who began with an acre or so of the French-American hybrid Seyval Blanc in 1951 at Hambledon in Hampshire and expanded from there. Other would-be winemakers followed, and between the late 1960s and the late 1990s, scores of new properties were planted with vines.

At this writing, there are something like 175 wineries in Britain, producing more than six million bottles annually, from Ryedale Vineyards in Westoro, in North Yorkshire, to St. Martin's Vineyard and St. Mary's Vineyard on the Isles of Scilly off the tip of Cornwall, with the majority concentrated in Sussex, Surrey, and Kent. (There were more wineries twenty-five years ago, but a number have since found the going too tough and closed down.) Twenty or so of Britain's wineries are in Wales; Llanerch Vineyard in the Vale of Glamorgan makes, among other offerings, a tart, clean, lively white from the German-bred Reichsteiner grape, under its Cariad label.

Apart from a few producers of berry wine, there are no producers in Scotland, though the owners of the Ardeonaig Hotel in Perthshire planted a small number of Riesling vines in 2006 (it's unclear whether any wine was ever produced, but if it was, it couldn't have been more than about ten cases), and chef and food writer Christopher Trotter made his first wine near Upper Largo in Fife in 2014, from Rondo, Seigerrebe, and Solaris grapes; even

Trotter admitted that it was "horrible." (Bottles labeled "British," as opposed to "English" or "Welsh" wine, are made in Britain from imported grape concentrate and are generally pretty nasty stuff.)

The great success story of British wine is in sparkling wines, made by the traditional Champagne method, and especially those based on the traditional Champagne varieties, which are proving to do well in the chalky soil of parts of Kent, Sussex, Hampshire, and Dorset—Chardonnay, Pinot Noir, and Pinot Meunier. The generally acknowledged leader in the field is Nyetimber, from West Sussex, whose wines are superb. Ridgeview, Pebblebed, Herbert Hall, Gusbourne, Knightor, Henners, Hoffmann and Rathbone, and Chapel Down are other names to look for. These tend to be crisp, bright, sometimes surprisingly complex wines, both white and rosé, that hold their own nicely against their French inspirations. (The French have noticed: Taittinger recently entered into a joint venture to produce sparkling wine in Kent.)

I was also impressed with the sparkling wines of Camel Valley Vineyard in Cornwall, especially their austere, very faintly pink Pinot Noir Brut—and the best English still wine I've encountered so far was Camel Valley's Darnibole Bacchus, an intensely flavorful, mineral-tinged white (made from a grape descended from Silvaner, Riesling, and Müller-Thurgau) that has the honor of being the first English wine awarded a PDO (Protected Designation of Origin) by the European Union. There are real possibilities here.

Wine AND Espionage

John Le Carré's retired spies pursue a number of occupations—schoolteacher, detective, member of Parliament . . . winemaker. In Le Carré's 1995 novel *Our Game*, Tim Cranmer, pensioned off by MI6 after the end of the Cold War, retires to his family's property, Honeybrook Manor, in Somerset and becomes "a wine-growing Englishman of a certain class." He apparently isn't very good at the wine part. When a visitor makes reference to "British wine," Cranmer replies "Unfortunately there's no such thing. There's English wine. There's Welsh wine. Mine's inferior English."

Cranmer struggles with the German grape press that his predecessor—his uncle—christened "The Sulky Hun" and complains that the eighteenth-century walled garden in which said uncle planted grapes is "a frost trap and a haven for disease." Cranmer grows Madeleine Angevine, a white-wine variety from the Loire, and also Pinot Noir, though he readily admits that Pinot won't ripen in England unless the vineyard site is exceptional, and that his isn't. (His uncle planted it, he says; "He was an incurable optimist.") The quality of Cranmer's wine ends up not mattering much, as he is last seen picking up an AK-47 to help fight the Russians in Ingushetia, from which he will likely not return (long, well-told story).

In his acknowledgments, Le Carré notes that "Major Colin Gillespie and his wife, Sue, of Wootton Vineyard in Somerset make much better wine than Tim Cranmer ever did." It was presumably they who helped him get the wine bits right. The Gillespies were pioneers of modern-day English winemaking, harvesting their first grapes in 1973 on their vineyard property near Wells. The winery, alas, did not survive into the twenty-first century.

APPENDIX

STOCKS, DOUGHS,
AND OTHER BASICS

CLARIFIED BUTTER

MAKES ABOUT 1¾ CUPS (395 G)

Clarified butter is essential for making potted shrimp, but is also a good cooking fat for many purposes, as it has a higher smoke point than regular butter—485°F (250°C) as opposed to 375°F (190°C). It is rarely used for baking, however, as it has less flavor than its unclarified counterpart.

1 pound (4 sticks / 450 g) butter

Melt the butter in a small saucepan over low heat. Remove the pan from the heat and spoon off and discard any white solids that have risen to the top. Carefully pour off the butter into a glass jar or bowl, stopping before you reach the cloudy liquid at the bottom of the pan. Discard the cloudy liquid, or add it to cream sauces.

SHERRIED BREAD CRUMBS

MAKES 3 CUPS

These bread crumbs are a perfect accompaniment to roast grouse and other game birds. They're also good scattered over simply grilled or roasted fish. Chef-turned-writer Simon Hopkinson got the recipe from his father, Bruce.

½ cup (1 stick /115 g) butter
3 cups (135 g) fresh coarse white bread crumbs
¼ cup (60 ml) dry sherry
Salt and freshly ground black pepper

Melt the butter over medium heat in a wide, heavy-bottomed skillet. Reduce the heat to low and stir in the bread crumbs. Cook, stirring continuously, for 6 to 8 minutes or until the crumbs are crisp and golden brown.

Drizzle in the sherry and mix it in thoroughly. Cook for a minute or so more, or until the sherry has evaporated or been absorbed. Season the bread crumbs generously with salt and pepper.

Store in a tightly sealed container. Warm the bread crumbs for about 10 minutes in a 250°F (120°C) oven just before serving.

PUFF PASTRY

MAKES ABOUT 2 POUNDS (900 G)

Store-bought puff pastry is perfectly acceptable, but there's something very satisfying about producing your own, if you have the time and the patience.

3½ cups (420 g) all-purpose flour, chilled, plus
    more for dusting
Pinch of salt
1 pound (4 sticks / 450 g) butter, slightly softened

Sift the flour and salt together into a large bowl, then, while stirring continuously with a floured wooden spoon, drizzle in enough cold water (1 to 1½ cups / 240 to 360 ml) to form a firm dough.

Shape the dough into a ball, return it to the bowl, cover the bowl with a clean, damp dish towel, and refrigerate the dough for about 1 hour.

Roll the dough out on a floured work surface to form a square about ½ inch (1.25 cm) thick. With your hands, shape the butter into a square about ⅛ inch (3 mm) thick and place it in the center of the dough square. Fold the dough over the butter to form a packet.

Roll the dough out again, this time into a rectangle about 6 by 18 inches (15 by 45 cm). Fold the dough inward from each long end, as neatly as possible, to form a thick 6-inch (15-cm) square packet. Seal the edges of the packet with the rolling pin.

Repeat the process, rolling out the dough into a 6 x 18-inch (15 x 45-cm) rectangle again, then folding it inward and sealing the edges as before. Wrap the dough in plastic wrap and refrigerate it for 30 minutes.

Repeat the process four more times, wrapping and refrigerating the dough for 30 minutes each time.

Refrigerate the dough for at least 30 minutes more after it's finished, before using. Puff pastry dough freezes well, tightly wrapped in plastic wrap and sealed in a freezer bag.

SHORTCRUST PASTRY

MAKES ENOUGH DOUGH FOR 2 (9- TO 10-INCH / 23- TO 25-CM) PIES OR TARTS

Shortcrust pastry—"short," like shortbread, because it has a high ratio of shortening (i.e., fat) to flour, typically (as in this recipe) 1 part shortening to 2 parts flour—is basically what Americans would consider pie dough. This pastry is used for both sweet and savory pies; for the latter, leave out the sugar.

2 cups (250 g) all-purpose flour, plus more for
    dusting
½ teaspoon salt
1 tablespoon confectioners' sugar (optional)
1 cup (2 sticks / 225 g) cold butter, cut into small
    pieces
1 egg yolk, beaten with 2 tablespoons cold water

Combine the flour, salt, and sugar (if using) in a large bowl, then rub in the butter with your hands until the mixture resembles coarse meal. Add the beaten egg yolk and toss the dough with a fork. Add enough cold water, from 1 to 3 tablespoons, to let the dough be gathered into a ball.

Cut the dough into two equal pieces and, on a board lightly dusted with flour, pat each half into a disk 4 to 5 inches (10 to 13 cm) in diameter. Wrap each piece of dough separately in plastic wrap and chill for at least 1 hour or up to 24 hours before using.

CHICKEN STOCK

MAKES ABOUT 2½ QUARTS (2.35 L)

This is a classic chicken stock recipe, useful as the base for countless soups but also, with seasonings added, a flavorful broth in itself. If you should by chance have rabbit bones available, substitute them for the chicken bones; they make a particularly delicious stock.

3 pounds (1.5 kg) chicken bones, with bits of meat attached
1 large onion, quartered
2 carrots, coarsely chopped
1 stalk celery, coarsely chopped
1 leek, white part only, washed well and coarsely chopped
1 bay leaf

Combine all the ingredients in a large pot and add enough cold water to cover them completely. Cover the pot and bring the water to a boil over high heat. Uncover the pot, reduce the heat to low, and simmer for 2½ hours, skimming off any scum that forms on the surface.

Strain the stock into a large bowl or another pot, discarding the solids. Rinse out the original pot, return the stock to it, and bring it to a boil over high heat. Reduce the heat to low and simmer for about 30 minutes longer. Cool the stock to room temperature, refrigerate, then remove the fat that has solidified on the surface of the stock. If you're not using the stock immediately, it may be cooled to room temperature, then frozen for future use.

VEAL or BEEF STOCK

MAKES ABOUT 2½ QUARTS (2.35 L)

I use this basic stock for added flavor and richness in many recipes that call for chicken stock.

4 pounds (1.8 kg) veal or beef bones, with bits of meat attached
1 large onion, coarsely chopped
2 carrots, coarsely chopped
1 stalk celery, coarsely chopped
2 or 3 large sprigs parsley
2 bay leaves
2 whole cloves
2 cloves garlic, unpeeled
2 tablespoons tomato paste

Preheat the oven to 450°F (230°C).

Spread the bones out in a large roasting pan and roast for 30 minutes, then add the onion and carrots and roast for 20 minutes more.

Put the bones, onion, carrots, celery, parsley, bay leaves, cloves, garlic, and tomato paste into a large pot. Deglaze the roasting pan on the stovetop over high heat with about ½ cup water, then add the contents of the pan to the pot. Add enough cold water to the pot to cover the ingredients completely. Cover the pot and bring the water to a boil over high heat. Uncover the pot, reduce the heat to low, and simmer, stirring occasionally, until the stock has reduced by half, 4 to 5 hours. Skim off any scum that forms on the surface of the stock as it cooks.

Strain the stock, discarding the solids. Rinse out the pot, then return the stock to it and simmer over low heat for about 30 minutes longer. Cool the stock to room temperature, refrigerate, then remove the fat that has solidified on the surface of the stock. If you're not using the stock immediately, it may be cooled to room temperature, then frozen for future use.

COURT BOUILLON

MAKES ABOUT 2½ QUARTS (2.35 L)

Court bouillon is fish stock; Eliza Acton described it in *Modern Cookery, in All Its Branches* (1845) as "a preparation of vegetables and wine, in which (in expensive cookery) fish is boiled." Not a bad definition. This "quick broth" is indeed the traditional poaching liquid for fish, but it also makes a good base for fish or shellfish soups and stews.

3 pounds (1.5 kg) fish carcasses or bones, with bits of meat and skin attached (use only white-fleshed saltwater fish)
1 large onion, coarsely chopped
1 stalk celery, coarsely chopped
1 leek, white part only, washed well and coarsely chopped
1 bay leaf
Juice of 1 lemon
1 (375-ml) bottle (or ½ [750-ml] bottle) dry white wine
10 whole white peppercorns

Put the fish, onion, celery, leek, bay leaf, lemon juice, white wine, and peppercorns into a large pot and add about 3 quarts (2.8 L) water, or enough to cover the ingredients completely. Cover the pot and bring the water to a boil over high heat. Uncover the pot, reduce the heat to low, and simmer for 30 minutes, skimming off any scum that forms on the surface as it cooks.

Strain the stock, discarding the solids. Rinse out the pot, then return the stock to it and simmer over low heat for about 15 minutes more.

If you're not using the court bouillon immediately, it may be cooled to room temperature, then frozen for future use.

VEGETABLE STOCK

MAKES ABOUT 2½ QUARTS (2.35 L)

This recipe is adapted from one used at The Colony, the stylish, art deco–style dining room at The Beaumont Hotel in London, where it is the basis for several soups.

½ cup (120 ml) vegetable oil
4 or 5 medium onions, chopped
6 to 8 medium carrots, chopped
1 large leek, washed well and chopped
½ small fennel bulb, chopped
1 small stalk celery stalk, chopped
2 cloves garlic, crushed
4 sprigs parsley

Heat the oil in a medium stockpot over low heat. Add the onions, carrots, leek, fennel, celery, garlic, and parsley and cook, stirring frequently, until they soften but haven't begun to brown, 5 to 7 minutes.

Add 3 quarts (2.8 L) water to the pot, cover it, and bring the water to a boil over high heat. Reduce the heat to low and simmer, uncovered, for 45 minutes.

Strain the stock, discarding the vegetables. If you're not using the stock immediately, it may be cooled to room temperature, then frozen for future use.

SOURCES

British products, including packaged goods and meat products (British style, but made in the United States), are widely available through a number of specialist websites. These include britishfoodshop.com, jollygrub.com, britishgoodsonline.com, ukgoods.com, britishfooddepot .com, britsuperstore.com, and britishsupplies.com. A surprising number of foodstuffs, both British and useful for British recipes, may be found through Amazon.com (for instance, pickling salt).

Dartagnan.com is an invaluable source for game birds including wild Scottish partridge, pheasant, grouse, and wood pigeon in season, and can also supply rabbit (including bone-in legs), three kinds of duck, duck-fat, free-range goose, and venison, among other products.

MAIL-ORDER SOURCES FOR SPECIFIC PRODUCTS:

Arbroath smokies: salmonlady.com

Bangers: properbritishbacon.com, balsonbutchers.com

Bere meal: (no website, but email craigiebutchers@ hotmail.co.uk)

British bacon: properbritishbacon.com, balsonbutchers.com

Clotted cream: englishteastore.com

Duck and goose fat: gourmetfoodsstore.com

Finnan haddie: scottishgourmetusa.com, salmonlady.com

Heather Honey: scottishgourmetusa.com

Haggis: britishfoodshop.com (for Stahly haggis), scottishhaggis.com (for McKean's haggis)

Lamb: jamisonfarm.com

Lamb shoulder (boneless): lavalakelamb.com

Lancashire cheese (and other British cheeses): igourmet.com, Whole Foods stores

Leaf lard: dietrichsmeats.com

Marrowfat peas: englishteastore.com

Mushroom powder: spicejungle.com

Pickled walnuts: jollygrub.com

Quatre-épices: spicejungle.com

Scottish langoustines: scottishgourmetusa.com

Scottish oatmeal: bobsredmill.com

Seville (bitter) oranges: floridaorangeshop.com, November to March, able to ship to some states only; melissas.com, December through February

Suet: grasslandbeef.com

Venison: brokenarrowranch.com

ACKNOWLEDGMENTS

My thanks go first and most of all to my longtime colleagues and friends Christopher Hirsheimer and Melissa Hamilton, who not only framed my words with beautiful and magically evocative images (as they have done for me so many times before) but also offered culinary advice and encouragement at every step.

I owe a great debt, too, to Julia Lee, "the Fry Queen" and so much more, who helped me tame many of the more vexing recipes herein.

A number of chefs and restaurateurs around England, Scotland, and Wales were extremely generous with their recipes of a nonvexing sort, as well as their advice and expertise in matters culinary and cultural. Above all, my sincere thanks to the irrepressible Jeremy Lee, and to Mark Hix, Fergus Henderson, and the late Ronnie Clydesdale and his son Colin.

Thanks, too, in this regard, to Nigel Haworth (and to Lady Sue Bancroft, Craig Bancroft, Craig Jackson, and Amanda Brown at Northcote), Charlie Soole, Ross Horrocks, Dylan Evans and Catarina Giannotti, Sue Lawrence, Ken Stahly, Michael Chapman, and Marie Rayner, and to Simpson's in the Strand.

Robert Titley, Robert L. Jones, Shaun Hill, Franco Taruschio, Kerry Sidney, the late Gareth Jones, Thelma Adams, and Chris and Gunna Chown helped me find my way through the gorgeous countryside and splendid kitchens of Wales.

In Scotland, I benefitted greatly from the assistance of Michael McCuish, Thorfinn Craigie, Iain R. Spink, and Liana Nickel.

I must thank my friends Sally Clarke, Simon Hopkinson, Jeremy King, and Sir Terence and Lady Vicki Conran for having fed me so well and being so welcoming and so helpful to me, in so many ways, for so many years.

Thanks, too, to Clodagh McKenna, Clive Osborne, Trevor Gulliver, Stephen Harris, Nina Syme, Jay Rayner, Hazel Thomas, Christian Holthausen, James Pembroke, Piers Russell-Cobb, and Annette Abstoss.

This book would not have come into being without the efforts of my agent, Michael Psaltis, and my editor at Abrams, Michael Sand. Mary Hern, Ashley Albert, and Danielle Young, also at Abrams, and Ivy McFadden and Sarah Scheffel helped with the fine tuning. I hope you're all as proud of the results as I am.

Finally, my thanks, appreciation, and love to Erin, for putting up with my writing schedule and my travels (and for being such a good companion on them when she could).

BIBLIOGRAPHY

Note: In drawing on older books, I used some hard copies, either from my own collection or consulted in the British Library. Where I used original or other early editions, I have given that bibliographical information; where I used modern editions or facsimiles, I've given the current information but have indicated the year of original publication. I was also able to find some historical works online from Project Gutenberg (gutenberg.org), Forgotten Books (forgottenbooks.org), Google Books (books.google.com), and other sources.

A Collection of Ordinances and Regulations for the Government of the Royal Household, Made in Divers Reigns: from King Edward II to King William and Queen Mary, also Receipts in Ancient Cookery. London: The Society of Antiqueries/John Nichols, 1790.

Acton, Eliza, *Modern Cookery, in All Its Branches*, second edition. London: Longman, Brown, Breen and Longmans, 1845.

An Comunn Gaidhealach, *Recipes of the Highlands and Islands of Scotland (The Feill Cookery Book, 1907).* Chicago: Kalevala Books, 2010.

Ar n-Aran Làitheil: Our Daily Bread: A Collection of Traditional Recipes from Geàrrannan. Geàrrannan Blackhouse Village, n.d.

Barry, Michael, *Old English Recipes*. Norwich: Jarrold Publishing, 1996.

Beeton, Isabella, *The Book of Household Management.* London: S.O. Beeton, 1866.

Blumenthal, Heston, *Historic Heston*. New York: Bloomsbury USA, 2013

Borrow, George, *Wild Wales: Its People, Language and Scenery* (1862). Edinburgh: Thomas Nelson and Sons, 1930.

Boswell, James, *The Journal of a Tour to the Hebrides with Samuel Johnson* (1785). New York: Everyman's Library, 1958.

Bradley, Richard, *The Country Housewife and Lady's Director in the Management of a House, and the Delights and Profits of a Farm* (1732). Totnes: Prospect Books, 1980.

Broomfield, Andrea, *Food and Cooking in Victorian England: A History*. Santa Barbara: Greenwood Publishing Group, 2007.

Brown, Catherine, *Broths to Bannocks: Cooking in Scotland 1690 to the Present Day*. London: John Murray, 1990.

Burke, Thomas, *Dinner is Served: Or Eating Round the World in London*. George Routledge & Sons, Ltd., 1937

Burton, John Hill, *Life and Correspondence of David Hume*, two-volume set. Edinburgh: William Tait, 1846.

Calvert, T. C., *The Story of Wensleydale Cheese*. Clapham: Dalesman Publishing Co., 1946.

Cool, H. E. M., *Eating and Drinking in Roman Britain*. Cambridge, etc.: The Cambridge University Press, 2006.

Cooper, Sir W. E., *Is Meat-Eating Sanctioned by Divine Authority?* Paignton: The Order of the Golden Age, 1906.

Davidson, Alan, *The Oxford Companion to Food*. Oxford: The Oxford University Press, 1999.

Davies, Gilli, *Lamb, Leeks & Laverbread: The Best of Welsh Cookery*. London: Grafton Books, 1989.

Defoe, Daniel, *A Tour Thro' the Whole Island of Great Britain*. (1724–1727). Exeter: Webb & Bower, 1989.

De la Falaise, Maxime, *Seven Centuries of English Cooking: A Collection of Recipes*. New York: Grove Press, 1973.

De Salis, Mrs. Harriet Anne, *The Housewife's Referee: A Treatise on Culinary and Household Subjects*. London: Hutchinson, 1898.

"Diner-Out," *London Restaurants*. New York: Brentano's, 1924.

Dods, Mrs. Margaret (Christian Isobel Johnstone), *The Cook and Housewife's Manua*l. Edinburgh: Printed for the author, 1826.

Edinburgh College of Domestic Science, *The Edinburgh Book of Plain Cookery Recipes*. London: Thomas Nelson and Sons, 1932.

Edington, Sarah, *Complete Traditional Recipe Book*. London: The National Trust, 2006.

Elia (Lamb, Charles), *Essays of Elia* (1823). Charleston, South Carolina: BiblioBazaar, 2010.

Ellison, J. Audrey, *Colman's Book of Traditional British Cookery*. London: Ward Lock Limited, 1980.

Evelyn, John, *Acetaria: A Discourse of Sallets* (1699). Brooklyn: Brooklyn Botanic Gardens, 1937.

Farley, John, *The London Art of Cookery* (1811). Carlisle, Massachusetts, Applewood Books, 2008.

Freeman, Bobby, *A Book of Welsh Soups & Savouries Including Traditional Welsh Cawl*. Talybont: Y Lolfa Cyf., 1987.

———, *First Catch Your Peacock*. Talybont: Y Lolfa Cyf., 1980.

Frewin, Leslie, ed., *Parnassus Near Piccadilly*. London: Leslie Frewin, 1965.

Gerard, John, *The Herbal or General History of Plants: The Complete 1633 Edition as Revised and Enlarged by Thomas Johnson*. Mineola, N.Y.: Dover Publications, 2015.

Glasse, Hannah, *The Art of Cookery Made Plain and Easy* (1788 edition). Whitefish, Montana: Kessinger Publishing, LLC, 2010.

Heath, Ambrose, *Good Cheese Dishes*. London: Faber & Faber, 1943.

———, *Good Savouries*. London: Faber & Faber, 1934.

Henderson, Fergus, *The Complete Nose to Tail*. New York: Ecco, 2013.

Hester, Les, ed., *A Taste of Moray*. Elgin: Moray College of Further Education, Moravian Press Ltd.,1986.

Hix, Mark, *British Food*. London: Quadrille Publishing Limited, 2005.

———, *British Regional Food: A Cook's Tour of Britain and Ireland*. London: Quadrille Publishing Limited, 2006.

Hooton-Smith, Eileen, *The Restaurants of London*. London: Alfred A. Knopf, 1928.

Hornsey, Ian S., *A History of Beer and Brewing*. Cambridge: The Royal Society of Chemistry, 2003.

Jerrold, Douglas William, William Makepeace Thackeray, Leigh Hunt, and Joseph Kenny Meadows, *Heads of the People: or, Portraits of the English*. Philadelphia: Carey & Hart, 1841.

Johnson, Dr. Samuel, *A Journey to the Western Islands of Scotland* (1775). Charleston, South Carolina: Nabu Press, 2010.

Kay, Billy and Cailean Maclean, *Knee Deep in Claret: A Celebration of Wine and Scotland*. Edinburgh, Mainstream Publishing, 1983.

Kenrick, William, *The Whole Duty of a Woman*. London: T. Read, 1737.

Kiple, Kenneth F. and Kriemhild Coneè Ornelas, *The Cambridge World History of Food*. Cambridge: Cambridge University Press, 2000.

Kitchiner, William, *Apicius Redivivus: or, The Cook's Oracle*. London: Samuel Bagster, 1817.

Lawrence, Sue, *A Cook's Tour of Scotland: From Barra to Brora in 120 Recipes*. London: Headline, 2008.

Leyel, Mrs. C.F., and Miss Olga Hartley, *The Gentle Art of Cookery* (1929). London: Chatto & Windus; The Hogarth Press, 1983.

Llanover, The Right Hon. Lady, *The First Principles of Good Cookery* (1867). Trefaron: Brefi Press, 1991.

Lockhart, G.W., *The Scots and Their Oats*. Edinburgh: Birlinn Limited, 1997.

The London Book of Menus Plus…, 3rd revised edition. London: L.B.M. Publications, 1986.

Ludington, Charles, *The Politics of Wine in Britain: A New Cultural History*. New York: Palgrave Macmillan, 2013.

MacInnes, Seumas, *The Stornoway Black Pudding Bible*, Edinburgh: Birlinn Limited, 2010.

Macsween, Jo, *The Macsween Haggis Bible*. Edinburgh: Birlinn Limited, 2013.

Markham, Gervase, *The English Hus-wife, Containing the Inward and Outward Virtues Which Ought to Be in A Compleat Woman*. London: Roger Jackson, 1615.

May, Peter, *The Black House*. New York and London: SilverOak, 2012.

McDouall, Robin, *The Gourmet's London*. London: MacGibbon & Kee, 1969

McNeill, F. Marian, *The Scots Cellar: Its Traditions and Lore* (1956). London: Repographia, 1973.

———, *The Scots Kitchen: Its Traditions and Lore with Old-Time Recipes* (1929). Edinburgh: The Mercat Press Ltd., 2004.

Michel, Marta Brookfield, *Stars in Your Kitchen*. New York: Dodd, Mead & Company, 1953.

Mitchell, M. M., *The Treasure Cookery Book: Containing the Principles and Rules of Modern Cookery Including Numerous Recipes*. London: Longmans, Green, and Co., 1913.

Morris, Lewis, Richard, William and John, *The Letters of Lewis, Richard, William and John Morris, of Anglesey (Morrisiaid Mon) 1728–1765*, transcribed from the originals and edited by John H. Davies. Aberystwyth: John H. Davies, 1907.

Newnham-Davis, Lieutenant Colonel, *Dinners and Diners: Where and How to Dine in London*. London: Grant Richards, 1899.

———, *A Gourmet's Guide to London*. London: Grant Richards Ltd., 1914.

O'Connor, Kaori, *The English Breakfast: The Biography of a National Meal with Recipes*. London, etc.: Bloomsbury Academic, 2013.

Ogilvie, Carol, *An Islay Cookbook*. Bruichladdich: The Lochindaal Press, 1995.

The Oxford English Dictionary. Online edition, oed.com.

Pegge, Samuel de La Vallee, ed., *The Forme of Cury: A Roll of Ancient English Cookery* (Circa 1390). Cambridge: Cambridge University Press, 2014.

Pepys, Samuel, *The Diary of Samuel Pepys, M.A., F.R.S.* (1659). London: George Bell & Sons, 1893.

Philp, Robert Kemp, ed., *Enquire Within About Everything*. London: Houlston and Sons, 1856.

Raffald, Elizabeth, *The Experienced English Housekeeper*. London: R. Baldwin, 1769.

Rayner, Jay, *A Greedy Man in a Hungry World*. London: William Collins, 2013.

Reardon, Joan, ed., *As Always, Julia: The Letters of Julia Child and Avis DeVoto*. Boston: Rux Martin/Houghton Mifflin Harcourt, 2010.

Sala, George Augustus, *The Thorough Good Cook: A Series of Chats on the Culinary Art, and Nine Hundred Recipes*. New York: Brentano's, 1896.

Shrager, Rosemary, *Rosemary: Castle Cook*. London: Everyman Publishers, 2001.

Sikes, Wirt, *Rambles and Studies in Old South Wales*. London: Sampson Low, Marston, Searle, & Rivington, 1881.

Sim, Margaret, *Margaret Sim's Cookery* (1879). Charleston, South Carolina: BiblioLife, 2009.

Smith, Eliza, *The Complete Housewife: or, Accomplished Gentlewoman's Companion*. London: J. Buckland, et al., 1727.

Smollett, Tobias, *The Expedition of Humphry Clinker* (1771). Charleston, South Carolina: BiblioBazaar, 2008.

Soyer, Alexis, *Soyer's Shilling Cookery for the People*. London: Geo. Routledge & Co., 1859.

———, *The Gastronomic Regenerator: A Simplified and Entirely New System of Cookery*. London: Simpkin, Marshall, & Co., 1846.

Spencer, Colin, *British Food: An Extraordinary Thousand Years of History*. New York: Columbia University Press, 2002.

Spink, Iain R., *The Arbroath Smokie Bible*. Edinburgh: Birlinn Limited, 2013.

Stout, Margaret B., *Cookery for Northern Wives*. Lerwick: T. & J. Manson, 1925.

Taruschio, Ann and Franco, *Leaves from The Walnut Tree: Recipes of a Lifetime*. London: Pavilion Books Limited, 1997.

Thackeray, William Makepeace, *Critical Reviews, Tales, Various Essays, Letters, Sketches, etc*. New York and London: Harper & Brothers Publishers, 1899.

Tibbott, S. Minwel, *Domestic Life in Wales*. Cardiff: University of Wales Press, 2002.

———, *Welsh Fare: A Selection of Traditional Recipes*. Cardiff: National Museum of Wales/Welsh Folk Museum: 1991.

Tomlin, G.A., *Pubs: A Collection of Hotel, Inn, and Tavern Signs in Great Britain and Ireland, to Which Are Added a Few Foreign Café Signs*. London: Ballantyne & Co., Ltd., 1922.

Topham, Edward, *Edinburgh Life 100 Years Ago: With an Account of the Fashions and Amusements of Society Selected and Arranged from "Captain Topham's Letters."* Edinburgh: William Brown, 1886.

Vine, Frederick T., *Savoury Pastry: Savoury Dish and Raised Pies, Pork Pies, Patties, Vol-au-Vents, Mincemeats, and Pies, and Miscellaneous Savoury Pastries*. London: Office of the "Baker and Confectioner," 1900.

Volant, F. and J. R. Warren, editors, *Memoirs of Alexis Soyer; with Unpublished Receipts and Odds and Ends of Gastronomy*. London: W. Kent & Co., 1859.

Walton, John K., *Fish & Chips and the British Working Class, 1970–1940*. London and New York: Leicester University Press, 1992.

White, Florence ("Mary Evelyn"), *Good Things in England: A Practical Cookery Book for Everyday Use*. London: Jonathan Cape, 1932

Wright, Clarissa Dickson, *The Haggis: A Little History*. Belfast: Appletree Press, 1996.

PERIODICALS

Anonymous, "Transcendental Cookery," *The New Monthly Magazine*, vol. 138 (1866).

MacLachlan, Christopher, "Hume and the Standard of Taste." *Hume Studies*, volume XII, number 1.

Orwell, George, "A Nice Cup of Tea." *The (London) Evening Standard*, January 12, 1946.

———, "British Cookery." Unpublished (commissioned by the British Council, 1946).

———, "In Defence of English Cooking." *The (London) Evening Standard*, December 15, 1945.

Saloman, Randi, "Arnold Bennett's Hotels." *Twentieth-Century Literature*, Spring 2012.

WEBSITES

scottishrecipes.co.uk

foodsofengland.co.uk

INDEX

Editor: Michael Sand
Designer: Danielle Young
Production Manager: Denise LaCongo

Library of Congress Control Number: 2015955623

ISBN: 978-1-4197-2223-3

Printed and bound in the United States
10 9 8 7 6 5 4 3 2 1

Abrams books are available at special discounts when purchased in quantity for premiums and promotions as well as fundraising or educational use. Special editions can also be created to specification. For details, contact specialsales@abramsbooks.com or the address below.

ABRAMS
The Art of Books

115 West 18th Street
New York, NY 10011
www.abramsbooks.com